The Genre of Biblical Commentary

The Genre of Biblical Commentary

Essays in Honor of John E. Hartley
on the Occasion of His 75th Birthday

Edited by
TIMOTHY D. FINLAY
and WILLIAM YARCHIN

☙PICKWICK *Publications* · Eugene, Oregon

THE GENRE OF BIBLICAL COMMENTARY
Essays in Honor of John E. Hartley on the Occasion of His 75th Birthday

Copyright © 2015 Wipf and Stock Publishers. All rights reserved. Except for brief quotations in critical publications or reviews, no part of this book may be reproduced in any manner without prior written permission from the publisher. Write: Permissions, Wipf and Stock Publishers, 199 W. 8th Ave., Suite 3, Eugene, OR 97401.

Pickwick Publications
An Imprint of Wipf and Stock Publishers
199 W. 8th Ave., Suite 3
Eugene, OR 97401

www.wipfandstock.com

ISBN: 978-1-62564-289-9

Cataloguing-in-Publication Data

The genre of biblical commentary : essays in honor of John E. Harley on the occasion of his seventy-fifth birthday / edited by Timothy D. Finlay and William Yarchin.

xviii + 264 p. ; 23 cm. Includes bibliographical references.

ISBN: 978-1-62564-289-9

1. Hartley, John E. 2. Bible—Commentaries—History and criticism. 3. I. Finlay, Timothy D. II. Yarchin, William. III. Title.

BS491.2 .G25 2015

Manufactured in the U.S.A.   10/16/2015

Contents

Permissions | vii
Preface | ix
Abbreviations | x
List of Contributors | xvii

Introduction to the Volume | 1
  —*William Yarchin*

Part 1: Production and Publication of Biblical Commentary

1 Writing a *Job* Commentary | 29
  —*David J. A. Clines*

2 Writing Commentary as Ritual and as Discovery | 40
  —*James W. Watts*

3 Commentary Changes in Format and Focus: An Overview | 54
  —*Elmer A. Martens*

4 *Awk, Dele,* and *Stet:* The Task and Craft of a Commentary Editor | 81
  —*Robert L. Hubbard, Jr.*

5 Macrostructure: How to Retrieve a Coherent Whole from Complex Information | 93
  —*Leslie C. Allen*

Part 2: Research and Its Results in Biblical Commentary

6 Does God Practice Mindfulness? A Reassessment of Isaiah 63:11–14 | 115
  —*Willem A. M. Beuken*

7 Isaiah 56:1–8 in Form-Critical Perspective | 131
  —*Marvin A. Sweeney*

8 Finding the Center: The Abimelech Account and the Gideon/Midianite Cycle as the Turning Point in Judges | 145
  —*John H. Hull, Jr.*

9 A Brief Introduction to Text-Criticism and Philology in 2 Samuel | 159
  —*Timothy D. Finlay*

10 Nathan's Ominous and Tragic Prophecy Becoming a Reality: 2 Sam 13:23–39 | 166
  —*Takamitsu Muraoka*

11 Commenting on the Unknown: Reflections on Isaiah 9:7–20 | 184
  —*H. G. M. Williamson*

Part 3: Relevance of Biblical Commentary

12 Exegetical Evidence for Non-Solar and Non-Sequential Interpretations of the Genesis 1 and 2 Creation Days | 199
  —*Miles V. Van Pelt*

13 *Ḥerem* versus Hospitality in the Story of Rahab | 217
  —*Victor H. Matthews*

14 As a Commentator, One Might Ask, "What Would Jeremiah or John Say?" | 234
  —*John E. Goldingay*

15 Biblical Commentary as an Exercise in Counterpoint: The Book of Job, Prosperity, and Liberation | 241
  —*Alissa Jones Nelson*

Permissions

Scripture quotations marked (ASV) are from the American Standard Version.

Scripture quotations marked (ESV) are from the ESV® Bible (The Holy Bible, English Standard Version®), copyright © 2001 by Crossway, a publishing ministry of Good News Publishers. Used by permission. All rights reserved.

Scripture quotations marked (KJV) are from the Authorized Version.

Scripture texts in this work are taken from the *New American Bible, revised edition* © 2010, 1991, 1986, 1970 Confraternity of Christian Doctrine, Washington, D.C. and are used by permission of the copyright owner. All Rights Reserved. No part of the New American Bible may be reproduced in any form without permission in writing from the copyright owner.

Scripture quotations marked (NASB) are from the the New American Standard Bible®, Copyright © 1960, 1962, 1963, 1968, 1971, 1972, 1973, 1975, 1977, 1995 by The Lockman Foundation. Used by permission.

Scripture quoted by permission. Quotations designated (NET) are from the NET Bible® copyright ©1996–2006 by Biblical Studies Press, L.L.C. http://netbible.com All rights reserved.

Scripture quotations marked (NIV) are taken from the Holy Bible, New International Version®, NIV®. Copyright © 1973, 1978, 1984, 2011 by Biblica, Inc.™ Used by permission of Zondervan. All rights reserved worldwide. www.zondervan.com. The "NIV" and "New International Version" are trademarks registered in the United States Patent and Trademark Office by Biblica, Inc.™

Grateful acknowledgement is made to the Jewish Publication Society for permission to use translation of Biblical texts from *Tanakh: The Holy Scriptures: The New JPS Translation According to the Traditional Hebrew Text (NJPS)*. Copyright © 1985 by the Jewish Publication Society.

Scripture quotations marked (NLT) are taken from the *Holy Bible*, New Living Translation, copyright ©1996, 2004, 2007, 2013 by Tyndale House Foundation. Used by permission of Tyndale House Publishers, Inc., Carol Stream, Illinois 60188. All rights reserved.

Scripture quotations marked (NRSV) are from New Revised Standard Version Bible, copyright 1989, Division of Christian Education of the National Council of the Churches of Christ in the United States of America. Used by permission. All rights reserved.

Scripture quotations marked (RSV) are from Revised Standard Version of the Bible, copyright 1952 [2nd edition, 1971] by the Division of Christian Education of the National Council of the Churches of Christ in the United States of America. Used by permission. All rights reserved.

Scripture marked (TNIV) are taken from the Holy Bible, Today's New International® Version TNIV®. Copyright 2001, 2005 by International Bible Society®. Used by permission of International Bible Society®. All rights reserved worldwide. "TNIV" and "Today's New International Version" are trademarks registered in the United States Patent and Trademark Office by International Bible Society®.

Preface

It is with great delight that we offer this Festschrift to John E. Hartley on the occasion of his seventy-fifth birthday. It is fair to say that anyone who knows John respects him as a scholar, as a teacher, and as a man of faith. In all the best senses of the word, John is our dear colleague, and we hope this volume will be received as a fitting tribute to him.

Wipf and Stock Publishers extended valuable assistance at all stages of the publishing process with the aim of making this volume a worthy reflection on the art and craft of biblical commentary—a scholarly enterprise that Wipf and Stock publications have themselves done much to advance.

Azusa Pacific University generously provided support for the services of a former student of John's, A. J. Zimmerman, as research assistant for this project. Our gratitude also extends to Peter Moore who, in cooperation with the authors, helped refine the style of most of the chapters in order to reach a larger audience of non-specialists. Most importantly, we wish to thank all the various scholars represented in this volume who enthusiastically agreed to honor John with their contributions.

Finally, we wish to thank, respectively, Eileen Finlay and Ann Yarchin, for putting up with us while we labored and for ensuring that we completed the task.

Timothy D. Finlay and William Yarchin
Azusa, California
August 2015

Abbreviations

GENERAL ABBREVIATIONS

BNF	Bibliothèque nationale de France
CUL	Cambridge University Library
IOSOT	International Organization for the Study of the Old Testament
LXX	Septuagint (the Greek Old Testament)
MT	Masoretic Text (of the Hebrew Bible)
NT	New Testament
OL	Old Latin
OT	Old Testament
SBL	Society of Biblical Literature
SISMEL	Societa Internazionale per lo Studio del Medioevo Latino
SP	Samaritan Pentateuch
Syr.	Peshiṭta (the Syriac Bible)
Tg.	Targum
Vulg.	Vulgate

TEXTS AND TRANSLATIONS OF THE BIBLE

AB	The Anchor Bible
ASV	American Standard Version
BHS	*Biblia Hebraica Stuttgartensia*
BHQ	*Biblia Hebraica Quinta*
CEB	Common English Bible
ESV	The Holy Bible, English Standard Version
KJV	King James Version

NASB	New American Standard Version
NET	New English Translation
NIV	New International Version (2011)
NJPS	*Tanakh: The Holy Scriptures: The New JPS Translation according to the Traditional Hebrew Text* (see also TNK)
NLT	New Living Translation
NRSV	New Revised Standard Version
RSV	Revised Standard Version
RV	Revised Version (1901)
TNK	Tanakh: A New Translation of the Holy Scriptures (1985; see also NJPS)
TNIV	Today's New International Version

PERIODICALS, REFERENCE WORKS, AND SERIALS

AAWGPHK³	Abhandlungen der Akademie der Wissenschaft zu Göttingen; Philolgisch-Historische Klasse (Dritte Folge)
ABD	D. N. Freedman, ed., *Anchor Bible Dictionary*, ed. 6 vols. New York: Doubleday, 1992
ABR	*Australian Biblical Review*
AbrN	*Abr-Naharain*
AbrNSup	Abr-Nahrain: Supplement Series
ACCS	Ancient Commentary on Christian Scripture
AJSL	*American Journal of Semitic Languages and Literature*
AJT	*Asia Journal of Theology*
AnBib	Analecta biblica
ANES	Ancient Near Eastern Studies Supplement Series
ANET	J. B. Pritchard, ed., *The Ancient Near East: Supplementary Texts and Pictures Relating to the Old Testament.* 2nd ed. Princeton: Princeton University Press, 1969
AOTC	Abingdon Old Testament Commentaries; see next entry
AOTC	Apollos Old Testament Commentary; see previous entry
APQ	*American Philosophical Quarterly*
ATD	Alte Testament Deutsch
AThDan	Acta Theologica Danica
AYBC	Anchor Yale Bible Commentary

BAT	Die Botschaft des Alten Testaments
BBB	Bonner biblische Beiträge
BCAT	Biblischer Commentar über das Alte Testament
BCBC	Believers Church Bible Commentary
BDB	F. Brown, S. R. Driver, and C. A. Briggs, *A Hebrew and English Lexicon of the Old Testament*. Oxford: Clarendon, 1907
BETL	Bibliotheca ephemeridum theologicarum lovaniensium
BKAT	Biblischer Kommentar, Altes Testament
Bib	*Biblica*
BibInt	*Biblical Interpretation*
BibLeb	*Bibel und Leben*
BibRec	*Biblical Reception*
BN	*Biblische Notizen*
BSac	*Bibliotheca Sacra*
BTB	*Biblical Theology Bulletin*
BTCB	Brazos Theological Commentary on the Bible
BThSt	Biblische Theologische Studien
BZAW	Beihefte zur Zeitschrift für die alttestamentliche Wissenschaft
CBC	Cambridge Bible Commentary (see next entry)
CBC	Cornerstone Biblical Commentary (see previous entry)
CBQ	*Catholic Biblical Quarterly*
CBSC	Cambridge Bible for Schools and Colleges
CCSL	Corpus Christianorum: Series Latina
Concilium	*Concilium International Journal for Theology*
ChrCent	*Christian Century*
CSM	*Christian Science Monitor*
CT	*Christianity Today*
DCH	D. J. A. Clines, ed., *Dictionary of Classical Hebrew*
DJD	Discoveries in the Judaean Desert
DSD	*Dead Sea Discoveries*
EBC	The Expositor's Bible Commentary
ERT	*Evangelical Review of Theology*
FAT	Forschungen zum Alten Testament

FH	*Fides et Historia*
FOTL	Forms of the Old Testament Literature
FRLANT	Forschungen zur Religion und Literatur des Alten und Neuen Testaments
GELS	T. Muraoka, *A Greek-English Lexicon of the Septuagint*. Leuven: Peeters, 2009
HALOT	L. Koehler, W. Baumgartner, and J. J. Stamm. *The Hebrew and Aramaic Lexicon of the Old Testament*. Translated and edited under the supervision of M. E. J. Richardson. 5 vols. Leiden, 1994–2000
HBS	Herders biblische Studien
HCOT	Historical Commentary on the Old Testament
HKAT	Handkommentar zum Alten Testament
HMS	Hearing the Message of Scripture
HSAT	Die Heilige Schrift des Alten Testaments. Edited by E. Kautzsch and A. Bertholet. 4th ed. Tübingen, 1922–23
HThKAT	Herders theologischer Kommentar zum Alten Testament
ICC	International Critical Commentary
Int	*Interpretation*
JAJSup	Journal of Ancient Judaism Supplements
JBL	*Journal of Biblical Literature*
JETS	*Journal of the Evangelical Theological Society*
JNES	*Journal of Near Eastern Studies*
JNSL	*Journal of Northwest Semitic Languages*
JQR	*Jewish Quarterly Review*
JSOT	*Journal for the Study of the Old Testament*
JSOTSup	Journal for the Study of the Old Testament Supplement Series
JTS	*Journal of Theological Studies*
JTSA	*Journal of Theology for Southern Africa*
KAT	Kommentar zum Alten Testament.
KBL	L. Koehler and W. Baumgartner. *Lexicon in Veteris Testamenti libros*
KeHAT	Kurzgefasstes exegetisches Handbuch zum Alten Testament
KHAT	Kurzen Handcommentar zum Alten Testament

LARR	Latin American Research Review
NAC	New American Commentary
NBBC	New Beacon Bible Commentary
NCBC	New Century Bible Commentary
NIB	New Interpreter's Bible
NIBC	New International Bible Commentary
NICOT	New International Commentary on the Old Testament
NIVAC	New International Version Application Commentary
OBO	Orbis Biblicus et Orientalis
OTL	Old Testament Library
PC	The Preacher's Commentary
Postscripts	Postscripts: The Journal of Sacred Texts and Contemporary Worlds
PSCF	Perspectives on Science and Christian Faith
RCS	Reformation Commentary on Scripture
RevExpos	Revue and Expositor
Sapientia Logos	Sapientia Logos: A Journal of Biblical Research & Interpretation inAfrica
SBET	Scottish Bulletin of Evangelical Theology
SBL	Society of Biblical Literature
SBLDS	Society of Biblical Literature Dissertation Series
SBLMS	Society of Biblical Literature Monograph Series
SBLSS	Society of Biblical Literature Symposium Series
SBS	Stuttgarter Bibel-Studien
SHBC	Smythe & Helwys Bible Commentary
Siphrut	Siphrut: Literature and Theology of the Hebrew Scriptures
SR	Sociology of Religion
STDJ	Studies on the Text of the Desert of Judah
TDOT	Theological Dictionary of the Old Testament
TENTS	Texts and Editions for New Testament Study
Textus	Textus: Annual of the Hebrew University Bible Project
ThGl	Theologie und Glaube
ThLZ	Theologische Literaturzeitung
THOTC	The Two Horizons Old Testament Commentary

ThWAT	*Theologisches Wörterbuch zum Alten Testament.* Edited by G. J. Botterweck and H. Ringgren. Stuttgart: Kohlhammer, 1970-
TOTC	Tyndale Old Testament Commentaries
Transformation	*Transformation: An International Journal of Holistic Mission Studies*
VT	*Vetus Testamentum*
VTSup	Vestus Testamentum Supplements
WBC	Word Biblical Commentary
WMANT	Wissenschaftliche Monographien zum Alten und Neuen Testament
WTJ	*Westminster Theological Journal*
ZAR	*Zeitschrift für altorientalische und biblische Rechtsgeschichte*
ZAW	*Zeitschrift für die alttestamentliche Wissenschaft*
ZBK	Zürcher Bibelkommentare

Contributors

Leslie C. Allen is Senior Professor of Old Testament in the School of Theology at Fuller Theological Seminary in Pasadena, California.

Willem A. M. Beuken is Professor Emeritus of Old Testament at the Katholieke Universiteit Leuven in Leuven, Belgium.

David J. A. Clines is Emeritus Professor of Biblical Studies at The University of Sheffield in Sheffield, UK.

Timothy D. Finlay is Professor of Biblical Studies at Azusa Pacific Seminary.

John Goldingay is the David Allan Hubbard Professor of Old Testament in the School of Theology at Fuller Theological Seminary in Pasadena, California.

Robert L. Hubbard, Jr. is Professor Emeritus of Biblical Literature at North Park Theological Seminary in Chicago, Illinois.

John H. Hull, Jr. is Minister of Faith Development at Beargrass Christian Church (Disciples of Christ) in Louisville, Kentucky.

Alissa Jones Nelson is Acquisitions Editor for Religious Studies at Walter de Gruyter GmbH, Berlin, Germany.

Elmer A. Martens is Professor Emeritus of Old Testament and President Emeritus of Mennonite Brethren Biblical Seminary, now Fresno Pacific University Biblical Seminary, Fresno, California.

Victor H. Matthews is Professor in the Department of Religious Studies and Dean of the College of Humanities and Public Affairs at Missouri State University in Springfield, Missouri.

Marvin A. Sweeney is Professor of Hebrew Bible at Claremont School of Theology, Claremont, California, and Professor of and Professor of Tanakh at the Academy for Jewish Religion (California) in Los Angeles, California.

James W. Watts is Professor in the Department of Religion at Syracuse University in Syracuse, New York.

H. G. M. Williamson is Regius Professor of Hebrew Emeritus at the University of Oxford, Oxford, England.

Takamitsu Muraoka is Professor of Hebrew Emeritus at the University of Leiden in Leiden, The Netherlands.

Miles Van Pelt is the Alan Belcher Professor of Old Testament and Biblical Languages and Academic Dean at Reformed Theological Seminary in Jackson, Mississippi.

William Yarchin is Dean's Endowed Professor of Biblical Studies at Azusa Pacific University, Azusa, California.

Introduction to the Volume

—William Yarchin

OVER THE COURSE OF his 45-years-long career, John E. Hartley has made noteworthy contributions in several different aspects of his role as a scholar. His former students—some of whom are represented in this volume—universally speak of the dedication he has shown to their growth and well-being as whole persons (rather than simply as minds) under his tutelage. His department colleagues and former deans know him as the chief sponsor and architect of the exegetical methodology advanced in the seminary biblical studies program at Azusa Pacific University where John has spent most of his teaching career. To the broader academic and pastoral guilds, however, John is probably best known for his biblical commentaries: *The Book of Job* in the New International Commentary on the Old Testament series (1988), *Levicitus* in the Word Biblical Commentary series (1992), and *Genesis* in the New International Biblical Commentary series (2000). Inasmuch as it is to these projects that John has devoted so much of his scholarly labor, it seemed fitting that a Festschrift honoring him on his seventy-fifth birthday would have as its theme the enterprise of biblical commentary. The following paragraphs serve to consider that enterprise and to situate the Festschrift contributions within it.

Considered phenomenologically, commentary makes visible and explicit what is otherwise hidden and implicit, that is, not immediately self-evident. At this level of abstraction, commentary by no means restricts itself to the Bible or even to literature. Broadcast sports commentators, for example, do not treat texts, but rather the athletes and events that make up a sporting event, and they bring to the viewer's attention details pertinent to a more complete understanding of what the sports fan observes as the game unfolds. In retail digital packaging of movies, actors and directors provide commentary that similarly brings to the viewer's attention details pertinent

2   The Genre of Biblical Commentary

to a more complete understanding of what the movie-watcher observes as the story unfolds. On the editorial pages of newspapers and blogs, political commentators likewise bring to their readers' attention details pertinent to a more insightful understanding of the events unfolding on the current political horizon. All of this commentating operates on the assumption—shared perhaps ubiquitously by everyone in some form or another—that to everything there is an implicit dimension which, but for commentary, would remain undisclosed.¹ Commentary thus makes visible and explicit the hidden and implicit.

Textual commentary in particular serves to disclose, from the brute data of the text confronting the reader, the meaning of those data for the reader. Inherent in such conveyance of meaning is interpretation, a hermeneutical action performed upon the text by the commentator on the reader's behalf. Necessarily, then, the phenomena of writing and reading textual commentary occur within something of a *pacte d'écriture* that the commentator accurately identifies the text's implicate and competently explicates it to the benefit of other readers' engagement with the text.² The very fact that

---

1. The implicit dimension(s) of reality can be considered a defining characteristic of premodern worldviews in general, and particularly in the West after Plato gave philosophical articulation to the implicit (heavenly) world of the divine and the implicit (interior) world of the soul. Almost all premodern biblical commentators gave explicating voice to the scriptural text on the basis of this ontological assumption, expressed rather directly in the third century by Origen. Citing Romans 1:20 whereby "the invisible is perceived from the creation of the world through the things that were made," Origen argues "therefore, just as the visible and invisible, earth and heaven, soul and flesh, body and spirit have mutually this kinship and this world as a result of their union, so also we must believe that Holy Scripture results from the visible and the invisible" (*Homilies on Leviticus* 5.1, in Origen, *Homilies*, 89). Acknowledgment of implicit dimension(s) of reality is, however, by no means the exclusive domain of premodern thought, as late modern engagement with quantum physics and psychology attests; see, e.g., the explorations by the theoretical physicist David Bohm, *Wholeness and the Implicate Order*, in which—strikingly like the views of many premoderns—the basis for all reality is participation rather than simply interaction.

2. Although not usually denoted by this French expression, the importance of communities of readers has become prominent in late modern literary theory. The Italian semiotician Umberto Eco has treated the subject often, including in the volume *Interpretation and Overinterpretation*, where he favors the expression "social treasury" that makes reading with understanding a "transaction between the competence of the reader (the reader's world knowledge) and the kind of competence that a given text postulates in order to be read in an economic way" (68–69). Michel Foucault also theorizes on such underlying expectations between texts and readers in *L'ordre du discours*, where Foucault articulates the interstitial place of commentary between the explicit and the implicit (27): "le commentaire n'a pour rôle, quelles que soient les techniques mises en œuvre, que de dire *enfin* ce qui était articulé silencieusement *là-bas*" (commentary's role, by whatever technique, is to at last speak what had been profoundly but silently articulated [emphasis original]).

a text is deemed worthy of commentary effort locates it in a canonical category: that is, the phenomenon of commentary presupposes a community of readers for whom the text's explicit expressions and implicit meanings are in some sense authoritative for informing professional practices such as medicine,[3] juridical norms,[4] or for guiding cultural hermeneutical standards such as philosophical teachings[5] or literary artistry.

Who are these readers for whom the commentator writes? From antiquity to the present day, the commentator's audience has varied considerably. Not uncommonly, commentary writing has taken place within a network of discourse comprised exclusively of elite readers sharing an advanced level of technical expertise. Often, however, the disclosive need addressed by commentary is more simply to introduce the text, typically to students within an educational setting or, for religious texts such as the Bible, within a devotional setting such as a monastery.[6] This means that the range of activities denoted by the term "commentary" is wide indeed, and under this umbrella term many different forms of explicating literature treating biblical texts

---

3. A good example from the second century CE is Galen's commentaries on works attributed to Hippocrates, and in particular, in support of a superior approach to medical arts, his *de Captionibus*, with its attention to language-based ambiguity and the role of interpretation; see Robert Blair Edlow, *Galen on Language and Ambiguity*.

4. See, e.g., commentaries by the second-century CE Roman jurist Julius Paulus on the Praetor's Edict as preserved in Justinian's *Corpus Juris Civilis*.

5. Scholarship devoted to works attributed to Homer offers the most conspicuous example as is evident from Schironi's overview of the manuscripts containing ancient Greek and Hellenistic commentating literature in her "Greek Commentaries," as well as Eleanor Dickey's detailed guide to ancient Homeric scholia, lexica, and commentaries in *Ancient Greek Scholarship*, 18–28. These works reflect the abundant commentary that discursive philosophical works also attracted in antiquity.

6. For example, Gregory the Great explains that his monastic brothers requested of him "to comment on the book of blessed Job and, as far as truth should give me strength, to reveal the book's mysteries in all their profundity for my brothers" (*Moralia in Job* section 1). Note Gregory's allusion to the implicit/explicit function of commentary.

over the centuries can be identified,[7] such as *hypotheseis*,[8] *homilies*, and *enarrationes*.[9]

In virtually every case, the need for textual commentary arises because over time the cultural points of reference by which the text had originally made immediate sense became obscured to later readers or disappeared altogether. The most conspicuous example is translating the text from its source language into a target-language. Before translation, the text can make no explicit statement to the target-language reader, nor can textual commentary convey implicit meaning. Translation, then, on its face attempts to disclose that which is implicit to the point of becoming the text's new explicate. In this way translation is doubly disclosive: while it attempts to render into a target language that which is explicit in the source language, it proceeds at all times under pressure to convey explicitly that which is implicit ("the sense") in the source text.[10] Thus translation cannot but serve as textual commentary in the sense we are treating here.[11] Unsurprisingly, as the exegetical tradition takes up these witnesses to the Old Testament—Greek Septuagint, Aramaic Targum, Old Latin and Vulgate, Syriac Peshitta—it attests not only to the ancient forms of the Hebrew text but also to ancient ways of interpreting it.

---

7. For a helpful treatment on the spectrum of these commenting literatures and reflections on the cultural factors leading to the production of textual commentary, see Barry Smith, "Textual Deference." A more succinct overview and updated bibliography regarding these various commentary-forms, with particular attention to the forms as they were adapted from classical scholarship to biblical interpretation, are offered by Schnabel, "On Commentary Writing." Lohfink schematizes elements of biblical commentary as a genre with example-titles in "Kommentar als Gattung."

8. By the fourteenth century chapter-divisions had become well-established features in Latin biblical manuscripts, and soon *hypotheseis* were to be found at the head of each chapter summarizing its content or teaching.

9. Much of the content preserved in the widely-used *Glossa Ordinaria* (standard commentary) to the medieval Latin Bible was abridged from patristic *commentarius currens* (running commentary). For a brief example in English translation, see William Yarchin, *History of Biblical Interpretation*, 103–4.

10. As noted by Ben Sira's grandson: "what was originally expressed in Hebrew does not have exactly the same sense (ἰσοδυναμεῖ) when translated into another language" (Sirach Prologue, NRSV).

11. This has ever been recognized in both Jewish and Christian scriptural traditions. For centuries the Targums have accompanied reading and exposition of the Tanakh for the light they cast upon the latter, not despite their homiletic character but because of it. In Latin-speaking Christendom, the interpretive nature of the Vulgate was rarely (if ever) suppressed, as evidenced, *inter alia*, by the constant acknowledgement of Jerome's textual explication via the ubiquitous presence of his prefaces regularly appended to the incipit of each biblical book.

Even when readers require no translation, the need remains for clarification of technical vocabulary or antiquated grammar and for explanation of the author's idiosyncratic usage of genre or rhetoric. But beyond these basics, to convey successfully the implicit meaning(s) of a text to a reading audience far removed from its author in time and space, the exposition must be attuned to the points of reference within the reader's horizon of intelligibility by which sense is made of things.[12] Such horizons are not static. They shift over time, requiring updated commentary and even metacommentary (commentary making explicit what is implicit in previously generated commentary). So a *commentary tradition* will inevitably grow around canonical works such as Homer's *Iliad* or Galen's treatises or the Torah, and eventually commentary on the canonical work is expected to engage with—or at least acknowledge the influence of—major voices within that tradition.[13] Biblical commentary conscious of its own tradition has found formal expression in a variety of ways, including *catenae* (chains) of quotations from patristic commentary written into the margins of biblical manuscripts, not unlike the standard scholiastic form practiced by Hellenistic scholars upon classical works.[14] Rabbinic biblical exposition has always been deeply aware of the tradition in which it stands, attributing at every turn a halakhic or aggadic insight to a named authority before adding further exposition.[15]

---

12. The œuvre of Philo Judaeus is a good case in point, as he made extensive use of the commentary form prevalent in his Alexandrian intellectual environment and applied it to Jewish scripture in an effort to have it speak though allegorical interpretation in the (largely Platonic) philosophical idiom to which his deeply Hellenized Jewish readership was attuned, making explicit the implicit sense (ὑπόνοια); see David Dawson, *Allegorical Readers*, 73–126. Some thirteen centuries later the imprint of Aristotelian metaphysical categories of causality upon thirteenth-century Latin biblical scholarship is particularly evident in the chapter-prologues drafted by Dominican masters at Paris, such as those by Guerric de St. Quentin pertaining to authorship of the psalms (Paris, BNF lat. 15264); see Alistair Minnis, *Medieval Theory of Authorship* and Martin Morard, "Entre mode et tradition," and more broadly Christopher Ocker, *Biblical Poetics*.

13. Mayer appropriately observes, in the preface to his edition and commentary on *Horace: Epistles* Book I: "A commentary on a standard classical author is a dialogue with the dead. The commentator engages not just with the ancient text but also with [its] long exegetical tradition" (vii).

14. For ease of modern access many patristic *catenae* have been assembled from manuscript margins and published in printed form; *catenae* on the New Testament are available online at http://catalog.hathitrust.org/Record/001937728, and those on the Greek Old Testament are listed in Swete, *An Introduction*, 363.

15. In many cases the adding of one rabbinic comment to another is by means of the Hebrew expression דבר אחר ("another comment"); note that, in scholia of authoritative commentary on classical works, essentially the same anthological signal appeared by use of the Greek term ἄλλως / Latin *aliter* or *dixit*; see Fausto Montana, "The Making," 124–25.

6   The Genre of Biblical Commentary

The history of biblical interpretation demonstrates that it is not simply distance in time and space that necessitates explicating commentary. In their biblical expositions Christian Fathers not infrequently insisted that the Old Testament's true Christological meaning had been deliberately made implicit—hidden away within the text's intentional obscurities—rather than explicit, disclosed only through the hermeneutical lens of the Christian Rule of Faith applied to the text via figurative exegesis guided by illumination from the Holy Spirit.[16] By the end of the fourth century the Old Testament's implicit meaning would be regularly made explicit by reference to the situation of the Christian reading community.[17] In earlier centuries, commentary appearing among the Dead Sea Scrolls similarly considered the meaning (*pesher*) of many sacred Jewish texts as speaking in a veiled prophetic way about the specific circumstances of the community that produced the scrolls; this implicit meaning was made explicit in the doctrine of the Teacher of Righteousness "to whom God has disclosed all the mysteries of the words of his servants, the prophets" (1QpHab VII:4–5).[18] Later Jewish midrash would go on to expand simultaneous possibilities for the biblical text's implicate by reference not only to the self-definition of (universal) Israel as shaped by classical rabbinic teachings, but also to the situation of the text's historical author, such as David when writing a particular psalm.[19]

This latter, historical frame of reference—often denoted with the term *peshat* among Jewish commentators—influenced Christian biblical commentary in the later Middle Ages, in some large part thanks to the mediation of *peshat* through the widely read *Postilla litteralis* of Nicholas of Lyre (1270–1340) who had in turn drawn extensively from the Jewish authority Shlomo Yiṣḥaqi (Rashi, 1040–1105).[20] Initially, late medieval

---

16. Clement of Alexandria is representative: "the Scriptures have hidden the sense ... of things declared for salvation by the Holy Spirit, wherefore the holy mysteries of the prophecies are veiled in the parables, preserved for chosen men" (*Stromata* 6.15).

17. Among the many examples that could be adduced, note Augustine's homily on Psalm 45 (Lat. 44) when he connects Latin words in the psalm's superscript *canticum pro dilecto* to the *filiis Core* and reasons, since Christians are children of Christ the beloved bridegroom, "this psalm was written for us, as its title declares" (CCSL 44.494).

18. Bockmuehl has recently reviewed shared characteristics of biblical commentary at Qumran relative to contemporary Jewish and Greek commentary practices in terms parallel to the explicit/implicit framework; see "The Dead Sea Scrolls."

19. See *Midrash Tehillim* 24.3 (שנו רבותינו כל פרשה שאמר דוד בספר תילים כנגד עצמו אמרה וכנגד כל ישראל [from Solomon Buber's 1891 Wilna edition]) and the parsing of the midrashic point there and in *b. Pes* 117a. Braude translates "all the psalms which David composed apply either to himself or to all Israel" (*The Midrash*, 338; see the midrash also at Ps 4.1, 18.1 and 35.1. Braude's rendering is echoed by Menn, "Sweet Singer," 66.

20. Lyre's Latin postils are best accessed in the printed edition of the standard

Christian commentators undertook expansive and detailed excursuses on the historical and cultural contexts of biblical passages in order to provide the most complete articulation of the literal sense—increasingly, the historical sense—of the text as a more sure foundation for figurative commentary explicating the implicit, mystical meaning.[21] As the modern epoch emerged, wherein truth would be conceived in scientific terms—that is, as that which is (historically) verifiable—modern biblical commentary would come to adopt the historical frame of reference as the almost exclusive starting point for conveying from the text what would otherwise not be immediately self-evident to the reader.[22] What is not self-evident to the reader of the Bible, of course, is precisely anything and everything not immediately disclosed in the very words of the text itself. And so modern biblical commentators share in common with their premodern predecessors the aim to convey understanding of the biblical text to the reader by making explicit what the text implicitly assumes as knowledge necessary for understanding it. For premodern biblical commentators the text's implicate could include historical/philological details, but they laid greater emphasis on revealing the divine (mystical) dimension implicit in the text as signified by those details. In the modern era, on the other hand, it is largely the historical/philological dimension implicit in the text that takes up most of the commentator's energies.

From an historical, scientific point of view, the results of the modern biblical commentary enterprise are impressive. On the pages of virtually any reputable commentary volume, twenty-first-century readers of the Bible may learn from an astounding array of information illuminating how ancient Jewish and Christian writers thought about God and how they expressed those thoughts. If access to that information is why modern readers of the Bible turn to biblical commentaries, the enterprise must be deemed

---

medieval commentary *Biblia Sacra cum glossa ordinaria*. For an example in English translation, see Yarchin, *History of Biblical Interpretation*, 105–8.

21. Note, for example, the prodigious assemblage of *litterae* (such as geographic and onomastic) details in answer to multitudinous *quaestiones* in the massive biblical commentary on the Gospel of Matthew by the fifteenth-century Spanish bishop Alfonso de Madrigal (*Commentarii* in 1 *am* partem *Matthaei*; Venice, 1615). With much less interest in figurative derivatives from the biblical text, the encyclopedic turn of the sixteenth and seventeenth centuries generated such compendious tomes as the nine volumes of the *Critici sacri* appended to the 1657 London Polyglot with their hundreds of excursuses on a wide variety of philological, historical, and cultural topics (*Critici sacri; sive, Annotata doctissimorum virorum in Vetus ac Novum Testamentum, quibus accedunt tractauts varii theologico-philologici: Editio nova in novem tomos distribute, multi anecdotis commentariis, ac indice at totum opus locupletissimo, aucta* (ed. John Pearson; Amsterdam: Boom, 1698).

22. See Yarchin, "Biblical Interpretation," 72–75.

not only impressive, but successful. That success ensures that the future biblical commentators will continue to apply the best available technical means of explicating the literary and historical dimensions implicit in the biblical text. If that success, however, totalizes the biblical commentary enterprise such that its explicating efforts are restricted to the implicit literary and historical dimensions of the text, the readership that biblical commentary will attract in the twenty-first century will in turn be restricted to only those readers satisfied with that limited focus. Conversely, such commentary will fail to reach other communities of readers, say, those for whom the important implicate of the Bible is not its historical or literary dimensions but its religious or devotional meaning.[23]

This observation highlights the location of the commentator between the text on the one hand and the reading community on the other. In his contribution to a kindred volume, Eckhard Schnabel cites the scene in Nehemiah 8, when, at the occasion of the public reading of the book of the law in post-exilic Jerusalem, prominent Levites "gave the sense, so that the people understood the reading" (v.8). Schnabel observes that, "[w]hile the reading of the text already implies a dynamic element which, at least in a rudimentary manner, breaks open the *stasis* of the text, it is the explanation or 'commentary' which produces understanding."[24] Our brief consideration here of the phenomenon of biblical commentary may permit us, for the moment, to personalize this into, "it is the commentator who produces understanding," or perhaps, more nuanced, "it is the commentator who makes understanding possible."

During antiquity, the bulk of commentary addressed a rather small educated elite capable not only of reading the text, but of reading it better in the light of philological details disclosed by commentators who would also expound on its literary and cultural implications. The dramatic expansion of literacy in recent generations has produced a Bible readership far beyond the limited horizon of the scholarly commentator's peers. This is ever so much more so as Christian readers of the Bible grow in numbers among social groups in geographies historically unaddressed by the academic

---

23. See the reflections of Richard Coggins, "A Future for the Commentary?," who observes, "[c]ommentaries are characteristically *either* trying to get back to the original: re-creating the eighth century BCE or the first century CE, placing our characters in their setting, explaining what their words would have meant to their contemporary situation, *or* they are seeking to establish the relevance of biblical material to the present-day audience, however 'relevance' and 'the present-day audience' may be defined" (172 [emphasis original]).

24. Schnabel, "On Commentary Writing," 17 (emphasis original).

commentating guild.²⁵ These other readers are just as hungry for explication of that which is not immediately self-evident to them when they pick up the Bible. Biblical commentary, then, has long been tailored to address specific target audiences, both within the academic guild and beyond in the general reading religious and secular public. With the expansion of biblical commentary in myriad forms beyond print media into broadcast and broadband media, the targeted audiences for commentary production multiply even more. So we might further revise the claim: "It is the commentator who makes possible *a certain kind of understanding,* depending on the audience addressed."²⁶

The honoree of this volume represents a generation of European-American biblical scholars striving during the late twentieth and early twenty-first century to disclose implicit dimensions of the biblical text before the eyes of at least two audiences simultaneously: their intellectual peers within the halls of Academe and their fellow believers within the pews of church and synagogue.²⁷ Most of the contributors to this volume consider themselves co-laborers with John Hartley in that effort, with varying places of self-identification along that spectrum between the academic community and the faith community. Like John, several of them have published work in modern commentary series, seeking to produce understanding within the readership targeted by each respective series.

We can sense the motivation shared by John and his peers by noting the Series Editorial Preface of the Word Biblical Commentary, for which no fewer than four of our contributors, along with John himself, have written volumes. The preface describes them as scholars sharing "a commitment to Scripture as divine revelation and to the truth and power of the Christian gospel," aiming to "make the technical and scholarly approach to a theological understanding of Scripture understandable by—and useful to—the fledgling student, the working minister, and colleagues in the guild of professional scholars and teachers as well." Another series for which John and contributors to this Festschrift have produced volumes, the New

25. See Jenkins, *The Next Christendom*; and Jenkins, *The New Faces of Christianity*.

26. "[Commentary] must be clear about two things. It must be clear about the audience-situation of the text, and about the audience-situation of the commentary. If it recognizes these two situations, then it may perform a service of mediation; not simply between reader and text, but between world and world, understanding and understanding, interpretation and interpretation." Marvin Brown, "The Commentary in Biblical Hermeneutics," 13.

27. "The modern commentary will manifest to a significant degree the 'double loyalty' of the interpreter in his or her contemporary social setting: loyalty to the professional guild and the university on the one hand and to the community of faith and the theological enterprise on the other." Anderson, "The Problem and Promise," 348.

International Biblical Commentary, speaks of "believing criticism," an approach to commentary through which the writers "hope to enrich the life of the academy as well as the life of the church." Still another commentary series for which John and at least one contributor to this volume have written, the New International Commentary on the Old Testament, "speaks from within that interpretive tradition known as evangelicalism" treating the "wonderfully human writings through which the living God speaks his powerful Word" with due attention to "implications for the life of faith today."

Key terminology positions these publication projects vis-à-vis targeted audiences with the aim of uncovering the implicit *theological understanding* (WBC), the implicit *meaning the text conveys* (NIBC), the implicit *knowledge of God* (HCOT) produced by exegetical and hermeneutical work aiming to "enrich the life of the academy as well as the life of the church" (NIBC). Not all the commentary work of John's peers, however, seeks so explicitly to serve the full range of ecclesiastical and academic readers. The preface to the International Critical Commentary, for example, notes that "[n]o attempt has been made to secure a uniform theological or critical approach to the biblical texts," and those who write for this series "have been invited for their scholarly distinction, not for their adherence to any one school of thought." Similarly, editors of the *Hermeneia* series "impose no systematic theological perspective upon the series (directly, or indirectly by selection of authors)," and the Foreword, most interestingly, describes its commentary aims in terms parallel to what we have emphasized in this introduction: "It is expected that authors will struggle to *lay bare the ancient meaning* of a biblical work or pericope. In this way *the text's human relevance should become transparent*, as is always the case in competent historical discourse" (emphasis added).

We sought out scholars who have known John and invited them to contribute to this Festschrift according to their own inclination within a range of specific possibilities illuminating biblical commentary. As already noted, most of them are themselves veteran commentary writers, and in several cases, like John, they have contributed to a published series of biblical commentaries. The result, in the aggregate, offers the reader insight into the production of a biblical commentary. Some are technically oriented, with those philological and historical details that support the craft of biblical commentary. Others are more personal, reflecting the commentator's struggle to balance the demands of the publishing enterprise with the needs of the commentary readership while remaining faithful to the voice of the biblical writer(s). Because these scholars span an ideological range, we invited our contributors to express themselves with as little or as much religious devotion to the biblical text as they preferred. They have responded with essays addressing three general areas pertaining to the genre of biblical commentary: production and publication, scholarly research folded into commentary, and the relevance of biblical commentary to broader issues in the readers' world.

PRODUCTION AND PUBLICATION OF BIBLICAL COMMENTARY

The enterprise begins with the writer working alone and yet in dialogue. *David J. A. Clines*[28] invites us inside the biblical commentator's study where we can see that the enterprise is actually a conversation that takes place, first among commentators, and then—once the work is in print—we readers get to listen in. As participating readers, we are thereby drawn into not simply a conversation among commentators but with the biblical writers themselves. We can thereby learn from commentators how to engage with the biblical writers—but Clines reminds us that the discourse of biblical commentary can become an inhibiting orthodoxy, a way of restricting rather than expanding insight. The irony here is not lost on Clines, since he wants his reader to realize how the Book of Job in particular defies the sort of orthodox thinking that commentary conventions, whether academic or confessional, can subtly impose upon Bible readers.

Several articles illustrate the enduring legacy of the Renaissance emphasis on how the grammar, syntax, and other contextual signals indicate the communicative intentions of the biblical speaker foregrounded in the text (Moses, Paul, Jesus, Isaiah, David). The signals include genre, poetic style, and literary structure at micro and macro levels of composition. Paralleling a similar observation by Clines, *James W. Watts*[29] notes that the effort to comprehend the referential world assumed by the ancient text can lead the modern commentator into subjects seemingly distant from theological literature, such as "the taxonomy of domestic fowl species." Our writers recognize that commentary-writing proceeds with constant awareness of the work from previous generations of commentators.[30] Here again we note

---

28. David J. A. Clines has written *Ezra, Nehemiah and Esther* for the New Century Bible Commentary (1984) and *Job* for the Word Biblical Commentary (1989, 2006, 2011).

29. James W. Watts has written *Leviticus 1–10* for the Historical Commentary on the Old Testament (2013).

30. St. Jerome, in a work that defends his own commentary and translation œuvre by reviewing the accomplishments of his Christian predecessors, wrote, "What is the function of commentators? They expound the statements of someone else; they express

not only the undertaking's conversational nature, but the intergenerational dimensions of that conversation. Watts aptly urges "attention to the history of the Bible's reception as part and parcel of exegesis." The notes from Clines's workbench exemplify what Watts articulates: "it is a focus on details informed by reflections on theories and methods that produces the most interesting creative and critical thinking." As already noted, this has ever been the case for biblical commentary, because substantive details in the text lose referential clarity over time, necessitating the very phenomenon of commentary on those details. Watts, however, by considering biblical commentary-production in the light of ritual theory, suggests that textual traditions bearing ultimate social authority, such as legal codes and Scripture, call for a class of experts in whose hands resides the task of speaking on behalf of the textual tradition to contemporary needs. Within that ritual dynamic we can also understand how biblical commentators approach the textual tradition on behalf of their respective reading communities, in a two-way communicative exchange. Watts strikingly suggests that the very fact that a literary tradition attracts a body of commentary contributes to the tradition's authority.[31]

Although scriptural commentary antedates the canonical Bible itself, the biblical commentary series is a publishing phenomenon that emerged only within the last two centuries.[32] The growth of literacy in the western

---

in simple language views that have been expressed in an obscure manner; they quote the opinions of many individuals and they say: 'Some interpret this passage in this sense, others, in another sense'; they attempt to support their own understanding and interpretation with these testimonies in this fashion, so that the prudent reader, after reading the different interpretations and studying which of these many views are to be accepted and which rejected, will judge for himself which is the more correct; and, like the expert banker, will reject the falsely minted coin" (*Apology Against Rufinus* 1.16). Here Jerome stands squarely in the tradition of ancient commentators' practice of juxtaposing previously offered interpretations of the same passage; see Montana, "The Making" 123.

31. The comparative religionist Guy G. Strousma ("Scripture and *Paideia*," 36) pushes the envelope farther: "A [scriptural] canon obtains its full significance when understood as the very driving force of the hermeneutical life of a religion, as its principle of authority. This authority belongs to the community—which itself invents, transforms, and preserves the rules according to which the holy writings should be read in order that their true meaning be revealed. As the Scriptures are invested, by their very definition, with an infinite number of meanings, their divine author is divested of the authority of the author of the literary texts. The meaning of sacred writings is given to them not by their author, but by the community of their readers. The *regula fidei* also becomes, then, a *regula legendi*."

32. Our reference here to publishing commentary in series is to be distinguished from publishing in sequential segments by subscription, a strategy of dissemination that dates back to the seventeenth century.

world greatly multiplied the number of Bible readers spanning multiple sectors of society. Because commentaries convey understanding of the text's implicit meaning for readers in a way relevant to the readers' interests, different targeted readerships results in commentaries with different emphases and methodological approaches. The modern biblical commentary series emerged as a publishing strategy to accomplish at least three things: 1) bring greater focus to specific details and exposition of delimited portions of the Bible than is possible in a single-volume whole-Bible commentary; 2) coordinate that focus across the series volumes according to a designated methodological protocol and format; and 3) use that format and protocol to address the interests of a targeted readership.

One of the things that distinguish commentary series from each other is the format in which the total assemblage of material (biblical text, accompanying elements such as footnotes, excursus, maps, indices, and most of all, the commentary sections themselves) is laid out in the volume(s) for the reader. *Elmer Martens*[33] provides an overview of commentary format from select English-language commentary series of the twentieth century. He observes the paradox of biblical commentary according to which all is for the sake of the text yet all is an exercise in paratext (those elements in the source document other than the words of Scripture themselves) which draws the reader's eyes away from the words of scripture in order to bring them back again with fresh insight—at least, that is the aim.[34] Martens astutely notes that the relevance of the biblical text lies in the paratext with which we frame it, and in the twenty-first century that paratext will surely broaden in scope to include not simply historical and philological detail but hermeneneutical reflections from a global [not just Western] horizon of biblical commentary. "The winds of cultural changes will almost certainly demand a review of the function of commentaries, and along with that review, one may expect further variations in [paratextual] format."

33. Elmer Martens has written *Jeremiah* for the Believers Church Bible Commentary (1986).

34. The graphically demonstrated paratextual nature of biblical commentary goes back centuries, as early commentary found its way onto the same page as the biblical text. Different sized-scripts were dedicated to the biblical text and its marginal patristic commentary respectively as in the eighth-century Codex Zacynthius (Cambridge, CUL British and Foreign Bible Society MS 213); or we might find the alternating scripts within a single text-column—majuscule for the biblical text and minuscule for commentary—as in the ninth-century Codex Monacensis 30 (Munich, Universitätsbibliotek 2° Cod. ms. 30). A parallel development in the *mise-en-page* of biblical commentary came about when the marginalia of an authoritative commentator were made the center of the page and the biblical text reduced to lemmata, as a comparison of David Kimḥi's psalms commentary in the fourteenth-century manuscript (Firenze, Bibl. Med. Laur. Plut.II.1) with a fifteenth-century early printing (Naples 1487) reveals.

Robert L. Hubbard, Jr.[35] continues the paratext theme within the biblical commentary series by viewing it in the light of the editorial development of the Hebrew Bible itself. From whatever originary authorial sources—whether, for example, Israelite prophets, royal court annalists, or priestly functionaries—certain ancient Israelite writings eventually became part of the Hebrew Bible because they passed through the hands of unknown tradents who left their own paratextual imprint on the documents they handed down. Those editorial paratexts served to guide later readers by clarifying antiquated references and terminology, by configuring assembled law- and proverb-collections into a more coherent shape, and by pointing the reader to themes presented in other parts of the ancient Hebrew literary canon. Hubbard sees certain parallels in the roles and tasks of the biblical commentary series editor (although he points out some aspects of the editing enterprise without ancient counterpart, such as publishers). Yet, as in the case of the ancient biblical editors, the text that the editor hands on to the publisher, and so eventually to the reader, bears paratextual refinements from the editor's hands that serve similar purposes. For example, stylistic refinements ensure that the writing is readily intelligible to the current generation of readers, and the editor works to make sure each volume within the series conforms to the aims for which the series is being produced. Readers of this Festschrift will observe here, as in several other chapters, the labor of reaching back to the efforts of the biblical writers themselves and in some sense continuing their work. And so Hubbard appropriately concludes by acknowledging the humbling privilege of the task.

Leslie Allen's essay[36] transitions from a focus on commentary production to scholarly research as it appears in the published commentary. He reflects upon a long career writing biblical commentaries, with a growing appreciation for the way textual structure (an explicate of the text) conveys meaning (an implicate of the text). Moving beyond formal structuring elements such as textual superstructure, Allen offers several examples of the

---

35. Robert L. Hubbard, Jr. has written *Joshua* for the NIV Application Commentary (2000), *First & Second Kings* for Everyman's Bible Commentary (1991), *The Book of Ruth* for the New International Commentary on the Old Testament (1988, and series editor), and served as co-editor, New International Biblical Commentary.

36. Leslie C. Allen has written *Jeremiah: A Commentary* for Old Testament Library (2008), the Ezra and Nehemiah portions of *Ezra, Nehemiah, Esther* for the New International Biblical Commentary (2003), *Psalms 101–50, Revised* for the Word Biblical Commentary (2002), *Ezekiel 1–19* for the Word Biblical Commentary (1994), *Ezekiel 20–48* for the Word Biblical Commentary (1990), *1, 2 Chronicles* for The Communicator's Commentary (1987), *Psalms 101–150* for the Word Biblical Commentary (1983), and *The Books of Joel, Obadiah, Jonah and Micah* for the New International Commentary on the Old Testament (1976).

ways in which substantive (not simply formal) elements—such as key words and themes—provide macrostructure to the composition as a whole, indicative of implicit meaning that the text's authors and editors sought to convey to readers.

RESEARCH AND ITS RESULTS IN BIBLICAL COMMENTARY

The second part of our collection shifts focus to specific examples where ancient hermeneutical impulses manifest in passages of the Hebrew Bible. *Willem A. M. Beuken*[37] discerns a case of "an exegetical comment, directly inserted into the running text ('interpolation') which changes the purport of the sentence without suppressing its primary meaning." Here, the Isaiah-book includes the beginnings of commentary on its own text so that later readers understand its implicit meaning in a certain way. Beuken helps us see that the tradents of the Isaiah textual tradition regarded themselves as inheriting a responsibility for not just handing on the text but for adding to its referential texture—amplifying its possibilities for meaning. Beuken himself acts in essentially the same capacity. Both tradents—the ancient Isaiah copyist(s) and Beuken—stand in the same place between the text and its readers, aiming to disclose from the text an insight into the divine mind. Inevitably the manner of such commentary-writing is different, reflecting different stages along the canon-trajectory: the ancients added a gloss that became part of the transmitted text itself, while the modern commentator adds a gloss that becomes part of the extra-textual hermeneutical tradition.

Central to much of Beuken's life-work is the book of Isaiah, shown by scholarship to be the product of literary accretion spanning several centuries. *Marvin A. Sweeney*[38] has similarly attended to the Isaiah tradition, and his contribution is a chapter that will ultimately appear in volume of the Forms of the Old Testament Literature series, dedicated to a comprehensive examination of the genres within which the semantic content of the Old

---

37. Willem A. M. Beuken has written *Isaiah: Part II, 28–39* for the Historical Commentary on the Old Testament (2000), *Jesaja 13–27* for the Herders Theologischer Kommentar zum Alten Testament (2007), and *Jesaja* for De Prediking van het Oude Testament (1979, 1983, 1989).

38. Marvin A. Sweeney has written *Isaiah 1–39, with an Introduction to Prophetic Literature* for the Forms of the Old Testament Literature series (1996), *The Twelve Prophets* (Vol. 1, and Vol. 2 with Jerome T. Walsh) for Berit Olam (2000), *Zephaniah: A Commentary* for Hermeneia: A Critical and Historical Commentary on the Bible (2003), *The Prophetic Literature* for the Interpreting Biblical Texts Series (2005), and *I and II Kings: A Commentary* for the Old Testament Library (2007).

Testament finds expression. (FOTL exemplifies a commentary series written for the scholarly guild with a design to convey the text's implicit meaning as it is illumined through a particular range of data or of a particular exegetical approach—in this case, form criticism.) The form-critical approach builds on an ancient yet ever-valid recognition that principled interpretation must be guided by accurate identification of the genre one is reading. As Sweeney's article demonstrates, the biblical text typically consists of a rich literary tapestry woven of genres whose cumulative interactive dynamic can provide insight into the message(s) the author(s) sought to communicate within a likely historical and social context. Form-critical analysis often helps us listen in on a conversation among biblical voices—here, between Ezra-Nehemiah and Trito-Isaiah—as interested parties of post-exilic Judea sought to define "community participation" in the emerging Torah-centric Judaisms.

Form-criticism is a subspecies of a larger hallmark of modern biblical scholarship: the recognition that so much of the Bible, particularly the First Testament, consists of poetic and narrative literature. In that light, principled exegesis includes a sensitivity to the biblical text's various literary dimensions. *John Hull*,[39] a former student of our honoree, traces the narrative arc in the composition of an entire biblical book (Judges), seeking the turning point between the book's two halves. By analyzing the characterization of the judges within a larger deuteronomistic evaluative frame of kingship as (il)legitimate leadership under YHWH, Hull shows that the turning point occurs with the leadership of Gideon and, especially, his son Abimelech. In his own words, Hull's essay "could serve as the literary setting section on Judges 9 in a commentary on Judges." The emphasis on "literary" reflects a noteworthy development in biblical commentary over the past fifty years. Most premodern commentary sought to explicate the biblical text as it might bear upon Jewish or Christian teaching in its rabbinic or patristic expressions respectively. Most modern biblical commentary has emphasized the more explicitly historical dimensions of the text, orienting itself by reference to either the history of ancient Israelite literature, or the history of Israel in its ancient near Eastern context, or both. But the last generation or two of biblical commentators have at times preferred to understand individual compositions primarily on the basis of their own literary features and only secondarily by virtue of their historical referentiality. Hull's probe into Judges 9 draws our attention to the ideological platform upon which the shapers of both the book of Judges and the collection of the Former Prophets stood in their evaluation of Israelite leadership vis-à-vis YHWH.

---

39. John Hull is a Disciples of Christ Minister.

Within the literary world of the Former Prophets, historical reference is circumscribed by the horizons of salvation history rather than any history that archaeological and historical sciences might be able to reconstruct. In his essay Hull is motivated by a desideratum that many contemporary biblical commentators pursue: offering their readers the opportunity to hear the biblical writer's voice on its own terms through attention to literary features appropriate to the genre, including characterization and lexical preferences.

Takamitsu Muraoka's[40] essay majors in the literary features just mentioned: characterization as indicated through lexical preferences and other linguistic nuances. His chapter provides a sterling example of biblical scholarship aimed squarely at members of the academic guild familiar with the Bible's ancient languages, not unlike the commentaries produced by the great Alexandrian librarians of antiquity such as Aristophanes of Byzantium and Aristarchus of Samothrace. Due to its technical nature, we have provided an extended introduction to Prof. Muraoka's essay *ad loc*. Here we point out that his contribution consists of a further installment in a series of studies on 2 Samuel 11–13, the narrative about a turning point in the life of King David. When such storytelling is offered orally in live performance, clues from facial expression, body language, and physical gestures would help the audience interpret the words declaimed by the storyteller. In the written form of David's story, however, only the details presented by the text itself offer any *fundament* for uncovering the storyteller's implied meaning. Within the Hebrew manuscript tradition, the explicit details in question may be differences in what the first-century BCE scribe of 4Q51 (4QIsa[a]) from the Qumran scrolls copied relative to what the Masoretic Text presents in the eleventh-century Codex Leningradensis. Moreover, in those instances when we are in possession of more than one telling of the same story, particularly by virtue of translation from one language to another, an important preliminary step to interpretation is needed, namely discerning what is implied by this or that grammatical construction or lexical choice in the target language relative to what was likely present in the source text. In these studies, Prof. Muraoka reads a portion of the David narrative closely for this implicate: relative to the Masoretic Text, how was the story understood by the 4Q51 scribe, by the roughly contemporary proto-Lucianic

---

40. Takamitsu Muraoka has written *Hebrew/Aramaic Index to the Septuagint: Keyed to the Hatch-Redpath Concordance* (1988), *A Greek-English Lexicon of the Septuagint* (1993, 2002, 2009), *Modern Hebrew for Biblical Scholars: An Annotated Chrestomathy With an Outline Grammar and a Glossary* for the Semantics of Ancient Hebrew Database (1998), *A Grammar of Egyptian Aramaic* (with Bezalel Porten, for Handbook of Oriental Studies, 2003), *A Grammar of Qumran Aramaic* for Ancient Near Eastern Studies Supplement Series (2011), and *Classical Syriac for Hebraists* for Subsidia et Instrumenta Linguarum Orientis (2nd, rev. ed., 2014).

Greek version, and by the similarly contemporary Kaige Greek recension? What a specific textual detail implies may be no more than an error on the part of a Greek translator. On the other hand, the implication of a given Greek lexical choice more often derives not from a mistake but from the peculiar manner in which translator understood the story and tried to convey it. Prof. Muraoka's essay shows how the ancient translators, as well as the tradents of the Hebrew text, were themselves biblical commentators who sought to make explicit the implicit meaning they perceived in the story. Modern biblical commentators may find guidance from them for conveying the implicit sense of David's story to today's reader.

But when it cannot be determined what a text denotes explicitly, what is the commentator to say? How can the text's implicate be discerned when the explicate itself remains obscured? In the essay by *H. G. M. Williamson*,[41] the case in point is historical reference in Isaiah 9:7–20, a passage whose basis for rhetorical force lies in its reference to historical events that elude retrieval—frustrating the commentator's wish to accurately convey the text's implicit meaning, even as that would have been recognized by ancient readers. Williamson's review of modern commentators' suggestions reveals a contemporary commentating mindset driven to clarify the text by successfully identifying its historical reference. But, as Williamson points out, this mindset does not always serve the text well. The literary artistry of biblical texts—perhaps most of all among the orations of prophets like Isaiah—requires that commentators remain open to imagine fresh referential possibilities in the text; in this case, a paradigmatic rather than solely historical reference. Here, the biblical writer seems to tie the word of judgment not to a specific set of historical circumstances but builds into his rhetoric an openness, a set of optional historical scenarios that the word of judgment addresses. This points to the ancient writer's diagnosis not of a particular action that will bring God's wrath but of the ancient nation's chronic sinful condition that will ultimately bring devastation upon it. Sometimes the prophetic orations adapt historical language to speak in supra-historical terms, and commentators are challenged to discern when that is the case. Doing otherwise would misrepresent the text—the modern commentator's anathema.

---

41. H. G. M. Williamson has written *1 and 2 Chronicles* for the New Century Bible Commentary (1982), *Ezra, Nehemiah* for the Word Biblical Commentary (1985), *Ezra and Nehemiah* for Old Testament Guides (1987), and *Isaiah 1–5: A Critical and Exegetical Commentary* for the International Critical Commentary (2014).

RELEVANCE OF BIBLICAL COMMENTARY

Avoiding misrepresentation of the biblical text is a theme that continues into our volume's third and final section. The biblical text was written in ancient times to address the concerns of ancient audiences according to ancient standards of intelligibility. But contemporary readers inhabit a significantly different cognitive world and successful commentators must bridge the ancient and contemporary horizons. Premodern commentators usually assumed on the part of the biblical writers categories of thinking and referentiality current to themselves. Modern scholarship proceeds on a different assumption: that ancient texts will as a matter of course reflect ancient ways of world-perception and thinking rather than modern ones. At the same time, contemporary biblical commentators hope to disclose to their modern readers the texts' ancient implicit insights about God and the human condition in ways that readers will find relevant to modern discourse.

For the Bible to address contemporary concerns appropriately, "a proper understanding of the text is essential, both in terms of what it teaches, and what it does not teach." This line from *Miles Van Pelt*[42] characterizes a way of studying ancient texts though close attention to what the grammar and syntax of the ancient languages exclude and what they allow for translation and interpretation. Here Van Pelt stands in a tradition rooted in the Renaissance applied to Greco-Roman classical and biblical literature at least by the fifteenth century. He demonstrates how the philological tradition continues to correct misunderstandings imported into the biblical text from social and intellectual debates of the present moment—in this case, the controversies characteristic of American evangelical interpretations of the early chapters of Genesis in the light of contemporary science. By the seventeenth century, growing awareness of non-European social customs encouraged explorations into biblical world beyond linguistics into the ancient social customs reflected in the Bible. *Victor Matthews's*[43] article extends the same sort of examination into sociological factors underlying biblical narrative, bringing a better understanding of how deftly biblical texts can speak of peace-generating mutual respect amid violent confrontations. The world in which Matthews writes is one that has witnessed global violence at an unprecedented scale, and in the twenty-first century the prospects for either

---

42. Miles Van Pelt has written *Biblical Hebrew: A Compact Guide* (2012), *Basics of Biblical Aramaic: Complete Grammar, Lexicon, and Annotated Text* (2011), and *Basics of Biblical Hebrew Grammar* (with Gary D. Pratico, 2001).

43. Victor Matthews has written *The IVP Bible Background Commentary: Old Testament* (with John H. Walton and Charles W. Chavalas, 2000), and *Judges and Ruth* for the New Cambridge Bible Commentary (2004).

peace or war stand to be informed by hermeneutics applied to canons of sacred scripture.

According to the Hebrew Bible, the task of communicating the divine will to a religious community in the midst of social, political, and economic upheavals is quintessentially prophetic. In his essay, *John Goldingay*[44] imagines the biblical prophet addressing the modern church audience on its way to exile instead of only to Jeremiah's ancient Judean contemporaries. Here we observe how a lifetime of biblical commentary-production—especially when concentrated on the Hebrew prophets—can cultivate a certain prophet-mindedness in a commentator like Goldingay. Beyond the study-bound task of exegesis, such a commentator shares the space of the prophet in his own ecclesial context, compelled to agonize over the apostasy that is plainly evident there but popularly ignored. Goldingay's piece reminds us that biblical commentary writing, at least in its modern iterations, is a peculiar enterprise. At one extreme, it can be undertaken strictly as an exercise in historical science, with clinical application of philological methodology to no purpose other than explicating the earliest recoverable meaning. At the opposite extreme, biblical commentary aimed at more popular audiences may find it expedient to ignore nuances of ancient literary expression for the sake of a relevance that has been determined by factors other than what the biblical text actually says. We have already noted that commentary serves to paratextually transmit the text's implicit voice. But Goldingay asks, "yes, but to whom am I transmitting the biblical voice? If I do no more than bring a text like Jer 2:5–14—so damning of ancient Judah's scholarly guild—before my own scholarly guild with all the requisite conventions of the commentary genre properly observed, have I actually done justice to the implicit message that the biblical voice articulated?" Goldingay, who himself possesses an enviable record of outstanding published exegesis, hopes for something more in biblical commentary, at least as it aims to convey the text to the church.

Similarly, former Hartley student *Alissa Jones Nelson*[45] observes that, if the purpose of biblical commentary is to convey the text to the reader who in turn can then engage with the author and with the historic community of

---

44. John Goldingay has written *Daniel* for the Word Biblical Commentary (1989), *Isaiah* for the New International Biblical Commentary (2001), *Psalms* for the Baker Commentary on the Old Testament (2006, 2007, 2008), *Minor Prophets II* (with Pamela Scalise) for the New International Biblical Commentary (2009), ten volumes in the Old Testament For Everyone series (2010–14), seventeen volumes for the Understanding the Bible Commentary Series (2010–16), and *Isaiah 56–66* for the *International Critical Commentary* (2014).

45. Alissa Jones Nelson is Acquisitions Editor for Religious Studies at Walter De Gruyter GmbH, Berlin.

commentators, a faithful conveyance of the text may not so much remove ambiguities as preserve them. With the book of Job at issue, Jones Nelson in her own way resonates with Goldingay's struggle over Jeremiah: is the commentator's purpose to "tame the text," attenuating the text's moral impulse (Jeremiah) or its deep theological ambiguity (Job)? As she considers both liberation theology and prosperity theology in the light of the book of Job, Jones Nelson brings before us a central theological conundrum prompted by this challenging book: is there any way of knowing one's standing with God except by the gauge of material well-being? This is an unavoidable difficulty in any theological system where the divine is taken to be an active agent in the world inhabited by humans, because—as the book of Job forces the issue—divine activity is seemingly unintelligible relative to the human situation apart from gauges such as health/disease, social wholeness/isolation, and wealth/poverty. Jones Nelson agrees with Clines that the biblical text offers no definitive resolution to this conundrum, but she goes on to suggest that this makes selective Bible reading and interpretation inevitable on the part of both liberation theologians and prosperity theologians. Both are turning to the Bible for authoritative endorsement of their own respective visions of how divine reality will ultimately manifest itself in the human situation, the one realized through participation in systemic social change, the other in spiritual exercises of prayer and tithing. Jones Nelson argues that a rigid, universalizing commitment to either the one or the other is inconsistent with the more complex socio-religious realities of Bible-reading communities as well as with the more complex theo-hermeneutical realities of the biblical text itself. This suggests an expansion of the hermeneutical circle within which biblical commentary takes place, something the honoree of this volume and all its contributors would endorse.

BIBLIOGRAPHY

Allen, Leslie. *The Books of Joel, Obadiah, and Micah*. NICOT. Grand Rapids: Eerdmans, 1976.
———. *1, 2 Chronicles*. The Communicator's Commentary. Nashville: W Publishing Group, 1987.
———. *Ezekiel 20–48*. WBC. Nashville: Nelson, 1990.
———. *Ezekiel 1–19*. WBC. Nashville: Nelson, 1994.
———. *Psalms 101–150, Revised*. WBC. Nashville: Nelson, 2002.
———. *Jeremiah: A Commentary*. OTL. Louisville: Westminster John Knox, 2008.
Allen, Leslie C., and Timothy S. Laniak. *Ezra, Nehemiah, Esther*. NIBC. Peabody, MA: Hendrickson, 2003.
Anderson, Bernhard W. "The Problem and Promise of Commentary." *Int* 36 (1982) 341–55.

Augustine. *Homily on Psalm 45*. CCSL. Turnhout: Brepols, 1953.
Beuken, Willem A. M. *Isaiah: Part II, 28–39*. HCOT. Leuven: Peeters, 2000.
———. *Jesaja 1–12*. HThKAT. Freiberg: Herder, 2003.
———. *Jesaja 13–27*. HThKAT. Freiberg: Herder, 2007.
———. *Jesaja 28–39*. HThKAT. Freiberg: Herder, 2010.
Bockmuehl, Markus. "The Dead Sea Scrolls and the Origins of Biblical Commentary." In *Text, Thought and Practice in Qumran and Early Christianity*, edited by Ruth A. Clements and Daniel R. Schwartz, 3–29. STDJ 84. Leiden: Brill, 2009.
Bohm, David. *Wholeness and the Implicate Order*. London: Routledge & Kegan Paul, 1980.
Braude, William G. *The Midrash on Psalms*. New Haven: Yale University Press, 1959.
Brown, Marvin. "The Commentary in Biblical Hermeneutics." In *The Commentary Hermeneutically Considered*. Edited by Edward C. Hobbs, 10–13. Protocol Series of the Colloquies of the Center 31. Berkeley: Center for Hermeneutical Studies in Hellenistic and Modern Culture, 1977.
Clement of Alexandria. *Stromata*. In *Ante-Nicene Fathers* 2, edited by Alexander Roberts, James Donaldson, and A. Cleveland Coxe. Buffalo, NY: Christian Literature Publishing, 1885.
Clines, David J. A. *Ezra, Nehemiah, and Esther*. NCBC. Grand Rapids: Eerdmans, 1984.
———. *Job 1–20*. WBC. Nashville: Nelson, 1989.
———. *Job 21–37*. WBC. Nashville: Nelson, 2006.
———. *Job 38–42*. WBC. Nashville: Nelson, 2011.
Coggins, Richard. "A Future for the Commentary?" In *The Open Text: New Directions for Biblical Studies?*, edited by Francis Watson, 163–75. London: SCM, 1993.
Dawson, David. *Allegorical Readers and Cultural Revision in Ancient Alexandria*. Berkeley: University of California Press, 1992.
Dickey, Eleanor. *Ancient Greek Scholarship: A Guide to Finding, Reading, and Understanding Scholia, Commentaries, Lexica, and Grammatical Treatises, from Their Beginnings to the Byzantine Period*. Oxford: Oxford University Press, 2007.
Eco, Umberto. "Between Author and Text." In *Interpretation and Overinterpretation*, edited by Stefan Collini, 67–88. Cambridge: Cambridge University Press, 1992.
Edlow, Robert Blair. *Galen on Language and Ambiguity: An English Translation of Galen's "De Captionibus (On Fallacies)" with Introduction, Text, and Commentary*. Leiden: Brill, 1977.
Foucault, Michel. *L'ordre du discours: leçon inaugurale au Collège de France prononcée le 2 décembre 1970*. Paris: Dallimard, 1971. Available in English translation by Rupert Swyer as an appendix to *The Archaeology of Knowledge*. New York: Pantheon, 1971.
Gregory I. *Moralia in Iob*, Books 1–5 and conclusion (35.20.49). Draft translation by James O'Donnell (http://www.georgetown.edu/faculty/jod/gregory.html).
Goldingay, John E. *Daniel*. WBC. Nashville: Nelson, 1989.
———. Isaiah. NIBC. Peabody: Hendrickson, 2001.
———. *Psalms, Volume 1: Psalms 1–41*. Baker Commentary on the Old Testament Wisdom and Psalms. Grand Rapids: Baker, 2006.
———. *Psalms, Volume 2: Psalms 42–89*. Baker Commentary on the Old Testament Wisdom and Psalms. Grand Rapids: Baker, 2007.
———. *Psalms, Volume 3: Psalms 90–150*. Baker Commentary on the Old Testament Wisdom and Psalms. Grand Rapids: Baker, 2007.

———. *Isaiah 56–66: A Critical and Exegetical Commentary.* ICC. London: T & T Clark, 2014.
Goldingay, John E., and Pamela J. Scalise. *Minor Prophets II.* Understanding the Bible Commentary Series. Grand Rapids: Baker, 2009.
Hartley, John E. *The Book of Job.* NICOT. Grand Rapids: Eerdmans, 1988.
———. *Leviticus.* WBC. Nashville: Nelson, 1992.
———. *Genesis.* NIBC. Peabody, MA: Hendrickson, 2000.
Hubbard, Robert L. *The Book of Ruth.* NICOT. Grand Rapids: Eerdmans, 1988.
———. *First & Second Kings.* Everymans Bible Commentary. Chicago: Moody, 1991.
———. *Joshua.* The NIV Application Commentary. Grand Rapids: Zondervan, 2000.
Jenkins, Philip. *The Next Christendom: The Coming of Global Christianity.* New York: Oxford University Press, 2002.
———. *The New Faces of Christianity: Believing the Bible in the Global South.* New York: Oxford University Press, 2008.
Jerome. *Apology against Rufinus.* In *Jerome, Dogmatic and Polemical Works.* Translated by John N. Hritzu. Father of the Church 53. Baltimore: Catholic University of America Press, 1965.
Justinian. *Corpus Juris Civilis.* Vol. 2. Edited by Paul Krüger. Berlin: Weidmann, 1895.
Lohfink, Gerhard. "Kommentar als Gattung." *BibLeb* 15 (1974) 1–16.
Lyre, Nicholas. *Biblia Sacra cum glossa ordinaria quidem a Strabo Fuldensis monacho benedictino: nunc vero novum partum, cum graecorum, tum latinorum explicationibus locuptetata, et postilla Nicolai Lyrani franciscani, nec non additionibus Pauli Burgensis episcopi, et Matthiae Thoringi replicis, opera et studio theologor,* edited by Leander de Sancto Martino and Jean Gallemart; Douai and Antwerp: B. Bellarus and J. Keebergius, 1617; reprinted with an introduction by K. Froehlich and M. T. Gibson. Turnhout: Brepols, 1992.
Madrigal, Alfonso de. *Commentarii in1 am partem Matthaei.* Venice, 1615.
Martens, Elmer A. *Jeremiah.* BCBC. Scottdale, PA: Herald, 1986.
Matthews, Victor H. *Judges & Ruth.* NCBC. Cambridge: Cambridge University Press, 2004.
Mayer, Roland. *Horace: Epistles Book I.* Cambridge Greek and Latin Classics. Cambridge: Cambridge University Press, 1994.
Menn, Esther M. "Sweet Singer of Israel: David and the Psalms in Early Judaism." In *Psalms in Community: Jewish and Christian Textual, Liturgical, and Artistic Traditions,* edited by Harold W. Attridge and Margot E. Fassler, 61–74. SBLSS 25. Atlanta: SBL Press, 2003.
Minnis, Alistair. *Medieval Theory of Authorship: Scholastic Literary Attitudes in the Later Middle Ages.* 2nd ed. Philadelphia: University of Pennsylvania Press, 2009.
Montana, Fausto. "The Making of Greek Scholiastic *Corpora.*" In *From Scholars to Scholia: Chapters in the History of Ancient Greek Scholarship,* edited by Franco Montinari and Lara Pagani, 104–62. Trends in Classics Supplementary Volumes 9. Berlin: de Gruyter, 2011.
Morard, Martin. "Entre mode et tradition: les commentaires du psaumes de 1160 à 1350." In *La Bibbia del XIII secolo: Storia del testo, storia dell'esegesi. Atti del Convegno della Società Internazionale per lo Studio del Medioevo Latino (SISMEL). Firenze, 1–2 giugno 2001,* edited by Francesco Santi and Giuseppe Cremascoli, 323–52. Florence: SISMEL, 2004.

Muraoka, Takamitsu. *Hebrew/Aramaic Index to the Septuagint: Keyed to the Hatch-Redpath Concordance*. Grand Rapids: Baker, 1998.

———. *Modern Hebrew for Biblical Scholars: An Annotated Chrestomathy with an Outline Grammar and a Glossary*. Wiesbaden: Harrassowitz, 1998.

———. *A Greek-English Lexicon of the Septuagint*. Leuven: Peeters, 2009.

———. *A Grammar of Qumran Aramaic*. Ancient Near Eastern Studies Supplement Series 38. Leuven: Peeters, 2011.

———. *Classical Syriac for Hebraists*. 2nd rev. ed. Subsidia et Instrumenta Linguarum Orientis 6. Wiesbaden: Harrassowitz, 2014.

Muraoka, Takamitsu, and Bezalel Porten. *A Grammar of Egyptian Aramaic*. Handbook of Oriental Studies. Leiden: Brill, 1997.

Ocker, Christopher. *Biblical Poetics before Humanism and Reformation*. Cambridge: Cambridge University Press, 2002.

Origen. *Homilies on Leviticus 1–16*. Translated by G. W. Barkley. Fathers of the Church 83. Washington, DC: Catholic University of America Press, 1990.

Paulus, Julius. "De Officio Praefectorum Praetorio Orientis et Illyrici." In *Corpus Juris Civilis* 1.XXVI, edited by Paul Krüger, 2:125. Berlin: Weidmann, 1895.

Schironi, Francesca. "Greek Commentaries." *DSD* 19 (2012) 399–441.

Schnabel, Eckhard. "On Commentary Writing." In *On the Writing of New Testament Commentaries: Festschrift for Grant R. Osborne on the Occasion of His 70th Birthday*, edited by Stanley E. Porter and Eckhard Schnabel, 3–10. TENTS 8. Leiden: Brill, 2013.

Smith, Barry. "Textual Deference." *APQ* 28 (1991) 1–13.

Strousma, Guy G. "Scripture and *Paideia* in Late Antiquity." In *Homer and the Bible in the Eyes of Ancient Interpreters*, edited by Maren R. Niehoff, 29–41. Jerusalem Studies in Religion and Culture 6. Leiden: Brill, 2012.

Sweeney, Marvin A. *Isaiah 1–39, with an Introduction to Prophetic Literature*. FOTL16. Grand Rapids: Eerdmans, 1996.

———. *The Twelve Prophets*. Vol. 1, *Hosea, Joel, Amos, Obadiah, Jonah*. Berit Olam. Collegeville, MN: Glazier, 2000.

———. *The Twelve Prophets*. Vol. 2, *Micah, Nahum, Habakkuk, Zephaniah, Haggai, Zechariah, Malachi*. Berit Olam. Collegeville, MN: Glazier, 2000.

———. *Zephaniah: A Commentary*. Hermeneia. Minneapolis: Augsburg, 2003.

———. *The Prophetic Literature*. Interpreting Biblical Texts Series. New York: Abingdon, 2005.

———. *I and II Kings: A Commentary*. OTL. Louisville: Westminster John Knox, 2007.

Swete, Henry Barclay. *An Introduction to the Old Testament in Greek*. Edited by Henry St. John Thackeray. Cambridge: Cambridge University Press, 1900.

Van Pelt, Miles V. *Basics of Biblical Aramaic: Complete Grammar, Lexicon and Annotated Text*. Grand Rapids: Zondervan, 2011.

———. *Biblical Hebrew: A Compact Guide*. Grand Rapids: Zondervan, 2012.

Van Pelt, Miles V., and Gary D. Pratico. *Basics of Biblical Hebrew Grammar*. Grand Rapids: Zondervan, 2001.

Walton, John H., Victor H. Matthews, and Mark W. Chavalas. *The IVP Bible Background Commentary: Old Testament*. Downers Grove, IL: IVP Academic, 2000.

Watts, James. *Leviticus 1–10*. HCOT. Leueven: Peeters, 2013.

Williamson, H. G. M. *1 and 2 Chronicles*. NCBC. Grand Rapids: Eerdmans, 1982.

———. *Ezra, Nehemiah*. WBC. Nashville: Nelson, 1985.

———. *Ezra and Nehemiah*. Old Testament Guides. London: T & T Clark, 1987.
———. *Isaiah 1–5: A Critical and Exegetical Commentary*. ICC. Bloomsbury: T & T Clark, 2006.
Yarchin, William. "Biblical Interpretation in the Light of the Interpretation of Nature, 1650–1900." In *Nature and Scripture in the Abrahamic Religions: 1700-Present*, edited by Jitse M. van der Meer and Scott Mandelbrote, 2:41–82. Leiden: Brill, 2008.
———. *History of Biblical Interpretation. A Reader*. Grand Rapids: Baker Academic, 2011.

PART 1

Production and Publication
of Biblical Commentary

1

Writing a *Job* Commentary

—David J. A. Clines

A REPORT FROM THE WORKBENCH

When I was invited to contribute to this volume I readily agreed because of my long-time friendship with the estimated honoree, John Hartley, whom I first got to know during a year-long residence in California in 1974–75 and with whom I often shared at SBL meetings over the years something of the joys and tribulations of the long-distance Joban commentator.[1] But I was also intrigued by the proposal of the editors of this volume to include articles "that reflect upon personal experiences in the production of a biblical commentary," which I have long thought a neglected form of writing. We are sensitive today to the social location of other scholars in our field, but are largely ignorant of the processes and mechanisms and lived realities that have shaped, facilitated or constrained their academic works.

There is the "human interest" aspect of other scholars' lives, of course, the attraction of gossip about our friends and rivals, which never ceases to entertain and which we crave even if we would never admit it. But there is also a deeper desire to understand our colleagues as more than the written products of their lives, but as human beings with a yen, if not an addiction,

---

1. John's *Job* was finished more than 20 years before mine, which meant that I envied him for more than 20 years.

for learning that we recognize in ourselves. How they are motivated to consign great swathes of their lives to vast scholarly projects, what sustains them during the countless solitary hours, what satisfactions they derive, what regrets they must endure—these things we want to know of *for ourselves*, to know of in reference to ourselves. For we need to assure ourselves all the time that we are normal (even if at the further reaches of normality), that we are not deranged, that we have peers who would understand us and not disapprove, at least not entirely, of what we have been doing with our lives.

It has never been enough to rely on the scrappy information we pick up from Prefaces, replete as they so frequently are with conventional and clichéd words of gratitude to neglected spouses and family pets. We would like to know more of what it means to be a scholar, what it does to one's days and years, and, deep down, how the addiction is to be managed.

So I thought I would break the habit of a lifetime and write some lines on my experience of writing a commentary on Job. I remembered that one day, a long time ago, nearly 20 years, *in medias res* of my commentary, I had written such a piece, not to be published but for the sake of capturing for myself the daily experience of commentary-writing. Now that I read it over, I would judge that when I wrote it I was inordinately enthusiastic about the joys of composition, but at least I do believe I did feel the way I describe on that particular day:

> I have 55 books on Job on the shelves behind me, and about 80 volumes of dictionaries, grammars and encyclopaedias. There are 13 English versions of the Bible on the desk to my right, 27 commentaries on the mahogany dining room table that is my main desk (the solidity of that mahogany is very important to me); these are all within hands' reach, but beyond them, on another table, are photocopies of 16 older commentaries—together with all the bills and departmental files and literary magazines I am banishing to the corners of my world.
>
> Of the English versions and 27 commentaries I read every word. Every morning I open on my Mac my two files for the day, one with *Translation and Notes* for the chapter in progress, one for the *Comment*. Before long, I also open the Bible search program Accordance, which will display all the occurrences of a word I am considering, in Hebrew and English in parallel columns. Whenever I need to look up a verse, I will use Accordance rather than a printed Hebrew Bible, since it will show me the verse in English and Hebrew, in half a dozen English versions as well if I want, and with the Septuagint and Vulgate for good measure. I can ask for a wider context if I want it, or, if

I have typed a row of biblical references in the *Comment*, I can copy and paste them into the search box and I can check that all my references were correct, and note all the verses where the English and the Hebrew numeration differs (since I must give the Hebrew numbering with the English in parentheses).

For the extreme right of my screen, I have a list of commentators, in chronological order, so that when I list their adherence to a particular view their names will appear in the correct date order.

When I start my commentary on a new passage of the Joban text, a strophe of four or five lines, let us say, I will begin by making my own provisional translation of the Hebrew, looking up in the dictionaries not only the words I do not know or know well but also the common words to see if I can find support for the exact rendering forming in my head. Then I will study each of my thirteen English versions, and, whenever I am disposed to differ significantly from one of them, make a footnote to the text of my translation; sometimes their rendering will bring me to amend my own provisional translation. The differences among the translations will usually hang upon disputes over philology, text criticism or interpretation, so later, when I get into the commentaries, I will be able to discover the reasons for all the variations.

Now it is time to work on the philological notes. Typically, I begin with Driver and Gray in the ICC, incorporating in the *Notes* to the translation any points that interest me, and move on to Dhorme, Gordis, Pope, de Wilde and Fohrer, usually in just that order. When I see that an emendation was earlier proposed by Siegfried or Duhm or some other older scholar not among my desk companions, I note the fact in the appropriate place with two exclamation marks before the author's name so that I can confirm it later when I am reading them (rather than break off my routine to check immediately).

When I have read all the more philological commentaries, and got together a fair draft of the *Notes* section, it is time to start writing the commentary proper. First I try to write a paragraph about the strophe as a whole, what I think it is saying in general and how it connects up with what went before. This is the most difficult part of all, and sometimes I will have to read in other commentaries before I can see what I myself want to say. Fohrer is the best at giving me a kick start into this general paragraph.

And now I am ready for the verse by verse commentary (the *Comment*). I read just as much in the commentaries as I need to get me started, surveying the kinds of issues they have taken up, and then I begin to write my own commentary. Almost always, I will start by saying what I think the verse as a whole is about, as well as how it connects with what has preceded or with the general context. Then I will consider the words and phrases themselves, explaining precisely what they mean, what their resonances are and how they contribute to the sense of the present verse. When I have done writing my own commentary on the verse or the strophe, I will then read systematically through all my 27 desk companions, incorporating as I go any points or thoughts I have learned from them that I feel I should include.

When I get to the end of the chapter or the speech there is of course still a lot of busy work to be done. First I shall have to search the whole of my files for double exclamation marks, so as to find the items I still need to check. Some of those I can check now, if they are older commentators like Dillmann or Hitzig, whose books I have in my pile of photocopies; others I shall have to save up for a library visit, since they may be monographs or journal articles. But I know from experience that I shall be able to despatch most of them pretty quickly, and I expect that on the whole they will not greatly subvert what I have already written. Sometimes, though, a little article in a journal will entirely undermine my whole train of thought, and I will have a lot of revision to do.

There is still the *Form/Content/Structure* section to write. It is a bit boring, but I have devised a set of questions to ask systematically, about strophic structure and literary forms and the like, and I think it is worth doing. The best bit is left till the very last. It is the *Explanation* section that comes at the end of each unit of text (typically a chapter), where, as I say in the Preface to Volume 1, I try hard to stand a little way off from the text to ask what has been going on and what it all means, or, as I say in the Introduction, I try to savour what has been going on in the speech, evaluate it as warmly and respectfully as I can, and then make no secret of what I myself think about it (I am under no obligation to agree with everything in the text, if only because we all know that the friends, and Job himself to some extent, are in the wrong on many issues). To write those concluding paragraphs, which will occupy only a page or two of the printed book, I will have to reread the whole of what I have written on the current chapter(s), put some Mahler on (it was Bach for the philological notes), go into a free associative linguitative mode—and just write (trying not to repeat what I have already said in the commentary proper).

At the end of each day, I should add, I ask my Mac to count the words in each of my writing files, and I will enter the new word counts and the minutes I have spent (average about 4 hours a day) into my spreadsheet called Writing Record 1996 (or whatever the year was), so that I can see how many words I have written in the day (average about 1300), what my hourly average was, what my cumulative daily average now is (c. 325), how many words of the commentary I have written so far, what proportion of the commentary is now finished, how many pages it will be when it is done, and at what date, at the present rate of progress, I may expect to have completed it. The day I have finished will not be better than the thousands of days I was just writing.

That was, as I say, quite some time ago (1996), and written while I was in the throes of composition. Today, I am looking back on the whole process and ruminating. My reflections are organizing themselves into two groups: pleasures and perils.

THE PLEASURES OF COMMENTARY

A Defined Task

Compared to writing a monograph or a journal article, writing a commentary is a pretty clearly defined task. Especially if you are writing for a series of commentaries, the format, audience, shape and scope are predetermined. You know where to start and where to finish. The commentator can be confident about what the work is to look like in the end, not agonizing over the whole even while struggling with the particular.

It may seem very mechanical to be able to estimate every day how many words you still have to write and when you may expect to be finished, but I have found that I need rewards and incentives to keep going at a large task, and these little signs of progress gave me most of what I needed.

Avoiding Blank Page Syndrome

Because you know what lies before you in the text, you always know, in general at least, what your next move must be. It is bliss to sit down in the morning not dreading the blank page or screen, or lacking any idea of which out of hundreds of potential sentences you should begin with. With a commentary, if you are at verse 12, you can be confident that your next horizon will be verse 13. Mind you, I still have found it a good idea to attempt banishing blank page syndrome altogether by finishing work for the day in the middle of a paragraph, or even of a sentence, so that there can be no question of how the next day should begin.

In the Presence of a Great Mind

For the most part, works that call for commentary are master works, works that repay commentary, works that are rich, complex, profound. No doubt, not all biblical books are equally profound, but in most cases the commentator is aware of following and exploring the work of a superior mind. This is always a pleasurable and rewarding experience, even if the commentator is not always in total sympathy with the author. I count myself very fortunate that I was invited to comment on Job, which must be one of the most intellectually rich books of the Bible. I don't know that I ever formed much of an image of the poet as a person, but I never failed to admire the inventiveness and delicacy of his mind.

An Educational Premium

One of the greatest pleasures of commentary writing, especially as distinct from other scholarly writing, is the constant demands of the text that you launch yourself into new fields and topics that you would otherwise probably never have touched. I recall getting into ancient metallurgy and astronomy, and, especially in commenting on the divine speeches, into the lives and habits of various living creatures (including referencing video clips of crocodiles). I suspect that mine may be one of the first large-scale biblical commentaries written with constant reference to Wikipedia. I had such a sense of the immense variety of knowledges the poet draws upon that I compiled for my commentary (taking the idea from A. de Wilde's commentary) a "Classified Index of the Book of Job," listing, with references, the animals mentioned, the birds, aspects of the earth, the sky and the weather, language about farming, emotions, manufactures, warfare and weapons, and so on, under 42 headings altogether, over nine pages of small type. All these matters are largely incidental to the main purposes of the book, of course, but they show an artist at work who is hugely sensitive to the multiplicity of the world and of its human inhabitants.

Companionship

Most commentaries, not just commentaries on biblical books, are written on texts that have already been commented on. So today's commentator inevitably works in the presence of a commentatorial cloud of witnesses. I called my predecessor commentators my "desk companions" because I enjoyed their characters and their individuality, and came over the years to feel I knew them and their minds very well, though I had never met most of them. Shut in my study, I was surrounded by human contact. They had travelled for many of the years of their lives on the same journey that would occupy me for a quarter of a century, and I came to admire their fortitude and the twists and turns of their minds as I turned to them day after day.

Efficiency

I love to be efficient. This is not a heartless quest and I hope I do not fetishize it. But I am very conscious of how much of our scholarly lives is wasted on the business of organizing ourselves to the point of becoming productive, and I have tried to streamline the busy-work as much as I can. Early on in writing the *Job* commentary, I realized that accessing the relevant scholarly literature, even when one has located references to it, threatens to delay if not prevent getting on with the primary task. Especially because I had made it my personal goal to review the literature of the past 100 years, considering all the philological proposals and textual emendations of Job I could lay my hands on (a task that needs to be done every generation, I believe), and envisaging a very comprehensive bibliography, I saw that I needed a database to record all the items I came across. In the database I would also note what I had read and what I had still to see, and it would arrange the items in the libraries I visit (usually Sheffield and Cambridge) according to their position on the shelves.

I taught my relational database Helix the location of every volume of all the journals I use, so once I had entered *JQR* 21 as the reference for a journal article, for example, it would know that we did not have that volume in Sheffield, and I would have to consult it in Cambridge, and at shelfmark P7.c.1 on the South Wing, Floor 3. All the other items for that location would be printed out before my visit to the library, including the books, for which I had looked up the shelfmark in the electronic catalogues. Very occasionally I managed through this system to consult 100 items in a single day, but more often no more than 40.

Each item was classified as I entered it as a record according to its destined place in the commentary, whether for the bibliography at the head of each chapter, or for the General Bibliography at the end, so that by exporting the data I had all the items under their appropriate heading and in alphabetical order by author. It was a pleasure to me to be able to control so much data without being overwhelmed by it, and I am happy to accept any judgment made about my character that can be inferred from that fact.

THE PERILS OF COMMENTARY

Mistaking the Horizon

Commentary writing is fine work, which must always be attending to particulars. The commentator has to make a conscious effort, many times in the course of a working day, to stand back from the detailed work on the words and phrases in order to consider the impact of decisions about their meaning on the whole book. Balancing the needs of the micro-exegesis against those of a total perspective on the book, in a perpetual interplay between the part and the whole, is one of greatest pleasures of commentary writing, but also a realm in which it is all too easy to go astray. I think of the great commentary of Édouard Dhorme (1926; English translation, 1967), which almost never considered a wider horizon than that of the individual verse; I cannot agree with the commonly expressed opinion that it is the greatest of all biblical commentaries of our time. I came to think that Fohrer's was the most successful of Job commentaries at combining exact exegesis with the larger issues. The peril for the commentator is failing to blend the microscopic and the panoramic.

Brainwashing

If one labours for month after month at understanding a complicated text, and feels one has succeeded at last in making a tolerable sense of it, it is almost forgivable for a commentator to accept, explicitly or implicitly, the views of one's author. In fact, with the Book of Job, that is the default position of commentators. Hardly ever have I encountered someone saying, "This is what I think the passage says, or, the book as a whole says, and personally I do not believe it." At the same time, there is very little consensus on what the Book of Job actually says; but no matter, we commentators differ greatly from one another, but whatever we think the book means, that is what we ourselves affirm.

The situation has only to be stated like that for us to realize its absurdity. Especially with the Book of Job, where—unlike almost every book in the Bible—contrary points of view are expounded at length, one might have thought that commentators would have felt themselves encouraged to sit loose to any or all of the ideas propounded in the book, since most of them must in some sense be "wrong." It could even be argued that the divine speeches are not necessarily the last word on the matters that the book deals with, all the more because they systematically avoid the primary question that Job has everywhere been raising, the question whether there is justice in the divine governance of the world.

Even if one is personally disposed to accept statements in the text, it surely behooves a critical commentator to consider counter-evidence and counter-arguments to what the text presents (e.g., where and how does Job or YHWH differ from other parts of the Hebrew Bible?). I tried to do that myself in the *Explanation* sections of my commentary, but I am sure I did not range widely enough in my evaluations of what the speakers in the book were putting forward. The peril for the commentator is allowing oneself to be brainwashed by sustained closeness to the text and over-familiarity with it.

Hyper-Professionalization

The commentator is typically a professional scholar, whose work will be read and reviewed by one's peers, who are experts in the academic study of the biblical book in question. The bibliographies with which major commentaries these days have to be festooned are the commentator's first line of defence against criticism that the work insufficiently deep and inadequately researched.

There is nothing wrong with displaying the resources for interpretation, but the peril lies in overlooking some of the crucial sources. I said in the Introduction to the first volume of my *Job* commentary:

> I became increasingly dissatisfied with restricting my horizon to the so-called "scholarly" works. Scholars quote scholars and create their own canon of approved literature on the Book of Job. Those writings that are not cited by previous commentators do not generally get cited by subsequent commentators ... Of course, when it comes to technical questions about philology, unscholarly remarks can be safely ignored. But when it is a

matter of large-scale interpretation, of the meaning of the book as a whole and not just of a particular word or verse, one does not need to be a technically trained scholar to have valuable insights. So my "undiscriminating" bibliography, which includes sermons and works of popular devotion alongside vast works of erudition, is meant as a kind of atonement for the principle of scholarly apartheid which reigns elsewhere in the commentary.

CONCLUSION

I call commentary-writing the quintessential form of biblical scholarship. Despite the plethora of commentaries, good, bad and indifferent, that publishers insist on setting before us, I would argue that we can never have too many commentaries. Except for commentaries that are mostly derivative, every commentary represents one person's tangling with the biblical text, and every such engagement is at the least interesting and at best profitable. I have heard commentary-writing disparaged as no more than a matter of copying from other commentaries, but I resist that criticism vigorously as simple ignorance of what goes into the creation of a commentary.

We need commentaries because we need commentary writers. The field of biblical studies needs a sizable cadre of commentators, that is, persons who have submitted themselves over a sustained period of time to the discipline of following a text, in all its windings, and grappling with questions of meaning on the large scale and the small. No other form of biblical scholarship trains the mind in the same way, or creates a sense of humility vis-à-vis the text and its author and vis-à-vis other scholars. Not all our colleagues are equally suited for commentary-writing, and it is no crime not to have written a commentary. But I must confess to asking myself about one or another esteemed colleague, who turns out not to have been perhaps of the first rank, Well, have they written a *commentary*?

BIBLIOGRAPHY

Clines, David J. A. *Job 1–20*. WBC. Dallas: Word, 1989.
―――. *Job 21–37*. WBC. Nashville: Nelson, 2006.
―――. *Job 38–42*. WBC. Nashville: Nelson, 2011.
Dhorme, Édouard. *A Commentary on the Book of Job*. London: Nelson, 1967 [Original, 1926].
Dillmann, August. *Hiob*. KeHAT 2. 3rd ed. Leipzig: Hirzel, 1869.
Driver, S. R., and George Buchanan Gray. *A Critical and Exegetical Commentary on the Book of Job*. ICC. Edinburgh: T & T Clark, 1912.

Duhm, Bernhard L. *Das Buch Hiob erklärt*. KeHAT 16. Leipzig: Mohr Siebeck, 1897.
Fohrer, Georg. *Das Buch Hiob*. KAT 16. Gütersloh: Gütersloher Verlagshaus Mohn, 1963.
Gordis, Robert. *The Book of God and Man: A Study of Job*. Chicago: University of Chicago Press, 1978.
Hartley, John E. *The Book of Job*. NICOT. Grand Rapids: Eerdmans, 1988.
Hitzig, Ferdinand. *Das Buch Hiob übersetzt und ausgelegt*. Leipzig: Winter, 1874.
Pope, Marvin H. *Job*. AB 15. 3rd ed. Garden City, NY: Doubleday, 1973.
Siegfried, C. *The Book of Job: Critical Edition of the Hebrew Text with Notes*. The Sacred Books of the Old Testament (The Polychrome Bible) 17. Leipzig: Hinrichs, 1893.
Wilde, A. de. *Das Buch Hiob; eingeleitet, übersetzt und erläutert*. Oudtestamentische Studien 22. Leiden: Brill, 1981.

2

Writing Commentary as Ritual and as Discovery

—James W. Watts

I AM DELIGHTED TO write about commentary writing for a master commentator, John Hartley. I keep his Leviticus commentary within easy arm's reach and consult it daily as I write my own commentary on that book.[1] He has in this way been a stimulating and dependable conversation partner. It is exactly this kind of conversation that commentary writing and reading is all about.

Much of my life has revolved around commentary writing and editing. Writing commentaries preoccupied much of my father's research. While I was in college, I worked summers compiling bibliographies for his Isaiah commentary.[2] As a graduate student, I proofread those volumes and two decades later I edited his revisions of them. Once established in a teaching career myself, I joined him in editing the WBC series as Associate Old Testament Editor (1997–2011). My own research now focuses on writing the Leviticus volumes in another technical commentary series, the Historical Commentary on the Old Testament (HCOT). The first volume was published in 2013.[3] So writing and editing commentaries has shaped much of my intellectual experience.

---

1. Hartley, *Leviticus*.
2. J. D. W. Watts, *Isaiah 1–33, Isaiah 34–66*.
3. J. W. Watts, *Leviticus 1–10*.

I have discovered that it is a surprisingly creative experience. It leads to thinking about issues and taking positions on debates that I had never thought about before. More than that, I have occasionally written about topics and made observations that, as far as I can tell, have never been written about before—a particularly surprising experience, given that the Hebrew Bible has been the subject of intensive interpretation and commentary for more than two thousand years. People frequently think that everything that can possibly be said about the Bible has already been said, and many times over. Yet I find that writing a commentary is to embark on a voyage of discovery that can lead to surprising innovations as often as any other mode of research.

My teaching career has taken place entirely within religious studies departments in liberal arts colleges and universities (at Hastings College from 1993 to 1999, in the College of Arts and Sciences at Syracuse University since then). Unlike the theological faculties where my father taught, my colleagues in other religious studies subjects and, especially, in other liberal arts departments, find biblical scholars' addiction to commentary writing somewhat peculiar. Commentary is not a typical genre of scholarship in these fields, except for some very specialized areas in the study of literature and law. It carries little prestige at research universities that quantify research output almost entirely on the basis of refereed journal articles and university press monographs (so I make sure that sufficient quantities of these genres appear on my c.v. too).

Intellectual and ideological concerns also lead observers outside of biblical studies, and some even within the guild, to regard commentary writing with suspicion. It seems to them to reproduce and strengthen tradition rather than emphasize innovative research. Though commentary received a brief reprieve when some philosophers reclassified all literature as simply recycling older materials,[4] that intellectual moment seems to have passed without fundamentally altering institutionalized assumptions about the genres of academic knowledge production. Critics within the field of biblical studies have suggested that commentary writing is fueled primarily by the religious book market rather than by research priorities.[5] They have

---

4. E.g., Barthes, "The Death of the Author," "We know now that a text is not a line of words releasing a single 'theological' meaning (the 'message' of the Author-God) but a multi-dimensional space in which a variety of writings, none of them original, blend and clash. The text is a tissue of quotations drawn from the innumerable centres of culture." He went on to declare that the death of the author also means the death of the critic, because interpretation of a text's singular meaning has become impossible. Cf. Derrida, *Writing and Difference*, 285.

5. Avalos, *End of Biblical Studies*, 325–37.

accused biblical scholars of colluding to support the cultural hegemony of the Bible.[6]

These suspicions of biblical commentaries observe that commentary writing takes place within a particular constellation of religious and academic politics that creates the market for commentaries and shapes the expectations of those who write them. That such cultural constraints also shape the production of every other textual genre does not alter the peculiarity of the social forces that generate biblical commentaries.

I do not intend to counter the political claims made by these authors. I instead propose a theoretical model, based on ritual theory, that can encompass both my experience of intellectual discovery through commentary writing and their observations about the social functions of commentaries.

WRITING AND READING COMMENTARY AS AN EXPERIENCE OF DISCOVERY

The commentary genre distinguishes itself by the fact that writers should engage every portion of the studied text, usually in sequential order. In the HCOT and WBC which included a new translation of the text, that expectation requires engaging every word of the Hebrew text, as well as many previous translations of it. As a result, the task of writing the HCOT commentary on Leviticus draws my attention to many issues that I have never thought about before, infusing this scholarly experience with an unusual degree of suspense. I never know where the next verse will lead—sometimes to observations and conclusions that few, if any, interpreters have made before.

A few examples will illustrate the kinds of innovative observations that commentary writing can generate. I refer readers to my commentary for the arguments in favor of these conclusions and leave it to them to judge their plausibility base on its exposition. The focus here will remain on why they came to mind in the first place.

One kind of observation addresses the text's rhetorical structure. Rhetorical analysis of a text's persuasive function provides important insights into its intended and actual effects, especially on those listening audiences for whom the Pentateuch (see Deut. 31:9–13) and most other ancient literature, was written. So this innovative approach that emphasizes persuasion[7] requires me to examine rhetorical effects at the micro level of verse

---

6. Schüssler Fiorenza, *Rhetoric and Ethic* 17–102; Berlinerblau, *The Secular Bible*, 57–84; Avalos, *End of Biblical Studies*, passim.

7. Previously argued in two monographs: J. W. Watts, *Reading Law*; and J. W. Watts, *Ritual and Rhetoric in Leviticus*.

arrangement, sentence structure, and individual word choices. For example, the prohibition of leavened bread on the altar and the requirement of salt on offerings in Lev 2:11–13 are obvious digressions because they break the chiastic arch that structures chap. 2, as Didier Luciani observed.[8] I noticed, however, that this digression has also been shaped poetically:

> This passage uses repeated terms in the first clause of each verse and the end of the final verse ... to produce a tightly unified composition that highlights the four prohibitions in the other clauses ... The four-fold repetition of "salt" in every clause of v. 13 emphasizes this concluding verse as well as the conceptual reversal that it contains: while vv. 11–12 prohibit additives of yeast and syrup, v. 13 requires salt as an additive to all "presents." The careful word choice and arrangement of these verses shows that this digression from the structure and contents of the rest of the chapter was nevertheless composed for maximal rhetorical impact.[9]

Similarly in Lev 6:8 (English 6:15), the word אזכרתה "its memorial portion" interrupts the usual refrain, "a soothing scent for YHWH" (cf. 1:9, 13, 17; 2:2, 9). The priestly (P) writer often varies or interrupts the refrains that structure his composition,[10] so other commentators have given little or no attention to the position of the word. However, attention to how the text sounds when read publicly caused me to realize that rhythm and rhyme led to this word appearing in this odd position:

> The verse can be analyzed as three lines that each end on a long "a" vowel (מנחה "commodity" twice, then אזכרתה "its memorial" or, with the Masoretic accentuation, ... מנחה ... שמנה אזכרתה "its oil ... commodity ... its memorial"). That leaves ליהוה "for YHWH" outside the three-line structure in emphatic position at the end.[11]

Taking into account the rhetorical setting of public readings also led me to a new explanation for the use of direct, second-person address in Lev 2:4–7. Whereas chaps. 1 and 3 couch all their provisions in the third singular

---

8. Luciani, *Structure littéraire du Lévitique*, 21–22.

9. J. W. Watts, *Leviticus 1–10*, 260–61.

10. As already observed by Paran, *Priestly Style*: "The priestly writer enjoys playing with words as though they were building blocks which can be put together in a variety of patterns according to the whim of the writer" (vii). Yet this observation has rarely been taken into account by commentators who consider such irregularities as signs of editorial changes.

11. J. W. Watts, *Leviticus 1–10*, 396.

typical of casuistic instructions, the instructions to lay people for preparing bread offerings switches to second singular because bread offerings must be baked at home. Priests cannot supervise their proper performance there, so it becomes entirely the responsibility of individual lay worshippers. The second singular pronouns drive that point home, especially in the aural experience of a public reading or recitation.[12]

Other innovations arise from summarizing and evaluating current research on pieces of the text and the subjects they address. That is surprising, since summary and review seem the opposite of creative research. My experience indicates otherwise, however. Evaluating other scholars' conclusions often leads me to take innovative positions on subjects that I did not anticipate addressing at all. For example, investigating the translation of מִן־הַתֹּרִים אוֹ מִן־בְּנֵי הַיּוֹנָה, usually translated "from turtledoves and pigeons," in Lev 1:14 led me to articles by Thomas Staubli. He argued that the use of two terms must designate two different kinds of birds, rather than the closely related turtledoves and pigeons. He found that Sumerian and Akkadian cognates of תֹּר/תּוֹר referred to wild hens and, later, domesticated chickens.[13] The LXX, however, supports the meaning "turtledove," so Staubli thought that turtledoves must have replaced wild hens in the rituals of the Second Temple. I found Staubli's arguments for the meaning "hen" or "chicken" persuasive, but not his acceptance of the LXX evidence for a change of ritual practice. Examination of Greek vocabulary for domestic fowl revealed that the common word for chicken, like English "hen," can be used more generally for many small birds. The LXX translator probably found that too inexact for the distinctions being mandated by Leviticus. He may have been led to "turtledove" by thinking that the Hebrew word, תּוֹר, is onomatopoeic for the sounds that doves make.[14] I stand by this argument and conclusion, yet it continues to surprise me that I have published an opinion about the taxonomy of domestic fowl species, a subject otherwise never drawing my interest!

Reviewing the history of interpretation of a particular word or verse can also stimulate innovations by highlighting how historical movements have generated unconscious trends in biblical interpretation. The phrase אוּרִים וְתֻמִּים in Lev 8:8 prompted me to make this kind of observation. Because my job as a commentary writer includes translating the Hebrew text into English, I was led to wonder why we usually transliterate this phrase as "Urim and Thummim" instead of translating the words. Though there

---

12. J. W. Watts, *Leviticus 1–10*, 256.
13. Staubli, "Hühneropfer."
14. J. W. Watts, *Leviticus 1–10*, 220.

is some debate about the words' meanings, they are not more difficult than many other ritual terms that are routinely translated. My survey of the history of translation showed that they had actually been translated with some variant of "light and truth" into Greek, Latin, Aramaic, German and English. The Geneva Bible in 1560 first transliterated the terms instead. Its date and context led me to suspect Reformation-era polemics behind this break with translation tradition. Sure enough, in searching for references to these divinatory objects in sixteenth-century European rhetoric, I discovered that Roman Catholics used them as biblical evidence for the infallibility of the Aaronide high priest and therefore as a typological proof of the Pope's infallibility as well. Protestants reacted by interpreting the names of the objects as indicating only the moral virtue of the priests, not evidence of infallibility. Transliteration further diluted the significance of these objects in Protestant Bibles.

These polemics created a habit of transliterating the terms that has persisted for five centuries, now even in Roman Catholic Bibles (e.g., NAB, JB). I felt that it was time to shake off this polemical heritage, and so translated the terms with the words, "luminaries and paragons."[15] The innovation, however, lies less in the English words that I chose than in the fact that I translated the terms at all. Reviewing the history of translation led me to realize how historical polemics continue to shape the behavior of interpreters. Choosing to reject this heritage led to innovation through translation. This is why it is necessary to pay attention to the history of the Bible's reception as part and parcel of exegesis, not just as a supplementary exercise. That history shapes how we translate and interpret the "original" text, whether we are aware of its influence or not. Conscious awareness allows for more intentional, and creative, exegesis.

The history of Leviticus's cultural reception also drew my attention to major omissions by comparison to the reception of some other biblical passages. The history of Western art or drama reflects little of Leviticus, an omission calling attention to the influence of literary genres on the visual arts. Artists much prefer to draw from narratives rather than from legal and instructional materials.[16] As a result, Exodus, Numbers, and especially Genesis, get depicted artistically far more often than Leviticus or Deuteronomy.

In contrast to its lack of influence on art, one might expect that the ritual instructions of Leviticus would have wielded more influence over ritual performances in Jewish and Christian communities. Its offering instructions certainly did influence the rituals of Jewish temples of the later

---

15. J. W. Watts, *Leviticus 1–10*, 457–62.
16. J. W. Watts, "Illustrating Leviticus"; and J. W. Watts, *Leviticus 1–10*, 33–39.

Second Temple period, and some of its purity rules still govern the daily lives of many observant Jews. However, the ritual gap between the book's instructions and later Jewish and Christian practices involves more than just the presentation of offerings. Leviticus 8, following instructions in Exodus 29, depicts the most elaborate ordination ritual found anywhere in Jewish or Christian bibles. Yet Jewish and Christian rituals for appointing rabbis, priests and other kinds of ministers to religious offices imitate instead the much simpler ritual of laying on hands, modeled by Moses' appointment of Joshua (Deut 34:9). The fact that neither Jews nor Christians grant Aaronide priests religious authority as mandated by Leviticus (especially 10:11–12) has inhibited imitating the book's ordination ritual for priests. This omission points out how changes in religious polity from the leadership of temples to the leadership of synagogues and churches shaped the book's cultural reception as much as the more famous changes in rituals of sacrifice and purification.

I have chosen examples of innovations in the interpretation of details, rather than from my commentary's wider thematic and historical arguments, because commentaries are infamous for their focus on details. Yet precisely by focusing on details, I repeatedly surprised myself by reaching innovative conclusions. In my experience, it is a focus on details informed by reflections on theories and methods that produces the most creative and critical thinking.

WRITING AND READING COMMENTARY AS RITUAL

How should we account for experiences of discovery in writing and, hopefully, reading commentaries? David J. A. Clines recounted his early experience of commentary writing as a "quest for truth" that changed over time into the experience of directing a symphony of voices representing readers of all times and places. He observed that readers of such a commentary

> can find and read what they want, and be perpetually tempted to read more than they thought they wanted, wander down avenues they didn't realize existed, waste time (i.e. enjoy themselves) with the text rather than efficiently pinpoint the answer to the question with which they had logged on.[17]

Clines' experience as a reader and writer of commentaries sounds very much like that of readers of the Bible itself. Though many Bible readers start with one question seeking one answer, reading scriptures frequently leads to

---

17. Clines, "Future of Commentary," 18–19, 23.

wandering through the text and making discoveries. Narrative criticism has theorized this experience of becoming immersed in "the world of the Bible" where the text generates questions to the reader rather than vice versa.[18] In this sense, commentary reading and writing extends and reproduces the ritual experience of scripture reading, or "Bible study."

Commentary supports the Bible's religious and cultural influence, as cultural critics have maintained. However, identifying commentary as a form of ritual allows for more nuanced analysis of this influence. Rituals have been analyzed by psychologists, sociologists, and anthropologists, as well as scholars of religion, throughout the twentieth century, and in the past few decades, ritual studies has developed into a recognized and influential field in its own right. Its resources can be deployed to understand the form and function of biblical commentaries, as well as the cultural role of biblical studies in general.

Although theorists debate the definition and function of ritual, they agree on its ability to focus the attention of individuals and, especially, groups of people. Rituals draw and maintain attention. Rituals mark times and spaces as extraordinary by requiring attention to very ordinary activities, such as walking, eating, and breathing.[19] They frequently require regular repetition. Instead of entering a room in whatever way is most practical, a procession requires attention to the timing, speed and sequence by which a group of people enter a room. Instead of eating a meal based on taste and etiquette only, ritual meals also require attention to the preparation and nature of the food and the sequence in which it gets eaten. Instead of letting the autonomous nervous system regulate one's breathing, many meditation rituals require attention to each inhalation and exhalation. Ritual calendars encourage repetition of particular rituals at set times during the day, week, or year. Though rituals often use such extraordinary attention to ordinary behavior to emphasize ideals or doctrines, some rituals serve primarily to pay attention to particular people (graduations, funerals), or to a nation (oaths of office, pledges of allegiance), or to a deity, or to a text.

Writing biblical commentaries fits easily within this description of ritual as extraordinary attention to ordinary activities. The normal activity of reading gets ritualized by commentary's focus on textual details and

---

18. Riceour, *The Conflicts of Interpretation*.

19. Smith observed that "Ritual relies for its power on the fact that it is concerned with quite ordinary activities placed within an extraordinary setting, that what it describes and displays is, in principle, possible for every occurrence of these acts" (*To Take Place*, 109; similarly Bell, *Ritual Theory*, 74, 92; for a broader survey of "ritual-like" activities, see Bell, *Ritual*, 138–69).

on debates over interpretive method, as well as by regular repetition in the form of writing and publishing ever more commentaries.

By saying that commentary "ritualizes" scripture, I do not mean to disparage commentary writing or reading in any way, though many will hear the claim as pejorative. Ritual frequently gets disparaged as "just ritual" or "empty ritual," and as "ritualistic" behavior in implicit or explicit contrast with religious practices that are authentic, heartfelt, and moral. These negative associations with the word "ritual" are deeply rooted in Western culture which deploys them polemically to distinguish true beliefs from superstitious falsehoods. The distinction has been used regularly by Christians to disparage the religious practices of pagans, Jews, and heretics, by Protestants to attack Catholics, and by modern rationalists to attack all forms of religious practice and belief.[20] Attacks on ritualism have been a favorite tactic for undermining religious authorities of all kinds.[21]

Against this prejudice which is deeply ingrained in both Christian and secular culture, theorists of ritual observe that all human societies make use of rituals, and in a wide variety of ways. Rituals play vital roles in marking changes in status within families (weddings, funerals), within religious communities (bar/bat mitsvahs, baptisms, confirmations, ordinations), and within nations (inaugurations, oaths of office). They serve to demarcate publicly those who affirm a particular community's religious identity (Passover seders, communion meals) or national identity (pledges of allegiance, national holidays).[22] Rituals unite individuals and communities but can also be used to fuel conflicts. Ritualization therefore should be understood as basic human behavior. By saying that commentary writing and reading ritualizes scripture, I am categorizing commentaries as the products of a fundamental human activity.

Many different religions ritualize sacred texts. Comparative study of religious communities provides insight into the distinctive effects of ritualizing scriptures in three different dimensions.[23] Commentary ritualizes the interpretation of scripture, as does translation, preaching, and devotional study. Ritualizing a text's *semantic dimension* in these ways enhances claims to the authority of both text and interpreters. It provides a basis, the biblical

---

20. See Búc, *Dangers of Ritual*, 251.

21. J. W. Watts, *Ritual and Rhetoric in Leviticus*, 154–61.

22. On ritual as publicly "indexing" people's relationship to a "canonical" order, see Roy Rappaport, *Ritual and Religion*, 53–58, 105–6, 122.

23. See J. W. Watts, "Three Dimensions." On the performative dimension, see also Graham, *Beyond the Written Word*; and Yoo, "Public Scripture Reading Rituals." On the iconic dimension, see also Parmenter, "The Iconic Book"; Parmenter, "The Bible as Icon"; and Larson, "Imperialized Sites of Memory."

text, for adjudicating disputes about religious doctrine and practice. Ritualizing interpretation leads to the emergence of expert interpreters (clergy and scholars), who specialize in making and weighing exegetical arguments. The more communities ascribe authority to their scriptures, the more they look to expert interpreters to address the challenges and disputes facing the community.[24]

That does not mean, however, that scholars always succeed in directing scripture-based communities. Texts can be ritualized in two other dimensions, their performative and iconic dimensions. Ritualization in all three dimensions distinguishes scriptures from other kinds of texts (such as literary classics, legal codes and theatrical scripts that are only ritualized regularly in one or two dimensions).

Ritualizing the *performative dimension* through reading, recitation, and memorization, as well as through the visual and theatrical arts, inspires audiences and performers to label the scriptures themselves as inspired. But such performances often exceed the bounds of expert interpretation and scholars have difficulty controlling the products of artistic creativity, such as films like *The Last Temptation of Christ* (1988), *The Passion of the Christ* (2004), and *Noah* (2014).

The *iconic dimension* gets ritualized by decorating the scriptural text, keeping it in special bindings, boxes, rooms or buildings, carrying it as an amulet, and manipulating it in various public and private ceremonies. Ritualizing the iconic dimension conveys legitimacy to the scripture, to the tradition that it represents, and to the community or individual that possesses it. Though scholars frequently ridicule the use of amulets and expensive decorations, they rarely have sufficient authority to challenge powerful or wealthy people who manipulate scriptures to legitimize their social status by taking oaths of office, by commissioning elaborate copies of scriptures, or by collecting and displaying rare books and manuscripts.

Commentary, as one of many ways for ritualizing scripture, conveys authority to its author and makes that authority available to its readers. Commentary also takes its place within an unending debate about the proper interpretation of scripture. It does so as part of the system by which religious communities adjudicate conflicts on the basis of scripture and delegate the debates to a relatively small circle of experts. The fact that interpretive debates often continue without end shows that religious communities rarely need the experts to reach consensus. Instead, the mere act of relegating the debate to experts frees the rest of the community from its divisive consequences. Of course, the frequency of schisms among scripture-based

---

24. J. W. Watts, "Ancient Iconic Texts."

communities shows that this strategy does not always succeed. Nevertheless, delegating conflict to expert exegetes remains the favored means of resolution in religious congregations and also in modern secular democracies, which provide give judges the power to enforce decisions made on the basis of arguments from expert lawyers. It is not accidental, therefore, that legal scholarship is the other academic discipline that favors the writing of commentaries.

Understanding commentary as a ritual of textual interpretation helps explain the experience of discovery in writing and reading commentaries. Just as physical rituals draw attention to realities otherwise ignored (breathing, eating, social indexing of processions, etc.), so the interpretive ritual of writing a commentary draws attention to otherwise ignored features of biblical texts. Each of the examples I described above can be understood from this perspective. (1) The requirement to analyze the literary structure of every passage and every word choice, together with a rhetorical approach, led me to recognize patterns of word repetition, rhyme and refrain variation previously unmentioned in the commentary literature. (2) The requirement to pay attention to the history of translation led to uncovering the impact of sectarian polemics on modern translation practices, with the result that I translated "luminaries and paragons" instead of transliterating as "Urim and Thummim." That same focus led to discovering the impact of Greek vocabulary on translation and interpretation and therefore translating "chickens" instead of "turtledoves." (3) The requirement to pay attention to the history of interpretation led to observing omissions that show the impact of literary genres on the visual arts, and also the impact of changing Jewish and Christian polities on the occlusion of Leviticus's charter to Aaronide priests. In each case, it was the ritual requirement that commentaries pay attention to every detail of a text, and the requirement of the HCOT series that I pay particular attention to translation and the history of interpretation, that set conditions which stimulated my creative insights into Leviticus.

It remains for other interpreters to decide whether my innovations are persuasive or not. My point here is that the commentary ritualizes scripture by drawing attention to every aspect of the text and giving weight to Jewish and Christian traditions of interpretation. These characteristics of traditional scriptural interpretation continue to direct modern critical interpretation, as Avelos and others have observed. They also stimulate innovative research on the text and its religious traditions, quite in contrast to the stereotype of religious rituals as conservative and stultifying.

Ritual theories provide explanations for this dynamic interaction of tradition and innovation. In fact, comparative study has shown that rituals' reputation for invariance is matched by their actual tendency towards constant change and innovation.[25] Similarly, commentaries' reputation for preserving and repeating tradition obscures their frequent innovations. Therefore, analyzing commentary writing and reading as a form of ritualizing the semantic dimension of a scripture provides a step forward in understanding how religious and academic communities use scriptures both to conserve a tradition and to adapt it to new circumstances.

COMMENTARY AND SCRIPTURE

Labelling commentary as ritual, specifically as a ritualized genre of text, leads to the observation that commentary not only contributes to the Bible's status as a scripture, it depends on that status as well. Ritualizing the Bible in its iconic, performative and semantic dimensions first gave it scriptural status and is what has maintained it over the millennia.[26] Biblical commentaries ritualize its semantic dimension and so play a role in maintaining the Bible's scriptural status. As William Graham observed, "Scripture cannot exist without constant interpretation."[27] The sheer scale, scope, and history of scholarship on the Bible depict its subject as worthy of such expense and attention.

Interpretive scholarship, however, is hardly the only engine supporting the Bible's prestige. These scriptures also gain their prestige and cultural influence from their ritualization in iconic and performative, as well as semantic, dimensions by Jewish and Christian communities across two millennia and now by 2.5 billion adherents worldwide. Hence, in contrast to literary scholarship that can plausibly be credited or blamed for generating the continuing prestige of certain novelists and poets, biblical scholarship plays at most a supporting role in the Bible's ritual publicity engine. Nevertheless, this cultural context means that critical commentary should pay attention, first of all, to the biblical text's status as a scripture and to the moral consequences of its influence in contemporary societies.

Leviticus is an especially interesting book upon which to comment as a scripture. Although a few verses get cited repeatedly as moral guidelines in contemporary debates (e.g., 18:22; 19:18), neither Jews nor Christians

25. Ronald Grimes noted that ritual criticism, and criticism by ritual, is as persistent and ubiquitous as ritual itself, and closely related to ritual innovation: "The contradiction between complaining about and revising rites, on the one hand, and treating them as a sacrosanct preserve, on the other, is blatant and persistent" (*Ritual Criticism*, 17).

26. For the claim that ritualizing all three dimensions was fundamental to the Pentateuch's elevation as the first Jewish scripture, as Torah, see J. W. Watts, "Ritualizing Israel's Iconic Texts."

27. Graham, "'Winged Words,'" 39.

follow its explicit instructions about offerings and about many other matters. So how does it function as scripture? Commentators who address the book's scriptural role usually take a theological approach to doing so. In my experience, rhetoric, ritual studies, and comparative scriptures studies provide broader avenues for understanding both the text and its cultural history as a scripture. In any case, the text's scriptural status in two different religious traditions cannot be ignored without misconceiving the social forces that support the enterprise of commentary itself.

> The meanings of Leviticus have been broadcast by the sounds of its words and the sight of the books and scrolls that contain it as much as by semantic interpretation of its contents, which have themselves been manifested in ritual and legal performances as well as in sermons and commentaries. Out of all this emerges the phenomenon of scripture, of which Leviticus is an integral part.[28]

BIBLIOGRAPHY

Avalos, Hector. *The End of Biblical Studies*. Amherst, NY: Prometheus, 2007.
Barthes, Roland. "The Death of the Author." Translated by S. Heath. In *Image—Music—Text*, 142–48. New York: Hill & Wang, 1977.
Bell, Catherine. *Ritual Theory and Ritual Practice*. New York: Oxford University Press, 1992.
———. *Ritual: Perspectives and Dimensions*. New York: Oxford University Press, 1997.
Berlinerblau, Jacques. *The Secular Bible: Why Nonbelievers Must Take Religion Seriously*. New York: Cambridge University Press, 2005.
Búc, Philippe. *The Dangers of Ritual: Between Early Medieval Texts and Social Scientific Theory*. Princeton: Princeton University Press, 2001.
Clines, David J. A. "Esther and the Future of Commentary." In *The Book of Esther in Modern Research*, edited by Leonard Greenspoon and Sidnie White Crawford, 17–30. London: Bloomsbury, 2003.
Derrida, Jacques. *Writing and Difference*. Translated by Alan Bass. London: Routledge, 1978.
Graham, William A. *Beyond the Written Word: Oral Aspects of Scripture in the History of Religion*. Cambridge: Cambridge University Press, 1987.
———. "'Winged Words': Scriptures and Classics as Iconic Texts." *Postscripts* 6 (2010) 7–22. Reprinted in *Iconic Books and Texts*, edited by James W. Watts, 33–46. Sheffield: Equinox, 2013.
Grimes, Ronald L. *Ritual Criticism: Case Studies in Its Practice, Essays on Its Theory*. Columbia: University of South Carolina Press, 1990.
Hartley, John E. *Leviticus*. WBC. Waco, TX: Word, 1992.

---

28. Watts, *Leviticus 1–10*, 2–3.

Larson, Jason T. "The Gospels as Imperialized Sites of Memory in Late Antiquity Christianity." *Postscripts* 6 (2010) 291–307. Reprinted in *Iconic Books and Texts*, edited by James W. Watts, 373–88. Sheffiled: Equinox, 2013.

Luciani, Didier. *Sainteté et pardon*. Vol 1, *Structure littéraire du Lévitique*. BETL 185. Leuven: Leuven University Press, 2005.

Paran, Meir. *Forms of the Priestly Style in the Pentateuch: Patterns, Linguistic Usages, Syntactic Structures* (Hebrew). Jerusalem: Magnes, 1989.

Parmenter, Dorina Miller. "The Iconic Book: The Image of the Bible in Early Christian Rituals." *Postscripts* 2 (2006) 160–89. Reprinted in *Iconic Books and Texts*, edited by James W. Watts, 63–92. Sheffiled: Equinox, 2013.

———. "The Bible as Icon: Myths of the Divine Origins of Scripture." In *Jewish and Christian Scripture as Artifact and Canon*, edited by Craig A. Evans and H. Daniel Zacharias, 298–310. Studies in Scripture in Early Judaism and Christianity 13. London: T & T Clark, 2009.

Rappaport, Roy. *Ritual and Religion in the Making of Humanity*. Cambridge Studies in Social and Cultural Anthropology 110. Cambridge: Cambridge University Press, 1999.

Ricoeur, Paul. *The Conflicts of Interpretation: Essays in Hermeneutics*. Translated by W. Domingo et al. Evanston: Northwest University Press, 1974.

Schüssler Fiorenza, Elizabeth. *Rhetoric and Ethic: The Politics of Biblical Studies*. Minneapolis: Fortress, 1999.

Smith, Jonathan Z. *To Take Place: Toward Theory in Ritual*. Chicago Studies in the History of Judaism. Chicago: University of Chicago Press, 1987.

Staubli, Thomas. "Hühneropfer im Alten Israel: Zum Verständnis von Lev 1,14 im Kontext der antiken Kulturgeschichte." In *Colloquium Biblicum Lovaniense 2006: The Book of Leviticus and Numbers*, edited by Thomas Römer, 355–69. BETL 215. Leuven: Peeters, 2008.

Watts, James W. *Reading Law: The Rhetorical Shaping of the Pentateuch*. Biblical Seminar 59. Sheffield: Sheffield Academic Press, 1999.

———. "The Three Dimensions of Scriptures." *Postscripts* 2 (2006) 135–59. Repr. in *Iconic Books and Texts*, edited by James W. Watts, 135–59. London: Equinox, 2013.

———. *Ritual and Rhetoric in Leviticus: From Sacrifice to Scripture*. New York: Cambridge University Press, 2007.

———. "Ancient Iconic Texts and Scholarly Expertise." *Postscripts* 6 (2010) 331–44. Reprinted in *Iconic Books and Texts*, edited by James W. Watts, 407–18. Sheffield: Equinox, 2013.

———. "Illustrating Leviticus: Art, Ritual and Politics." *BibRec* 2 (2013) 3–15.

———. *Leviticus 1–10*. HCOT. Leuven: Peeters, 2013.

Watts, John D. W. *Isaiah 1–33*. WBC. Waco, TX: Word, 1984.

———. *Isaiah 34-66*. WBC. Waco, TX: Word, 1985.

Yoo, Yohan. "Public Scripture Reading Rituals in Early Korean Protestantism: A Comparative Perspective." *Postscripts* 2 (2006) 226–40.

3

Commentary Changes in Format and Focus

An Overview

—Elmer A. Martens

EVEN A CASUAL BROWSING in Old Testament commentaries produced in the last five decades alerts the reader to considerable changes in format and focus. Or, for that matter, one may examine the commentaries by John Hartley, the honoree of this volume, to observe style variations in format.[1] This essay documents the changes by offering a taxonomy of commentaries, and by reflecting on what these shifts signify. Recent series, in experimenting with focus and format, signal both creativity and a rethinking of format. "A visual generation of believers deserves a commentary series that contains not only the all-important textual commentary on Scripture, but images, photographs, maps, works of fine art, and drawings that bring the text to life."[2] Whatever the future for commentary writing, taking stock of past efforts is certainly an important step; producers of commentaries might take note. Moreover, commentary users will benefit from an overview of issues,

---

1 I take great satisfaction in contributing to this volume in honor of a scholar whose expertise I highly esteem and with whom I have had some memorable conversations about spirituality and exegesis. Hartley, *Job,* NICOT; *Leviticus,* WBC; *Genesis,* NIBC.

2. Fretheim, *Jeremiah,* series preface, xiv.

entailing format as well as function, facing commentary writers. So what is a commentary intended to achieve; and how does the format contribute or detract from that goal?

This investigation's focus is a sampling of English-language commentary series published since 1970, primarily in academic mode (technical/semi-technical), mainly Protestant, and mostly from North American publishers.[3] Free-standing and one-volume commentaries are not included but their omission, or that of certain other series, is not to be taken as a measure of their value.[4] The sampling is subjective and concentrates on format features, as well as the specific focus of each commentary series. Illustrations on form and focus will be taken, where possible, from commentaries on the Book of Jeremiah. The essay concludes with an analysis and some reflections.

COMMENTARIES WITH A PHILOLOGICAL EMPHASIS

ICC [1899] 1974. Format: author's translation; running commentary by pericope; documentation in the text, no footnotes.

AB 1964. Format: author's translation; notes; comment.

OTL 1965. Format: author's translation, running commentary by pericope; numerous footnotes.

NICOT 1976. Format: author's translation; textual notes; verse by verse commentary; aim (cf. Hartley's *JOB*); numerous footnotes.

WBC 1983. Format: bibliography precedes major text unit; author's translation; notes; form/structure/setting; comment (usually verse by verse); explanation (adumbrates theological themes); excursus (occasionally).[5]

The nature of biblical commentaries includes discussing the meaning of terms. Some Hebrew words, such as *ḥesed,* are so freighted with meanings that a single English term like "mercy" or "love" is scarcely adequate. The nuances are so multi-faceted that entire monographs are devoted to exegeting

---

3. For a sampling, see the end-of-article list. Abbreviations are explained there as well.

4. See, Longman, *OT Commentary Survey*; Fretheim, "OT Commentaries."

5. Abbreviations: ICC, The International Critical Commentary; AB, Anchor Bible Commentary; its replacement, AYBC, Anchor Yale Bible Commentary; OTL, The Old Testament Library; NICOT, New International Commentary on the Old Testament; WBC, Word Biblical Commentary.

the single word *ḥesed*. A commentary, however, distils such research and amplifies the appropriate connotation of the term in its particular context.

A prime example of close attention to linguistic matters is the venerable International Critical Commentary (ICC). In their 1974 preface to the Jeremiah volume, the editors assert that the series holds a special place "because it has sought to bring together all the relevant aids to exegesis, linguistic and textual no less than archaeological, historical, literary and theological, to help the reader understand the meaning of the books in the Old and New Testament."[6] William McKane, author of the Jeremiah volume, states that his commentary is "one which concentrates on fundamentals of biblical scholarship. It aims at exegetical goals but is built on the foundation of the Hebrew Bible and the Ancient Versions."[7] McKane's introduction of ninety-nine pages is heavily weighted toward linguistic matters, utilizing ancient versions, an interest that characterizes his commentary. The last half of the introduction touches on "historical problems" and "lament exegesis." He touches ever so lightly on theology, stating that some of the theological questions, "because they are meta-linguistic in important respects, are beyond the limits of a plain exegesis of the Hebrew text."[8] By contrast, forty years later commentaries would emphasize the theological aspects of the biblical text.

In ICC's volume on Jeremiah, pericopes of three to fifteen verses are given a heading (e.g., "A Cooking Pot on the Boil, 1:13–16") and followed by a running commentary. The Hebrew terms are in bold print; portions of the LXX text are in Greek font. The temple sermon pericope, "A False Sense of Security, 7:1–15," discusses whether the LXX version is the original, but the commentary is based on the MT. On translation and exegetical matters, McKane constantly dialogues with scholars such as John Bright, M. J. Dahood, W. Holladay, J. Skinner, W. Thiel, H. Weippert and Y. Yadin. The bibliography for volume I extends from pages 103–23.

In sum, the commentators in the ICC series regard their task as giving the reader some sense of the variations in the text's transmission, incorporating matters of historical interest, and now and again apprising the reader of how other scholars have understood matters. The commentary is technical and proceeds by text units; there are no format headings within a unit.

The Anchor Bible (AB) series initially majored in linguistic matters, explaining the biblical text by illuminating word meanings and providing explanations of places and events. For the Jeremiah volume (1965), John

---

6. McKane, *Jeremiah I*, vii.
7. Ibid., xi.
8. Ibid., xcviii.

Bright rendered his own translation of the Hebrew text, as did others in the series. Bright's "Notes" sections are often about the finer points of Hebrew grammar and syntax[9] and the commentary sometimes rearranges the units based on his hypothetical chronology of Jeremiah's career. On Jer 7:1–34; 8:1–3, "The 'Temple Sermon' and Appended Sayings," Bright's "Comment" section largely rehearses the flow of Jer 7:1–8:3 but includes information regarding dating from Jeremiah 26 where a briefer account of the sermon is given.[10] In "The 'Temple Sermon'; Jeremiah Narrowly Escapes Death," Bright rearranges the text so that Jer 26:24 appears before Jer 26:20–23. Major changes in format appear in the reissue of the series (1999; see below "Commentaries with Literary Approaches.")

The commentaries in the Old Testament Library (OTL) series, though more flexible and not as limited to lexicography as the ICC, essentially explain vocabulary and how the biblical text (often less than five verses) is to be construed vis-à-vis the context. In Leslie Allen's commentary on Jeremiah (2008), which completes the series, format headings are absent. The author's translation of the text, printed in segments (e.g., Jer 7:1–20; 32:1–44) is followed by notes of a technical nature (text critical notes, comparison with LXX, etc.). The commentary's heart lies in the often lengthy discussion of the motifs, stylistic matters, and thought-flow of the text. Footnotes appear on almost every page. Though working from the final form of the biblical text, Allen states, "I have made some effort to ascertain earlier stages of the literary process that led to the final form."[11] He has also paid attention to inter-textuality, echoes and parallelism elsewhere in the OT and NT. Bold-faced headings signal the larger sections (e.g., Jer 7:1–20, " The Exilic Outcome of Nominal and Pagan Worship"), as well as the immediate unit under discussion. Theological summaries are absent, as is application: "The necessary task of contemporary application is left to other commentaries."[12]

The New International Commentary on the Old Testament (NICOT) series is moderately technical and written from an evangelical viewpoint. J. A. Thompson's Jeremiah volume (1980) was the fourth in the series. No format headings appear; text units with the author's translation are given a heading (e.g., "The Temple Sermon (7:1–15)"). Such units are embedded within major sections, eight in all, which come with several-page introductions.

---

9. A prime example in this series of the priority of linguistic matters is Dahood's three-volume *Psalms* with its frequent references to Ugaritic.

10. Bright, *Jeremiah*, 57–59.

11. Allen, *Jeremiah*, 2.

12. Ibid.

Though somewhat difficult to classify, the Word Biblical Commentary (WBC) fits best in this category in the light of the editor's statement: "What may be claimed as distinctive with this series is that it is based on the biblical languages, yet it seeks to make the technical and scholarly approach to a theological understanding of Scripture understandable by—and useful to—the fledgling student, the working minister, and colleagues in the guild of professional scholars and teachers as well."[13] Planning of the series, now complete with 32 volumes for the OT, began in 1977.

The format is intended to serve a wide spectrum of readers. The scholar may have particular interest in "Notes" or "Form/Structure/Setting;" the "working minister" might turn to "Explanation." Douglas Stuart comments, "This series [WBC] is notable for its excellent format, thorough bibliographical information and over-all quality."[14] The "Explanation" for Jeremiah 32:23–40 (which includes the passage of the New Covenant) consists of one paragraph.[15] A dilemma every commentary writer must deal with is recurring themes or issues that extend over several biblical passages. One solution often used in WBC is to punctuate the commentary with "excursuses." The volume, *Jeremiah 26–52,* has six excursuses (e.g., "Seventy Years").

Other commentary series, of course, could be classified in this more generic rubric of commentaries, characterized by overviews, notes, and frequently by verse-by-verse commentary.[16]

COMMENTARIES MAJORING ON SOURCE ANALYSIS

Hermeneia, 1974. Format: bibliography precedes text units; author's translation; text (elaborating on versions and translation choices); structure and form; setting; interpretation (verse by verse commentary); aim (summary of message, occasionally with application).

13. Craigie, Kelly, and Drinkard, *Jeremiah 1—25,* xi.
14. Douglas Stuart, *Guide,* 109.
15. Keown, Scalise, and Smothers, *Jeremiah 26–52,* 135.
16. E.g., The New International Biblical Commentary (NIBC) is based on the NIV. In Hartley's *Genesis,* several excursus appear. The series usually displays the following format: 1) an overview of a larger text block; 2) a running commentary of the pericopes within the larger block; and 3) additional notes (on single verses, linguistic in nature, sometimes according to theme, interaction with other scholars, and some bibliography).

The Expositor's Bible Commentary (EBC) which appeared first in 1979 has been revised with Tremper Longman III and David E. Garland as general editors. The newer series, utilizing textual units, has the following format: overview, NIV printed text, commentary, and notes (mostly linguistic).

Several commentary series display significant interest in source analysis.[17] A representative is the Hermeneia series. In a series foreword, Frank Moore Cross (OT) and Helmut Koester (NT) explain that "The series is designed to be a critical and historical commentary. . . . It will utilize the full range of philological and historical tools, including textual criticism . . . the methods of the history of tradition . . . and the history of religion. . . . Insofar as possible, the aim is to provide the student or scholar with full critical discussion of each problem of interpretation."[18]

William Holladay, in the "Author's Foreword" in the Jeremiah volume references two crucial matters: the chronology of the prophet's career; and "a scheme for the literary history of the book."[19] Occasionally there is an added section, "Preliminary Observations," as in the temple sermon passage (Jer 7:1–15), where in more than two double-columned pages the author justifies certain translation decisions (e.g., the meaning of "in this place"), and argues that vv. 13–15 belong to a "second scroll."[20] Critical questions about sources and literary composition are in the forefront.

COMMENTARIES HIGHLIGHTING LITERARY APPROACHES

> FOTL, 1981. Format: bibliography; the text unit is titled but not translated; structure; genre; setting, intention; glossary.

> AYBC. Format: author's translation, rhetoric and composition, notes, message and audience.

The Forms of Old Testament Literature (FOTL) series, edited initially by Rolf P. Knierim and Gene M. Tucker, with Marvin A. Sweeney added later, was prompted by the mid-twentieth century interest in analyzing Biblical *Gattungen* (literary genres). The first of 24 projected volumes, *Wisdom Literature: Job Proverbs, Ruth, Canticles, Ecclesiastes and Esther* by Roland Murphy, was released in 1981. A helpful format feature in this series is the end-of-book glossary which lists and describes genres (e.g., riddle), genre elements (e.g., motive clauses) and formulas. While the format of Structure, Genre, Setting, and Intention (followed by a bibliography) remain standard

---

17 Among them would be Historical Commentary on the Old Testament (HCOT), begun in 1997 with twenty volumes available, whose interests also include philology and textual criticism.

18. Holladay, *Jeremiah 1*, ix.

19. Ibid., xi.

20. Ibid., 234–49.

through the series, the material for each in recent volumes has often been heavily expanded.

Because the Jeremiah volume is not yet available, Marvin Sweeney's *Isaiah 1–39* (1996) can serve as an exemplar. Although covering only 39 chapters, Sweeney's commentary is three times longer than R. Murphy's aforementioned volume which covered six books. Sweeney titles Isaiah 6:1–13 "Isaiah's Commission Account." The Structure section consists of a detailed structural outline dividing the text into seven parts (Presence Vision Report, Audition Report, Commission Report etc.) with two pages explaining and justifying the structure. In the Genre section, Sweeney identifies the chapter not as a typical call narrative, but for reasons of both form and content as a Vocation Account. The Genre section also discusses the genre of the subunits such as Vision Report and Audition Report. Sweeney elaborates on all these terms in the Glossary at the back of the book, which for Isaiah extends to thirty-three pages. The three pages in the Setting section discuss history, authenticity, and royal motifs, with two pages devoted to the passage's Intention: "Consequently, the original intent of 6:1–11 was to express condemnation of the northern kingdom of Israel, but the addition of vv. 12–13 expressed the judgment of the southern kingdom of Judah and enabled the editors to combine chapter 6 with the narratives concerning Isaiah's confrontation with Ahaz in the balance of the 'memoir' (7:1–9:6 [RSV 7])."[21]

The Anchor Yale Bible Commentary (AYBC) in its reissue of commentaries retained the earlier format, but allowed for methodological emphases other than the linguistic and also allowed a flexible format as in the Jeremiah commentary by Jack R. Lundbom. Lundbom's "Introduction," including extensive bibliographies, extends to 217 pages. Lundbom makes "considerable use of rhetorical criticism"[22] allocating forty-six pages to rhetoric (method, composition). Ten pages are devoted to the theology, first of the prophet, then of the book.

The format for the commentary proper has also been modified so that, for example, the section "Rhetoric and Composition" (6 pages) follows the translation of the temple sermon (Jer 7:1–15), followed by a section, "Notes" (ten pages), then two pages of concluding comment under the heading "Message and Audience" (then and now).[23] Various rhetorical features come into play in the prose of the Jer 7:1–15 text, a passage often considered a unit but which Lundbom divides into three oracles (7:1–7; 7:8–11; 7:12–15) be-

---

21. Sweeney, *Isaiah 1–39*, 141.
22. Lundbom, *Jeremiah 1–20*, 68.
23. Ibid., 453–73.

cause of rhetorical features such as the three messenger formulas, inclusion structures, and a lack of coherence in vv. 1–15 (e.g., between vv. 3–7 and vv 12–14),[24] stating that "Discerning the narrative structures and delimiting the oracles are greatly aided by rhetorical criticism."[25] Lundbom's commentary is in the AYBC series, but scarcely resembles the format of John Bright's earlier *Jeremiah* (1965) in the same series. As for the larger text block, two excurses (not listed in the table of contents) are offered on Jer 7:22–23.[26] In general however, despite changes, the format over the decades has provided a semblance of continuity.[27]

COMMENTARIES ATTUNED TO LITERARY/ THEOLOGICAL APPROACHES

> Berit Olam, 1998. Format: delimitation of the text, plot, repetition, characterization, footnotes, excurses.
>
> AOTC, 2001. Format: Text not printed, literary analysis (structure, style of literary unit), exegetical analysis, theological and ethical analysis.
>
> TOTC. Format: series revision, text not printed, context (literary, historical), comment (exegesis), meaning (highlighting theological themes).[28]
>
> HMS. 2013. Format: the main idea of the passage; literary context; translation and outline; structure and literary form; explanation of the text; canonical and practical significance.

Berit Olam, a series with the subtitle "Studies in Hebrew Narrative and Poetry," clearly belongs in the literary category. David Cotter, general editor and author of the volume on Genesis, states, "I am interested in the way Genesis functions as a narrative, what its plot is, how its characters develop and change."[29] The discussion of a pericope (e.g., Gen 19:30–38, "Lot Settles") is organized in keeping with that interest: Delimitation of the Text (3+ pp); The Plot (9 pp); Repetition (1 pg); Characterization (2 pp).[30] In this segment, as in others also, a lengthy footnote recounts a Jewish midrash

---

24. Ibid., 455.
25. Ibid., 457.
26. Ibid., 486–89.
27. Another example of attention to rhetorical criticism is Watts, *Leviticus*.
28. Abbreviations: AOTC Abingdon Old Testament Commentaries; TOTC Tyndale Old Testament Commentaries. HMS Hearing the Message of Scripture.
29. Cotter, *Genesis*, ix.
30. Ibid., 112–28.

on the text. An excursus of nine pages is entitled, "God as a Developing Character in Genesis 12—25." In this series, literary concerns are foremost as illustrated in the purpose statement and the corresponding format.

In the foreword to the Abingdon Old Testament Commentaries (AOTC) series, editor Patrick Miller explains that the first section, Literary Analysis, attends to genre, structure and stylistic features. The Exegetical Analysis section "considers the leading concepts of the unit, the language of expression, and problematical words, phrases, and ideas in order to get at the aim or intent of the literary unit."[31] Comments here also pertain to historical, social and cultural situations. Finally, regarding Theological and Ethical Analysis, Miller writes, "Though not aimed primarily at contemporary issues of faith and life, this section should provide readers a basis for reflection on them."[32]

Louis Stulman's 400-page volume on Jeremiah for this series divides the book into two major literary units: Book One (Jeremiah 1-25) subdivided into 7 units (e.g., "Dismantling Kingship in Israel" Jeremiah 21-24), and Book Two (Jeremiah 26-52) with nine units (e.g., "The Book of Consolation" Jeremiah 30-33). The literary unit which includes the Temple Sermon, entitled "Dismantling the Temple and its Culture of Certitude" (Jeremiah 7-10), begins with a literary analysis examining the prose in Jer 7:1—8:3 as well as the poetry that follows in 8:4—10:25. Four pages are devoted to exegetical analysis. The emphasis on the literary continues as the author points out that the prose temple sermon "stabilizes the wild world of poetry."[33] Unlike the ICC, which foregrounds lexicography and grammar, the "exegetical" analysis here is more about "the searing assault on worship."[34] Stulman identifies three crucial assumptions in Jeremiah's harsh critique of the Jerusalem establishment, such as the belief that the temple is a place where God is ever present. A lengthy paragraph follows on temple history in Israel. In short, the exegetical analysis is an exegesis of the main idea governing the sermon. Stulman discusses the remaining subunits of the larger literary unit (Jeremiah 7-10) before getting to the "Theological and Ethical Analysis" (3 pages), the subject of which is true worship.

In summary, though this series (AOTC) makes space for history and linguistics, it majors on the biblical text's literary overtures, which then are easily conjoined with the theological and the practical. Frequent headings, along with engaging prose, help draw the reader into the text's flow.

---

31. Stulman, *Jeremiah*, xiv.
32. Ibid., xv.
33. Ibid., 90.
34. Ibid.

The Tyndale Old Testament Commentaries (TOTC) is reissuing its series. In also updating its format, it takes account of the literary emphasis by organizing the text units into larger blocks, rather than individual verses. Each segment is treated under three headings: context (literary, historical); comment (exegesis) and meaning, "by which is meant the message that the passage seeks to communicate within the book, highlighting its key theological themes."[35] Hetty Lalleman's introduction to Jeremiah is relatively lengthy (key Hebrew terms, metaphors);[36] but here we note that the TOTC series joins the ranks of other series that create space for theological nuances.[37]

Hearing the Message of Scripture with the subtitle: A Commentary on the Old Testament, is a recently launched series, very bold in setting out the format. The series emphasizes the literary strategies which are entailed in the theological message of a book. "The commentators in this series recognize that too little attention has been paid to biblical authors as rhetoricians, to their larger rhetorical and theological agendas, and especially to the means by which they tried to achieve their goals." The prospectus continues, "Rather than focusing on words or phrases, contributors to this series will concentrate on the flow of thought in the biblical writings, both at the macroscopic level of entire compositions and at the microscopic level of individual text units."[38] Daniel Block, the general editor and the author of the first volume, *Obadiah*, summarizes the book's theme as dominion belongs to YHWH. Rhetorical strategies in the service of this theme include a style that is transparently passionate, and an appeal to higher authorities. The commentary (116 pages) has nineteen tables, charts and figures.

---

35. Lalleman, *Jeremiah and Lamentations*, 8.

36. Ibid., 9–63.

37. In this category one could include the mini-series, Baker Commentary on the Old Testament Wisdom and Psalms, with its emphasis on the message of the biblical book, sometimes given under the heading "Theological Implications," and sometimes, as in the Proverbs commentary, in an appendix of "Topical Studies." So also, The Cornerstone Biblical Commentary (CBC), with its format of text (NLT), notes (emphasis on terms), and commentary (pointing to theological themes), might be listed here.

38. Block, *Obadiah*, 9–10.

64 Part 1: Production and Publication of Biblical Commentary

COMMENTARIES HIGHLIGHTING THE THEOLOGY OF THE TEXT

> BTCB, 2006. Format: text (various translations), five essays pinned to a text (Genesis), essays on text units (Ezekiel), few footnotes.
>
> THOTC, 2008. Format: commentary (exegesis on text units, half the book), theological message (e.g., unifying themes, key theological teaching, second half of the book).
>
> BELIEF, 2010. Format: essays on text blocks, further reflections (multiple), final thoughts, boxed side bars.[39]

The heavy emphasis on theology in The Two Horizons Old Testament Commentary [THOTC]—in stark contrast to the Anchor Bible series, for example--illustrates a decided shift in the last decade toward commentary more focused on theology.[40] Editors J. Gordon McConville and Craig Bartholomew explain that two features distinguish the series: "theological exegesis and theological reflection."[41] They further explain, "Commentaries traditionally treat philology, grammar, syntax, composition and matters of history. But scholars in this series locate their primary interests on theological readings, past and present, interests said to include identifying the way a biblical book contributes to biblical theology and how it might be utilized in current constructive theology."[42]

James McKeown's *Genesis* commentary (2008) serves as the exemplar here, because the commentary on Jeremiah is not yet available. Aside from an introduction to the biblical book, the volume is in two parts: 1) Commentary (175 pp); and 2) Theological Horizons of Genesis (160 pp). The latter rubric consists of some twenty essays categorized under four headings: Main Unifying Themes (e.g., Blessing); Key Theological Teachings (e.g., The Character of God); Genesis and Theology Today (e.g., Genesis and Science); and Genesis and Biblical Theology (e.g., Genesis in Canonical Context). The first half of the commentary in this series treats exegetical niceties by

---

39. Abbreviations: BTCB, Brazos Theological Commentary on the Bible; THOTC, The Two Horizons Old Testament Commentary. Belief: A Theological Commentary on the Bible.

40. One might place the New American Commentary (NAC) which is billed as "An Exegetical and Theological Exposition of Holy Scripture," in this classification. The editors state that "the commentary emphasizes how each section of a book fits together so that the reader becomes aware of the theological unity of each book and of Scripture as a whole." Authors employ the NIV translation. The Jeremiah volume consists of a running commentary on a section though broken into segments of one or two verses.

41. Parry, *Lamentations*, i.

42. Ibid.

blocking off sections. The second half is given over to theological matters, which is clearly the commentary's emphasis.[43]

Belief: A Theological Commentary on the Bible, inaugurated by Westminster John Knox in 2010, grew out of a consultation in 2007, with theologians rather than biblical scholars being the authors. In a decided shift of viewpoint and format, the series introduction, written by William C. Placher and Amy Plantinga Pauw, addresses historical-critical approaches: "By themselves, they do not convey the powerful sense of God's merciful presence that calls Christians to repentance and praise; they do not bring the church fully forward in the life of discipleship. It is to such tasks that the theologians are called."[44] The editors explain that the writers are minimally interested in "matters of form, authorship, historical setting, social context and philology." Instead they

> will seek to explain the theological importance of the texts for the church today . . . The authors' chief dialogue will be with the church's creeds, practices, and hymns; with the history of faithful interpretation and use of the Scriptures; with the categories and concepts of theology; and with contemporary culture in both 'high' and popular forms.[45]

With Jeremiah not being one of the six commentaries currently available, our exemplar is Deana Thompson's *Deuteronomy*, one of the latest volumes in the series. Thompson organizes her work around six major divisions in Deuteronomy, the second of which is "5:1–11:31, Moses' Second Address: Reiterating the Role of Rules." Beyond the 2.5 pages of brief commentary review, eight reflective essays for this text block (e.g., "Parent God"; "Thinking in New Ways about the Law") take up some 60 pages. In all, 25 essays of "Reflections" are contained in the slim volume of 270 pages. Distinctively, most pages have a boxed bar or occasionally two, some being brief quotations in bold print from authors such as Jürgen Moltmann, Martin Buber, John Calvin, Sally McFague, Pope John Paul II, and Robert Alter. Other side bars contain Scripture text quotations (e.g., Joshua 24:15; Amos 7:4–6). The format's preponderance of essays reflects its intent to help the church understand the theological importance of the texts.

The Brazos Theological Commentary on the Bible (BTCB), also a recent commentary, differs markedly in format as well as being ecumenical, drawing authors from Catholic and Protestant traditions. In a preface to the series, R. R. Reno, the General Editor, refutes the notion that doctrine is a

---

43. McKeown, *Genesis*.
44. Thompson, *Deuteronomy*, xi.
45. Ibid., xii.

"moldering scrim" in getting at the meaning of Scripture. To the contrary, "the central premise in this commentary series is that doctrine provides structure and cogency to scriptural interpretation"[46]—the "doctrine" being that of the Nicene tradition. In keeping with a reconstructive, not reactionary stance, the series represents experiments in "post critical interpretation." The format for the series is fluid; authors are free to move within the premodern traditions or focus on contemporary historical study: "Some will comment verse by verse; others will highlight passages, even single words that trigger theological analysis of Scripture."[47]

As the commentary on Jeremiah by Kevin Vanhoozer is still forthcoming, a sampling of the series is best taken from Robert Jenson's *Ezekiel*, which table of contents lists 76 Scripture units along with titles. Some are short (e.g., "The Locked Gate and the Prince," 44:1–3); one of the longest spans two chapters ("The Plan of God's House," 40:1—42:20). No format headings appear beyond these unit headings, with comments on a selected theological topic extending four to six pages per unit. However, the Genesis commentary, while holding to a similar template, is quite different, with five sections of some 40 pages per section treating five themes, each anchored in a verse (e.g., # 5 "Need for Atonement: 'Now There Comes a Reckoning for his Blood' (42:22)." Inside these sections, comments appear only on selected constitutive verses—the intent is not to comment on every verse. Footnotes are minimal. Genesis is not read as centering on background and history but "is ordered toward consummation."[48] By contrast, Jenson's four-page essays are on wide-ranging topics; and the author is sensitive to Jewish interpretations.

COMMENTARIES TILTING TOWARD CURRENT RELEVANCE AND PRACTICE

> INTERPRETATION, 1985. Format: Bible text cited but not printed, essay-length explanations of larger units (often chapters), no format differentiations.
>
> NIB, 1994. Format: overview (of large sections), text (NIV & NRSV), commentary, reflections, occasional excursus.
>
> NIVAC, 1999. Format: printed text (NIV), original meaning, bridging contexts, contemporary significance.

---

46. Jenson, *Ezekiel*, 14.
47. Ibid.
48. Reno, *Genesis*, 74.

SHBC, 2000. Format: no printed text, commentary on text blocks, connections, endnotes (few and brief), coded special-interest boxes (e.g., culture/context, photographs).

AOTC 2002. Format: author's translation, notes on text, form and structure, comment, explanation.[49]

The twenty-six volume Interpretation: A Bible Commentary for Teaching and Preaching series launched in 1985 with a volume on Daniel, its title more than hinting at the dimension of the "practical." The purpose of the series is not to replace the historical critical commentary but to provide "a commentary which presents the integrated result of historical and theological work with the biblical text." It also aims to meet the need of "students, teachers, ministers, and priests."[50] In conventional fashion, Roland E. Clements' *Jeremiah* is divided into major sections—six in this instance—with titles such as "The Fate of the Nation and its Institutions" (Jeremiah 21—29) and "The Testing of the Nations" (Jeremiah 46-52). The commentary deals mostly with chapter-size segments (e.g., "The Good and Bad Figs" Jeremiah 24; "Jeremiah and the Message about Jerusalem's Fall," Jeremiah 26), and discusses selected themes in a way that prompts contemporary relevance, even if that relevance is more implied than explicit. Each titled text segment is explained in essay fashion, with no format differentiation. Several other series designed for preachers are also now available.[51]

The New Interpreter's Bible (NIB) series aims "to bring the best in contemporary biblical scholarship into the service of the church to enhance preaching, teaching and study of Scriptures."[52] In keeping with this practical aim and the controlling principle of "form serves function," the commentary design, apart from the usual introductory materials and bibliography, features side by side NIV and NRSV translations, commentary, and reflections. The biblical text is divided into primary units which in turn are placed within larger sections of Scripture. The commentary on Jeremiah 7:1—8:3, "A Sermon in the Temple," runs in serial paragraph fashion broken by four headings (e.g., 7:1-15) and treats the exhortations, the rhetorical movement, and principles governing Israel's covenant. Six enumerated "reflec-

---

49. Abbreviations: NIB New Interpreter's Bible ; NIVAC New International Version Application Commentary; SHBC Smyth & Helwys Bible Commentary; AOTC Apollos Old Testament Commentary.

50. Clements, *Jeremiah*, v.

51. E.g., The Preacher's Commentary (PC) series, now complete with 23 volumes, is also target specific. The series, edited by Lloyd Ogilvie, employs the New Kings James Bible translation.

52. *Introduction to Prophetic Literature*, xvii.

tions" offer trajectories the preacher or teacher might pursue (e.g., The heart of Israel's moral life, a New Testament connection, God's freedom). In the series' predecessor, *The Interpreter's Bible* (1960s), subsequent to the biblical text one author would write the exegesis (single column), and another scholar would write the exposition beneath (double column, different font). The intent there too was to inform professional communicators.

The Zondervan series, The NIV Application Commentary (NIVAC), clearly aims at practical relevance. In a series introduction the editors state, "The primary goal of the NIV Application Commentary Series is to help you with the difficult but vital task of bringing an ancient message into a modern context ... The format is designed to achieve the goals of the series."[53] J. Andrew Dearman discusses the temple sermon within the larger literary setting of 7:1—8:3. The comment on "the original meaning" of the temple sermon (7:1-15) is primarily about the temple and basic covenant stipulations (1 page of 5 paragraphs). In the "bridging contexts" section (2 pages) the author allows that "there is no one-to-one correspondence between ancient Israel and the church."[54] He draws on the New Testament to make the point that "Behavioral matters are a powerful indicator that reveals the allegiances of the heart" and remarks on the significance of the temple in the OT and in Jesus' teaching about temple.[55] "The Contemporary Significance" (1 page) stresses that theology (i.e., how to think of God) matters for the church. Moreover, behavior and Christian ethics "are a means to an end: to worship and serve the living God."[56]

The unique format of the Smyth & Helwys Bible Commentary consists of "a visually stimulating and user-friendly series that is as close to multimedia in print as possible." "Using a multimedia format, the volumes employ a stunning array of art, photographs, maps and drawings to illustrate the truths of the Bible for a visual generation of believers."[57] Hence a distinctive feature of the series is the large number of sidebar visuals, often several on one page, sometimes accompanied by color font text (e.g., an artistic representation of Solomon's temple (Jer 7:1-15).[58] The base format identifies a text block (e.g., The Temple Sermon, 7:1—8:3), provides an introduction, continues with a section marked "Commentary" written in essay style but with clear identification of verses; adds "Connections" (e.g.,

53. Dearman, *Jeremiah and Lamentations*, 11.
54. Ibid., 100.
55. Ibid.
56. Ibid., 103.
57. Fretheim, *Jeremiah*, xiv.
58. Ibid., 134.

"The Disjunction between Exhortation and Finality of Judgment"); and concludes with Notes (bibliographic comments), apparently to compensate for the absence of footnotes. The page layout of a series such as this is far removed from the text-dense ICC.

Regarding the Apollos Old Testament Commentary (AOTC) series, the editors explain, "Traditionally, commentators have been content to highlight and expound the ancient text. More recently the need for an anchor in the present day has also become more evident, and this series self-consciously adopts this approach, combining both."[59] The format is as follows: Translation by the author, Textual Notes, Literary Form and Structure, Comment (exegesis), and Explanation. The history of interpretation is sometimes included in the Explanation section to show how the text might function for the reader and the preacher. For example, the "Explanation" section for Ecclesiastes 3 ("For everything there is a season") focuses on God's sovereignty and human decision with the claim that the biblical assertion "God has made everything beautiful in its own time" is "the greatest statement of divine providence in the whole of Scripture."[60] Further comments speak to injustices but conclude with Qoheleth's message, which is "that we are to make the most of the here and now, the most of our work, the most of our wisdom and joy."[61] The commentaries in this category focus on the relevance of the biblical message.

COMMENTARIES ATTUNED TO DENOMINATIONAL VANTAGE POINTS

> BCBC, 1986. Format: Preview; structural outline, explanatory notes per outline, the text in biblical context; the text in the life of the church, an appendix of topical essays.
>
> RCS, 2011. Format: Excerpts from Protestant Reformation-era sermons, commentary, confessions, and treatises.
>
> ACCS, 2001. Format: RSV text, overview, extracts with a supplied title from pre-modern scholars' writings.[62]

---

59. Fredericks and Estes, *Ecclesiastes and Song of Songs*, 7.
60. Ibid., 124.
61. Ibid., 124, 126.
62. Abbreviations: BCBC Believers Church Bible Commentary; RCS Reformation Commentary on Scripture; ACCS Ancient Commentary on Christian Scripture.

As the existence of denominations itself indicates, various shadings and emphases are found within Christian theology.[63] Within the last decades several series forthrightly identify the denominational perspective guiding commentary focus, as exemplified in the Believers Church Bible Commentary (BCBC), which grew from a desire to strengthen the identity of Anabaptist churches. In this case, my own Jeremiah commentary launched the series. The editors in a "Series Foreword" state their desire "to be of help to as wide a range of readers as possible,"[64] but clarify that the writers stand in the Anabaptist and Mennonite tradition, which is characterized by "specific theological understandings such as believers baptism, commitment to the Rule of Christ in Matthew 18:15–18 as part of the meaning of church membership, belief in the power of love in all relationships, and a willingness to follow the way of the cross of Christ."[65] An editorial council processes and approves manuscripts; and the commentaries do not have a printed biblical text.

As a member of the council initially, I spent a major part of a sabbatical researching and devising an appropriate format. A most helpful counsel, arising from an interview with Professor James Mays or perhaps Professor John Bright, was, "Get a line on the text." So my practice became to study a unit using the "Formal Bible Study Method, a method that leans heavily on form criticism."[66] Only after determining the passage's focus did I examine other commentary sources and make appropriate revisions.

My Jeremiah commentary divides the book in an eightfold chiastic arrangement. Given a biblical rather than a systematic theology approach to Scriptural teaching, the "Text in Biblical Context" section discusses contours of a biblical theme in both testaments. The final section addresses how the church has utilized the text in past centuries but emphasizes more how the text is currently relevant. A set of essays at the end of the book—a major feature of the series—deals with topics encountered in the book (e.g., "Kings of Judah," "Lament"). These essays replace the excurses in other series.

The format of Jeremiah's temple sermon (Jer 7:1–15) aligns with the aim of the series. The larger text block is Jer 7:1—8:3 (so also Dearman, above). The explanatory notes cover in turn "The Temple Sermon (7:1–15)," "Perversions and Precepts Involving Worship (7:16–26)," and "Carcasses

---

63. In this category one would also place the Old Testament volumes of the Wesleyan Bible Commentary series, the New Beacon Bible Commentary, also in the Wesleyan tradition, and other denominational works.

64. Martens, *Jeremiah*, 9.

65. Ibid., 10

66. For method details see Martens, "Psalm 73," 15–26. Accessible via http://www.directionjournal.org/12/4/psalm-73-corrective-to-modern.html/.

Everywhere (7:27–8:3)." In the section, "The Text in Biblical Context," two paragraphs discuss 1) corrupt theology, including correctives, *pace* Isa 66:1–2 and Acts 7; and 2) acceptable worship with emphasis on moral rectitude (Amos 5:21–25; Matt 5:23–24). As for the "The Text in the Life of the Church," a paragraph touches on religious clichés (e.g., "born again") and in this instance offers an outline of a possible sermon, entitled "Moving Against the Stream."[67]

The Reformation Commentary on Scripture (RCS) is another example of a commentary series stressing denominational emphases. Its editorial board comprises representatives of the Reformed, Lutheran, Anabaptist and Puritan traditions. As of this writing only the OT commentaries on Genesis 1–11 and the Ezekiel/Daniel are available. The format, even if more generic, allows for a particular theological bent, and as a compilation of excerpts, it draws on a range of genres, "extensive commentary, brief annotations, impassioned sermons, official confessions and careful doctrinal and practical treatises."[68]

Though not denomination-specific, the Ancient Christian Commentary on Scripture (ACCS) is era-specific, compiling extracts from early Christian exegetical works from the second through the eighth centuries. The RSV text is printed with a title given to the pericope (e.g., "Jer 7:1–15 Turn From Your Evil Ways") followed by an Overview. Excerpts from early church scholars are supplied using topical headings (e.g., "Mechanical Use of the Temple is Inappropriate," an excerpt from Jerome).[69]

REFLECTIONS AND ANALYSES

Several observations follow from this taxonomy. First, the enterprise of commentary writing is infused with much energy. Several series have been launched in the last decade, almost an explosion in the industry. It is good that pastors, teachers, Bible readers, scholars and students have more choices. That being said, is this expansion driven by consumer need or simply momentum from scholars eager to capitalize on their insights, which may or may not edify the church? Do publishing establishments drive this explosion of commentaries and should one expect commentary series with newer emphases and formats to continue multiplying?[70] Whatever the reasons, the increased attention to Scripture is heartening.

67. Martens, *Jeremiah*, 72–78.
68. *IVP Academic Catalogue,* Spring 2014, 25.
69. Wenthe, *Jeremiah, Lamentations*, 64–66.
70. Cf. Reid, "Commentaries and Commentators."

Second, though commentary formats have changed over the years, certain features remain standard: the editor's forewords (variously named) in which the objectives and the distinctives of the series are clearly delineated; an introduction to the biblical book detailing author, sources, the historic circumstances, and sometimes the theology of the biblical book; and bibliographies for further reference. The size of commentaries, however, has greatly increased.[71]

Third, because the first and last volumes produced in a series may be decades apart, a few series have themselves evolved in format. The AYB series, begun in the mid-twentieth century as "The Anchor Bible," is one example. Douglas Stuart writes, "The older volumes (before about 1978) are semi-detailed or detailed; the newer volumes are in-depth."[72] FOTL envisioned twenty-four volumes; to date (mid-2014) eighteen have been published. In 2013, some thirty years after the initial volume, Rolf P. Knierim and Marvin A. Sweeney, the current co-editors of FOTL, acknowledge "that the original form-critical method was inadequately conceived since the search for societal traditions or conditions behind the texts was conducted without form-critical study of the social and literary conditions in which these texts were produced and in which they function."[73] Recent volumes give more attention "before everything else" to the structure of each identified text unit.[74] For example, in keeping with the revised emphases, the major component of Judg 6:1—10:5, presents a detailed structure of more than ten pages followed by eight pages of discussion on structure. It is true that the earlier distinctive format has been retained: text (without translation but with grammatical and historical notes), structure, genre, setting, intention, concluding with a bibliography. Nevertheless, the weight given to each format item has decidedly shifted.

Fourth, several changes in approach are not series-specific but represent larger tendencies. Currently, far less emphasis is placed on atomistic exegesis of single phrases or verses and there is a trend toward essays on larger scriptural blocks. Also, now the intended readership likely includes lay persons and preachers, not just academics. For example, the *New Interpreter's Bible* (NIB) addresses the challenge with a two-type format of exegesis and exposition to make for ease of access according to the interests of readers. Brevard Child's six-fold format in writing the Exodus commentary (OTL)

---

71. E.g., Renkama, *Lamentations*, whose treatment of five biblical chapters extends to 649 pages.

72. Stuart, *Guide*, 101.

73. Frolov, *Judges*, xiii.

74. Ibid. See Sweeney and Ben Zvi, eds., *Changing Face*.

has two sections specifically assisting the scholar—a new translation and an explanation of literary and historical problems—but his final four sections have the general reader in mind: the Old Testament context, the unit-by-unit discussion in a canonical context; New Testament usage; history and exegesis; and theological reflection. Child's commentary, which gave impetus to writing commentaries with a more theological cast, illustrates well how form follows function.[75]

Current "fads" or trends in methodology clearly account for some format changes. Fifty years ago self-descriptions included the word "critical" (e.g., International Critical Commentary; Hermeneia–a Critical and Historical Commentary of the Bible). Somewhat later, though still in "critical" mode, forms and structures of the text attracted attention.[76] David Petersen, endorsing the Genesis volume in the Berit Olam series, states, "It [the Genesis Commentary] joins a growing number of commentaries that treat Genesis from a literary vantage point . . . It can no longer be said that 'historical-critical' studies dominate work on this biblical book."[77] Research methodologies have moved from attention to "criticisms" to narrative, to theologies. One clearly identifiable approach, the so-called "New Literary Approach," is by itself a "plethora of approaches." The focus on the text's final form resulted in a change of direction from diachronic to synchronic and "from analysis to synthesis."[78] McKeown, who follows a synchronic approach, explains, "[H]olistic studies enable the researcher to highlight the recurrence of the key words, phrases, motifs, and themes that give the work its distinctiveness as a literary unity."[79] Interest in source analysis has subsequently waned.

Fifth, and related to the previous point, theology more explicitly informs commentary writing now, as exemplified by recent series touting a theological approach (e.g., Brazos Theological Commentary, The Two Horizons Commentary). As noted above, the ICC and OTL eschewed theology, confining themselves more to the conventional features of commentary. But the trend of reading the Bible as literature meant that scholars paid attention to the message, and consequently to theology. Rudolf Smend, reviewing a century of Old Testament study which moved from literary criticism to history of religion to broadly theological emphases, concluded: "Today the

---

75. Childs, *Exodus*.

76. See Sweeney, "Latter Prophets," for a review of the series of approaches (e.g., historical study, form- and redaction-critical study, literary, etc.).

77. https://:www.logos.com/product/31028/berit-olam-studies-in-hebrew-narrative-and-poetry.

78. McKeown, *Genesis*, 8–9.

79. Ibid.

Old Testament plays an undisputed role in the study of theology viewed as a whole, just as Kittel demanded in 1921 that it should."[80] That trend continues in the current century and is welcomed by most. Richard John Neuhaus comments on the previous non-theological approach: "Preachers and teachers in particular, but thoughtful Christians more generally, have long lamented the slide of biblical scholarship into hyper-specialized critical studies of ancient texts in remote historical context."[81] The ferment in these times is not about whether commentaries should include theological dimensions, but in what manner, in what form and to what extent these should be presented.

One reason for the theological turn may reside in the meager, often conflicting, results gained from exploring critical questions. Timothy Stone, reviewing a commentary in the Brazos series, addresses this issue: "The handwriting is on the wall for historical-critical commentaries; in the eyes of many, they have been weighed and found theologically wanting. This seems to be the motivating verdict behind the bourgeoning genre of theology."[82] Another motivation might well be the need to make commentaries relevant to the present. Clearly one cannot always move directly from an explanation of a single verse to a practical application. Rather, we need a larger horizon—theology as a bridge from text to praxis—to do so. To go down this theology track will require new skills, and likely produce new formats.

Sixth, the cultural move from the enlightenment/modern era either to post-modernism or pre-modernism has hugely influenced commentary writing and will continue to do so. The trend toward theological-oriented commenting is already a reaction to the enlightenment's rationalizing mentality. Philosophically, the move is toward a larger wholism. For Christian faith, such wholism reaches back to premodern times, to the era of the Reformers, to patristic times and to Jewish rabbinic commentary. This is exemplified in the Ancient Christian Commentary on Scripture (ACCS) revisiting expositions of the Church Fathers.

Obviously, the general cultural ethos is a major determinant in the production of interpretative literature. The postmodern mood is suspicious of methods generally because they naturally straightjacket research and predetermine outcomes so that the "meaning" of a text is obscured or perverted.[83] Moreover, a global orientation has already raised the vol-

---

80. Rudolf Smend, "Trends," 259.

81. https://www.logos.com/product/37336/brazos-theological-commentary-on-the-bible.

82. Stone, review of Wells and Sumner, *Esther and Daniel*, in *Review of Biblical Literature* [http://www.bookreviews.org].

83. See George, "Postmodern Literary Criticism," and similar essays in that volume.

ume of voices from the South calling to be heard. Bible commentaries are increasingly written by scholars with African, Latino or Asian perspectives.[84] With other special interest groups (e.g., feminism, liberation theology, ecology) also bringing an expanded set of questions to the biblical text, one might expect an increased variety in commentary format. The post-secular and post-modern mind-set allows for, or even calls for explanations that engage various world views. Thus, while word studies are still important for writers of commentaries, will it be necessary for them to address theologies, and even philosophies embedded in other religions? With the enlargements of function may come greater opportunities and hence more call for creativity in format. At the same time the current culture's bent toward practicality cannot be ignored. The demand is for instant relevance.[85] The winds of cultural changes will almost certainly demand a review of the function of commentaries, and along with that review, one may expect further variations in format.

Seventh, as to format, the technological revolution's influence will continue. A generation more attuned to the visual will want more than a page of solid print. Side bars, charts, quotations are already in evidence. Fretheim's commentary on Jeremiah includes side bars which appear on almost every page giving details of a linguistic, historical or archaeological nature, or citing some well known OT scholars.[86] This volume, as is also the case in other series, comes with a CD,[87] and several commentary series are now in e-book format. Appraising various possibilities, Fretheim opines with a dash of optimism, "Readers should be prepared for ever greater diversity among the commentaries that will become available. And rejoice in that reality!"[88] More commentaries are likely to appear digitally on the Internet allowing, perhaps even mandating, a variety of innovations.

Eighth, function and format interconnect. The format serves the commentary's objective or function. Although the function of commentaries and their intended audience may seem obvious, clarification of this should impact the format of presentation. One may envision multiple purposes, as does B. S. Childs in his Exodus commentary; if so the format should assist in fulfilling the objectives, as his does so well. Moreover, what priority should

---

84. E.g., Comentario Biblico Iberoamericano.

85. Cf. the preacher's complaint, "Most Old Testament commentaries don't deal with the text in ways that are needed to touch base with contemporary experience." Fretheim, "OT Commentaries. Their Selection and Use," 71.

86. Fretheim, *Jeremiah*.

87. All 59 volumes of the *Word Biblical Commentary* (WBC) are on one CD. Similarly, all 29 volumes in the ACCS series are available on CD-ROM.

88. Fretheim, "OT Commentaries," 76.

be given to such factors as historical or philological details, to theology, to application, and to ease of access? Whatever the answer, the format should help give greater specificity and accuracy to those concerns. Likewise, if the intent is to contextualize a passage within a book and so to follow the text's flow, the format should readily represent that. If the intent is to explicate a theology, the most advantageous page layout to that end should be adopted.

Finally, while we as commentators deal with the challenges of formats, we still relish the insights we discover in explaining and applying the Biblical teachings to our readers. Refinements there may well be in function and format, but the genre of commentary writing on Scripture, highly valued as God's divine communication to the world, will continue.

BIBLIOGRAPHY

Allen, Leslie C. *Jeremiah*. OTL. Louisville: Westminster John Knox, 2008.
Block, Daniel I. *Obadiah: The Kingship Belongs to YHWH*. HMS. Grand Rapids: Zondervan, 2013.
Bright, John. *Jeremiah*. AB 21. Garden City, NY: Doubleday, 1965.
Childs, Brevard S. *The Book of Exodus: A Critical, Theological Commentary*. OTL. Philadelphia: Westminster, 1974.
Clements, Ronald E. *Jeremiah*. Interpretation. Atlanta: John Knox, 1988.
Cotter, David W. *Genesis*. Berit Olam. Collegeville, MN: Liturgical, 2003.
Craigie, Peter C., Page H. Kelley, and Joel F. Drinkard, Jr. *Jeremiah 1–25*. WBC 26. Dallas: Word, 1991.
Dahood, Mitchell J. *Psalms I, 1–50*. AB 16. Garden City, NY: Doubleday, 1966.
———. *Psalms II, 51–100*. AB 17. Garden City, NY: Doubleday, 1968.
———. *Psalms III, 101–50*. AB 17A. Garden City, NY: Doubleday, 1970.
Dearman, J. Andrew. *Jeremiah and Lamentations*. NIVAC. Grand Rapids: Zondervan, 2002.
Fredericks, Daniel C., and Daniel J. Estes. *Ecclesiastes and the Song of Songs*. AOTC 16. Downers Grove, IL: InterVarsity, 2010.
Fretheim, Terence E. "Old Testament Commentaries: Their Selection and Use." *Interpretation* 36 (1982) 356–71.
———. *Jeremiah*. SHBC. Macon, GA: Smyth & Helwys, 2002.
Frolov, Serge. *Judges*. FOTL VIB. Grand Rapids: Eerdmans, 2013.
George, Mark K. "Postmodern Literary Criticism: The Impossibility of Method." In *Method Matters: Essays on the Interpretation of the Hebrew Bible in Honor of David L. Petersen*, edited by Joel M. LeMon and Kent Harold Richards, 459–77. Society of Biblical Literature Resources for Biblical Study 56. Atlanta: SBL Press, 2009.
Hartley, John E. *The Book of Job*. NICOT. Grand Rapids: Eerdmans, 1988.
———. *Leviticus*. WBC 4. Dallas: Word, 1992.
———. *Genesis*. NIBC. Peabody, MA: Hendrickson, 2000.
Holladay, William L. *Jeremiah 1*. Hermeneia. Philadelphia: Fortress, 1986.
Jenson, Robert W. *Ezekiel*. BTCB. Grand Rapids: Brazos Press, 2009.

Keck, Leander E., ed. *Introduction to Prophetic Literature: Isaiah, Jeremiah, Baruch, Letter of Jeremiah, Lamentations, Ezekiel.* NIB 6. Nashville: Abingdon, 2001.
Keown, Gerald L., and Pamela J. Scalise. *Jeremiah 26-52.* WBC 27. Dallas: Word, 1995.
Lalleman, Hetty. *Jeremiah and Lamentations.* TOTC 21. Downers Grove, IL: InterVarsity, 2013.
Longman, Tremper, III. *Old Testament Commentary Survey.* 5th ed. Grand Rapids: Baker, 2013.
Lundbom, Jack R. *Jeremiah 1-20.* AYBC 21A. Garden City, NY: Doubleday, 2004.
Martens, Elmer A. "Psalm 73: A Corrective to a Modern Misunderstanding." *Direction* 12/4 (1983) 15-26.
———. *Jeremiah.* BCBC. Scottdale, PA: Herald, 1986.
McKane, William. *A Critical and Exegetical Commentary on Jeremiah, Vol. I: Jeremiah I-XXV.* ICC. Edinburgh: T & T Clark, 2000.
McKeown, James. *Genesis.* THOTC. Grand Rapids: Eerdmans, 2008.
Parry, Robin. *Lamentations.* THOTC. Grand Rapids: Eerdmans, 2010.
Reid, Daniel G. "Commentaries and Commentators from a Publisher's Perspective." In *On the Writing of New Testament Commentaries: Festschrift for Grant R. Osborne on the Occasion of his 70th Birthday,* edited by Stanley E. Porter and Eckhard J. Schnabel, 451-69. Texts and Editions for New Testament Study 8. Leiden: Brill, 2013.
Renkema, Johan. *Lamentations.* HCOT. Leuven: Peeters, 1998.
Reno, Russell R. *Genesis.* BTCB. Grand Rapids: Brazos Press, 2010.
Smend, Rudolf. "Trends. Old Testament Scholarship in the Twentieth Century: A Retrospect." In *'The Unconquered Land' and Other Old Testament Essays: Selected Studies by Rudolf Smend,* 245-59. Burlington, VT: Ashgate, 2013.
Stone, Timothy J. Review of Samuel Wells and George Sumner, *Esther and Daniel. RBL* [http://www.bookreviews.org] 2014.
Stuart, Douglas. *A Guide to Selecting and Using Bible Commentaries.* Dallas: Word, 1990.
Stulman, Louis. *Jeremiah.* AOTC. Nashville: Abingdon, 2005.
Sweeney, Marvin A. *Isaiah 1-39, with an Introduction to Prophetic Literature.* FOTL 16. Grand Rapids: Eerdmans, 1996.
———. "The Latter Prophets (Isaiah, Jeremiah, Ezekiel)." In *The Hebrew Bible Today: An Introduction to Critical Issues,* edited by Steven L. McKensie and M. Patrick Graham, 69-94. Louisville: Westminster John Knox, 1998.
Sweeney, Marvin A., and Ehud Ben Zvi, eds. *The Changing Face of Form Criticism for the Twenty-First Century.* Grand Rapids: Eerdmans, 2003.
Thompson, Deana A. *Deuteronomy.* BTCB. Louisville: Westminster John Knox, 2014.
Watts, James W. *Leviticus, Volume 1: Chapters 1-10.* HCOT. Leuven: Peeters, 2013.
Wenthe, Dean O. *Jeremiah, Lamentations.* ACCS 12. Downers Grove, IL: InterVarsity, 2009.

LIST OF COMMENTARY SERIES CITED

Note: Commentaries are listed alphabetically by series noting the publisher and the year the series was inaugurated, if available. Editors (OT) are listed next; so are other details about volumes available and status of the series.

Abingdon Old Testament Commentaries (AOTC). Nashville: Abingdon, 2001. Edited by Patrick D. Miller. Available: 14 volumes; status: in process.

Anchor Bible (AB; AYB). Garden City, NY: Doubleday, 1956; Yale University Press. 2007. Edited by W. F. Albright; D. N. Freedman. Available: 61 volumes; status: "all but complete."

Ancient Christian Commentary on Scripture (ACCS). Downers Grove, IL: InterVarsity, 2001. General editor, Thomas C. Oden. Available: 14 volumes; status: complete.

Apollos Old Testament Commentary (AOTC). Downers Grove, IL: InterVarsity, 2002. Edited by David W. Baker and Gordon. J. Wenham. Available: 7 volumes; status: in process.

Baker Commentary on the Old Testament Wisdom and Psalms. Grand Rapids: Baker 2005. Edited by Tremper Longman III. Available: 7 volumes; status: complete.

Belief. A Theological Commentary on the Bible. Louisville, KY: Wesminster John Knox, 2010. Edited by Amy Plantinga Pauw and William C. Placher. Available: 4 volumes; status: in process.

Believers Church Bible Commentary (BCBC). Scottdale, PA: Herald Press, 1986. Edited by Elmer A. Martens and Douglas Miller. Available: 14 volumes; status: 11 more projected.

Berit Olam. Collegeville, MN: Liturgical, 1998. Edited by D. W. Cotter. Available: 14 volumes; status: in process.

Brazos Theological Commentary on the Bible (BTCB). Grand Rapids: Brazos Press, 2006. Edited by R. R. Reno. Available: 11 volumes; status: in process, 13 more projected.

Comentario Biblico Iberoamericano continuation of Comentario Biblico Hispanoamericano. Buenos Aires: Ediciones Kairos, 1989. Edited by C. Rene Padilla. Available: 5 volume; status: in process.

Cornerstone Biblical Commentary (CBC). Wheaton, IL: Tyndale, 2005. General editor Philip Comfort. Available: 12 volumes; status: complete.

The Expositor's Bible Commentary (EBC). Grand Rapids: Zondervan, 1969 (now revised). Edited by Tremper Longman III and David Garland. Available: 8 volumes; status: complete.

Forms of Old Testament Literature (FOTL). Grand Rapids: Eerdmans, 1981. Edited by Rolf Knierim, Gene M. Tucker, Marvin A. Sweeney. Available: 17 volumes; status: projecting a total of 24.

Hearing the Message of Scripture (HMS). Grand Rapids: Zondervan 2013. General editor Daniel I. Block. Available: 2 volumes; status: a total of 35 projected.

Hermeneia. Philadelphia: Fortress, 1973. Edited by Frank Moore Cross. Available: 33 volumes; status: in process.

Historical Commentary on the Old Testament (HCOT). Leuven, Belgium: Peeters, 1997. Available: 20 volumes; status: in process.

International Critical Commentary (ICC). Edinburgh: T & T Clark, 1899. Edited by J. A. Emerton. Available: 27 volumes; status: in process.

Interpretation. Atlanta, GA: John Knox, 1985. Ed. James L. Mays. Available: 26 volumes; status: complete.

New American Commentary (NAC) Nashville: Broadman & Holman. Available: 24 volumes. Status: in process.

New Beacon Bible Commentary (NBBC). Kansas City, MO: Beacon Hill. Available: 15 volumes: Status: projected a total of 26.

New International Biblical Commentary (NIBC). Peabody, MA/Cumbria, UK: Hendrickson/Paternoster, 1994. Edited by Robert L. Hubbard, Jr. and Robert K. Johnston. Available: 11 volumes; status: in process.

New International Commentary of the Old Testament (NICOT). Grand Rapids: Eerdmans, 1976. Edited by Robert L. Hubbard, Jr. Available:15 volumes; status: A total of 26 projected.

New Interpreter's Bible (NIB). Nashville: Abingdon, 1994. Ed. David L. Petersen. Available: 7 volumes; status: complete.

New International Version Application Commentary (NIVAC). Grand Rapids: Zondervan, 1999. Edited by Tremper Longman III and John Walton. Available: 22 volumes; status: almost complete.

Old Testament Library (OTL). Louisville: Westminster John Knox, 1965. Editorial Board. Available: 37 volumes; status: complete.

Preacher's Commentary (PC). Harper Collins Christian Publishing. Edited by Lloyd J. Ogilvie. Available: 22 volumes; status: complete.

Reformation Commentary on Scripture (RCS). Downers Grove, IL: InterVarsity, 2012. Edited by Timothy George, Available: 2 volumes; status: 13 more projected.

Smyth & Helwys Bible Commentary (SHBC). Macon, GA: Smyth & Helwys, 2000. Edited by Samuel E. Balentine. Available: 14 volumes; status: 18 more projected.

The New American Commentary (NAC), Nashville: Broadman, 1993. Edited by E. Ray Clendenen. Available: 25 volumes; status: mostly complete.

The Two Horizons Old Testament Commentary (THOTC). Grand Rapids: Eerdmans, 2008. Edited by J. Gordon McConville and Craig Batholomew. Available: 5 volumes; status: in process.

Tyndale Old Testament Commentaries (TOTC). Downers Grove, IL: InterVarsity, mid-1960s, now revised editions. Edited by David Firth and Tremper Longman III. Available: 29 volumes; status: complete.

Wesleyan Bible Commentary. Indianapolis: Wesleyan Publishing House, 1998. Editors, various. Available: 3 volumes; status: no more planned.

Word Biblical Commentary (WBC). Dallas: Word, 1983. Edited by David A. Hubbard, Glenn Barker, and John D. W. Watts. Available: 32; status: in process.

4

Awk, Dele, and *Stet*
The Task and Craft of a Commentary Editor

—*Robert L. Hubbard, Jr.*

As Qohelet famously warns, "Of making many books there is no end, and much study wearies the body" (Eccl 12:12 TNIV). That truth also applies to book editing, a task I have been engaged in for two decades. I have co-edited an Old Testament commentary series completed in 2012, am a contributing editor of a series nearing completion, and for two decades have been the solo editor of a major series also nearing completion.

At times editing is, indeed, wearisome: the manuscripts are long and, in some cases, tedious to read. Yet editing remains a necessary step in producing commentaries and, in fact, continues a long history of endeavor. In this essay, I define who an editor is today, review an Old Testament slice of the history of editing, and the in light of their work I reflect on my own experience as an editor of commentaries. I make no claim to be the "ideal editor," but the topic seems apropos for a volume devoted to the genre of commentaries that honors Professor John E. Hartley, a premier commentary-writer I have been privileged to know personally for near four decades. I count it a special joy to call him a friend and treasure the collegiality that he has generously shared with me during our careers. I offer this contribution to congratulate my dear friend on his outstanding service to the church and the academy and to thank him for his occasional counsel and enduring friendship.

THE TASK OF A COMMENTARY EDITOR

What is a commentary editor? First, an experienced scholar whom a publisher hires to oversee the production of a commentary series on biblical books. Second, a broker under contract to represent the publisher in recruiting authors to sign contracts to write volumes for the series. Prospective authors are all scholars themselves, some more established than others, and most earn their living as full-time faculty. The preference for academic faculty over other well-qualified prospects is pragmatic: the former have more discretionary time to pursue research and writing, and their employers are more likely to support, if not reward, such endeavors.

Once an author accepts an invitation to write for such a series, the publisher issues a contract with him/her that stipulates the obligations incumbent on each party. Among the obligations the author assumes is an agreed-on deadline to submit the completed manuscript. In my experience, that date represents a compromise between the earlier and later dates proposed by the publisher and the author, respectively. Some authors find that stipulation threatening, and the extent of deadline flexibility varies from publisher to publisher. But, usually in most cases grace abounds, provided the author evidences significant progress toward completion. On the other hand the publisher's patience is not inexhaustible. Publishers cannot stay in business without books to sell, so they occasionally cancel the contract of someone deemed unlikely to finish. Once a contract is in force, the commentator works under an editor's oversight who on behalf of the publisher advises on technical matters (e.g., the series format, what to include/exclude, how to submit a manuscript, etc.) and serves as the author's primary liaison with the publisher. This oversight may include giving feedback on certain written commentary portions the author may submit. Wise authors update their editors every year or so concerning their work, and those failing to do so will hear about it. In turn, wise editors periodically apprise the publisher concerning the status of authors under contract.

When the happy day arrives that the author submits the final manuscript, the editor evaluates its readiness for publication. The editor may either forward it to the publisher recommending its publication, or (if necessary) return it to the contributor for revisions or additions beforehand. The primary revisions usually concern aligning the manuscript with the series' format, shortening it to fall within the maximum length the publisher permits, and clarifying portions deemed unclear. The most common addition I have recommended is to include a section or two in the Introduction for completeness (e.g., treatment of interpretive problems confronting readers, theological themes or reflections, the book's message for Christian life today). Once a manuscript is approved and in the publisher's hands, the editor's job effectively ends except for occasional consultation with the publisher's editorial staff. Further matters that arise are worked out just between the author and the publisher, although the publisher does occasionally consult the editor.

MY ROLE AS A COMMENTARY EDITOR

As a broker between a series publisher and authors, I represent several distinct interests. First, I represent the interests of the publishers with whom they are under contract and who establish the purpose, target audience, format, content level, etc. of their series—the "givens" that guide my work as an editor. Within those parameters, however, publishers welcome authorial creativity and variety if it advances the purpose and quality of the series. Someone once asked novelist Chaim Potok about how Judaism influenced his thinking and writing. In reply, he compared Judaism to the banks of a river: it established the boundaries within which he was free to explore the river fully. The givens of commentary series function in much the same way: they establish a consistent framework within which the authors may explore, research and express their creative individuality.

Second, I represent the audience that the series intends to reach. Authors frequently target an audience of their scholarly peers in writing commentaries. They understandably want to establish and maintain their "scholarly reputation," one key to receiving other invitations to write, lecture, and even consider a new, more prestigious faculty position. When attending the Society of Biblical Literature annual meeting, they want all who read their name tags to recognize them and acknowledge their work. Perhaps most important, they want their department chair or dean to notice their work so that their institution may grant them rank promotions and the ultimate prize—academic tenure. The fact is, however, that each series targets a specific audience profile in a spectrum of education levels and motivations for reading. As an editor, I often counsel authors to keep in mind the ideal reader-profile of the series for which they are writing and to tailor their work accordingly. I tell them, "Imagine . . .

> a lay person with a high school education who's reading your book as a member of a weekly small-group Bible study"

- a college-educated lay person who's reading your book to prepare to lead that study or to teach a class"
- a pastor serving a rural church who only has your book to consult in sermon preparation"
- a Christian university student who hopes your book will supply answers to troubling questions arising in a religion course."

This type of reader profile guides a commentary writer with regard to a host of issues, e.g., how technical the commentary should be, what issues to include or exclude, how much application, comment or theological reflection is desirable.

Third, I represent the link of continuity across the volumes of a series. It is the series editor and the publisher who ensure that Commentary X will be consistent in level, depth, and purpose with Commentaries Y and Z as well as A to W. Years ago, one of my seminary professors pointed out that the stated purpose of one well-known series was to help modern readers understand the Bible. He then read aloud with gentle amusement a paragraph from one of its volumes dominated by numerous comparisons of the Hebrew text with transliterated parallels drawn from cognate Semitic languages. To affirm that such technical verbiage brought the Bible's contents to life for a modern reader was more than a stretch. I do not intend to denigrate modern readers, the commentary series, or the author. My point, rather, is to illustrate that an editor faces unique challenges in brokering the alignment of a commentary's contents with the purpose of the commentary series to which it contributes.

Ultimately, my primary role as editor is that of quality control. I am the gatekeeper whose scrutiny all commentaries must satisfy to be recommended for publication. Although some commentaries have won my approval with minor or no revisions, others required more back-and-forth between me and the authors before gaining my approval of their book. To see publication, John Hartley's fine commentaries on Job and Leviticus had to win the approval of each series' editor, Professors Roland Harrison (NICOT) and John D. W. Watts (WBC).[1] Ideally, an editor wants each additional volume to maintain the quality of its predecessors—to sustain, if not further enhance, the positive stature of the entire series. That does not mean that every new volume is the commentary that I would have written had the assignment been mine. On the contrary, I expect them to exceed what I would have produced because, for the most part, authors are invited to contribute due to their unique scholarly expertise on a particular biblical book.

---

1. Hartley, *The Book of Job* (NICOT, 1988); Hartley, *Leviticus* (WBC, 1992).

EDITING: THE BIBLICAL PRECEDENT

When discussing the composition history of Old Testament books, scholars typically invoke the roles played in the process by "writers," "compilers," and "editors" (or "redactors"). A "writer" is someone who first puts into writing what is now part of the Masoretic Text (MT). This could mean simply reducing to writing a previously oral composition, rewriting some prior source, creating a brand new document, or various combinations of these. "Compilers" typically knit together those pre-existing literary pieces into larger wholes—e.g., a collection of prophetic oracles, the so-called Elohistic psalter, the Deuteronomistic History, etc. Among those "larger wholes" would be individual biblical books (e.g., Deuteronomy, Isaiah, the Psalms) and the Hebrew canon as a whole (The Torah, Prophets, Writings). The work of editors, however, may occur anywhere along the process of composition and may eventually attain the same level of authority as the texts on which they worked. As we shall see, however, the boundary separating writers, editors, and compilers is not hard and fast: any of them may compose other original texts to be included, the openings and closings of collections, or the short seams that give the latter their continuity. In what follows, I will explore several well-known biblical phenomena—the tell-tale fingerprints of ancient editors. This exploration eschews an exhaustive treatment in favor of sampling the evidence with the aim of enriching our understanding of the editor's role and underscoring their contribution's importance.

First, some ancient editors supplied *parenthetical explanatory comments*. Literarily, they are brief (two words or a single verse) and occur uniformly in narratives (but never in direct speech by a narrative character). Instead, they mark the brief intrusion of the editor's voice into the context of the enfolding story. Disjunctive syntax (i.e., initial *waw* or a non-verb) typically signals their presence; the editor, as it were, has pressed the "pause button" on the ongoing story to clarify something just said rather than what follows. Some comments simply add the explanation asyndetically, i.e. without any conjunction. In Josh 12:3, we read "to the sea of the Arabah, the Dead Sea" where "the Dead Sea" is the explanation of "the Arabah." Similar examples are found in 1 Chron 28:18 and Ezek 37:16. But most common is the construction where the explanatory place name is preceded by *hu'/hi'* which roughly translates to "that is." These explanations were inserted by editors to clarify an unfamiliar place-name that was probably older and possibly Canaanite. The editors in effect updated the received text by citing the place name by which their contemporaries knew it. The following table samples these explanatory editorial parentheses from various types of place names:[2]

Text(s)	Place Name	Equivalent	Type
Gen 14:2, 8	Bela	Zoar	City
Gen 14:3	Siddim	Dead Sea Valley	Valley
Gen 14:7	En Mishpat	Kadesh	Desert Oasis
Gen 14:17	Valley of Shaveh	King's Valley	Valley
Gen 35:19; 48:7	Ephrath	Bethlehem	City
Gen 35:6 Josh 18:13 cf. Gen 28:19; Josh 16:2	Luz	Bethel	City
Deut 4:48	Mount Sirion	Hermon	Mountain
Josh 15:8; 18:28 1 Chron 11:4	Jebusite (city)	Jerusalem	City
Josh 15:9	Ba'alah	Kiriath Jearim	City
Josh 15:60; 18:14	Kiriath Ba'al	Kiriath Jearim	City
Josh 15:10	Mount Jearim (Mountain Slope)	Kesalon	City
Gen 23:2; 35:27 Josh 15:13, 54; 20:7; 21:11 Cf. Judg 1:10	Kiriath Arba	Hebron	City
Josh 15:25	Kerioth Hezron	Hazor	City
Josh 15:49	Kiriath Sannah	Debir	City
2 Chron 20:2[A]	Hazezon Tamar	Ein Gedi	Spring

A. In my view, parenthetical comments in postexilic texts derive from authors supplying additional information and or imitating the older editorial practice for literary effect; cf. 1 Chron 1:27 (Abram = Abraham); 1 Chron 5:26 (Pul = Tiglath-Peleser); Ezra 10:23 (the Levite Kelaiah = Kelita); Esth 3:7; 9:24 (*pur* = the lot).

Table 4.1

2. Cf. the editorial comment that Jerub-Ba'al was Gideon (Judg. 7:1; 8:35), a comment perhaps aimed at heading off reader ruminations about his apparently Canaanite name. For editorial clarification of the connection between the person Esau and the nation Edom, cf. Gen. 36:1, 8, 19. Concerning the parenthetical remark that reckoned King Og of Bashan as "the last of the Rephaites" (Josh. 13:12 TNIV; NRSV "Rephraim"), see R. Liwak, "repa'im," *TDOT* 13:602–614, who defines it as "an aboriginal race of giants" with mythological status (p. 611; cf. Num. 13:33). In Og, he argues, "the historical and mythological figures coalesce . . ." (p. 612; cf. Deut. 3:11; Josh. 12:4; 13:12).

To a modern editor, it is striking that the Israelite editors retained the older name and added a comment rather than simply replacing the older name with the contemporary one. They may have felt constrained by the same reverence for the Hebrew text for which later scribes are renowned. Or possibly they thought that retaining the older names created a kind of halo effect: it implied that the editors were very learned and authoritative—in other words, to win audience acceptance of their insertions.

Longer parenthetical comments similarly seek to explain something old and unfamiliar to a later audience—such as legal customs or words no longer in vogue. In 1 Samuel 9:9, the reference to Samuel as a "seer" (*haro'eh*) has the editor clarifying that a seer was how an earlier generation described what the readers know as a "prophet" (*hannabi'*). This procedure would also help the reader understand the unfamiliar by something more familiar. As with the brief parentheses so also here the editor inserts a comment rather than substitute the newer term for the older one. In Ruth 4:7, an editorial aside explains that the sandal ceremony was Israel's ancient way of consummating a legal transaction. Its inclusion assumes that the sandal-exchange custom about to play out was no longer practiced and needed explaining. The editor's ultimate priority in these longer examples also is that the audience understand the text as clearly as possible.

Colophons, which also mark an editor's/editors' fingerprints, are brief notations typically appended to clay tablets in the ancient Near East. They identify people connected with the text's production (e.g., the scribe, the tablet's owner, the person who ordered the inscription), include a title or cite catchphrases from the tablet contents, and state the text's purpose.[3] The conclusion of Leviticus 14 (vv. 54–57 NIV) provides a clear example of a colophon that draws on the language of the text's preceding contents:[4]

> These are the regulations for any defiling skin disease, for a sore, for defiling molds in fabric or in a house, and for a swelling, a rash or a shiny spot, to determine when something is clean or unclean. These are the regulations for defiling skin diseases and defiling molds.

Hartley has pointed out that this summary "functions as a conclusion to both chaps. 13 and 14."[5] The reason is simply that, whereas the instruction in ch. 13 (vv. 1–58) has its own closing summary (v. 59), the colophon under discussion summarizes the content of both ch. 13 and the two instruc-

---

3. For examples, see *ANET*, 101, 305, 331, 338, 340, and 341.

4. My identification of these verses as a colophon follows the summary of editorial phenomena in Fishbane, *Biblical Interpretation*, 28–32, 44–77.

5. Hartley, *Leviticus*, 199.

tional sections of ch. 14 (vv. 1–32, and 34–53). Its first two verses (14:54–55) summarize the various kinds of scale disease on which chs. 13–14 instruct. As Milgrom observes, the final two verses (vv. 56–67) "comprise inclusions—with the beginning of chap. 13, with the beginning of chap. 14, and with the summation (vv. 54–55). Thereby, the subscript has skillfully and effectively locked in and enveloped chaps. 13–14, the entire unit on scale disease."[6] This observation implies that the person responsible for including vv. 54–57—technically, whether "author," "editor," or both—apparently did so to give the context a concluding literary flourish. This knit together its various elements into a satisfactory whole, which not only works to inform readers but also makes their reading more satisfying, if not enjoyable.

Finally, two *editorial remarks*, one that opens a section late in Proverbs and one that closes the book of Hosea, offer two last fingerprints. Proverbs 25:1 prefaces the book's second collection of Solomonic proverbs (Prov 25–29) thusly: "These are more proverbs of Solomon, compiled by the men of Hezekiah king of Judah" (TNIV). This report of editors working in King Hezekiah's service in Jerusalem during the late eighth century BCE functions as a title for the collection that follows and presumes someone writing either at that time or viewing the event retrospectively later.[7] It also presumes the availability of an inventory of Solomonic proverbs, probably in both oral and written forms, and a decision that they be "collected" together in writing.[8] In other words, as Meinhold observes, the editors worked more as compilers than as authors: they wrote down extant oral proverbs, copied written ones, and organized them into a collection.[9] What moved leadership in late eighth-century Jerusalem to launch this major editorial project is uncertain. Meinhold notes that, like his contemporary Isaiah, the

---

6. Milgrom, *Leviticus 1–16*, 885. In his view (886), the colophon represents "the love of and concern for literary devices" typical of Milgrom's preexilic "school of H." He credits the instruction concerning clean houses (14:33–53) to an "author (or editor)," but it is unclear whether those terms apply to the hand responsible for the colophon. Concerning his view that "H" predates "D," cf. Milgrom, *Leviticus 23–27*, 2254–57.

7. LXX identifies the editors specifically as the king's "friends" or "close associates" (*philoi*).

8. Heb. ⌐*ataq* hi. (KBL "move, remove"; LXX *exgraphein* "to write out, copy for oneself") pictures the process as the removal of the material from where (and how) it was beforehand to the location (and condition) the editors chose; cf. B. Gemser, *Sprüche Salomos*, 91. Translations render the verb variously: "compiled" (NIV), "copied" (CEB, NRSV, TNK), "collected" (NLT), etc.

9. So, Meinhold, *Die Sprüche*, 2:415–16; cf. Waltke, *Proverbs 15–31*, 301, who avers that "the final editor reckoned this collection an appendix to Solomon's first collection, which Solomon himself authored and presumably compiled (10:1–22:16)."

king sought to foster the importance of wisdom in Jerusalem,[10] perhaps to inform palace deliberations over Judah's response to the decades-long Assyrian threat. Certainly, the management of that threat dominates the reign of Hezekiah in the Deuteronomistic History (2 Kgs. 18–19). Possibly royal awareness of the demise of Israel in 722 BCE made compiling Solomon's leftover proverbs all the more urgent, or perhaps the collection-venture grew out of Hezekiah's attempt at religious reform (2 Kgs. 18:2–7). Even if originally compiled for the instruction and guidance of court officials (e.g., 25:2–15), the collected proverbs continue to teach all Israel universal truths—paradigms for conduct applicable to many other situations.[11]

The final textual fingerprint comes from Hosea (14:9; MT 10):

> "Who is wise? Let them realize these things. Who is discerning? Let them understand.
>
> The ways of the LORD are right; the righteous walk in them, but the rebellious stumble in them." (TNIV)

According to Sheppard, this comment marks a secondary editorial layer which assesses the prophetic book Hosea from a wisdom perspective.[12] The saying, probably the editor's literary creation rather than an extant proverb, presumes that the prophetic book has an authoritative, canonical function and calls for it to be read both as prophecy and as a guide to acquiring wisdom.[13] But Hosea 14:9 [10] is not simply something appended; its wording and themes intentionally resonate with the book's contents. This close linguistic and thematic connection invites the reader to find in Hosea "wisdom similar to that found in the Solomonic books."[14] It also opens the door to an in-depth interpretive conversation between Hosea and Proverbs on shared themes—e.g., the themes of judgment and mercy, and knowledge and

---

10. Meinhold, *Die Sprüche*, 416.

11. Waltke, *Proverbs 15–31*, 301 ("Jesus may have instantiated vv. 6–7 to guests at a wedding feast [Luke 14:7–11] and Jude applied the image in 25:14 to unproductive people [Jude 12]).

12. Sheppard, *Hermeneutical Construct* 121, 135 ("this final verse offers an assessment to a book which has already acquired its essential shape"). In his view, besides Hosea's prophecy, other texts to receive a similar secondary wisdom interpretation include wisdom, hymnic, and narrative traditions (Eccl 12:13–14; Psalms 1–2; 2 Sam 23:1–7).

13. Ibid., 135 (quote), 136. Tentatively, he dates the addition of this comment to the final stages in the compilation of Hosea in the fifth century BC and possibly later; cf. Sheppard, "The Last Words," 192. Citing Prov 25:1, Dearman (*Hosea*, 3–8, 346), suggests the reign of Hezekiah as the setting both for the addition of Hos 14:9 (MT 10) and for the penultimate form of the whole book.

14. Sheppard, "The Last Words," 188, 192.

understanding.[15] The abrupt change from strident, first person prophetic oracles to a softer third person voice offering a teacher's advice creates a striking rhetorical effect: Hosea seems to address the reader personally, and yet what he says is still the Word of God.[16] Finally, Sheppard stresses that to read Hosea in the light of wisdom and its universal perspective opens other doors—e.g., to the exchange of proverbs with the larger world outside the people of God.

As expounded by Sheppard, the editorial addition of Hosea 14:9 [10] rounds out the picture of the challenge and opportunity afforded a commentary editor. The challenge is to encourage commentators to incorporate into their work historical exegesis of specific contexts, the tracing of thematic or theological trajectories through other scriptures, and discussion of one's exegetical conclusions in dialogue with others' thinking. The opportunity is that the broader conversation—what Sheppard calls "the appeal to passersby"[17]—will likely attract a wider readership than otherwise would be the case. And it may also nudge some Christian readers out of their cloistered comfort zones. I see this as deepening the Church's understanding of itself and also strengthening its evangelistic muscle.

CONCLUSION: REFLECTIONS OF A PRACTITIONER

The role of "editors" in the formation of MT centers on incorporating brief additions to already-existing literary pieces or collections of pre-existing materials. Their purpose ranges from polishing, clarifying and updating to recasting existing literary wholes into a radically new interpretive light. Their efforts, in a later time and sometimes different place than the original work, ensures that the text in their possession can effectively address an audience of their contemporaries. Foundational to their enterprise is that both editor and audience share membership in a religious community which regards the literary corpora on which they work as authoritative writings necessary to guide the community's ongoing life. And although a major difference exists between their editorial work and mine, there is also significant overlap.

However, we know about their work because it enjoys canonical status as part of the MT; by contrast, none of the volumes that win my approval and serve readers today attains canonicity and enjoys absolute authority in any religious community. Hopefully, in some measure they sustain or

---

15. Cf. Sheppard's discussion of the Hosea-Proverbs relationships ("The Last Words," 197–202).

16. Ibid., 193–94.

17. Ibid., 200.

advance contemporary religious communities, but the biblical text remains primary in their ongoing life. In that sense, my editorial role compares to those ancient editors whose fingerprints I have explored. I can advise authors on how to bring the ancient text to life for readers today—to maximize the reader's ability to tune in to the text and to grasp its message clearly—but I cannot alter what it says. The text is sacred, and the love and admiration I feel for it I also accord to those nameless ancient editors in whose train I follow. I am honored and humbled to carry on their work.

POSTSCRIPT: SOME PERSONAL EXPERIENCES OF A COMMENTARY EDITOR

A few years ago, I tried over several years to recruit a scholar to write a specific volume for a series but, though very interested, the individual did not have a full-time teaching position at the time. The person rightly declined because the lack of an institutional home base lessened the chances of completing the project. Later, I engaged another author who eventually produced the volume in question.

Another thing the last two decades have taught me is how often scholars show traits of what we call "the Human Condition." Most scholars sail along in pursuit of the task with no obstructions other than the need for perseverance and consistent self-discipline. Others, by contrast, struggle for decades to finally produce an acceptable 450-page manuscript. Behind the struggle often stands the burdensome disability of perfectionism that limits their productivity to a snail's pace. Others labor under the inability to say "no" to invitations to write or speak. The latter relegates the commentary to the proverbial back-burner. Surprisingly, some scholars lack what one of my former teachers called *Sitzfleisch*—the ability to sit and concentrate for long periods of time. That disability may explain why a few authors may feign making progress, even promise a manuscript "at the end of the summer," but not produce a single page in a decade. With a few others the commentary task may unexpectedly surface deep personal and/or physical problems that impede its timely completion.

Besides such human foibles, scholars are not immune to the capricious vicissitudes of "the Human Drama." Distinguished scholars are mere mortals like everyone else. They die prematurely of heart attacks or fatal accidents, and some suffer ordinary mortality before their commentary is finished. Some are innocent bystanders when personnel cutbacks and even institutional closures force them into employment less conducive to scholarly work. Unexpected family problems may require a shift in an author's priorities and lead the person voluntarily to terminate a contract and repay a royalty advance. The Human Condition and the Human Drama compel the series editor to wear many hats: the literary critic, the pastoral counsellor, the wise grandfather, the angry coach, and (alas, occasionally) the cold executioner.

BIBLIOGRAPHY

Dearman, J. Andrew. *The Book of Hosea*. NICOT. Grand Rapids: Eerdmans, 2010.
Fishbane, Michael A. *Biblical Interpretation in Ancient Israel*. Oxford: Clarendon, 1985.
Gemser, Berend. *Sprüche Salomos*. 2nd ed. HAT 1/16. Tübingen: Mohr Siebeck, 1963.
Hartley, John E. *The Book of Job*. NICOT. Grand Rapids: Eerdmans, 1988.
———. *Leviticus*. WBC. Dallas: Word, 1992.
Liwak, R. "Repa'im." In *Theological Dictionary of the Old Testament*, edited by G. Johannes Botterweck, Helmer Ringgren, and Heinz-Joseph Fabry, 13:602–14. Grand Rapids: Eerdmans, 2004.
Meinhold, Arndt. *Die Sprüche, Teil 2: Sprüche Kapitel 16–31*. ZBK. Zurich: TVZ, 1991.
Milgrom, Jacob. *Leviticus 1–16*. AYBC. Garden City, NY: Doubleday, 1991.
———. *Leviticus 23–27*. AYBC. Garden City, NY: Doubleday, 2001.
Pritchard, James B. *The Ancient Near East: Supplementary Texts and Pictures Relating to the Old Testament*. 2nd ed. Princeton: Princeton University Press, 1969.
Sheppard, Gerald T. *Wisdom as a Hermeneutical Construct: A Study in the Sapientializing of the Old Testament*. BZAW 151. Berlin: de Gruyter, 1980.
———. "The Last Words of Hosea." *RevExpos* 90 (1993) 191–204.
Waltke, Bruce K. *The Book of Proverbs*. NICOT. Grand Rapids: Eerdmans, 2005.

5

Macrostructure
How to Retrieve a Coherent Whole from Complex Information

—*Leslie C. Allen*

"I work from the bottom up," a NT commentator once remarked to me as we sat at lunch in a British theological college where I was spending a sabbatical. I reflected that, whatever other commentators did, this OT commentator certainly did the same, with an academic background in linguistic areas and text criticism. I have always felt at home exploring the foothills, while very much aware of the arduous trek awaiting me as I worked from passage to passage until reaching the top and taking in the book's landscape stretching out far below. Not that such viewing was reserved for the very end. Along the way, lower vistas also invited appreciative surveys.

Macrostructure relates to the overall gist of a text, as a literary landscape. The investigations of rhetorical criticism and literary criticism have helped commentators discern it. More recently they have benefited from the careful definitions of discourse analysis, which demonstrate that a particular macrostructure organizes complex information into a coherent whole. In so doing, it reduces that information into an essential and generalized shape. It looks at a literary forest rather than its individual trees.¹ Macrostructural studies vary in length from complete books down to smaller units with their own objective coherence in terms of form or another schema, such as the acrostically shaped poems of Lamentations. This article sets out some examples of macrostructural work done in commentaries I have written, and also includes some developed and new work. First, three portions of OT books are presented from a macrostructural perspective, and then three books. I offer this synchronic study as a tribute to the work of John Hartley, who in his commentaries has faithfully scrutinized the text from the bottom right up to the top.²

JEREMIAH 16[3]

This chapter is composed of five separate units, in vv. 2–9, 10–13, 14–15, 16–18, and 19–21. Within the literary blocks of Jeremiah, such compositions are often introduced by an oracle reception statement, "The word of the LORD came to me."[4] It duly appears in v. 1, but only in the MT and not in the earlier edition of the book represented in the LXX.[5] The presence of such a statement is unexpected at first, because presumably the prohibition to marry or take part in social gatherings in 16:2–9 was originally added to 15:15–21 by way of illustration, as the similarity of 15:17 and 16:8–9 suggests. The unit explains the prohibition in light of the coming undoing of Judah's cultural world. However, we have to ask if the MT's addition reflects awareness that a new composition has been developed from the unit in 16:2–9.

The coherence of the composition is not immediately obvious. It may warrant Luther's complaint about the prophets: "They have a queer way of talking, like people who, instead of proceeding in an orderly manner, ramble from one thing to the next, so that you cannot make head or tail of them or see what they are getting at."[6] A clue to its intended coherence is a Hebrew keyword throughout the composition, namely 'ereṣ, which bombards the reader in all five units and so functions as a macroword. Occurring nine times, at vv. 3, 4, 6, 13 (twice), 14, 15, 18, and 19, it has diverse senses: "this

---

1. Van Dijk, *Macrostructures*, 14, 44. For an analysis of the relationship between a macrostructure and a particular text see Longacre, *Joseph*, 40–54.
2. Cf. his article, "From Lament to Oath."
3. See Allen, *Jeremiah*, 186–95, especially 188, 194–95.
4. Unless otherwise indicated, English quotations are taken from the NRSV.
5. See section 6, the book study of Jeremiah, below.
6. Cited by von Rad, *Old Testament Theology*, 2:33 n1.

land" of Israel in vv. 3, 6, 13—but also the "earth" in v. 4 and the "land" of exile in v. 13, a sense which is maintained in vv. 14-15. Verse 18 reverts to the first meaning with "my land," while v. 19 widens it to "the earth." Apart from the instance in v. 4, the other cases suggest a general movement from home to exile and back, while in v. 19 the non-Israelite usage is developed in a positive direction.

But what macrostructural purpose does all this varied rhetorical repetition serve? Evidently the composition editorially highlights the references to abstaining from contemporary funeral rites in vv. 5-7 by reinterpreting them as pagan practices, implicitly in the light of such Torah traditions as Lev 19:28; 21:5; Deut 14:1 embody. This is a new meaning for the unit, one it did not originally envision. The second unit has this interpretation in view when making paganism the ground for Israel's punishment with exile, where ironically the people could worship other gods as much as they wanted. Such punishment both explains and takes further the death of other members of God's people in "this land" at vv. 3-4. The third unit takes a positive turn, promising eventual return from exile. The fourth reverts to the people's being hurled out of their land in v. 13 and describes the thorough tracking down enacted in reprisal for the paganism shockingly practiced in Yahweh's own land. The MT accommodates the switch to the previous motif of punishment by adding "first" in v. 18, a reading relegated to a footnote in the nrsv. The final unit, by way of climax, announces an exilic Israel's reaffirmation of its distinctive faith in Yahweh. It even envisions other nations' coming "from the ends of the earth" and declaring their own faith in him, so that not only Israel but the rest of the world renounce their paganism and acknowledge Yahweh as God. The composition uses its keyword to declare the triumph of Yahwism over pagan religion, negatively by punishing infected Israel with forfeiture of its land and death, and positively by Israel's recovery of its land and pristine faith and by the world's turning to that faith.

JEREMIAH 34-36[7]

I regard these three chapters as functioning as a literary block within the book. Usually the book announces a fresh block by employing an oracle reception heading, "The word that came to Jeremiah from the Lord." This does happen in 34:1—though in this case it is uncharacteristically repeated in 34:8 and 35:1, while the next block, chs. 37-39, lacks it in 37:1. The previous block of chs. 32-33 began with this heading, at 32:1. Chronology is clearly not an organizational criterion in this particular block, since ch. 34 stays

---

7. See Allen, *Jeremiah*, 381-400, especially 383.

in King Zedekiah's reign in line with 32:1, while chs. 35–36 move back to Jehoiakim's reign, before chs. 37–39 push forward to Zedekiah's fateful last years. A Hebrew verb, *šmʿ* in the sense of hearing positively and so obeying Yahweh and his word(s), operates as a keyword that sets out the dominant theme for the block. In ch. 34 Jeremiah urges Zedekiah to "hear the word of the Lord" (v. 4), but in a later incident declares in Yahweh's name: "You have not obeyed me" (v. 17). In ch. 35 Yahweh's exasperated question to the people, "Can you not . . . obey my words?" (v. 13), is followed by a series of divine statements in vv. 14–17 that, over the generations and even now, they have not obeyed him or listened. This refusal is contrasted with the religious example set by the Rechabites, who willingly obeyed their founder Jonadab in abstaining from wine (vv. 8, 10, 14, 18). Chapter 36 has an inclusio, opening with Yahweh's hope of Judah's positive hearing of his threats of disaster and repenting (v. 3), and ending by regretting their failure to take such threats seriously (v. 31). Between this inclusio, initial cases of Jehoiakim's royal staff hearing positively readings from a scroll of Jeremiah's oracles (vv. 11, 13, 16) are reversed by the later lack of a positive response in hearing it (v. 24) and by the king's refusal to listen to advice to do so (v. 25).

This thematic macroword running all through the block is accompanied by development within the overall theme. The development picks up in detailed narrative form the divine warning in 26:4–6, that failure to "listen to me, to walk in my *law* that I have set before you and to heed the words of my servants the *prophets*" would result in ultimate disaster.[8] So Jer 26:4–6 functions as a macroproposition for chs. 34–36, which gradually spell it out. Chapter 34 relates disobedience at the time of the siege of Jerusalem to a requirement of the *law* found in Deuteronomy 15 ("covenant," 34:13, 18). In turn, ch. 35 goes back to an earlier period in Jeremiah's prophesying, when he uses the Rechabite sect's scrupulous respect for its trademark tradition to show up Judah's disdain for warnings from the longstanding movement of the *prophets* (v. 15). Finally, ch. 36 provides a dramatic climax for the block in narrating Jehoiakim's burning of the scroll of oracles of "the *prophet* Jeremiah" (v. 8, where the mt perceptively adds "the prophet" to the shorter edition of the LXX). Such enacted refusal to heed the last of the preexilic prophets sealed Judah's fate.

---

8. Kessler, "Jeremiah 26–45," 84.

PSALM 89

One of my early attempts at commentary, published in 1979, involved Psalms 73-150.[9] My treatment of Psalm 89 contained no surprises, defining it as a royal lament prefaced with a challenging hymn and concluded with a doxology that, despite the verse numbering, was not part of the psalm, but signaled the close of Book 3 of the Psalter.[10] In fact, my definition related not to the macrostructure of the psalm, but to its superstructure. "Superstructure" is the term used in discourse analysis for a schematic definition of a text, here in terms of form rather than content.[11] In my subsequent years of lecturing on the Psalms, I learned more about Psalm 89, especially from a book by Craig Broyles,[12] coming to appreciate that it is actually a complaint against Yahweh, a subtype of lament represented in a third of all the laments in the Psalter. It also confirmed that the function of a hymn in such a complaint is to permit the complaint to challenge or even contradict its content.[13] But I thought I had nothing new to learn about the doxology. "Blessed be the LORD forever" is a call to praise, and "Amen and Amen" is a praising response (cf. Neh 8:6). The literary doxology's hymnic structure lacks only a reason for praise, which is implicitly sought in the content of Book 3, Psalms 73-89, the doxology pushing praise in these psalms to the fore.

That last observation has prompted second thoughts about the psalm and especially the role of the doxology. If one compares Ps 106 and its doxology in v. 18 with 1 Chr 16:34-36, where Ps 106:1, 47-48 recur, it is striking that the doxology is included in the quotation. Its call to praise is meant to reiterate the praise expressed just before in 1 Chr 16:34, with reference to Yahweh's steadfast love. What if we are meant to interpret the doxology at the close of Ps 89 as an integral element, in addition to providing closure for Book 3? A striking feature of this doxology's short call to praise is its coloring by the psalm's content. "Forever" is a keyword of the psalm. In the other doxologies "forever" recurs only in Ps 72:19, where "Blessed be his [Yahweh's] glorious name forever" echoes a similar reference to the king in v. 17, "May his name endure forever," and serves to undergird it by affirming the monarchy's theocratic basis.[14] In the case of Psalm 89, we need to

---

9. Allen, "Psalms 73-150," 650-702.
10. Ibid., 663-64.
11. See van Dijk, *Macrostructures*, 107-32; van Dijk and Kintsch, *Strategies*, 235-41.
12. Broyles, *Conflict of Faith*, 168-73.
13. Ibid., 44-46.
14. Leuenberger, *Gott in Bewegung*, 180.

ask whether the editorial ending has also colored the interpretation of the psalm itself. Does its ending on a glad note change the sense of the psalm?

"Forever" (*ʿôlām* or *lĕʿôlām*, but *lĕʿad* in v. 29 [MT 30] for stylistic variation) reverberates through the psalm, in expressions of unending praise in vv. 1, 52 (2, 53), as well as a component of Yahweh's steadfast love in vv. 2, 28 (3, 29).[15] This steadfast love has in view his promises that the Davidic covenant will be maintained "forever" (vv. 4, 29–30, 36–37 [5, 30–31, 37–38]). With this evidence put together, a clear macrostructure emerges. The opening verse (MT v. 2) and the doxology form an inclusio, praising God forever, and the initial specification of his steadfast love as a theme of praise points forward to his covenant promises concerning the Davidic monarchy. With respect to the psalm, the doxology's function is to echo the initial praise of Yahweh, implicitly in this very role, somewhat like the function of 1 Chr 16:36. Unending steadfast love warrants unending praise. If we understand in this way the final form of Psalm 89, the doxology has a new purpose, to align itself with the earlier Davidic promises and so to tone down the prayerful complaint of vv. 38–51 (39–52). The complaint is still heard with respect and felt with regret, but no longer has the disabling effect it had in the original psalm and is reduced to a hiccup in God's long-term purposes. The divine promises about Israel's king remain valid, and so the faith community can cope with the complaint. From this postexilic perspective, the doxology has transformed the psalm. Its superstructure is now largely that of a hymn that is praise in its own right, which moderates the complaint, and its macrostructure now concerns not failure, but well-grounded hope.[16]

---

15. In v. 46 (47) the lamenting question, "Will you hide yourself forever?" includes a different word, *lāneṣaḥ*, a term characteristic of the psalms of complaint, which here cuts across the other cases of "forever."

16. Contrast Wilson, *Editing of the Psalter*, 213–14, who affirms for the psalm an overall negative perception of the collapse of the Davidic monarchy (but he does acknowledge hope in v. 1 [2] and in the appeals of vv. 49–50 [50–51]). Hossfeld has a similar negative view throughout his article "Ps 89," and current scholarship generally agrees. Leuenberger (*Gott in Bewegung*, 192–93), in line with this negative perspective, makes a comparison with Job 1:21, "The Lord gave, and the Lord has taken away; blessed be the name of the Lord." Hossfeld and Zenger (*Psalms 2*, 209–10) discuss in the case of Psalm 72 whether the doxology is part of the final (or even original) form of the text (cf. Barbiero, "Psalm 72," 81–86), but do not raise the issue here (*Psalms 2*, 407, 413). Steymans, in his specialist study of Psalm 89 (*Psalm 89 und der Davidbund*, 53, 97), while recording the repetition of the divine name and of *ʿôlām* in v. 52 (53), treats the verse as nothing more than a doxology to Book 3. However, Barbiero ("Conclusione del Salmo 89," 543–45) considers v. 52 (53) to be part of the original psalm. My proposal represents a third view, that the doxology placed at the end of Book 3 was also formulated to transform the meaning of the immediately preceding psalm and to bring it in line with the positive royal Psalm 72 and with the doxology at the end of Book 2. Saur (*Die Königspsalmen*, 181–82, 314–15) has significantly observed that the

THE BOOK OF AMOS

A few years ago I was helping a PhD student in her rhetorical-critical study of Amos.[17] Her dominant interest lay in analyzing features of reversal in particular passages, in terms of various categories and characters involved. My mind went further, to try to consider the book as a whole by comparing beginning, middle, and end. My commentary writing on Amos has been restricted to a small work on the Twelve, published in 1987, which tended to move from passage to passage.[18] As to the ending of the book, Amos 9:11–15, a book by Joseph Groves, published in the same year, first brought home to me the literary nature of this section.[19] Step-by-step, in literary fashion it searches out negative passages earlier in the book and gloriously caps them with corresponding positive ones. For instance, "I will raise up the booth of David that is fallen" in v. 11 reverses "fallen, no more to rise" in 5:2 and "they shall fall and never rise again" in 8:14 and reapplies those texts in terms of a royal hope. The formulaic phrase "I will restore the fortunes (of my people Israel)" in 9:14 crystallizes the particular cases of reversal. This phrase, in Hebrew *wĕšabtî 'et-šĕbût*, which repeats the verb with a derived noun, also contributes to a macrostructural agenda for the book.

At the beginning of the book, repetition of the verb itself is a feature of the first block of the book, 1:3—2:16. A repeated pattern marks each of the eight judgment oracles, one element of which is "I will not revoke the punishment." The NRSV's footnote renders it literally as "cause it to return." The Hebrew phrase, *lō' ăšîbennû*, includes an indefinite pronoun that I suggest refers loosely back to "transgressions," as a boomerang that will come back and hit the transgressor. Significantly, other Hebrew words for sinning can oscillate in meaning between sin and punishment. Accordingly, Norman Snaith pointed out long ago that the pronoun refers "not only to the initial act, but also to its natural consequences."[20] As to the indefinite pronoun, an idiomatic British saying is comparable. Anyone who witnesses bad behavior is likely to say to the perpetrator, "You'll cop it," with a sense of inevitably

---

praise of the doxology at the close of Psalm 89 harks back to the hymn at the beginning of the psalm, and so reopens the factor of praise that will be continued in the next book of Psalms, both in its psalms of divine kingship and in its "proto-messianic" psalms, Psalms 101, 110, 132, 144.

17. Recla, "Reversing."
18. Allen, *Hosea–Malachi*, 41–55.
19. Groves, *Actualization in the OT*, 179–91.
20. Snaith, *Amos. Part Two*, 15. For other suggestions, see the discussions of the phrase in Wolff, *Joel and Amos*, 128; Knierim, "'I Will Not' . . . Amos 1 and 2"; Barré, "Meaning"; Paul, *Amos*, 46–47; Möller, *Prophet in Debate*, 178–80; Linville. "What Does It Mean?" 403–5, 409–21.

being held responsible for the bad behavior. Here the meaning relates to not turning away reprisal for the transgressions. Such certainty of punishment, affirmed in each of the national oracles, culminates in the case of Israel (2:6).

Our keyword recurs in the middle of the book, again highlighted by repetition, as in chs. 1–2. This time it occurs five times in the course of 4:6–11, uttered to Israel in lamenting tones: "yet you did not return [*lō' šabtem*] to me."[21] Yahweh inflicted lesser punishments as opportunities to repent, but to no avail. Instead, Yahweh must now negatively confront them with ultimate judgment (v. 12). The Israelites' failure to return to their covenantal roots accentuated their original wrongdoing of 2:6.

The book of Amos uses the versatile keyword *šûb* to establish the focal points of its macrostructure. Yahweh's ongoing dealings with Israel involved, but did not end with, judgment that both the wrongdoing and repeated stubbornness justified. The studied series of reversals at the book's close is summed up in a positive counter-reversal, *'āšûb 'et-sĕbût*. As Linville has briefly observed, "[w]ith this reversal the reader may then reappraise all that has gone before," namely, the varied use of the key term in chs. 1–2 and 4.[22] Yahweh was to break the cycle of punishment and begin again with a fresh and enduring work of grace.

THE BOOK OF EZRA-NEHEMIAH

So far keywords have provided significant clues as the tools of macrostructure, but they do not have a major role in the two remaining examples. Masoretic tradition and other factors have suggested to most scholars that Ezra–Nehemiah is a single, unified work.[23] In this example I argue that parallel, progressive sets of elements are placed side by side in this book to illustrate Judah's accomplishments under God in the early postexilic period. I wrote on these lines in a commentary published in 2003,[24] but here develop and in part correct my earlier proposal.[25]

---

21. Groves himself connected 4:6–11 and 9:14 (*Actualization in the OT*, 185). The central case is reinforced by the presence of a similar Hebrew verb, *hpk*, in 4:11 (twice, "overthrew"); 5:7 ("turn"), 8 ("turns"); 6:12 ("turned"), with a combination of not only human subjects but also divine, echoing the divine cases in chs. 1–2.

22. Linville, "What Does It Mean?" 423.

23. See, e.g., Blenkinsopp, *Ezra–Nehemiah*, 38.

24. Allen and Laniak, *Ezra, Nehemiah, Esther*, 4–7. I commented on Ezra–Nehemiah, and Laniak on Esther. A still earlier version appeared in my essay, "'For He Is Good.'"

25. Some of these parallel elements are obvious and have been recognized. For example, Eskenazi (*Literary Approach*, 38) identifies a tripartite structure in terms of

Macrostructure

From a synchronic perspective, I envision Ezra–Nehemiah as falling into three blocks: Ezra 1–6; 7–10; and Neh 1–13. The first, overarching parallel relates to the *divine and human commissions* authorizing the work described in each part. They are set out in Ezra 1:1–4; 7:1–28a; and Neh 1:1—2:10. In the first case, the content of the commission is to "rebuild the house of the LORD" (Ezra 1:3). In the second case, it is to "beautify the house of the LORD" (Ezra 7:27 niv) and to impose the Torah, "the law of" Ezra's "God" on the Jewish colony (7:14, 25–26). In the third case, it is to "rebuild Jerusalem" (Neh 2:5). The doubly authorized nature of the commissioning is seen most clearly when "the LORD stirred up the spirit of King Cyrus of Persia" to publish an edict (Ezra 1:1; cf. v. 2). In Ezra's own case, the commission comes from Artaxerxes, who sends with him an elaborating letter responding to Ezra's request to the king (7:11–26); however, the king's permission is traced to divine influence (7:6, 27–28). Likewise, the king grants Nehemiah his request gives him letters that enable him to carry out his commission, but Nehemiah directly credits God's "gracious hand" with this enabling (Neh 2:7–8). In all three cases divine providence is traced in the royal authorization.

A recurring feature of this first element is the *invoking of sacred texts* claimed to underlie each venture. In the first case at Ezra 1:1, it appears to be Jer 51:1 (cf. v. 11).[26] True, the stirring up of the spirit (*hēʿîr rûaḥ*)[27] concerns the conquest of Babylon, but it is significant that this conquest is to be declared "in Zion" (51:10, cf. v. 35), and such stirring up of the spirit is intended as Yahweh's "vengeance for" the destruction of the "temple" (v. 11, cf. v. 24). In Ezra's own case at 7:27, mention of the sacred text is allusive in nature. Isaiah 60:7, "I will glorify my glorious throne" (cf. v. 13), uses the same Hebrew verb *pēʾēr* as Ezra 7:27, and an intertextual reference has been suggested.[28] In Neh 1:8–9, Nehemiah refers to Deut 30:1–4 in his prayer and asks God to "remember" this "word that you commanded your servant Moses." The invoking of Scripture plays a key role as a basis for each of the commissions.

---

potentiality that defines objectives, process of actualization, and success that is celebrated. Blenkinsopp ("Ezra–Nehemiah: Unity or Disunity?" 307) sums up Karrer-Grube's indication of parallel structures ("Conceptual Unity," 136–50) as "two periods (Cyrus to Darius, Artaxerxes), opposition to both temple building and wall building, priestly and lay leadership, temple and city wall," but adds: "These parallel structures and motifs could no doubt be further amplified."

26. Williamson, *Ezra, Nehemiah*, 10. Karrer-Grube ("Conceptual Unity," 156, 159) has lent her support.

27. A translation such as NIV and NRSV margin, "I will stir up the spirit of a destroyer," is assumed by the Ezra reference.

28. Fensham, *Ezra and Nehemiah*, 109; Clines, *Ezra, Nehemiah, Esther*, 107.

The next common feature relates to the *reconstituting of God's people*. Although not included in my previous work, Tamara Eskenazi's advocacy of this feature has convinced me of its presence, though she takes only the first and third cases into account, regarding them as an inclusio for Ezra 1:5– Neh 7:73 (72).[29] She also has drawn attention to the repetition of genealogical material on a national scale. Telling evidence first appears in Ezra 2:1–70 with the addition of material in vv. 59-63 about returnees who "could not prove ... whether they belonged to Israel" (v. 59). It is surely important that elsewhere in the literary work, at Ezra 8:1–14, 18–20, there is a comparable list of family heads of Jews who returned with Ezra, together with their lineage. Nehemiah 7:6–73a (72a) completes the parallel listing by repeating the Ezra 2 list as the basis for allocating members of the community to Jerusalem, though from a redactional perspective Nehemiah's list appears to have been earlier.[30] The community of returned exiles is claimed to be a true restoration of God's preexilic people; and the lists are the chief manifestation of this claim, although other elements in Ezra-Nehemiah reinforce it.[31]

A straightforward triple division has marked the first two parallel features, but from now on there is a bifurcation in each of the three blocks of the book. Each commission is implemented in two stages. Accordingly, Ezra 1–6 subdivides at this point into 1:5—3:13 and 4:1—6:22. The rebuilding of the temple falls into two stages. First, in 1:5—3:13 there is the preliminary task of *rebuilding the altar*, to permit sacrificial worship, closely conjoined with *laying the temple foundation*. There follows in 4:1—6:21 the *rebuilding of the temple*. An initiating verb signals the two operations. A general statement that the returnees "got ready [Hebrew *qûm*] to go up and rebuild the house of the Lord" (1:5) is later subdivided: they "set out [*qûm*] to build the altar" (3:2) and "set out [*qûm* again] to rebuild the house of God" (5:2).

Ezra's explicitly double mandate (7:14-20, 25–27) is fulfilled first in the *beautifying of the temple* in 8:24-36 by transporting and delivering silver, gold, and vessels. Then *the imposition of the Torah* in Judah is selectively achieved in 9:1—10:44, in a presentation of intermarriage with the local population as a case of breaking God's commandments (9:10, 14). Nehemiah's granted request to rebuild Jerusalem (Neh 1:5–6) is likewise divided into two stages: first, *rebuilding Jerusalem's wall* in the course of Neh 2:11—6:19 and then *repopulating the city* in 7:4-5 (cf. 11:1–2). This double outworking is delineated by the same preliminary claim: "my God (had) put into my heart/mind ..." (2:12; 7:5). More was involved in rebuilding

---

29. Eskenazi, *Literary Approach*, 37, 88–93.
30. See Williamson, *Ezra, Nehemiah*, 268–69.
31. Eskenazi, "Unity and Disunity," 322.

Jerusalem than reconstructing its walls. The verb "build" in Hebrew (*bnh*) can have a human dimension as well as a material one, and this is implicitly the case in Nehemiah's second task. To build a house can mean to establish a family (e.g., Deut 25:9) or a dynasty (e.g., 2 Sam 7:27). Jerusalem needed people in order to be a viable city.

There is no gain without pain, a truth that emerges in Ezra-Nehemiah with the careful recording of *obstacles that had to be overcome* before accomplishing each of the double tasks. Ezra 1–6 describes regional opposition to each task, in 3:3 and 4:1-6. In Ezra 7–10, concern that the precious freight the returning exiles were carrying should reach Jerusalem safely was successfully resolved: "our God . . . delivered us from the hand of the enemy and from ambushes along the way" (8:31). In turn, the imposition of a standard set out in the Torah to prevent assimilation met with internal opposition, though only from a minority (10:15).

In Nehemiah's case much of the text deals with recurrent regional opposition faced in rebuilding the walls (Neh 2:10—6:19). In Neh 5:3, he discusses an internal setback undermining the unity of the people but even that was indirectly related to the rebuilding (5:16). In my commentary I perceived no obstacles relating to Nehemiah's second aspect of rebuilding Jerusalem or the large block of material in 7:73b (72b)—10:39 (MT 40), except in relating it to his prayer in ch. 1, where he agonized over the exiles' disobedience.[32] I was on the right track, but did not pursue it far enough, for three reasons. First, I envisioned this phase too narrowly, in terms of opposition, whereas Nehemiah 5 tells us to think more broadly in terms of setbacks, although one may indeed speak of "adversaries inside rather than outside of the community."[33] Second, I missed the verbal link, *šûb*, "(re)turn," between Neh 1:8, citing Deut 30:2, and the later prayer in Neh 9, at vv. 26, 28, 29. Third, I overlooked the crucial statement in 1:9 about God's bringing his obedient people back "to the place at which I have chosen to establish my name" (cf. Ezra 6:12). Elsewhere the nominal phrase refers to the sanctuary, but here it evidently refers to Jerusalem, under the influence of texts that apply the verb "choose" to Jerusalem (e.g., 1 Kgs 8:44).[34]

---

32. Allen, *Ezra, Nehemiah* (in Allen and Laniak), 125.

33. Janzen, "Cries of Jerusalem," 131.

34. Eskenazi overlooked this passage in her extension of the meaning of "the house of God" in Ezra-Nehemiah to include the city in certain places. Her understanding of "the house of God" caused her to divide Ezra-Nehemiah into a general introduction that defines the objective in Ezra 1:1-4; a process of actualization in Ezra 1:5—Neh 7:73 (72) that is summarized in Ezra 1:5-6 and described in three movements, in 1:7—6:22; 7:1-10; and Neh 1:1—7:5; and the accomplishment of the objective in Neh 8:1—13:3, plus a coda in 13:4-31 (*Literary Approach*, 37-126).

Nehemiah 1:9 is of the utmost significance for understanding 7:73b (72b)—10:39 (40). Repopulating Jerusalem had a special symbolism, because its citizens represented the rest of the returnees living elsewhere in Judah. Their residing in "the holy city" (11:1, 18; cf. Isa 52:1; Joel 4:17 [3:17])) bestowed on them the representative role that fulfilled Nehemiah's praying in ch. 1. His prayer moved beyond the reference to return to the land in Deut 30:5 to the capital as the site of divine presence. Mention of "the holy city" is implicitly meant to remind readers of the condition in Neh 1:9 (cf. Lev 20:7–8).

There was an obstacle, glaringly obvious to Nehemiah in his opening prayer: a disobedient people. This obstacle is what the material in 7:73b (72b)—10:39 (40) is intended to address. The presupposition governing its location at this point is that a holy city demanded a holy people. The whole community's understanding of the recited Torah and their acting upon it by confession and covenant vows qualified them to occupy Jerusalem through their representatives.[35]

After detailing the overcoming of obstacles, the separate stories can reach the *achievement* of their mandates. In Ezra 3:3 the rebuilding of the altar resulted in daily burnt offerings, while 3:10a duly records the conjoined laying of the temple foundation. In 6:14–15 the temple project is completed. As for the next double phase, Ezra 8:33–34 records the handing over of the precious freight to the temple staff, while in 10:5, 19a, 44 the community swears obedience to the Torah, which is duly expedited. Nehemiah's commission finds fulfilment at Neh 6:15 in the completion of the wall rebuilding and at 11:1–2 in the allotment of Jerusalem's new residents.

Celebration can now follow, as the next phase in the overall series. The first to be mentioned is a ceremony and an opportunity of sacrificial worship in Ezra 3:3b–4, after the altar building. A further ceremony (3:10b–13) celebrates the refounding of the ruined temple; it consists of sacred music and communal praise and joy—as well as some vocal disapproval. Ezra 6:16–17, 19–22 describes the celebratory dedication of the rebuilt temple at great length. In 8:35 it is time to celebrate again with sacrifices, now that the sacred valuables have been delivered. And at 10:19b, the offenders' presentation of guilt offerings marks an appropriate ritual response.

Nehemiah's double commission receives only one celebration, described at length in Neh 12:27–43, the ceremonial processing along the walls, culminating in worship, sacrifices, and (now unalloyed) festal joy. This celebration covers both stages of his commission, because it relates

---

35. Chronologically the vows apparently came later than the events of ch. 13, but the literary presentation is controlled by a spiritual necessity, the overcoming of the community's disobedience.

both to the walls' completion and to the city's repopulation. The latter factor is evident in that the citizens, not the people at large, took part in it—only Levites are mentioned as brought into the city from outside (v. 27). In light of 11:4, "Judah, Benjamin" (12:34) refer to the Judean and Benjaminite settlers in Jerusalem.[36]

The final phase, seen most clearly in Ezra 1–6, is the *establishment of guidelines* for the future.[37] In Ezra 3:5-8, rebuilding the altar permits the inauguration of a regular cycle of sacrifices ("began," v. 6), while in 6:18 the system of cultic personnel can be set up from then on in accordance with the Torah. The presence of this phase in the rest of Ezra-Nehemiah is less easy to detect. The adornment of the temple in Ezra 7–8 lacks it. Nor is it immediately discernible in chs. 9–10. Josephus found a guideline with regard to intermarrying: "Ezra purified the practice relating to this matter, so that it remained fixed for the future" (*Ant.* 11.53). He was evidently basing his statement on the adverbs "never" and "forever" in 9:12. Karrer-Grube has commented on the lack of a concluding element in Ezra 9–10, "we will not . . . anymore,"[38] but perhaps 9:12 was meant to fill this gap.

As for Nehemiah's mission, the close relationship between its two aspects suggests there may not be a double occurrence of this phase. In Neh 12:44-47 the appointment of temple officials and arrangements for their maintenance carries forward the earlier notice of Ezra 6:18. Now the community was obediently honoring the obligations set down in the Torah and by David and Solomon. The thematic continuation in Neh 13 may also have a similar significance. Nehemiah's monitoring of the new norms with regard to support of temple personnel, Sabbath keeping, and marriage presents him as a model for future generations. Moreover, the survey of his work at vv. 30b–31 has some correspondence to Ezra 3:5-8 in establishing the cultic practices of the wood offering and the bringing of first fruits, to enable the offering of the sacrifices and offerings of the Torah (cf. Neh 10:34). An obedient people thus play their part in honoring God at the temple, the spiritual heart of Jerusalem. "Even once the agreement of ch. 10 has been completed, constant vigilance is necessary for the community to survive."[39] And Nehemiah, for one, demonstrated such vigilance.

---

36. Eskenazi, *Literary Approach*, 118 n. 261.

37. It is the redactionally latest block of Ezra 1–6 that diligently supplies almost every component of the pattern, while the earlier material that follows it has gaps here and there, but does provide substantial clues that were developed in Ezra 1–6, thus drawing attention to their presence in the rest of Ezra-Nehemiah. For the late nature of the first block, see in principle Williamson, "Composition."

38. Karrer-Grube, "Conceptual Unity," 141.

39. Janzen, "Cries of Jerusalem," 134.

Ezra–Nehemiah exhibits repetitive parallelism as a superstructure. Moreover, its sequential episodes, with their progression of elements, use in each case a narrative superstructure of intention, implementation, complication, and resolution. The combination of the two superstructures provides a mold for the macrostructure. The purpose is to pour into that mold a summary of what was regarded as important elements in the early history of postexilic Judaism. Temple, Torah, and Jerusalem were the constituent parts of the new order. Israel's God had providentially prompted imperial compliance to inaugurate it, and sacred texts were invoked in confirmation. After the long exile, God's people were reconstituted in the homeland and capital. Although each of the accounts of the three missions pursues some of its own concerns, the basic structuring they share reveals the emphases that the composite work was intended to commend to its readers. Its repeated themes hammer home theological interpretations of their recent history and lessons for them to live out in the future. Ezra–Nehemiah intends to proclaim the restoration that laid a new foundation for the ongoing history of Israel. Such is the main message Ezra–Nehemiah wants to give its readers.

THE BOOK OF JEREMIAH

The shape that the MT version of Jeremiah has come down to us reveals a great deal of complexity, so much so that John Bright described the book as "a hopeless hodgepodge thrown together without any discernible principle of arrangement at all."[40] To explain the present shape requires a process of development. In my commentary, published in 2008, I described the book as like "an old English country house, originally built and added to in the Regency period, augmented with Victorian wings, and generally refurbished throughout the Edwardian years."[41] I subscribe to the view of most scholars, elaborated by Emanuel Tov, that the strikingly different LXX substantially reflects an earlier Hebrew edition than the one represented by the MT; both editions have been found as Hebrew fragments at Qumran.[42]

Yet the editions have much in common, including evidence of a system of literary blocks consisting of smaller compositions and of carefully placed prose sermons written in a distinctive style. A chief difference between the two editions is the placing of the oracles against the nations, chs. 46–51 in the MT and English translations. In the LXX they appear after 25:13, in a

---

40. Bright, *Jeremiah*, lvi.

41. Allen, *Jeremiah*, 11. Much of the following material depends on pages 12–14 of my commentary.

42. See Tov, "Literary History."

different order. Yet careful study of ch. 25 reveals that their incorporation there represents an intrusion, disturbing the compositional unity of ch. 25.[43] The later editing to which the MT bears witness moved them from there to their present position near the end of the book. A clue to this removal is 25:14, which the LXX lacks and which Anneli Aejmelaeus has well described as "a patch to repair the place when the oracles had been removed."[44] Indeed, the replacement deliberately echoes the language of 50:29, 41; 51:6. Another clue is the retention of v. 13, which presupposes the continuation of the oracles now missing in the MT

If for now we ignore those added oracles, what may we say of the shape of the book? For the most part, it represents a superstructure, a collection of oracles in chs. 1–25 followed by a collection of narratives in chs. 26–45; 52. Of Jeremiah's eight so-called confessions selectively placed throughout chs. 11–20, the first four pave the way for responses from Yahweh (11:18–20 + 21–23; 12:1–4 + 5–6; 15:10 + 11–14, 15–18 + 19–21 [20:7–20?]). The positive oracles in chs. 30–31; 33 look extraneous, since they do not fit the superstructure.[45] As a separate literary source, they were evidently attracted into the text by the positive symbolic action narrated in 32:1–15 and now cluster around it. But in principle a schematic structure prevails, with different schemata, rather than content, supplying the pattern.

The LXX edition honors this pattern by placing the foreign oracles near the close of the collection of oracles, thus recognizing the superstructure and complying with it. The exact placing was determined by the references to Babylon and other foreign nations in ch. 25. However, the MT edition has drastically defied the old pattern by putting them near the close of the collection of narratives. Did it have a different structuring in mind? The answer in my commentary drew on the work of Ronald Clements to give an affirmative answer and to explain the new pattern.[46] He pointed to a pattern in the prophetic books, whereby some promises of hope follow dominant messages of doom. Brevard Childs indeed suggested this pattern for the book of Jeremiah, without explaining how it works out in structural detail.[47] Sometimes the pattern can be a recurring feature of a book. In

---

43. See Allen, *Jeremiah*, 283.
44. Aejmelaeus, "Jeremiah at the Turning-Point," 478.
45. Chapters 30–31; 33:1–13 appear in the LXX, but 33:14–26 only in the MT.
46. Clements, "Patterns," 49–55.
47. Childs, *Introduction*, 351. For some other proposals for the structure of the book see Allen, *Jeremiah*, 12; House, "Plot, Prophecy and Jeremiah"; Murphy, "Quest for Structure."

Hosea, each of the three literary complexes, chs. 1–3; 4–11; and 12–14, ends on a positive note.[48]

Is a recurring pattern of such a kind present in the MT of Jeremiah? If so, the unevenly balanced pronouncement in 1:10 now has the role of a macroproposition: "I appoint you ... to pluck up and to pull down, to destroy and to overthrow, to build and to plant."[49] In both the LXX and the MT this deliberately unbalanced verse serves as a key thematic sentence, while in the MT it appears to announce the macrostructure of the book. "Verse 10 captures in succinct form the agenda of the book."[50] Even though the LXX shows its awareness of a separate superstructure in its placement of the oracles against the nations, enough material exists common to both editions to warrant seeing signs of a different, macrostructural pattern, less developed in the LXX edition and recognized in the MT edition by its placing of the foreign oracles near the close of the book. The oracles are positive in their message to Israel, both by reflecting judgment on its enemies and by containing specific positive messages for it (46:27–28; 50:17–20). Moreover, adding post-judgment reversals in the MT for some nations (46:26; 48:47; 49:6), supplementing Elam's reversal already in the LXX (= MT 49:39), fits the pattern on a smaller scale.

How about the rest of the book? It is not difficult to see a series of long sections ending in positive material: chs. 2–9 + 10; 11–29 + 30–33; and 34–45 + 46–51, with Egypt now functioning as a rhetorical bridge in the last case.[51] The historical postscript in ch. 52 already exhibits this pattern (vv. 1–30 + 31–34): "Chapter 52 declares through two incidents the message of Jeremiah's ministry calling (1:10)."[52] The MT edition has also highlighted positive material by adding to the older edition 10:6–8, 10; 30:10–11 (copied from 46:27–28); 33:14–26. This extends a practice already present in the older edition, the repetition of 10:12–16 in 51:15–19.

The MT edition has its own macrostructure, achieved by adopting in a fuller and recurrent way a pattern found in other prophetic books. To this end it could expand a limited amount of evidence it found in the older edition and to develop it on a larger scale. This way it gave the book a new coherence: it cut across the earlier superstructure of oracles and narratives

---

48. Wolff, *Hosea*, xxix–xxxi.
49. The LXX lacks "and to overthrow."
50. Murphy, "Quest for Structure," 316.
51. A few other positive messages, in 3:14–18; 12:15–16; 16:14–15; 23:3–8; 24:4–7, do not carry enough quantitative weight to have macrostructural value for the book as a whole. Jeremiah 23:3–8 marks a positive ending for the collection of royal oracles in 21:11—23:8.
52. Murphy, "Quest for Structure," 316.

dominating the LXX edition, while largely retaining it, and worked out for the book an impressive macrostructure of judgment and eventual salvation.

Discourse analysis provides ways to categorize the sweep of a book or passage and to distinguish between macrostructure and superstructure, and understand the relationship between them. It has enabled me to reformulate and verify conclusions reached earlier in my commentaries on other grounds and in some cases has given me greater clarity to develop some of them on what now appears to be surer grounds. Of course, there is much more to a book or passage than these deliberately reductionist general summaries, but their value is in recovering ancient definitions of the overall meaning of texts.

BIBLIOGRAPHY

Aejmelaeus, Anneli. "Jeremiah at the Turning-Point of History: The Function of Jer. xxv 1–14 in the Book of Jeremiah," *VT* 52 (2002) 459–82.

Allen, Leslie C. "'For He Is Good . . .' Worship in Ezra–Nehemiah." In *Worship and the Hebrew Bible: Essays in Honor of John T. Willis*, edited by M. P. Graham et al., 15–34. JSOTSup 284. Sheffield: Sheffield Academic, 1999.

———. *Hosea-Malachi*. Bible Study Commentary. London: Scripture Union, 1987.

———. *Jeremiah: A Commentary*. OTL. Louisville: Westminster John Knox, 2008.

———. "Psalms 73–150." In *A Bible Commentary for Today: Based on the Revised Standard Version*, edited by G. C. D. Howley et al., 650–702. London: Pickering & Inglis, 1979.

———. "The Value of Rhetorical Criticism in Psalm 69." *JBL* 105 (1986) 577–98.

Allen, Leslie C., and Timothy S. Laniak. *Ezra, Nehemiah, Esther*. NIBC. Peabody, MA: Hendrickson, 2003.

Barbiero, Gianni. "Alcune osservazioni sulla conclusione del Salmo 89 (vv. 47–53)." *Bib* 88 (2007) 536–45.

———. "The Risks of a Fragmented Reading of the Psalms: Psalm 72 as a Case in Point." *ZAW* 120 (2008) 67–91.

Barré, M. L. "The Meaning of l' šybnw in Amos 1:3–2:6." *JBL* 105 (1986) 611–31.

Blenkinsopp, Joseph. *Ezra–Nehemiah: A Commentary*. OTL. Philadelphia: Westminster Press, 1988.

———. "Ezra–Nehemiah: Unity or Disunity." In *Unity and Disunity in Ezra–Nehemiah: Redaction, Rhetoric, and Reader*, edited by Mark J. Boda and Paul L. Redditt, 306–14. Hebrew Bible Monographs 17. Sheffield: Sheffield Phoenix, 2008.

Bright, John. *Jeremiah*. 2nd ed. Anchor Bible. Garden City, NY: Doubleday, 1974.

Broyles, Craig. *The Conflict of Faith and Experience in the Psalms: A Form-Critical and Theological Study*. JSOTSup 52. Sheffield: JSOT Press, 1989.

Childs, Brevard S. *Introduction to the Old Testament as Scripture*. Philadelphia: Fortress, 1979.

Clements, Ronald E. "Patterns in the Prophetic Canon." In *Canon and Authority: Essays in Old Testament Religion and Theology*, edited by George W. Coats et al., 42–55. Philadelphia: Fortress, 1977.

Clines, David J. A. *Ezra, Nehemiah, Esther*. NCBC. Grand Rapids: Eerdmans, 1984.
Dijk, Teun A. van. *Macrostructures: An Interdisciplinary Study of Global Strategies in Discourse, Interaction and Cognition*. Hillsdale, NJ: Lawrence Erlbaum Associates, 1980.
Dijk, Teun A. van, and Walter Kintsch, *Strategies of Discourse Comprehension*. New York: Academic Press, 1983.
Eskenazi, Tamara C. *In an Age of Prose: A Literary Approach to Ezra–Nehemiah*. SBLMS 36. Atlanta: Scholars, 1988.
———. "Unity and Disunity in Ezra–Nehemiah: Responses and Reflections." In *Unity and Disunity in Ezra–Nehemiah*, edited by Mark J. Boda and Paul L. Redditt, 315–28. Hebrew Bible Monographs 17. Sheffield: Sheffield Phoenix, 2008.
Fensham, F. Charles. *The Books of Ezra and Nehemiah*. NICOT. Grand Rapids: Eerdmans, 1982.
Groves, Joseph W. *Actualization and Interpretation in the Old Testament*. SBLDS 86. Atlanta: Scholars Press, 1987.
Hartley, John E. "From Lament to Oath: A Study of Progression in the Speeches of Job." In *The Book of Job*, edited by W. A. M. Beuken, 79–100. BETL 114. Leuven: Leuven University Press, 1994.
Hossfeld, Frank-Lothar. "Ps 89 und die vierte Psalmenbuch (Pss 90–106)." In *"Mein Sohn bist du" (Ps 2:7): Studien zu den Königspsalmen*, edited by E. Otto and E. Zenger, 173–83. SBS 192. Stuttgart: Katholisches Bibelwerk, 2002.
Hossfeld, Frank-Lothar, and Erich Zenger, *Psalms 2: A Commentary on Psalms 51–100*. Translated by L. M. Maloney. Hermeneia. Minneapolis: Fortress, 2005.
House, Paul R. "Plot, Prophecy and Jeremiah." *JETS* 36 (1993) 297–306.
Janzen, David. "The Cries of Jerusalem: Ethnic, Cultic, Legal, and Geographic Boundaries in Ezra–Nehemiah." In *Unity and Disunity in Ezra–Nehemiah: Redaction, Rhetoric, and Reader*, edited by Mark J. Boda and Paul L. Redditt, 117–35. Hebrew Bible Monographs 17. Sheffield: Sheffield Phoenix, 2008.
Karrer-Grube, Christiane. "Scrutinizing the Conceptual Unity of Ezra and Nehemiah." In *Unity and Disunity in Ezra–Nehemiah*, edited by Mark J. Boda and Paul L. Redditt, 136–59. Hebrew Bible Monographs 17. Sheffield: Sheffield Phoenix, 2008.
Kessler, Martin. "Jeremiah Chapters 26–45 Reconsidered." *JNES* 27 (1968) 81–88.
Knierim, Rolf P. "'I Will Not Cause It to Return' in Amos 1 and 2." In *Canon and Authority: Essays in Old Testament Religion and Theology*, edited by George W. Coats et al., 163–75. Philadelphia: Fortress, 1977.
Leuenberger, Martin. *Gott in Bewegung: Religions- und theologiegeschichtliche Beiträge zu Gottesvorstellungen im alten Israel*. FAT 76. Tübingen: Mohr Siebeck, 2011.
Linville, James R. "What Does It Mean? Interpretation at the Point of No Return in Amos 1–2." *BibInt* 8 (2000) 400–424.
Longacre, Robert E. *Joseph: A Story of Divine Providence: A Text Theoretical and Text-linguistic Analysis of Genesis 37 and 39–48*. 2nd ed. Winona Lake, IN: Eisenbrauns, 2003.
Möller, Karl. *A Prophet in Debate: The Rhetoric of Persuasion in the Book of Amos*. JSOTSup 372. London: Sheffield Academic Press, 2003.
Murphy, S. Jonathan. "The Quest for the Structure of the Book of Jeremiah." *BSac* 166 (2009) 306–18.
Paul, Shalom M. *Amos: A Commentary on the Book of Amos*. Hermeneia. Minneapolis: Fortress, 1991.

Rad, Gerhard von. *Old Testament Theology*. 2 vols. New York: Harper, 1962–1965.
Recla, Josephine V. "Reversing the Reversal: A Study of the Reversal Motif in the Book of Amos." PhD dissertation, Fuller Theological Seminary, School of Theology, 2010.
Saur, Markus. *Die Königspsalmen: Studien zur Entstehung und Theologie*. BZAW 340. Berlin: de Gruyter, 2004.
Snaith, Norman H. *The Book of Amos. Part Two: Translation and Notes*. Study Notes on Bible Books. London: Epworth, 1946.
Steymans, Hans U. *Psalm 89 und der Davidbund: Eine strukturale und redaktionsgeschichtliche Untersuchung*. Österreichische Biblische Studien 27. Frankfurt am Main: Peter Lang, 2005.
Tov, Emanuel. "Literary History of the Book of Jeremiah in the Light of Its Textual History." In *Empirical Models for Biblical Criticism*, edited by Jeffrey H. Tigay, 211–37. Philadelphia: University of Pennsylvania Press, 1985.
Williamson, H. G. M. "The Composition of Ezra i–vi." *JTS* n.s. 34 (1983) 1–30.
———. *Ezra, Nehemiah*. WBC 16. Waco, TX: Word, 1985.
Wilson. Gerald H. *The Editing of the Hebrew Psalter*. SBLDS 76. Chico, CA: Scholars Press, 1985.
Wolff, Hans W. *Hosea: A Commentary on the Book of the Prophet Hosea*. Hermeneia. Philadelphia: Fortress, 1974.
———. *Joel and Amos: A Commentary on the Book of the Prophets Joel and Amos*. Hermeneia. Philadelphia: Fortress, 1977.

PART 2

Research and Its Results in Biblical Commentary

6

Does God Practice Mindfulness?
A Reassessment of Isaiah 63:11–14

—*Willem A. M. Beuken*

"Though God is the Bible's hero,
his portayal may yet appear a special case"[1]

THE NUMBER OF TEXTUAL problems in the Hebrew Bible seems to decrease under the influence of the methodological conception that the final form of a text has exclusive validity (synchrony). Speculative emendations of the Masoretic Text and postulates of new lexemes and uncommon grammatical forms or syntactic constructions stand little chance of being accepted over-against "the plain meaning." In case a word group or sentence hardly yields a meaning, it is the larger context that determines the import. From a hermeneutical point of view, however, the increasing appeal to the final form of a text is itself problematic. First of all, texts gradually develop into

---

1. Sternberg, *Poetics*, 323. I wish to express my appreciation to Dr. Torsten Uhlig (Wolkenstein OT Schönbrunn, Germany) for reading the first version of this article and making a number of significant, critical comments which I have taken over for the final version.

their definitive shape: their genesis knows successive stages.² Moreover, when specific traditions (MT or LXX) have ended up in their so-called canonical version, unconscious mistakes or even intended alterations can still occur during the transcription of the text although this is considered to be definitive. Against this background, we should never give up the study of so-called *cruces interpretum*.

To this category belongs Isa 63:11a MT: ויזכר ימי עולם משה עמו. A survey of some English translations exemplifies the problems:

Then he remembered the days of old, of Moses, his servant (RSV)

Then they remembered the days of old, of Moses his servant (NRSV)

Then they remembered the ancient days,

Him, who pulled His people out [of the water] (NJPS)

Thus he remembered the ancient days, Moses [and] his people (NICOT)³

Then they recalled the days of old: [Moses, his people] (AB)⁴

This small list of authoritative translations can be expanded by other translations in the scholarly literature, especially those of German origin. It makes no sense to survey all the existing proposals and the corresponding explanations: excellent reviews are available.⁵ We ascertain the tendency to maintain MT as regards the word עמו: changing it into עבדו, the interpretation of Syr., is widely rejected nowadays. The question that remains is the function of the word in the sentence. With regard to the other problem—whether the subject of the first word, ויזכר, is God or Israel—it appears that the latter view now prevails. These questions remain fundamental for the explanation of the immediate passage (vv. 11–14). Therefore, it seems advantageous to examine the linguistics of this *crux interpretum* again, first in connection to the immediate passage, secondly against the background of the literary genre of laments in Psalms, thirdly to describe its theological meaning, and finally for its role in the larger lament of Isa 63:7—64:11.

LINGUISTIC ANALYSIS OF ISA 63:11

וַיִּזְכֹּר יְמֵי־עוֹלָ ם מֹשֶׁה עַמּוֹ

---

2. Otto, "Jenseits."
3. Oswalt, *Isaiah Chapters 40–66*, 601.
4. Blenkinsopp, *Isaiah 56–66*, 252.
5. Koole, *Isaiah 56–66*, 360–64; Goldenstein, *Das Gebet*, 65–70.

Does God Practice Mindfulness? 117

אַיֵּה הַמַּעֲלֵם מִיָּם אֵת רֹעֵי צֹאנוֹ
אַיֵּה הַשָּׂם בְּקִרְבּוֹ אֶת־רוּחַ קָדְשׁוֹ

The common translation of the first word זכר by "to remember" renders just one specific meaning of the verb, i.e. when its object refers to the past, so as to imply "not to forget." But in Isa 63:11, the meaning "to call to mind, to recall" suits better than "to remember."[6]

From the syntactic point of view, YHWH is the subject of ויזכר ימי עולם, "he recalled." This is a continuation of v. 10b: "He turned ... he fought" (ויהפך ... הוא נלחם), and also of vv. 8–9: "He said ... he was ... he lifted up, he carried" (ויאמר ... ויהי ... וינטלם וינשאם). The *versiones* (LXX, Vulg., Tg., Syr.) confirm the singular finite form. Nevertheless, since the impression prevails that the people are speaking in vv. 11b–14, this actant is usually taken as the subject of ויזכר, too. In that case, it coincides with the subject of "they rebelled and grieved," YHWH's antagonist in v. 10 (subject המה; indirect object להם ... בם).

Due to these considerations, NRSV and NJPS come to the translation: "they remembered" (cf. above). This interpretation of the 3d pers. sing. ויזכר can be upheld with a plea of its indeterminate meaning ("one, people") or as an *ad sensum* phrasing. More often, the last word of v. 11a, עמו, is taken as the subject of ויזכר, although it occurs at the end of the sentence, in fact after the supposed object: "His people recalled the days of old (of) Moses."[7] In that case, the interpretation of the whole verse line seems to rely on the following argument: Although the word order (verb—object—adjunct of the object—subject) is very strange from the syntactic point of view, that is just the way the final text form runs.

Some critical questions can be raised concerning this explanation. First, does the presumed word order keep within the limits of the Hebrew syntax and is it plausible in the context of Hebrew poetry? The words משה עמו limp, without any syntactic determination, behind a clause consisting of a finite verb plus an object, while the connection of משה to ימי עולם is grammatically unclear and strange with regard to content.

Second, does the concept of "the final form of the text" not carry with it that a passage can acquire a supplement outside of its syntactic pattern?

---

6. Cf. Ps 89:51. Eising, "זכר."

7. Following Delitzsch, *Jesaia*, 602: "Da gedachte der Vorzeit-Tage Mose's sein Volk." This interpretation relies on the thematic analogy with Deut 32:7; Isa 51:9–10; Jer 2:6, on the Masoretic accentuation of the inversion object–subject in 2 Kgs 5:13, and on other accumulations of genetives, e.g., in Isa 28:1.

In other words, a sort of marginal note at the level of a metatext?[8] The hermeneutical option for the final text form does not exclude the acceptance of glosses, it includes it. In v. 11, some translations have indeed interpreted and rendered the words משה עמו in that way while their function remains a subject of discussion.[9] The fact that these words are lacking in the LXX, in addition to the way that they are rendered in other *versiones*, supports this opinion.[10]

Third, the reasoning that vv. 11b–14a cannot but contain what "the people" are saying is not waterproof. If it were preposterous that in vv. 11b–13, YHWH would refer to himself as subject in the 3rd person sing., the same would hold true if the people would refer to themselves as object in the 3rd person plural. Moreover, YHWH is often the subject of זכר, "to recall." In many places, God is heedful of his favors to Israel or of his covenant to the ancestors and the people, or he is invited to do so (Gen 8:1; 9:15–16; 19:29; Exod 2:24; 6:5; 32:13; Lev 26:45; Ps 25:6–7; 74:2; 98:3; 105:8 [1 Chr 16:15]. 42; 106:45; 111:5; 115:12; Isa 64:8; Jer 14:21; Ezek 16:60; 2 Chr 6:42 (cf. the negative remembrance in Ps 74:18.22; 89:51). Only in v. 14b, YHWH is addressed in the 2nd pers.

Fourth, the interpretation that God is the subject of "he recalled the days of old" seems unlikely if the words משה עמו are taken as belonging to the primary text but that interpretation becomes viable if these words function as a metatext, i.e. as a gloss to that sentence. The word "Moses" may have been added to the object "the days of old" in anticipation of Moses' anonymous role in vv. 11b–12a. The word "his people" may have been added precisely in order to change the subject of the sentence from God to Israel.

Lastly, the hypothesis that vv. 11b–14a mention what "he (God) recalled" in v. 11a, seems to be refuted by v. 14b: "Thus you guided your people, to make for yourself a glorious name." This sentence, directed to God, cannot be part of what God recalled. This last point, however, can be

---

8. Cf. Tov, *Textual Criticism*, 275–84: "Additions to the Body of the Text."

9. Oswalt, 601; Blenkinsopp, 252–54.

10. The Vulgate has taken these words into the syntactic connection: *Et recordatus est dierum saeculi, Moysi et populi sui*. In this way, "the people" is the object, not the subject of "he recalled." The Targum combines the two interpretations in an extended description: "Then he *had pity for the glory of his name, for the sake of the remembrance of his benefits which were from* of old, *the prodigies which he did by the hands* of Moses *for* his people *that they might not say*: Where is he who brought them up...?" "Remembrance" presupposes Israel as subject, yet "his people" functions first as object, next as subject of the question: "Where is he who ...?" (cf. Chilton [ed.], *The Isaiah Targum*, 121). The Syriac has read "Moses his servant" and makes these words into the object of "he recalled."

met with a counterargument. The resemblance of "to make for yourself a glorious name" in v. 14b to "to make for himself an everlasting name" in v. 12b strikes the attention. If the words "(Moses) his people" in v. 11aβ are a gloss that makes "his people" into subject of "he recalled," v. 14b may be an addition that makes the preceding vv. 11b–14a, by means of addressing YHWH directly, into a statement of Israel.

THE CONTEXT OF ISA 63:11–14

> 11 Then he recalled the days of old [Moses his people].
> Where is he who brought them up from the sea
> with the shepherd(s) of his flock?
> Where is he who put in him
> his holy spirit?
>
> 12 He caused to go at the right hand of Moses
> his glorious arm.
> He divided the water before them
> to make for himself an everlasting name.
>
> 13 He caused them to go through the depths
> like a horse in the desert,
>
> (so) they did not stumble,
>
> 14 like cattle that go down in the valley
> (so) the spirit of YHWH gave us rest.
> Thus you guided your people,
> to make for yourself a glorious name.

According to our hypothesis, the words "Moses his people" are clarifying notices (a metatext, not a syntactically integrated text) to the indeterminate sentence "he recalled the days of old." The phrase "his people" determines the subject (God) and the word "Moses" determines the object of the verb.[11] The addition "Moses" serves as a specification, because in vv. 11b–14a both the people (plural in vv. 11bα, 12b, 13a) and Moses ("shepherd[s]" in v. 11bα; singular in v. 11bβ; personal name in v. 12a) are mentioned as beneficiaries of God's acting. The text oscillates between those two. If "Moses" were lacking in v. 11a, he would be mentioned by his name only in v. 12, although he is already envisaged in v. 11b, "the shepherd(s) of his flock."

---

11. The interpretation of "Moses" as the subject of "he recalled" provides a complicated clause, too. In the whole passage, moreover, Moses would speak about himself in the 3d pers.; *pace* Clifford, "Narrative and Lament," esp. 97.

The latter words, את רעי צאנו, provide two difficulties: (a) MT treats the first word as the object-marker but a preposition seems more likely; and (b) it is unclear whether the second word represents a noun in the plural (רעי) or the singular (רעה) construct state. In both regards, even the Hebrew text tradition is not clear.[12] Because the actant "they" in v. 10 (המה, להם, בם) is explicitly present, the object suffix of המעלם מים, "the one who brought them up out of the sea," in v. 11 cannot but refer to "they." It is, moreover, difficult, from the semantic point of view, to defend the notion that the two terms, the *hifʿil* of עלה and ים, would refer to the rescuing of Moses as an abandoned child in Exodus 2.

Therefore, v. 11bα refers to Israel's crossing through the Red Sea and the words את רעי צאנו do not function as adjunct object to the suffix in "(he brought) them (up)," but as prepositional adjunct: "with the shepherd(s) of his flock." The plural form רעי is supported by 1QIsa^a, Aquila, Vulgate and Radaq; the singular form רעה is supported by LXX, Targum, Syriac, Rashi and Ibn Ezra. A case can be made for a plural referring to Moses and Aaron (cf. Ps 77:21), but Aaron's acting has not been mentioned or alluded to up to this point. Therefore, the reading רעה (singular) is probably the original one: "with the shepherd (i.e. Moses) of his flock." The plural reading רעי may stem from interpreting the suffix in המעלם as anticipating instead of referring to the manifold "they" in v. 10.[13] The unusual absolute form of the object-marker את must have been chosen by the Masoretes specifically to prevent its being understood as a preposition, i.e. "together with the shepherd (i.e. Moses) of his flock."[14] This would detract from YHWH's exclusive activity; moreover, it would not fit well with the next line which says that the shepherd received YHWH's "holy spirit."

The retrospect on the exodus from Egypt focuses on the crossing of the Red Sea. Verse 11, mentions in two "where is he who?" clauses the result of God's acting ("He brought them up out of the sea with the shepherd[s] of his flock") and the cause of the shepherd's success ("He put within him his holy spirit"). Verses 12–13a then elaborate this in three participial clauses: "He caused to go at the right hand of Moses his glorious arm. He divided the waters before them... He caused them to go through the depths." The comparison attached, "like a horse in the desert, (so) they did not stumble/ like cattle that go down in the valley" (vv. 13b–14aα), evokes the passage through the wilderness (from "depths" to "desert"), the more so because

---

12. Barthélemy, *Critique textuelle*, 439–40.

13. In another explanation, the plural form is called an orthographic preservation of *tertiae yod* in the participle; cf. Dahood, "Proverbs 8:22–31," 520.

14. For examples, cf. *DCH*, I, 451: את as "in the care of."

"cattle" is in keeping with "the shepherd of his flock." However, there is no special mention of the wilderness journey, only of its outcome, the settling in the land: "The spirit of YHWH gave him/us rest" (14aβ).

Even if vv. 11b–14a report the content of God's self-reflection (v. 11a: "He recalled"), it is the prophet who speaks in v. 14b, or rather the people (in view of the dominating "we"-speaker in the rest of 63:16–64:11): "Thus you guided your people, to make for yourself a glorious name." In that case, the people do not elaborate on their own disappointment (v. 11a: "He [the people] recalled"), but take up God's self-reflection.

In this interpretation, the beginning of the lament, 63:7, has a different tenor. The report of God's acting covers three full verse lines ("YHWH's gracious deeds/ praiseworthy acts// all that YHWH has done for us/ the great goodness to the house of Israel// according to his mercy/ according to the abundance of his steadfast love"). This extended introduction serves a clear rhetorical purpose if these lines not only anticipate the retrospect on God's rescue in v. 9 (". . . He carried them all the days of old"), but also God's self-reflection in vv. 11–14a ("He recalled the days of old . . . the spirit of YHWH gave us/him rest"). This explanation yields a different feature to God's judgment. In this case, it is not *at the time of their lament* that Israel confronted God with his previous benevolent attitude towards them ("they recalled"), but *at the time of his punishing Israel and in connection with that,* God realized that much earlier he had rescued his people from great affliction ("he recalled"). The relationship of v. 10b with v. 11a can freely be described as follows: "He turned to be their enemy, *yet* he recalled the days of old."

GOD'S SELF-REFLECTION IN OTHER LAMENTS IN THE HEBREW BIBLE

The next question is whether this notion of YHWH's self-reflection, as posited by the preceding investigation of Isa 63:11–14, arises elsewhere in the Scriptures, especially in other laments. At least the recurring motif that God calls to mind his favors, his covenant or his promises towards the ancestors or Israel, is found (Exod 2:24; 6:5; 32:13; Lev 26:45; Isa 64:8; Ezek 16:60; Ps 25:6–7; 74:2; 98:3; 105:8,42; 106:45; 111:5; 115:12; 2 Chr 6:42).

Further, the question form of Isa 63:11: "Where is he who?. . ." is a rhetorical device (with YHWH himself, his word, his love, etc., as subject; cf. Isa 63:15; 2 Kgs 2:14; Jer 2:6,8; 17:15; Mic 7:10; Mal 2,17; Ps 42:4.11; 79:10; 89:50 [cf. v. 51: "Recall"]; 115:2; Job 35:10). It is found all over the Ancient Near East.[15] Remarkable is the biblical parallel in which YHWH

---

15. Burnett, "Divine Absence."

himself raises the question concerning the gods: "Where are their gods, the rock in which they took refuge? ... Let them rise up and help you!" (Deut 32:37–38; cf. Isa 36:39; Jer 2:18).

Ongoing research of the book of Psalms has shown that the psalmist (or other persons around him) quite often quotes words of God without explicitly introducing or concluding these as such.[16] There is a clear disparity here between the psalms and prophetic literature which likes to distinguish formally between the word of God and that of the prophet. Besides, the verb "to recall" (זכר) belongs to the group of *verba cogitandi vel dicendi*, so much so that also in Isa 63:11, the verb "he recalled" can function as the opening of a quotation, either of God or of the people.

The phenomenon of "multi-voicedness" should also be taken into account. A shift of the person speaking is not always explicitly announced but sometimes surfaces by a shift in tone, often supported by grammatical markers. Moreover, the new speaker does not necessarily take on a clear identity. Thus in a number of psalms, a "didactic voice" has been diagnosed which cannot be reduced to a social or religious function (Moses, a priest, a prophet, a sage) but simply strengthens the dialogical process within the psalm itself.[17] The phenomenon of voice shifting can, of course, confirm the hypothesis that in Isa. 63:11 the people's recalling is related but it can also be applied to God's recalling in continuation to his hostile actions (v. 10). In both interpretations, the clause "Where is he (third-person singular) who brought them up?" characterizes the detached attitude of the speaker: either of Israel with respect to their God whom they had known as their savior in former times, or of God himself with respect to his former partiality for Israel.

THE THEOLOGICAL EFFECT OF GOD'S SELF-REFLECTION IN ISAIAH 63:11–14A

In the interpretation where "his people" is the postponed subject of v. 11a, the verse contains a lament of Israel: "His people recalled the days of old: 'Where is he who brought them up?'" As we have observed before, the

---

16. Doeker, *Die Funktion*, provides the following survey. Words of God are introduced in some way or other in Pss 2:5–6,7–9; 12:6; 27:8ab; 35:3; 50:5, 7–15, 16–23; 60:8–10; 68:23–24; 81:6–15; 82:1–4, 6–7; 89:20–38; 90:3; 95:8–11; 105:8–11; 108:8–10; 110:1, 4; 132:11–12, 14–18. An introduction is absent in Pss 32:8–9; 46:11; 75:3–4(6); 89:4–5; 91:14–16. This study is the most recent one in a line of predecessors: Booij, *Godswoorden*; Nasuti, *Tradition History*; Koenen, *Gottesworte*. The last study adds the following texts: Ps 21:9(10)–13; 58:2–3; 87:4, 6.

17. Mandolfo, *God in the Dock*, esp. 9–27.

complaint is not directly addressed to God. It gave vent to Israel's doubt as to whether God was still willing and able to save the people as he had done in old times. In the opposite interpretation, the author of the metatext has found the statement: "He (God) recalled the days of old" in the sense that God was conscious, precisely when he punished Israel for its rebellion, of the fact that in former days he had rescued the people and had brought them through the agency of Moses to rest. In this set-up, the prophetic prayer (v. 7: "I recall"; plural from v. 16 on: "our Father") describes God's second thoughts at the judgment that he himself was executing.

In this view, the fact that God did not raise the two "Where is he who? ..." clauses (v. 11b) in the I–form but in the he–form means that he created distance between his actual severe chastisement and his former saving action. He realized that he had changed his attitude towards Israel, and this reflection initiated the questions: "Where is he who?..." They do not contain an overtone of reproach or regret but of worry about proper identity and reputation (cf. v. 12: "to make for himself an everlasting name"). "He recalled," in this way, implies a self–reflection of God, a sort of soul-searching in which he weighed up his judgment against his usual saving agency.

With regard to literary form, a comparison of God's mindfulness with God's self-pity urges itself. In the latter, an accusation of Israel's infidelity goes together with sorrow at the punishment that God has to bring on Israel. Particularly the latter topic is found in the book of Jeremiah (Jer 8:4–7; 9:1–7; 12:7–13; 15:5–9), yet it resounds, too, in the opening of the book of Isaiah (Isa 1:2–3, 11–20).[18] Nevertheless, God's mindfulness, as assumed in Isa 63:11, distinguishes itself from his self-pity. For what God had in mind was not Israel's lack of loyalty at the time, but his own dedication to "the shepherd of his flock" (v. 11), who was to rescue the people from "the sea" (v. 11b), "the water/ the depths" (vv. 12–13), with the assistance of "his holy spirit" (v. 11), in order "to make for himself a glorious name" (v. 12). Of course, the topic of God's benevolence can support the interpretation that "his people" is the original subject of the verb "he recalled." However, it is equally suited to the hypothesis that God functioned as that subject. Anyhow, the topic gives God's mindfulness a different nuance than found in the passages about God's self-pity mentioned before.

If Isa 61:11a refers in first instance to YHWH ("He recalled the days of old"), the most important parallel text is without any doubt found in Jer 31:20: "Is Ephraim my dear son? Is he my darling child? For as often as I speak against him, I call him to mind still (זכר אזכרנו עוד). Therefore my inner self yearns for him (המו מעי לו), I will sure have mercy on him (רחם

---

18. Hermisson, "Vom Zorn und Leiden Gottes"; Schlimm, "Different Perspectives."

אֲרַחֲמֶנּוּ)." The conformity of this text to Isa 63:11 is not limited to the topic "God recalls Israel," but also includes the literary genre of an introspection.[19]

The hypothesis of God's mindfulness raises the question of whether the Scriptures contain parallels of this concrete form of anthropomorphic speaking about God. There are, of course, the topics of God's "repentance" and "turnabout" (incidentally they concur; "to repent," נחם: Exod 32:12–14; 2 Sam 24:16; Jer 4:28; 15:6; 18:8–10; 20:16; 26:3,13,19; 42:10; Ezek 24:14; Joel 2:13; Amos 7:3,6,9; Jonah 3:10; 4:2; Zech 8:14–15; Mal 1:9)[20]; "to turn," שוב: Exod 32:12; Deut 1:18; Josh 7:26; 2 Kgs 23:26; Isa 63:17; Jer 4:28; 12:15; Joel 2:14; Jonah 3:9; Zech 1:3; Mal 3:7; Pss 6:5; 85:5; 90:13; Job 6:29; 2 Chr 30:6).[21] Moreover, the theme whether and how God's anger can be averted is familiar (Num 14:17–19; Deut 9:7–29; Isa 9–10; Jer 6:11; 18:20; Hos 11:9; Hab 3:2; Pss 30:6; 103:8–9).

We are inclined to equate YHWHs mindfulness to one of these anthropomorphisms, especially to "repentance," but with an important modification. In the spiritual process by which people come to change their thoughts and actions, mindfulness and repentance represent different stages, yet the former can introduce the latter. Metaphorically applied to YHWH, they share a theological meaning: they embody God's freedom to determine, all by himself, his actions with regard to Israel and the world. Döhling has felicitously summarized the biblical function of God's repentance in this way: "Die Reue erscheint vielmehr als eine auch für Gott dynamische, gewissermaßen temporäre Größe. Gott ist, besser *wird* in sich je und je *frei* zur Reue. Dies fügt sich gut zur Logik einer dramatischen inneren Dissoziation und den Aspekten der *unerwarteten* Veränderung zuvor eingenommener und geäußerter Haltung im Gegenüber zur Welt."[22] If mindfulness is the gate to repentance, this metaphor presents the belief that Israel does not dispose of God's intimate movements. It is not necessary that the people remind God of his saving activity in former days, on the contrary, of his own accord, God balances his judgment with his long-standing protection of Israel: "Der Impuls zur Reue geht von Gott selbst aus oder entspringt in Gott."[23]

It seems well-advised to subsume God's mindfulness and repentance under the overarching concept of his sovereign mental power to move freely.

---

19. Fischer, *Jeremia 26–52*, 161.

20. For basics, cf. *ThWAT*, V, 369–76 (Simian-Yofre). The topic was first studied by Jeremias, *Die Reue Gottes*

21. Biberger, "'Vielleicht kehrt Gott um!"

22. Döhling, *Der bewegliche Gott*, esp. 523.

23. Ibid., 494.

Recent exegetical literature pays attention to this specific trait of YHWH's relationship to Israel and the nations, of history as "theohistory." Scripture depicts YHWH as operating the progress of time and acting within it, not as *movens immobilis*, but as engaged in interplay with humankind.[24] This topic of God's mindfulness directly fits into the larger depiction of God's involvement.[25] Together with the other anthropomorphisms just mentioned (anger, repentance, turnabout), mindfulness characterizes YHWH's interference with history. These "Modi von Gottes Beweglichkeit" (Döhling) represent YHWH's course of action with regard to the world in the form of the mental and emotional processes by which human beings crystallize their interaction.

GOD'S SELF-REFLECTION IN THE CONTEXT OF THE LAMENT OF ISAIAH 63:7—64:11

Finally, a twofold question is at stake: how well does the interpretation of vv. 11-14a as referring to God's mindfulness in "the communicative strategy" of the larger lament 63:7-64:11 work, both considered by itself and considered in the development of the prophetic book towards its end?[26]

Given the dynamic pattern of occurrences of the verb "to recall" (Isa 63:7, 11; 64:4, 8), "the intention of the whole prayer emerges as an act of remembrance as well as it reflects a hope that it can launch a similar turn as in its former history."[27] It must be admitted that the opening sentence (Isa 63:7: "I will recall the gracious deeds of YHWH, the praiseworthy acts of YHWH, because of all that YHWH has done for us, and the great favor to the house of Israel") lays the thematic foundation for the interpretation of Isa 63:11 as "his people recalled the days of old." This holds the more so, first because this application of the topic "to recall" is resumed in Isa 64:4 ("You meetest him who joyfully works righteousness, those who recall you in your ways") and secondly because Isa 64:11 results in the prayer that forms the purport of the lament: "Do not be exceedingly angry, O YHWH, and recall not iniquity forever" (Isa 64:8).

One major difficulty in this interpretation of Isa 63:11 is the past tense: "His people recalled (*wayyiqtol* form)." With regard to the communicative

---

24. Döhling, *Der bewegliche Gott*, 487-529; cf. Leuenberger, *Gott in Bewegung*; Hartenstein, "JHWHs Wesen im Wandel."

25. Cf. the contrast of God's awaking from sleeping as metaphor for divine sovereignty in Pss 7:7; 35:23; 44:24; 59:5; Batto, *In the Beginning*, 139-57.

26. Uhlig. *Hardening*, 287-315.

27. Ibid., 293.

progress from Isa 63:7 ("I will recall the benevolent acts of YHWH") to the beginning of the supplication proper in Isa 63:15 ("Look down from heaven and see"), one would expect v. 11 to run as follows: "His people recalls (or 'we recall') the days of old" (using either an imperfect or a participle) but that is not the case. In this interpretation, therefore, v. 11 refers to a moment in the past when the people remembered God's primeval protection at the time of Moses (vv. 11–14a). It is the past to the second power! The mention of Israel's past, not actual retrospect to God's care for the people at their beginning, has no communicative function in the actual speaking context, even though in the conclusion, God is directly addressed in the present (v. 14b: "Thus you guided your people"), which opens Israel's appeal to YHWH to intervene as savior right now (v. 15). The fact that, at some earlier date, Israel recalled God's primeval blessings can hardly support a plea for rescue in the present.[28]

Conversely, the interpretation of v. 11 as an act of YHWH himself ("He recalled") harmonizes with the logical development of the lament. In that case, YHWH's earlier mindfulness counts as one of his generous deeds towards Israel. In immediate connection to, indeed almost simultaneously with, his punishment of Israel, God was conscious of the fact that he had guided and protected his people through the waters and the desert. Israel zooms in on this mindfulness of YHWH which accompanied his judgment, by means of the conclusion: "Thus you guided your people" (v. 14b). In a fitting way, moreover, Israel adds the supplication proper: "Look down from heaven and see" (v. 15). According to this interpretation, the time table of the lament works out in a fluent, transparent way.

Current research has paid much attention to the position of Isa 63:7—64:11 in the larger context of Isaiah 56–66. Some scholars consider the passage as a basically independent (post)exilic lament. Others understand it as fully integrated in the development of this section of the prophetic book. By means of multiple references to Isa 40:1—63:6, the lament would explain the delay of the salvation announced there as due to YHWH's slowness or unwillingness to intervene. The indictment comes clearly to the fore in Isa 63:17: "Why, O YHWH, do you make us stray from your ways and harden our heart, so that we do not fear you? Turn back for the sake of your

---

28. In a written communication, Dr. Torst Uhlig has specified his view as follows: "The speaker remembers/ recalls 'the mercies of YHWH' (v. 7). Looking back he also remembers how the people remembered the days of old (v. 11). It is then not explicitly stated but implied that whenever they recalled the days of old this led to a change. In that way, the speaker now also wants to remember/ recall the mercies, hoping that this will lead to a change, too." While this explanation meets my objection concerning the past time perspective, it demands some unusual brainwork. So, *ceteris incommodis paribus*, it seems justifiable to maintain the thesis of this article.

servants, the tribes that are your heritage." A careful analysis, which cannot be resumed here, results in the conclusion that the lament plays a role in the interaction of the text with the intended readers: "this prayer discloses those who are still hardened. Those who would still join in that prayer *after* the previous proclamation (40:1–63:6 W.B.), express that they feel unaffected by it. This means, they manifest their enduring hardness."[29]

Against this background, the problem of how to interpret Isa 63:11 returns. It is obviously possible to consider the verse as meaning "His people recalled the days of old: Where is he who? . . ." so as to anticipate the reproach: "Where are your zeal and your might?.. Why do you make us stray from your ways?" (vv. 15–17). In the opposite explanation advanced in this article, however, v. 11 may anticipate the verses quoted, perhaps even more intimately. In that case, v. 15b, "The yearning of your inner self and your compassion (המון מעיך ורחמיך) are withheld from me," would aptly look back upon v. 11 in the interpretation: "God recalled the days of old." For the terms "inner self/ compassion" and the verb "to recall" belong to the same semantic field of mental activity and are anthropomorphically applied in both texts. With regard to this, the earlier established analogy with Jer 30:21 is striking. According to this interpretation, the persistent hardening of Israel makes the prayers fail to recognize that God's mindfulness accompanied his punishment.

CONCLUSION

The *crux interpretum* of Isa 63:11a, ויזכר, "he recalled," does not ask for an unambiguous solution but rather to be maintained and treated as an annotation. The syntactic pattern of the passage from v. 10 on leads to the interpretation "God recalled." However, the gloss עמו at the end of the verse line suggests the meaning "His people recalled." The construction of v. 11a does not compel us to take "his people" as the exclusive linguistic subject of the clause at the level of the final text. Rather, the word belongs to the metatext level: it brings another subject, i.e. "his people," along, in the same way as the word "Moses" at the same level indicates the object of the sentence. The second meaning ("His people recalled") does not blot out the first meaning ("God recalled"), but preserves it: the reading process provides a bending of subject reference. The final text does not lead to fill in and then reject a bygone meaning; on the contrary, it displays it. This is not a matter of diachrony vs. synchrony which sometimes serves as a key

---

29. Uhlig, *Hardening*, 299.

to the solution of problems in modern hermeneutics.[30] It is rather a case of an exegetical comment, directly inserted into the running text ("interpolation") which changes the purport of the sentence without suppressing its primary meaning.

The passage subsequent to v. 11a renders what "he recalled": the content matches with both God and the people as subject. In the latter case, this is covered by vv. 11b–14, in the former case only by vv. 11b–14a, while the speaker of the lament reacts to God's recalling in v. 14b. In as far as vv. 11b–14a hold God's self-reflection, the very fact that God called to mind his former protective attitude towards Israel adds a special trait to his portrayal. Even while God was punishing Israel, he was conscious of the circumstance that he had always acted as the redeemer of his people. Of course, Israel often confronts God with that salutary data (cf. Pss 44:2–4; 80:9–12; 106:8–12; Neh 9:7–15). To this list must now be added Isa 63:11, when we follow the indication of the inner-textual note and understand it as: "The people recalled." The underlying text, however, does not cease to proclaim that during his chastisement, God bent his mind to his long-standing support of Israel.[31]

I am grateful for having been invited to write an article for these essays in honor of John E. Hartley. Since the Congress on the Book of Job in Leuven (1993), John and I have shared a concern for respectful exegesis of the Scriptures in a bond of friendship that transcends hermeneutical discussions.

BIBLIOGRAPHY

Barthélemy, Dominique. *Critique textuelle de l'Ancient Testament. 2. Isaïe, Jérémie, Lamentations*. OBO 2nd ser. 50. Göttingen: Vandenhoeck & Ruprecht, 1986.
Batto, Bernard F. *In the Beginning: Essays on Creation Motifs in the Ancient Near East and the Bible*. Siphrut: Literature and Theology of the Hebrew Scriptures 9. Winona Lake, IN: Eisenbrauns, 2013, 139–57.
Beuken, Willem A. M. "Psalm 39: Some Aspects of the Old Testament Understanding of Prayer." *Heythrop Journal* 19 (1978) 1–11.
Biberger, Bernd. "'Vielleicht kehrt Gott um!' (Joel 2,14)." *ThGl* 102 (2012) 140–52.
Blenkinsopp, Joseph. *Isaiah 1–39*. AYBC 19. Garden City, NY: Doubleday, 2000.

---

30. For a clarifying, in-depth reflection on this problem cf. Hong, "Synchrony and Diachrony."

31. At the congress of IOSOT XXI, 2013 (München), two short papers have focused on texts of interpretative multivalence in the book of Isaiah: J. Gärtner, "'Deine Fremden' oder 'deine Vermessenen'" (Program Book, p. 119); M. P. Maier, "Festbankett oder Henkersmahlzeit?" (Programme Book, p. 150). Readers are referred to the prospective publication of these important studies.

Booij, Thijs. "Godswoorden in de Psalmen. Hun functie en achtergronden." PhD diss., Free University Amsterdam.

Burnett, Joel S. "The Question of Divine Absence in Israelite and West Semitic Religion." *CBQ* 67 (2005) 215–35.

Chilton, Bruce D. *The Isaiah Targum. Introduction, Translation, Apparatus and Notes.* Aramaic Bible 11. Edinburgh: T & T Clark, 1987.

Clifford, Richard J. "Narrative and Lament in Isaiah 63:7–64:11." In *To Touch the Text: Biblical and Related Studies in Honor of Joseph A. Fitzmyer*, edited by M. P. Horgan and P. J. Kobelski, 93–102. New York: Crossroad/Continuum, 1989.

Dahood, Mitchell. "Proverbs 8,22–31." *CBQ* 30 (1968) 512–21.

Delitzsch, Franz. *Commentar über das Buch Jesaia.* BCAT. Leipzig: Dörfling & Franke, 1889.

Docker, Andrea. *Die Funktion der Gottesrede in den Psalmen.* BBB 135. Berlin: Philo, 2002.

Döhling, Jan-Dirk. *Der bewegliche Gott: Eine Untersuchung des Motivs der Reue Gottes in der Hebräischen Bibel.* HBS. Freiburg: Herder, 2009.

Eising, H. "זכר." In ThWAT, edited by G. J. Botterweck and H. Ringgren. Stuttgart, 1970–

Fischer, Georg. *Jeremia 26–52.* HThKAT. Freiburg: Herder, 2005.

Gärtner, Judith. "'Deine Fremden' oder 'deine Vermessenen' (Jes 29,5)? Das Ineinander von Gericht und Heil im Arielwort (Jes 29,1–8)." In *IOSOT XXI Short Papers.* Munich, 2013.

Goldstein, Jonathan A. *Das Gebet der Gottesknechte: Jesaja 63,7–64,11 im Jesajabuch.* WMANT 92. Neukirchen-Vluyn: Neukirchener, 2001.

Hartenstein, Friedhelm. "JHWH's Wesen im Wandel. Vorüberlegungen zu einer Theologie des Alten Testaments." *ThLZ* 137 (2012) 3–19.

Hermisson, Hans-Jürgen. "Von Zorn und Leiden Gottes." In *Denkwürdiges Geheinnis: Beiträge zur Gotteslehre: Festschrift für Eberhard Jüngel zum 70. Geburtstag*, edited by I. U. Dalferth, J. Fischer, and H.-P Großhans, 185–207. Tübingen: Mohr Siebeck, 2004.

Hong, Koog P. "Synchrony and Diachrony in Contemporary Biblical Interpretation." *CBQ* 75 (2013) 521–39.

Jeremias, Jörg. *Die Reue Gottes. Aspekte alttestamentlicher Gottesvorstellung.* BibThSt 31. Neukirchen-Vluyn: Neukirchener, 1997.

Koehnen, Klaus. *Gottesworte in den Psalmen: Eine formgeschichtliche Untersuchung.* BThSt 30. Neukirchen-Vluyn: Neukirchener, 1996.

Koole, Jan L. *Isaiah III. Volume 3: Chapters 56–66.* HCOT. Leuven: Peeters, 2001.

Leuenberger, Martin. *Gott in Bewegung. Religions- und theologiegeschichtliche Beiträge zur Gottesvorstellungen im alten Israel.* FAT 76. Tübingen: Mohr Siebeck, 2011.

Maier, Michael P. "Festbankett oder Henkersmahlzeit?—Die zwei Gesichter von Jes 25,6–8." In *IOSOT XXI Short Papers.* Munich, 2013.

Mandolfo, Carleen. *God in the Dock: Dialogic Tension in the Psalms of Lamentations.* JSOTSup 357. Sheffield: Sheffield Academic, 2002.

Nasuti, Harry P. *Tradition History and the Psalms of Asaph.* SBLDS 88. Atlanta: Scholars, 1988.

Oswalt, John N. *The Book of Isaiah Chapters 1–39.* NICOT. Grand Rapids: Eerdmans, 1986.

Otto, Eckart. "Jenseits der Suche nach dem 'ursprünglichen Text' in der Textkritik." *ZAR* 18 (2012) 363–72.

Schlimm, Matthew R. "Different Perspectives on Divine Pathos: An Examination of Hermeneutics in Biblical Theology." *CBQ* 69 (2007) 673–94.

Sternberg, Meir. *The Poetics of Biblical Narrative: Ideological Literature and the Drama of Reading*. Indiana Literary Biblical Series. Bloomington: Indiana University Press, 1985.

Tov, Emmanuel. *Textual Criticism of the Hebrew Bible*. 3rd ed. Minneapolis: Fortress, 2012.

Uhlig, Torst. *The Theme of Hardening in the Book of Isaiah. An Analysis of Communicative Action*. FAT 2/39. Tübingen: Mohr Siebeck, 2009.

7

Isaiah 56:1–8 in Form-Critical Perspective

—*Marvin A. Sweeney*

ISAIAH 56:1–8 HAS LONG been recognized as the leading text of Trito-Isaiah since the publication of Duhm's commentary in 1892 (Duhm, 390–95). It is a particularly important text in the book of Isaiah insofar as it expresses Isaiah's universal perspectives concerning the inclusion of foreigners and eunuchs in YHWH's covenant. Many presume that the text envisions an open call for the inclusion of foreigners and eunuchs, but closer examination of the text indicates that it expects such persons to abide by the terms of YHWH's covenant, beginning with observance of the Shabbat. Such observance of the covenant constitutes conversion to Judaism. Recognized halachic procedure for conversion to Judaism is formalized only in the rabbinic period (see "Proselytes," *EncJud* 13:1182–93, esp. 1183–85). Nevertheless, there are a number of biblical texts that take up issues concerning conversion, such as "the persons that (Abram and Sarai) had made in Haran" in Gen 12:5; the portrayal of Jethro in Exodus 18; the law concerning marriage to a foreign woman in time of war in Deut 21:10–14; Ruth in the Book of Ruth; texts in Isaiah, such as Isa 56:1–8.

The following presents commentary on Isa 56:1–8 written for the forthcoming volume on Isaiah 40–66 for the Forms of the Old Testament Literature commentary series. It is an honor and privilege to present it to John Hartley, who came to Claremont to study form-critical exegesis while I was still a graduate student and he was preparing his commentary on

Leviticus for the Word Biblical Commentary series. The genre terms in capital letters are the stylistic device used in the FOTL series to indicate that there is a glossary entry for that term in the back of that volume. The Bibliography section has been changed from the format used in the FOTL series in order to match the style used in this Festschrift.

PROPHETIC INSTRUCTION CONCERNING THE INCLUSION OF OBSERVANT FOREIGNERS AND EUNUCHS IN YHWH'S TEMPLE: ISAIAH 56:1–8

Structure

Prophetic Instruction Concerning Inclusion of Observant Foreigners and Eunuchs in Temple Community	Isa 56:1–8
I. Prophetic report concerning YHWH's instructions for proper observance	1–3
A. Prophetic messenger formula	1aα
B. YHWH's instruction speech concerning proper observance	1aβ–3
1. Instruction proper concerning justice and righteousness	1aβ–b
a. two-fold instruction: do justice and righteousness	1aβ
1) observe justice	1aβ1–2
2) do righteousness	1aβ3–4
b. two-fold rationale: G-d's deliverance and righteousness is near	1b
1) for my deliverance is near	1bα
2) for my righteousness is to be revealed	1bβ
2. specification of what is just and right: observant foreigners and eunuchs will not be excluded nor cut off	2–3
a. beatitude specifying justice and righteousness: observe Shabbat and refrain from evil	2
1) beatitude protasis	2a
a) happy is the man who does this	2aα
b) happy is the person who grasps this	2aβ
2) beatitude apodosis: observes Shabbat and refrains from evil	2b
b. prophetic instruction concerning inclusion of foreigners and eunuchs: rhetorical statements concerning inclusion of foreigners and eunuchs	3
1) let foreigner not say that YHWH has excluded me from people	3a
2) let eunuch not say I am a withered tree	3b

Isaiah 56:1-8 in Form-Critical Perspective 133

II. Basis for prophet's instruction: report of YHWH's instructions concerning place of observant foreigners and eunuchs in Temple community	4–8
A. Prophet's presentation of YHWH's oracle	4–5
1. prophetic messenger formula	$4a\alpha^{1-4}$
2. YHWH's instruction speech concerning assured place of observant foreigners and eunuchs in Temple	$4a\alpha^{5}-5$
a. to the eunuchs	$4a\alpha^{5}$–b
1) who observe my Shabbats	$4a\alpha^{5-9}$
2) and choose what I want	$4a\beta$
3) and hold fast to my covenant	4b
b. YHWH's promise: monument and name	5
1) monument and name in my Temple and walls better than sons and daughters	5a
2) an eternal name	5b
B. concerning place of observant foreigners in Temple	6–8
1. to the foreigners who join YHWH	6
a. qualification of foreigners who join YHWH	6a
1) to serve YHWH	$6a\alpha$
2) to love the name of YHWH	$6a\beta$
3) to be a servant to YHWH qualified	$6a\gamma$
b. appositional specification	6b
1) all who observe Shabbat	$6b\alpha$
2) all who hold fast to my covenant	$6b\beta$
2. presentation of YHWH's oracular promise: they are welcome in my Temple	7–8
a. YHWH's oracular statement	7
1) promise: I will include them in my Temple	7a
a) I will bring them to my holy mountain	$7a\alpha^{1-4}$
b) I will have them rejoice in my house of prayer	$7a\alpha^{5-7}$
c) their whole burnt offerings and peace offerings are welcome on my altar	$7a\beta$
2) basis for promise: my house of prayer is for all the peoples	7b
b. expanded oracular formula	8
1) oracular formula proper	$8a\alpha$
2) qualification: YHWH gathers exiles of Israel	$8a\beta$–b
a) prophet's qualification: YHWH gathers exiles of Israel	$8a\beta$
b) YHWH's statement: I will gather more to those already gathered	8b

Isaiah 56:1–8 constitutes prophetic instruction concerning the inclusion of observant foreigners and eunuchs in YHWH's Temple. It is demarcated at the outset by the introductory messenger formula in v. 1aα, which identifies the prophet as the speaker who conveys YHWH's speech. YHWH's speech then follows in vv. 1aβ–2 with YHWH's instructions concerning proper observance. Some argue that only vv. 1–2 constitute a unit separate from the following material in vv. 3–8 (e.g., Westermann, 309–16). But such a view fails to account for the fact that YHWH's speech in vv. 1–2 expresses the basic principles of justice and righteousness, here defined as Shabbat observance and refraining from evil that serve as the foundation for the following elaboration on YHWH's instruction by the prophet in vv. 3–8. The prophet quotes YHWH throughout vv. 3–8 in elaborating on the inclusion of foreigners and eunuchs who observe Shabbat and YHWH's covenant at large. Consequently, the expanded oracular formula in v. 8 closes the unit. The metaphorical references to wild beasts and blind watchmen in Isa 56:9 opens a new unit concerned with YHWH's forgiveness of those who repent.

The prophetic report concerning YHWH's instructions for proper observance in Isa 56:1–2 begins with the prophetic messenger formula in v. 1aα which identifies the following material as a speech by YHWH. The first person references in v. 1aβ–b confirm YHWH's identity as a speaker, but such references are lacking in vv. 2–3. Indeed, the third person references to YHWH in v. 3 appear as part of the purported speech by the foreigner. Lacking any indication of a shift in speaker, vv. 2–3 must be considered as part of YHWH's speech. The second instance of the prophetic messenger formula in v. 4 indicates the voice of the prophet once again. YHWH's instruction speech in vv. 1aβ–3 consequently comprises two major sub-units. The first in v. 1aβ–b constitutes YHWH's instruction proper concerning justice and righteousness. This segment begins with a two-fold instruction in v. 1aβ to do justice and righteousness, which includes individual statements for each in v. 1aβ1–2 and v. 1aβ3–4 respectively. The two-fold rationale, introduced by the particle, *kî*, "because, for," follows in v. 1b with YHWH's statements that my deliverance is near in v. 1bα and that my righteousness is to be revealed in v. 1bβ.

The second sub-unit in vv. 2–3, which begins with no conjunctive element, then specifies what is meant by just and righteousness. After all, these are very general terms that do not lend themselves to inherent definition. Consequently, vv. 2–3 specifies these general principles by stating that observant foreigners and eunuchs will not be excluded or cut off from the nation by YHWH. The first element in this sub-unit is the beatitude in v. 2 which specifies that justice and righteousness in this instance constitutes observance of Shabbat and refraining from doing evil. The first element or

Isaiah 56:1–8 in Form-Critical Perspective   135

protasis of the beatitude in v. 2a states that happy is the man who does this in v. 2aα and happy is the person who holds fast to this or grasps this in v. 2aβ. Because the reader does not yet know what "this" is, v. 2b steps in as the beatitude apodosis to state that "this" refers to Shabbat observance and refraining from doing evil. Verse 3, linked to v. 2 by a *waw*-consecutive verbal formation, then follows with prophetic instruction concerning the inclusion of foreigners and eunuchs in two statements. The first in v. 3a instructs that foreigners should not have to say that YHWH excludes them, and the second in v. 3b instructs that eunuchs should not have to say that they are withered trees, i.e., that they have no progeny or legacy among Israel. Nevertheless, readers must observe that observance and the foreigners and eunuchs have not yet been put together.

The basis for the prophet's instruction then follows in Isa 56:4–8 with a report of YHWH's instructions concerning the place of the observant foreigners and eunuchs in the Temple community. This section begins with an introductory *kî*, which signals its explanatory role in relation to Isa 56:1–3. The introductory prophetic messenger formula in v. 4aα$^{1-4}$ and the closing expanded oracular formula in v. 8 indicate that the prophet is the speaker. The passage comprises two major sub-units. The first is the prophet's presentation of YHWH's oracle concerning the observant eunuchs in vv. 4–5 and the second is the prophet's discussion concerning the place of observant foreigners in vv. 6–8.

The prophet's presentation of YHWH's oracle concerning observant eunuchs in vv. 4–5 begins with the prophetic messenger formula in v. 4aα$^{1-4}$, which introduces YHWH's instruction speech in vv. 4aα^5–5. The instruction speech comprises two sub-units. The first is the reference to the eunuchs in v. 4aα^5–b, which identifies them as the subject of discussion. The sub-unit presents YHWH's three qualifications for the eunuchs, viz., they observe my Shabbats in 4aα$^{5-9}$; they choose what I want in v. 4aβ; and the hold fast to my covenant in v. 4b. YHWH's promise to the eunuchs then follows in v. 5. Verse 5a states that they will have a monument and a name in YHWH's Temple and walls, which is better than sons or daughters, and v. 5b states that they will have an eternal name.

The prophet's discussion concerning the place of observant foreigners in the Temple then follows in vv. 6–8. Verse 6 presents the prophet's statements concerning observant foreigners. The third person reference to YHWH confirms that the prophet is the speaker. The prophet begins in v. 6a with a statement of the qualification of the foreigners who would join YHWH, viz., they will serve YHWH in v. 6aα, they will love the name of YHWH in v. 6aβ, and they will be servants to YHWH in v. 6aγ. Verse 6 then presents two appositional specifications for the foreigners, viz. they are those who observe Shabbat in v. 6bα and they are all who hold fast to "my" covenant in v. 6bβ. The reference to "my" suggests that the prophet quotes a fragment of a YHWH speech, although it is possible that an original reading of "his covenant" became "my covenant" under the influence of YHWH's oracular statement in v. 7 and the reference to "my covenant" in v. 4b. The prophet then presents YHWH's oracular promise in vv. 7–8. YHWH's oracular statement appears first in v. 7. It includes YHWH's basic promise in v. 7a that I will include them in my Temple, specified in three successive statements, viz., I will bring them to my holy mountain in v. 7aα$^{1-4}$, I will have them rejoice in my house of prayer in v. 7aα$^{5-7}$, and their whole burnt offerings and peace offerings are welcome on my altar in v. 7aβ. The basis for YHWH's promise, i.e., that my house of prayer is for all peoples, then follows in v. 7b. Finally, the expanded oracular formula in v. 8 identifies vv. 6–8 as an oracle by YHWH. The oracular formula proper appears in v. 8aα, and the qualification YHWH as the one who gathers exiles appears in v. 8aβ–b. The prophet's qualification proper appears in v. 8aβ, and then the prophet includes a quotation from YHWH, "I will gather more to those already gathered," in v. 8b to reinforce YHWH's identity as a powerful and trustworthy G-d.

GENRE

Past interpreters have identified a number of generic elements in Isa 56:1–8, but the basic genre of the passage is Prophetic INSTRUCTION concerning the inclusion of observant foreigners and eunuchs in YHWH's Temple community. To arrive at this generic character, the passage combines several generic elements, such as the prophet's REPORT of YHWH's speeches, the ORACLES which constitute YHWH's speeches, and the basic generic character of the passage as an INSTRUCTION, which provides proper guidance concerning the inclusion of observant foreigners and eunuchs in the Temple.

First is the REPORT. The passage combines third person statements about YHWH and the issue of foreigners and eunuchs with first person statements attributed to YHWH to provide the relevant instruction. Although the prophet is not named, the use of oracular forms in the passage, e.g., the MESSENGER FORMULA, "Thus says YHWH," and its variants in vv. 1aα and 4aα$^{1-4}$ together with the closing expanded ORACULAR FORMULA, "utterance of my L-rd, YHWH" (read as "utterance of my L-rd, G-d") in v. 8a points to the prophetic identity of the basic speaker in the passage. In all cases, these formulae refer to YHWH in the third person as do the statements in vv. 3, 6abα (although v. 6bβ is formulated in first person, it may originally have been a third person statement), and 8a.

The second is an ORACLE by YHWH. The oracles reported by the prophet in the passage include vv. 1aβ-2, 4aα⁵-5, 7, and 8b. All are identified as oracular material by the combination of MESSENGER FORMULAE in vv. 1aα and 4aα¹⁻⁴, the expanded ORACULAR FORMULA in v. 8a, and by the first person language presupposing YHWH as the speaker found in each of the oracular speeches noted above.

The fourth is INSTRUCTION by YHWH as conveyed by the prophet. INSTRUCTION is "a writing or discourse ... that offers guidance to an individual or group by setting forth particular values or prescribing rules of conduct" (Sweeney, *Isaiah 1-39*, 522). In the present instance, that INSTRUCTION calls for the inclusion of observant foreigners and eunuchs in YHWH's Temple. Interpreters must be clear as to the full parameters of this instruction. It does not simply call for the inclusion of foreigners and eunuchs; it specifies that such foreigners and eunuchs must be observant, and it specifies that such observance constitutes doing what is just and right, observance of the Shabbat, refraining from doing evil, doing what YHWH wills, holding fast to YHWH's covenant, serving YHWH, loving the name of YHWH, and being servants to YHWH (see vv. 1, 2, 4 and 6). Although Deut 23:2-9 specifies that certain foreign groups and anyone with crushed testicles or a cut off member shall be excluded from the congregation, the present passage specifies that such persons shall be admitted to the congregation if they are observant of YHWH's covenant. In the case of foreigners, the passage does not go into the details of whether they are Ammonite, Moabite, Edomite, or Egyptian, which hold different status in Deuteronomy. Instead, it appears to presuppose Deuteronomy's commands to allow "resident aliens" (Hebrew, *gērîm*) certain rights of observance in Israel. In later periods, such "resident aliens" are considered as converts to Judaism. In the case of eunuchs, the passage apparently considers that such status may not be a matter of personal choice and that the decision to observe YHWH's covenant in fact constitutes observance of YHWH's covenant—and possibly repentance—as envisioned by Deuteronomy. Thus, the passage appears to presuppose Deuteronomy, but it also appears to have expanded or interpreted the meaning of Deuteronomy in keeping with the views expressed throughout the larger context of the book.

Finally, the BEATITUDE also plays a role in this passage in v. 2. A BEATITUDE is "a short, formulaic speech that extols the fortunate or blessed state of an individual or whole people" (Sweeney, *Isaiah 1-39*, 515). It typically begins with *ăšrê*, "happy are," which is the case in v. 2. In the present instance, the BEATITUDE follows the basic INSTRUCTION to do justice and righteousness. The BEATITUDE in v. 2 reinforces the INSTRUCTION in v. 1 by specifying in part what doing justice and righteousness means, i.e., it constitutes Shabbat observance and refraining from doing evil. This constitutes INSTRUCTION or guidance in proper conduct, and the rest of the passage continues to offer further INSTRUCTION concerning the meaning of the initial statement in v. 1.

SETTING

Although past interpreters have attempted to argue that Isaiah 56:1–8 is a composite text (Westermann, 309–16; Sekine, *Die tritojesajanische Sammlung*, 31–41; Koenen, *Ethik*, 11–15), more recent discussion, including the present analysis, points to the literary unity of this passage (e.g., Stromberg, *Isaiah after Exile*, 40–42; Blenkinsopp, 131; Smith, *Rhetoric and Redaction*, 51–54). In most cases, the grounds for dividing the passage into discreet components were generic, but form critical scholarship has come to recognize that genre is not the fundamental defining criterion for a distinct text, but functions as an element within textual form, often in combination with other generic elements, to constitute the text and to serve its purposes. In the present text, Isa 56:1–8 is an example of prophetic INSTRUCTION, but it employs a variety of other generic elements to facilitate its basic form and task of instruction.

The passage is clearly interested in the status of foreigners and eunuchs within the Jewish Temple community. The laws in Deut 7:1–6; 23:2–9 indicate that questions were raised about the status of both groups within the Jewish community. Deuteronomy was likely composed in the late-seventh century BCE and presupposes a settled kingdom of Judah that could presume a largely Judean or Israelite population and control admission to the Jerusalem Temple, but the demise of the kingdom of Judah and the experience of the Babylonian exile would have reopened questions concerning the status of foreigners and eunuchs within the Jewish community and its Temple environs. The experience of foreign invasion on the one hand and Babylonian Exile on the other would have opened the way for far greater numbers of intermarriages and foreign births among the people of Israel and Judah as they were exposed in both context to foreign cultures. In the case of eunuchs, service, whether forced or not, in various Babylonian contexts would have required eunuch status. With the possibility of the return of both eunuchs and Jews born of one or two foreign parents, the issue of the status of such persons in Judaism would have risen once again in the early-Persian period when both returning exiles and Jews who remained in the land would have turned to the newly-built Second Temple in Jerusalem.

The issue of the status of foreigners in the Jewish community—and particularly in relation to the Temple—comes to a head in the times of Nehemiah and Ezra during the late-fifth and early-fourth centuries BCE. In both cases, Nehemiah and Ezra forbid intermarriage with foreigners as recorded in Ezra 9–10 and Neh 13:23–31. Most interpreters presuppose that Isaiah 56:1–8 is opposed to the practice of forbidding foreign marriage, but closer examination of the issue indicates that this is not necessarily the case. The prohibition of intermarriage by Ezra and Nehemiah is based on the above-mentioned laws in Deut 7:1–6, which forbids marriage with the Canaanites because they will cause the people to follow their foreign gods. But Deut 21:10–14 specifies the procedure for an Israelite man to marry a foreign woman in the aftermath of war. Likewise, Deuteronomy continuously calls for the inclusion of *gērîm* or "resident aliens" in the celebration of Israelite holidays (see Deut 16:11–12) and guarantees them equal legal rights and care (Deut 1:16; 10:17–19). In Rabbinic times, *gērîm* were understood to refer to converts to Judaism.

Given Ezra's (and Nehemiah's) observance of Torah, consideration the law of the Passover offering in Exod 12:43–49 is especially instructive. The law specifies that no "foreigner" (Hebrew, *ben-nēkār*) may eat of the Passover offering. But it goes on to specify that slaves who have been circumcised and resident aliens (Hebrew, *gērîm*) who have been circumcised may eat of the Passover offering. Those who remained uncircumcised are excluded from eating the Passover offering. Here, circumcision appears to be the defining characteristic of who might eat of the Passover offering. A foreigner is uncircumcised. A resident alien has the option to become circumcised. And a foreigner can presumably become a resident alien. It appears that we see in Exod 12:43–49 a process by which foreigners might become part of the people of Israel or Judah. Such a process appears to constitute an early form of conversion to Judaism as later recognized by Rabbinic Judaism.

Similar considerations may be brought to bear on Ezra and Nehemiah. Marriages to foreign women are forbidden, but foreign women in Ezra-Nehemiah appear to be women who continue to speak the languages of their former cultures and who continue to worship foreign gods (Neh 13:23–31). But what about those women who assimilate into Jewish culture, learning to speak the Hebrew language and worshipping YHWH exclusively, as stipulated by Deuteronomy? Do they remain foreigners? Or do they become part of Israel?

This question returns us to Isa 56:1–8. The passage specifies that foreigners who uphold YHWH's covenant with Israel, specifically including the observance of Shabbat, will be admitted to the Temple. At this point, we must consider such persons to be converts in some form or another to Judaism. Such persons would have been considered part of the Jewish community in the time of Ezra and Nehemiah as well. Our passage appears to complement Ezra-Nehemiah, not oppose it.

Consequently, Isa 56:1-8 appears to be set in the period of Ezra and Nehemiah, i.e., in the late-fifth or early-fourth century BCE, about a century following the building of the Second Temple, when Nehemiah made observance of the covenant, particularly Shabbat, the defining characteristic of the Jewish people in Jerusalem, and when Ezra made observance of Torah the criterion by which proper Jewish observance would be measured.

As many have observed, Isa 56:1-8 functions as an introduction to the Trito-Isaian materials in Isaiah 56-66, and it relates intertextually to Isaiah 65-66, which envisions the restoration of the righteous nation of Israel at the end of the book. The question of inclusion in the Jewish community is of paramount interest in these chapters. Insofar as Isa 56:1-8 defines the parameters for inclusion in the Jewish community, viz., adherence to the covenant, observance of the Shabbat, doing what is considered to be just (Hebrew, *mišpāṭ*) and right (Hebrew, *ṣĕdāqâ*), refraining from doing what is wrong. These characteristics define the people of Israel who will be returned to Jerusalem and the land of Israel throughout Trito-Isaiah. As Rendtorff observes, these characteristics, particularly those who do what is considered to be just (Hebrew, *mišpāṭ*) and right (Hebrew, *ṣĕdāqâ*), permeates the entire book of Isaiah and suggests that the materials in Trito-Isaiah, Isaiah 56-66, constitute a major portion of the final redaction of the book. Indeed, he notes that *mišpāṭ* and *ṣĕdāqâ* appear frequently together in Isaiah 1-39, but never in Isaiah 40-55 which prefers the combination *ṣĕdāqâ* and *yĕšû☐â* instead. The different conceptualizations of *ṣĕdāqâ*, one which emphasizes justice and the other which emphasizes divine deliverance, point to a Trito-Isaian redaction of the book of Isaiah which presupposed a core in Isaiah 40-55 for which Isaiah 1-39 and 56-66 would provide a broader literary context (Rendtorff, "Isaiah 56:1"; Rendtorff, "The Composition of the Book of Isaiah").

INTERPRETATION

Isaiah 56:1-8 sets the theme for Isaiah 56-66 by specifying who is eligible for inclusion in the restored Jewish community of the Jerusalem Temple. It stipulates that foreigners and eunuchs, two groups whose status among the Jewish people might come into question, are included insofar as they do what is just and right, choose what YHWH desires, hold fast to YHWH's covenant, observe the Shabbat, and avoid doing what is wrong. In the case of the foreigners, such persons would constitute converts to Judaism insofar as these foreigners affirm the covenant between YHWH and the Jewish people (cf. Goldingay, 84; Paul, 447-50). In the case of the eunuchs, who likely served in some capacity as part of the Babylonian administration, such persons would be granted status in the Jewish community by adhering to the covenant. Isaiah 56:1-8 is therefore in dialog with Pentateuchal texts, such as Deut 7:1-6; 23:2-9; and Exod 12:43-49, which provide guidance on the admission of foreigners and eunuchs into the people of Israel. Isaiah 56:1-8 presupposes the debate concerning the admission of foreigners into the community in the time of Nehemiah and Ezra. Although many view Isa 56:1-8 as opposed to Ezra's policy against intermarriage with foreign women, Isa 56:1-8 stipulates that foreigners undertake action that amounts to conversion to Judaism. Nehemiah and Ezra are opposed to intermarriage with women who maintain foreign identity and religious practice, and so there is little basis for concluding that Isaiah 56:1-8 and the texts concerning intermarriage in Ezra 9-10 and Nehemiah 13:23-31 are in conflict with each other. Isaiah 56:1-8 appears to support the policies of Nehemiah and Ezra by stipulating how foreigners become a part of Israel and are therefore no longer viewed as foreign. The book of Ruth likewise supports the practice of conversion to Judaism, in this case by a woman.

Isaiah 56:1-8 constitutes the prophet's report concerning the inclusion of observant foreigners and eunuchs in the Temple community. Within the literary context of the book of Isaiah, the prophet must be Isaiah ben Amoz. Diachronically speaking, the prophet is one of the anonymous prophets from the Persian period whose works appear in Isaiah 56-66, commonly identified with Trito-Isaiah. Following Isaiah 55, which functions as an introduction to Isaiah 56-66 by inviting the people to take part in YHWH's covenant conceived as a continuation of the Davidic covenant (cf. Stromberg, *Isaiah after Exile*, 77-79), Isaiah 56:1-8 states the conditions for the inclusion of foreigners and eunuchs in the Temple community. Overall, Isaiah 56-66 expects that the people will be righteous servants of YHWH (Blenkinsopp, "The Servant and the Servants"; cf. Stromberg, *Isaiah after Exile*, 79-82), insofar as the observe YHWH's covenant. These chapters also charge that the wicked in the community, i.e., those who do not observe the covenant, impede the full realization of the ideals of the book of Isaiah.

Isaiah 56:1-8 begins in vv. 1-3 with the prophet's report concerning YHWH's instructions for proper observance. The prophetic messenger formula in v. 1aα identifies the following material in vv. 1aβ-3 as YHWH's oracular instruction speech concerning proper observance. The speech presents a very general overview statement of YHWH's expectations in v. 1aβ–b, i.e., that the people should observe justice and do righteousness because YHWH's deliverance is near and YHWH's righteousness is about to be revealed. Such a statement anticipates the fulfillment of the ideals of the book of Isaiah, but it does little to specify what exactly YHWH requires. Verses 2–3 then specify the general statement. Verse 2 employs a beatitude to specify that "the happy man," i.e., the ideal Jew from the standpoint of our oracle, is one who observes the Shabbat and refrains from doing evil. Observance of the Shabbat is a fundamental command in Judaism; Genesis 1:1—2:3 presents the Shabbat as an inherent component of the divine creation of the world, and Exodus 31:12–17 identifies observance of the Shabbat as an "eternal covenant" or "covenant of creation" (bĕrît ʿôlām) between Israel and YHWH. Verse 3 then presents prophetic instruction concerning the inclusion of foreigners and eunuchs who observe these conditions in the form of rhetorical statements respectively made by the foreigner and eunuch that they will not be excluded from the community nor considered a withered tree. The withered tree of course serves as a metaphor for a person who cannot produce seed and therefore cannot produce offspring.

Isaiah 56:4–8 then presents the basis for the instruction in the form of the prophet's report of YHWH's instruction concerning the place of observant foreigners and eunuchs in the Temple community. The passage begins in vv. 4–5 the prophet's presentation of YHWH's oracle, introduced in v. 4aα$^{1-4}$ with the prophetic messenger formula. YHWH's oracular instruction speech in vv. 4aα^{5}–5 stipulates that eunuchs who observe Shabbat, choose what YHWH wants, and hold fast to YHWH's covenant will have a place in YHWH's house and walls, i.e., within YHWH's Temple. That place come in the form of a monument, Hebrew, yād, literally, "hand," that is better than sons and daughters and an eternal name. The term, yād, can be used to describe a monument, such as the sacred pillar that sometimes appears in Israelite Temples or a monument for a grave site (1 Sam 15:12; 2 Sam 18:18). It can also be used as a metaphor for the phallus, which is the organ of reproduction that is missing in the eunuchs (Isa 57:8). The combination of terms in this passage, Yad veShem, "Hand/Monument and Name," is employed as the name for the modern Holocaust Museum in Jerusalem to signify that those lost in the Shoah (Holocaust) would forever have a place among the people of Israel despite the fact that their murders deprived them of the chance to produce descendants for the future of Judaism.

Isaiah 56:6–8 then presents the prophet's statements concerning the place of foreigners in the Temple. Verse 6 speaks of the qualifications of such observant foreigners, initially v. 6a they are to serve YHWH, love the name of YHWH, and be servants to YHWH. Verse 6b specifies that they are to observe the Shabbat and hold fast to YHWH's covenant. Verses 7–8 then constitute the prophet's presentation of YHWH's oracular promise. YHWH's oracular statement in v. 7 indicates that YHWH will include them in the Temple by bringing them to the holy Temple mount, have them rejoice or worship in the house of prayer, and present their offerings. The basis for this promise is that YHWH's Temple is the Temple for all the peoples, i.e., it stands as the holy center of creation and Israel's worship there aids in securing all creation (Levenson, "The Temple and the World"). The expanded oracular formula in v. 8 identifies YHWH as the source of the oracle and the one who gathers the exiles of Israel. The quotation of YHWH's statement in v. 8b indicates that YHWH's efforts to gather in the diaspora are ongoing, i.e., there are more to come. Apparently, Isa 56:8 draws on images of YHWH's holy mountain in Isa 11:9, and it anticipates Isa 66:20. Isaiah 56:6–8 likewise points to the gathering of the exiles in Isa 11:12 and Isa 66:20 (Sweeney, "The Reconceptualization of the Davidic Covenant"; Sweeney, "Prophetic Exegesis in Isaiah 65–66"; Stromberg, *Isaiah after Exile*, 82–86).

BIBLIOGRAPHY

Blenkinsopp, Joseph. *Isaiah 56–66*. AB 19B. New York: Doubleday, 2003.
———. "The Servant and the Servants in Isaiah and the Formation of the Book." In *Writing and Reading the Scroll of Isaiah*, edited by C. C. Broyles and C. A. Evans, 155–75. VTSup 70. Leiden: Brill, 1997.
Duhm, Bernhard. *Das Buch Jesaia*. HKAT III/1. Göttingen: Vandenhoeck & Ruprecht, 1892.
Goldingay, John. *A Critical and Exegetical Commentary on Isaiah 56–66*. ICC. London: Bloomsbury, 2014.
Koenen, Klaus. *Ethik und Eschatologie in Tritojesajabuch*. WMANT 62. Neukirchen-Vluyn: Neukirchener, 1990.
Levenson, Jon D. "The Temple and the World." *Journal of Religion* 64 (1984) 275–98.
Odeberg, Hugo. *Trito-Isaiah (Isaiah 56–66): A Literary and Linguistic Analysis*. Uppsala universitets årsskrifte 1931, Theologi 1. Uppsala: Lundequistska, 1931.
Paul, Shalom M. *Isaiah 40–66: Translation and Commentary*. Eerdmans Critical Commentary. Grand Rapids: Eerdmans, 2012.
Pauritsch, Karl. *Die neue Gemeinde. G-tt sammel Ausgestossene und Arme (Jesaja 56–66). Die Botschaft des Tritojesaja*. AnBib 47. Rome: Pontificial Biblical Institute, 1971.
Polan, Gregory. *In the Ways of Justice towards Salvation: A Rhetorical Analysis of Isaiah 56–59*. American University Studies, Series VII, Theology and Religion 13. Frankfurt: Lang, 1986.
"Proselytes." In *Encyclopedia Judaica*, edited by C. Roth, 13:1182–1193. Jerusalem: Keter, 1971.

Rendtorff, Rolf. "Isaiah 56:1 as a Key to the Formation of the Book of Isaiah." In *Canon and Theology: Overtures to an Old Testament Theology*, 181–89. Overtures to Biblical Theology. Minneapolis: Fortress, 1993.

———. "The Composition of the Book of Isaiah." In : *Overtures to an Old Testament Theology*, 146–69. Overtures to Biblical Theology. Minneapolis: Fortress, 1993.

Schramm, Brooks. *The Opponents of Third Isaiah: Reconstructing the Cultic History of the Restoration*. JSOTSup 193. Sheffield: Sheffield Academic, 1995.

Sekine, Seizo. *Die Tritojesajanische Sammlung (Jes 56–66) redaktionsgeschichtlich untersucht*. BZAW 175. Berlin: de Gruyter, 1989.

Smith, P. A. *Rhetoric and Redaction in Trito-Isaiah: The Structure, Growth and Authorship of Isaiah 56–66*. VTSup 62. Leiden: Brill, 1995.

Steck, Odil Hannes. *Studien zu Tritojesaja*. BZAW 203. Berlin: de Gruyter, 1991.

Stromberg, Jacob. *Isaiah after Exile: The Author of Third Isaiah as Reader and Redactor of the Book*. Oxford: Oxford University Press, 2011.

Sweeney, Marvin A. *Isaiah 1–39, with an Introduction to Prophetic Literature*. FOTL 16. Grand Rapids: Eerdmans, 1996.

———. "Prophetic Exegesis in Isaiah 65–66." In *Form and Intertextuality in Prophetic and Apocalyptic Literature*, 46–62. FAT 45. Tübingen: Mohr Siebeck, 2005.

———. "The Reconceptualization of the Davidic Covenant in Isaiah." In *Reading Prophetic Books: Form, Intertextuality, and Reception in Prophetic and Post-Biblical Literature*, 94–113. FAT 89. Tübingen: Mohr Siebeck, 2014.

Wells, Roy D. "Isaiah as an Exponent of Torah: Isaiah 56:1–8." In *New Visions of Isaiah*, edited by R. F. Melugin and M. A. Sweeney, 140–55. JSOTSup 214. Sheffield: Sheffield Academic, 1996.

Westermann, Claus. *Isaiah 40–66: A Commentary*. Translated by David M. G. Stalker. OTL. Philadelphia: Westminster, 1969.

Van Winkle, Dwight W. "Isaiah 56:1–8." In *SBL 1997 Seminar Papers*, 234–52. Atlanta: Scholars, 1997.

———. "The Meaning of *yad wašem* in Isaiah LVI 5." *VT* 47 (1997) 378–85.

———. "An Inclusive Authoritative Text in Exclusive Communities." In *Writing and Reading the Scroll of Isaiah: Studies of an Interpretive Tradition*, edited by C. C. Broyles and C. A. Evans, 423–40. VTSup 70. Leiden: Brill, 1997.

8

Finding the Center
The Abimelech Account and the Gideon/Midianite Cycle as the Turning Point in Judges

—*John H. Hull, Jr.*

WHEN I FIRST ENCOUNTERED Professor John Hartley, he was a young man of thirty-one years. I was an undergraduate student only beginning to unravel the mysteries of studying the Hebrew Bible. Professor Hartley became my teacher, mentor, and guide. His example as a teacher, a scholar, and a friend has provided lifelong lessons for me, and for generations of his students. The following essay, which could serve as the literary setting section on Judges 9 in a commentary on Judges, is dedicated to Professor Hartley.

The Masoretic Text of the book of Judges includes a notation at the end of the book, indicating the book contains 618 verses. Going strictly by the number of verses, Judg 10:7 is the last verse in the first half of the book and Judges 10:8 begins the second half of the book.[1] These two verses are the middle verses of a passage (Judg 10:6–9) that narrates YHWH's anger against the Israelites for their evil-doing and the resulting eighteen-year

---

1. See *BHS* and *BHQ*, both based on the text of Codex Leningradensis.

Ammonite oppression—the elements that throughout the book of Judges indicate a new cycle.[2]

In one respect, this Jephthah/Ammonite cycle seems to represent a turning point. Though Jephthah eventually leads Israel in a defeat of the Ammonites, this does not result in the formulaic refrain "the land had quiet for forty years" as happened at the end of earlier oppressions by Aram, Moab, Canaan/Hazor, and Midian. But, as the following table of Israel's leaders and cycles of oppression indicates, in another important respect the real turning point comes slightly earlier—in the Gideon/Midianite cycle and, I shall argue, in the Abimelech narrative in particular.

Table 1. Oppressors and Leaders in Judges

Cycle of Oppression	Leader	Length of Time	Death and Burial
	Joshua		DBR (2:7–8)
Aramean Cycle		oppression: 8 years	
	Othniel	land was quiet 40 years	died
Moabite Cycle		oppression: 18 years	
	Ehud	land was quiet 80 years	died (retrospective)
	Shamgar		
Canaanite Cycle		oppression: 20 years	
	{Deborah		
	{Barak	land was quiet 40 years	
Midianite Cycle		oppression: 7 years	
	Gideon	land was quiet 40 years	DBR
Abimelech		ruled 3 years	
	Tola	judged 23 years	DBR
	Jair	judged 22 years	DBR
Ammonite Cycle		oppression: 18 years	
	Jephthah	judged 6 years	DBR

2. These elements appear in Judg 3:7–8 which introduce the Othniel/Aramean cycle (Judg 3:7–11); Judg 3:12–14 which introduce the Ehud/Moabite cycle (Judg 3:12–31); Judg 4:1–3 which introduce the Deborah-Baraq/Canaanite cycle (Judg 4:1—5:31); Judg 6:1–5 which introduces the Gideon/Midianite cycle (Judg 6:1—10:5); Judg 10:6–9 which introduce the Jephthah/Ammonite cycle (Judg 10:6–12:14); and Judg 13:1 which introduces the Samson/Philistine cycle which finds a partial ending in Judg 16:31 but, because Samson only begins to deliver Israel from the Philistines, continues through 1 Samuel 7.

	Ibzan	judged 7 years	DBR
	Elon	judged 10 years	DBR
	Abdon	judged 8 years	DBR
Philistine Cycle		oppression: 40 years	
	Samson	(judged 20 years during Philistine oppression)	DBR

Table 8.1

Two things stand out in this table. First, the leaders from Othniel through Gideon succeeded to the extent that "the land was quiet" for a considerable time after their delivering Israel from oppression. The standard period was forty years, doubled to eighty after Ehud's victory over Moab. Second, among the early leaders, a full death and burial report appears only for Joshua—and even then, it is repeating information found at the end of Joshua 24 prior to the beginning of Israelite leadership in the period of the Judges. We are told that "Othniel son of Kenaz died" (Judg 3:11), but no burial is mentioned. Ehud's death is reported only retrospectively, at the beginning of the next oppression cycle (Judg 4:1), and no mention of the deaths of Deborah or Baraq is made at all. But starting with Gideon's death and continuing through Samson, a full death and burial report is included for each of Israel's leaders (Abimelech not withstanding).

The pattern changes with the death of Gideon and the Abimelech reign in Shechem. Through the time of Gideon, leaders achieved, with YHWH's help, a lasting peace (at least until the next generation *did evil in the eyes of YHWH*). But following Abimelech, this did not happen. Instead, the chronological information is conveyed by a formulaic statement about the length of time each leader *judged* Israel.

This naturally raises the question, what caused the change? Was Gideon's leadership so faulty that no subsequent leader could achieve lasting peace? If that was so, then why did YHWH grant a forty-year period of quiet—even after Gideon's ill-conceived creation of the ephod in Ophrah?

GIDEON'S LEADERSHIP

Gideon's leadership gains a decidedly mixed evaluation. On the one hand, it is Gideon to whom the messenger of YHWH appeared when the Israelites had cried out for help against the Midianite oppression (Judg 6:11). It was Gideon who built an altar for YHWH and demolished the altar of Ba'al in his hometown of Ophrah (Judg 6:23–32). It was Gideon/Jerubbaʻ]al, under the influence of the spirit of YHWH, whose successful campaign against the Midianites resulted in routing the Midianite army and killing the two Midianite commanders as well as the two Midianite kings (Judg 7:1—8:21).

On the other hand, Gideon at times vacillates. He is slow to recognize the messenger of YHWH, hesitant to tear down the altar of Baʻal, finally doing so under cover of darkness. Then, despite receiving YHWH's spirit and successfully assembling an army of Israelites from throughout the tribes to fight against the Midianites, Gideon hesitates again, demanding a sign from God—and yet another sign when the first materializes (6:36–40). When he finally captures the kings, Zebah and Zalmunna, he attempts to pass off their execution to his inexperienced son, Jether. Only when the kings dare Gideon to do the deed himself—challenging his manhood—does he finally take responsibility for the task (Judg 8:18–21).

So it is no wonder biblical scholars have evaluated Gideon in so many different ways. Among recent commentators, Niditch rejects the analysis of Gideon as an imperfect leader, maintaining that the narrative portrays him as a great hero. She does not see the narrative as strongly pro-monarchic and argues "minor ambivalences about the nature of the hero" are typical of Judges and its tradition.[3] Schneider's analysis of Gideon is less favorable. As Gideon's military actions develop in the narrative, with little reference to the deity toward the end of the campaign, Schneider sees the absent deity as the narrator's attempt to highlight the problem of military leaders who forget their deity. She regards the Abimelech story as a possible indictment of Gideon in a narrative that does not take a stand on Gideon's actions.[4] Frolov, even more critical of Gideon, sees him as "clueless" about what it means to be a loyalist for YHWH. Frolov sees the narrative as pro-monarchic, contra Niditch, and regards Gideon's refusal to accept kingship, opting instead for retirement from public life, as a failure preventing him from establishing a stable line of succession.[5] The Abimelech debacle is a direct result.

The most notable leaders in Judges are portrayed with regard to their military deliverance of Israel from oppression. Commentators typically pay little attention to those leaders with only a brief report (Shamgar, Tola, Jair, Ibzan, Elon, Abdon). Gideon, however, is the one leader achieving not only military victory but also cult reform. Prior to starting his military campaign, Gideon tore down the altar of Baʻal in Ophrah belonging to his father and cut down the Asherah beside it. The command to tear down the altar given

---

3. Niditch, *Judges*, 103.
4. Schneider, *Judges*, 122.
5. Frolov, *Judges*, 196–97.

by YHWH (Judg 6:25) uses the verb הרס which also appears in the Elijah narratives in regard to altars of YHWH demolished by the Ba'al-worshiping opposition (1 Kgs 18:30; 19:10, 14). The narrator's report of the destruction, however, uses the verb נתץ, the same verb used in Deuteronomy 7:1–5 in which Moses conveys the divine command regarding Israel's expected behavior toward the cultic objects of the seven nations being displaced.

Attitude toward the cult is, of course, a hallmark of the narrative evaluation of Israel's leaders in the book of Kings. The language of cultic destruction used in Deuteronomy 7 repeats in Deut 12:3 and Judg 2:2. The verbs employed in 7:5—נתץ (tear down, break down), שבר (smash), גדע (hew down), and שרף באש (burn with fire)—also appear in Kings in connection with the work of the great cult reformers, Hezekiah (2 Kgs 18:4) and Josiah (2 Kgs 23:14–15), the exception being that the verb for removing the Asherah becomes כרת (cut down) rather than גדע (hew down). The same language is used at the end of Kings to describe the Babylonian actions in purging the YHWH cult elements from Jerusalem (2 Kgs 25:9–17). The Kings narrative portrays Jerusalem's destruction as an act of cult reform.

The description of Gideon's actions includes both נתץ and כרת (Judg 6:28), the two elements that characterize leadership in Kings. The Assyrian royal narratives relate actions of Assyrian leaders on two primary fronts: those regarding maintaining Assyrian temples and those regarding "foreign affairs," chiefly military campaigns. These two spheres are interrelated in Assyrian ideology and are also part of the Deuteronomistic principles of leadership. In the end, leaders not displaying the proper attitude toward the cult don't have successful military campaigns.

In addition to the question of cult reform, a second measure of Kings and other leaders in the Deuteronomistic sphere is how they stack up against the Instruction for the King in Deut 17:14–20.[6] Three things are prohibited to kings by this instruction: multiplication of weapons (horses), wives, and wealth (silver and gold). Gideon fails on the second count—he had many wives (Judg 8:30)—which explains his seventy sons. In addition, Gideon's actions regarding wealth are questionable. He collects gold from his fellow Israelites' war spoils without initially specifying that it was to be used in service of YHWH. Gideon then turned that large quantity of gold into an ephod which he set up in his home town, an episode reminiscent of Aaron's forming the golden calf (Exod 32:1–6). Golden earrings are the source for the molten cult object in both stories. While there may have been

---

6. Frolov, *Judges*, 196–97, suggests Gideon failed by not responding to the people's request that he rule, arguing that the principle of Deut 17:14–20 means Gideon should have immediately inquired of YHWH whether his rule was acceptable to YHWH.

some attempt to honor YHWH, both cultic actions are contrary to Deuteronomistic ideology.

In some respects, Gideon's leadership is reminiscent of Solomon's. Despite Solomon's early exemplary actions in building a house for YHWH, and asking for wisdom rather than wealth, at the end of his reign he had numerous wives and *pilagshim*,[7] many of whom were foreign. Furthermore, these wives "turned away his heart" from YHWH so that he followed other gods and built cultic installations for them (1 Kgs 11:1–8). Solomon also had many horses and chariots, and much of the tremendous quantity of gold he received went into his house rather than YHWH's (1 Kings 10). Although Solomon reigned for forty years, the account of his reign concludes with an explicit judgment by YHWH (1 Kgs 11:9–13) followed by Jeroboam revolting (11:14ff.). Things completely deteriorate following Solomon's death. Rehoboam fails to establish rule over the northern tribes—at Shechem, where Abimelech fell! Jeroboam takes over as king of the north, reigning from Shechem. Whatever its flaws, Solomon's reign had been the zenith of Israel's kingdom period in terms of both territory and temple. Following Solomon's time, Israel declines. Despite reformers like Jehu—who teamed up with Elijah to purge the Baʻal cult in the north and received positive affirmation from YHWH (2 Kgs 10:30)—as well as Hezekiah and Josiah in the south, the kingdom was gradually taken apart until the Babylonian "cult reform" of the temple.

While the parallels are not perfect, Gideon managed like Solomon to leave Israel with forty years of quiet. He multiplied wives—even if only a tenth the number that Solomon had—and displayed bad judgment with regard to the wealth taken from enemies. He abandoned his early positive cult actions in the golden ephod incident, just as Solomon abandoned exclusive worship of YHWH at the temple in favor of cultic installations for other gods. While Solomon had numerous *pilagshim* who led him astray, Gideon had just one *pilegesh*, but this resulted in the catastrophe that was Abimelech. And just as the nation fell apart at Shechem after Solomon's death, so Israel collapsed in chaos under Abimelech at Shechem.

GIDEON OF THE ABIEZRITES AND ABIMELECH OF SHECHEM

Abiezer was one of the clans of Manasseh who received its portion of land west of the Jordan (Josh 17:2).[8] Shechem is also named as a clan of the same

---

7. See the section on *pilegesh* below.
8. Schley, "Abiezer"; Frolov, *Judges*, 180.

tribe, which suggests a location for Ophrah in the vicinity of Shechem.⁹ These same traditions connect Shechem to Manasseh's tribal territory. Joseph's bones, brought from Egypt, were buried there (Josh 24:32). The burial tradition indicates Joseph's remains were buried in a plot of land Jacob had purchased from "the sons of Hamor, the father of Shechem" (Gen 33:19). Connecting Jacob to Hamor reminds us—as if we could forget—that Jacob's daughter Dinah was raped by Shechem, the son of Hamor (Gen 34:1-2). Subsequently Shechem requested that his father, Hamor, make the necessary arrangements to obtain Dinah as his wife. Dinah's brothers, outraged by Shechem's treatment of their sister, set in motion a ruse that allowed them to slaughter all Hamor's men. The Israelites seized the women and children of the place as well as all the livestock. Hamor is described as the Hivite prince of the land (Gen 34:2).

Thus, at one level, Shechem looks like an Israelite town with ties to Gideon's Abiezrite clan. On the other hand, there are echoes of a Canaanite (Hivite) past centered on enmity between the sons of Jacob and the sons of Hamor. Shechem would later become the first capital of the northern kingdom under Jeroboam I (1 Kgs 12:25) and was the site of Rehoboam's failed attempt to have the northern tribes acclaim him king (1 Kgs 12:1) after the death of his father, Solomon. Just as in Kings, Shechem is where the kingdom broke apart, so in Judges it is where a bloody war broke out between the Abimelech-led Shechemite lords and the remainder of the family of Gideon, the man who had first been asked by the Israelites to establish dynastic rule (Judg 8:22).

And so Abimelech, a Shechemite on his mother's side, uses a grant given by Shechemite lords from the temple of Baʻal-berith to hire men and take revenge on his Israelite half-brothers (Judg 9:4-5). The reform instituted by Gideon, who demolished the temple of Baʻal in Ophrah (Judg 6:27-32), has clearly failed. The narrative has already indicated that as soon as Gideon died, the Israelites returned to lust after the Baʻalim, adopting Baʻal-berith as a god (Judg 8:33).

At the very least, Abimelech's extermination of his brothers and attempt to establish a kingdom centered in Shechem demonstrates the breakdown of society in Israel's central hill country. Nevertheless, more is at stake than a simple struggle for power and succession among the descendants of Gideon. Abimelech's ruthless miscalculation has unleashed a firestorm. The links in the narrative to Baʻal-berith suggests that failing to rely on YHWH alone stands at the root of the breakdown.

---

9. Frolov, *Judges*, 180; cf. Hamilton, "Ophrah," who suggests the Jezreel valley.

The question about Abimelech's mother, and her Shechemite relatives, is whether or not they are Israelite. Are they, in fact, part of the remnant of foreign elements living in their midst as referenced in Judg 3:5–7? This states that Israelites were living among the Canaanite nations (including Hivites), taking their daughters as wives and worshiping their gods. The Abimelech narrative is ambiguous. Abimelech implies his brothers—the seventy sons of Gideon—are exercising rule over Shechem. But that alone does not mean that Shechem is an Israelite center. The past history of Shechem suggests it is a cultic center, but whether of a positive or negative nature is not known.

The connections to Hamor and the rape of Dinah have been discussed. Following Jacob's return from his time in Aram, he erected an altar at Shechem on land he purchased from Hamor's family (Gen 33:19). Events unfold quickly. The next chapter in Genesis contains the story of the rape of Dinah and the subsequent slaughter of the men of Shechem and Hamor. Immediately after that, Jacob received instructions from God to go to Bethel and establish an altar there (Gen 35:1). Jacob instructed his household to purge themselves of foreign gods in preparation for the move. As a result Jacob's family gave him "all the foreign gods that they had, and the rings that were in their ears; and Jacob hid them under the oak that was near Shechem" (Gen 35:4, NRSV).

Has this long-buried cache of foreign gods and earrings—buried under the oak near Shechem—come back to haunt Israel in the time of Gideon and Abimelech? Abimelech was made king by the lords of Shechem "by the oak of the pillar at Shechem" (Judg 9:6). The narrative blurs the lines with regard to Shechem. However, was the enmity between Abimelech and his seventy brothers about more than his mother's status as a *pilegesh*? Perhaps, Gideon, like Solomon, has married a foreigner—a Hivite in their midst. While never stated clearly, the narrative scatters hints throughout Judges that the breakdown at Shechem is not a simple struggle for leadership succession among Gideon's sons. As the relationship between Abimelech and the lords of Shechem deteriorates, and Gaal has moved in and received the backing of Shechem's leaders, Gaal asks "Who is Abimelech ... that we should serve him? Did not the son of Jerubbaʻal and Zebul his officer serve the men of Hamor father of Shechem?" (Judg 9:28). While Gaal's question is somewhat enigmatic, it is one more sign in the narrative linking Shechem to Hamor, that is, to a non-Israelite identity. Abimelech had relied on his mother and her Shechemite heritage to gain a foothold in the first place.

Following the death of Gideon, a notice of Israel's apostate behavior appears in the narrative which departs from the standard pattern. Unlike the more usual formulaic expressions of this behavior that lead to the established cycles of apostasy and oppression (Judg 3:7, 12; 4:1; 6:1; 10:6;

13:1), the notice in Judg 8:33 begins with a temporal *wayehi* clause that provides background information for the move of Abimelech to take over in Shechem (9:1).[10] While Judg 8:33 varies from the formulaic pattern of the other unit introductions, it does contain language that connects to the initial instance of the language in Judges. Judg 2:11–23 contains a summary of typical events that take place during the cyclical periods of apostasy, oppression and deliverance. And while the opening clause matches the formulaic Israel-did-evil language of the introductions (Judg 2:11), subsequent language in this passage references Israelite worship of the Ba'alim (2:11b–13) and lusting after other gods (2:17). This language, in particular the Hebrew root זנה, bears further investigation.

ZNH (זנה) IN JUDGES

The root זנה is frequently used in the Hebrew Bible to indicate Israel's failure in its relationship to God: *Israel abandoned the Lord and* זנה *after other gods*. Judges employs the term in this fashion in 2:17; 8:27, 33. The best translation for זנה אחרי has become a matter of some debate. Traditionally translators have used such phrases as *played the harlot after, whored after, prostituted themselves to*.[11] This language continues to be widely employed.[12] Sensitive to the work of Phyllis Bird, who argued against automatically connecting *ZNH* to prostitution, the NRSV uses *lusted after* to retain the sexual sense while avoiding a linkage to prostitution.[13]

Lipka has summarized the range of views concerning זנה.[14] Following Bird, Lipka argues we should not use phrases that automatically imply prostitution. "*Znh* is a . . . general and inclusive term, covering all instances of sexual intercourse in which there is an absence of a marriage bond between otherwise acceptable partners. This includes adultery, premarital sex by a daughter who is still part of her father's household, and the licit sexual activities of a prostitute."[15] Lipka indicates women are always the subject when *zonah* is used with a literal sense in the Hebrew Bible. Biblical *zonah-*

---

10. See Frolov, *Judges*, 169; Niccacci, *Syntax*, 48–52.

11. "Play the harlot" (RSV, NASB), "whored after" (ESV, KJV, ASV), "prostituted" (NIV).

12. Clines, זנה, *DCH* 3:121.

13. Bird, "To Play the Harlot, 76–79. Bird, "The Harlot as Heroine." CEB ("were unfaithful, following after other gods") and TNK ("went astray after other gods") also avoid the connection to prostitution.

14. Lipka, "Prostitution, Promiscuity."

15. Ibid., 1.

women "appear to be without husbands or male guardians, and thus they are not violating the rights or honor of any male by having sexual relations outside the bounds of marriage."[16]

In short, a *zonah*-woman stands outside the more conventional status of women bound to males (husbands or guardians). While such women were not engaged in activity against the legal rules of the society, these unconventional women were not always viewed with high regard. In Judges, we find both licit *zonah*-women and indictments of Israel for figuratively engaging in *zonah* after gods other than YHWH. The *zonah*-women may not be doing anything "illegal" but they certainly are held apart from the more conventional male-relational women. Jephthah the Gileadite was the son of a *zonah*-woman and Gilead. Gilead's sons born to his conventional wife drove away Jephthah the *ben-zonah* (Judg 11:1–3).

Samson took up with a *zonah*-woman in Gaza (16:1). Presumably both she and Samson's subsequent paramour, Delilah, were Philistines. While Delilah is not explicitly labeled a *zonah*-woman, she seems to have no relationship to a husband or male guardian. By linking the two stories together, the narrator encourages the reader to view Delilah in this light. The narrator of Judges indicts Israelites for serially straying after foreign gods, thus "doing evil in the eyes of the Lord." Such actions are labeled זנה in the summary introduction (2:17) and in the verses that precede the Abimelech story (8:27, 33). This linkage along with the Deuteronomistic injunction against taking up with the inhabitants of the land (Canaanites, Hittites, Hivites, Perizzites, Girgashites, Amorites, and Jebusites)[17] suggests Samson is violating at least the spirit of God's instruction if not the letter.

In the book of Judges, these Canaanite-like neighbors begin to fade as the group of forbidden nations. While still present in Judges 3:5, which lists six of them as the peoples among whom the Israelites lived, and in the naming of the third oppressor nation ("King Jabin of Canaan, who reigned in Hazor," Judg 4:2), these somewhat stylized nations start being replaced by nations and peoples who lived as near-neighbors. The oppressors in Judges become the Arameans, Moabites, Ammonites, Midianites, Philistines and their kings and lords. Sidonians, Amalekites and Maonites are also mentioned (Judg 10:12). So when Samson takes up with a string of Philistine women—two without the status of wife—it is no wonder the hero is unable

---

16. Ibid., 2. Riegner's (*Vanishing Hebrew Harlot*) argument that a זנה stem meaning "to engage in non-Yahwistic cultic practice" without reference to any sexual meaning is unconvincing.

17. The full list of seven nations is found Deut 7:1; Josh 3:10; 24:11. More often the list appears with six nations (omitting the Girgashites) and sometimes shorter combinations. Judg 3:5 omits the Girgashites.

ultimately to deliver Israel from Philistine oppression. He has violated more than his Nazirite vow. He has taken up with women of the near-neighbors.

The use of *ZNH* in Judges suggests that Judg 8:33 is appropriate as an introduction to a cycle of apostasy and oppression. The variation may be because this cycle is subordinate, part of the larger Midianite cycle, as argued extensively by Frolov.[18] However, I am unconvinced that the end of the section regarding Gideon's leadership is to be found at Judg 8:28, with Gideon's return to Ophrah and death there (Judg 8:29–32) as part of the narrative about Abimelech. Certainly there is an overlap, as Abimelech is first introduced in this section; nevertheless, the pattern of introducing of a subsequent ruling character in a previous period of rule is common enough in Kings. And the modified notice of apostasy (8:33) is sufficient to mark the shift to Abimelech, even if only as background to the narrative that takes up in Judg 9:1.[19]

PILEGESH (פילגש) IN JUDGES

The term *pilegesh* occurs twelve times in Judges: once in connection with Gideon who fathered Abimelech with his Shechemite *pilegesh* (8:31), and the remainder as part of the terrible and bloody story of the Levite and his *pilegesh* (Judges 19–20). While it is becoming increasingly common to translate the term as "secondary wife" rather than the older "concubine," uncertainty exists about the social conventions surrounding relationships between men and their concubines in the Hebrew Bible. Both Gideon's Shechemite *pilegesh* and the Levite's *pilegesh* are also referred to as אמה (Judg 9:18; 19:19). The term אמה means "female slave." Jotham, in his fiery speech against his half-brother, refers to Abimelech as the son of his father's slave woman. While the speech may be pejoratively skewed against Abimelech, it does suggest that Abimelech's mother was in a coerced relationship with Gideon. That the Levite of Judges 19 refers to his *pilegesh* with the same term in his conversation with his host in Gibeah, indicates that at least some *pilagshim* not only lacked the full status of a wife but were likely the enslaved property of their masters with whom they had children. On several occasions there were problems with sons and would-be successors sleeping with

---

18. Frolov, *Judges*, 156–75.
19. Niccacci, *Syntax*, 48–52.

their father's *pilagshim*,[20] a situation suggesting liberties that would never have been taken with wives.[21]

The status of Abimelech's mother raises the question of why Gideon had such a relationship. And it again raises the question, was Abimelech's mother an Israelite? If so, how did she fall into the status of slave woman? Is her status another hint that we should view the Shechemites as less than legitimate Israelites? Whatever the case prior to Abimelech's power grab in his mother's home town, the ruling class of Shechem quickly becomes lawless, ambushing and robbing all who passed by their city (Judg 9:25). Granted this is part of the evil spirit God sent to damage the relationship between the lords of Shechem and Abimelech (Judg 9:23), but is that all there is to it? Hints abound that danger lurks in Israel among the remnants of those nations that Israel has failed to eliminate, largely due to its apostasy. And when the Levite bypasses the Jebusite city in Judges 19 in order to find shelter in an Israelite town, the ensuing violence confirms that society has completely disintegrated in Israel.

IS ABIMELECH AMONG THE OPPRESSORS?

Finally, we turn to the question of whether to evaluate Abimelech as a leader of Israel or as one of the oppressors. Clearly he is a rogue son of Gideon whose actions result in terrible consequences for Shechem, for Abimelech himself, and for Israel during his reign. Judges is clear that Abimelech was made king (מלך) by the lords of Shechem. By contrast, the word used to describe Gideon's leadership and the request that he rule is משל (Judg 8:22–23). While it may be a thinly disguised substitution, the language of kingship is carefully avoided. And even Abimelech himself sticks with *mashal* when asking the lords of Shechem to select him as ruler instead of his brothers (9:2). This substitution is grounded in the narrative's careful use of kingship language. The oppressors in Judges are kings: Cushan-rishataim (king of Mesopotamia), Eglon (king of Moab), Jabin (king of Hazor/Canaan), Zebah and Zalmunna (kings of Midian), kings of the Ammonites who battle with Jephthah.[22] Only the Philistines, whose rulers are lords, deviate from the pattern. And so when Abimelech is made king by Shechem—but not by Israel—the not-so-subtle implication is that rather than being among the

---

20. Cf. Reuben with Bilhah (Gen 35:22), Abner with Saul's (2 Sam 3:7), and Absalom with David's (2 Sam 16:21–22; 20:3).

21. See Schneider, *Judges*, 129, 141.

22. For example, Judg 3:8, 12; 4:17, 23; 8:5; 11:12, among other references to these kings.

judges and deliverers who legitimately lead Israel, Abimelech is among the kings who oppress!

The refrain that recurs at the end of Judges, "there was no king in Israel" (Judg 17:6; 18:1; 19:1; 21:25) is somewhat ambiguous. It might explain the disintegration of the nation ("if only there was a king to set things right"), anticipate the monarch ("soon we shall have a king"), be ironic, or be some combination of these things. Nevertheless, the message up to this point has been clear. Kings oppress. Judges and deliverers exercise legitimate leadership.

And so Abimelech is among the oppressors, not the legitimate leaders of Israel. The variation in the introduction of this—perhaps—subordinate cycle is likely due to this oppression being different. Abimelech may be a "son of Hamor" the Hivite prince. He is also, however, a son of Gideon. His presence is a clear example of the consequences of "Canaanites among you" as detailed in Judg 2:11–23. Gideon may have been a cult reformer at the beginning, destroying his father's Baʻal altar and replacing it with a YHWH altar, but in the end he did not get YHWH-worship right. He erected a golden ephod in the same town where his father's Baʻal shrine once stood. And as soon as he died, Israel returned to its old ways.

Abimelech is in fact the cancer in the midst of the nation. He represents Israel's tendency to fall away, to allow the abuse of power, and to turn aside from its exclusive worship of YHWH. Gideon, like Solomon, represented both the high point of YHWH cultic activity and its rapid slide downward and backward, with Abimelech the consequence. Things are never the same in Judges after Abimelech. No more forty-year periods of quiet in the land. And there is more focus on leaders and their regular succession. Each dies and is buried. The narrative may have one eye on 1 Samuel and the transition to royal power found there. Yet it is still clear that such power must be exercised with caution. It must rely on YHWH and avoid the worship of Baʻalim and Asherot. And it must be Israelite: neither Canaanite nor Moabite nor any people non-exclusive to YHWH, may rule.

BIBLIOGRAPHY

Bird, Phyllis. "To Play the Harlot: An Inquiry into an Old Testament Metaphor." In *Gender and Difference in Ancient Israel*, edited by Peggy Day, 75–94. Minneapolis: Fortress, 1989.

———. "The Harlot as Heroine: Narrative Art and Social Presupposition in three Old Testament Texts." In *Missing Perons and Mistaken Identities: Women in the Hebrew Bible: A Reader,* edited by Alice Bach, 99–118. New York: Routledge, 1999.

Brenner, Athalya. "Women Frame the Book of Judges—How and Why?" In *Joshua and Judges*, edited by Athalya Brenner and Gale A. Yee, 125–38. Minneapolis: Fortress, 2013.

Frolov, Serge. *Judges*. FOTL. Grand Rapids: Eerdmans, 2013.

Hamilton, Jeffries M. "Ophrah." In *ABD* 5:28.

Lipka, Hilary. "Prostitution, Promiscuity, or Apostasy? The Offense, Its Consequences, and the Meaning of *z-n-h* in Leviticus 19:29." Paper presented at the annual meeting for the Society of Biblical Literature, San Diego, California, November 22–25, 2014.

Niccacci, Alviero. *The Syntax of the Verb in Classical Hebrew Prose*. Translated by W. G. E. Watson. JSOTSup 86. Sheffield: Sheffield Academic, 1990.

Niditch, Susan. *Judges: A Commentary*. OTL. Louisville: Westminster John Knox, 2008.

Riegner, Irene E. *The Vanishing Hebrew Harlot: The Adventures of the Hebrew Stem* זנה. Studies in Biblical Literature 73. New York: Lang, 2009.

Schley, D. G. "Abiezer." In *ABD* 1:15.

Schneider, Tammi J. *Judges*. Berit Olam. Collegeville, MN: Liturgical, 2000.

9

A Brief Introduction to Text-Criticism and Philology in 2 Samuel

—*Timothy D. Finlay*

TEXTUAL COMMENTARY HAD ITS beginnings in ancient scholia and other notes aimed at clarifying obscure words and correcting copies that had either added or dropped words from the works of authors such as Homer and Plato. In his Hexapla, the church father Origen saw to it that such scholarship was applied to the Greek versions of the Old Testament that were in circulation during late antiquity. Details of textual transmission remain prominent in modern-era biblical commentaries as writers frequently devote some attention to establishing either what the original text said, or how it should be translated. Certain biblical books, and sections of biblical books, have peculiarities that require special treatment. In Job, it is the frequency of rare or unique Hebrew words (*hapax legomena*) necessitating detailed philological analysis. In the portion of 2 Samuel discussed in Takamitsu Muraoka's article, the remarkable nature of the textual witnesses is what demands particular attention.

Modern textual criticism of the Hebrew scriptures begins with the Masoretic Text (MT) as a base. The MT is presented in hundreds of medieval manuscripts, chief among them Codex Aleppensis from the first half of the tenth century and Codex Leningradensis from 1008. Manuscripts found at Qumran in the Judean Desert, pre-dating these medieval codices by a millennium, usually confirm what the later Hebrew codices contain. Not uncommonly, however, the MT can be corrected to a likely earlier textual reading preserved in the Dead Sea Scrolls in support of readings preserved also in Hebrew copies of the Samaritan Pentateuch (SP) or of the Greek Septuagint (LXX). For the books of 1–2 Samuel a Qumran manuscript known as 4Q51 (4QSam[a]) plays a particularly important role for textual criticism, and in this essay Prof. Muraoka refers frequently to it, particularly in the light of readings from LXX.[1] LXX, however, has its own history of textual transmission and translation, a history that is particularly convoluted in the case of the four books of Kingdoms (known as 1 & 2 Samuel and 1 & 2 Kings respectively in most English Bibles, following the titles given in the Hebrew Bible).[2] Knowledge of this history is helpful for appreciating Prof. Muraoka's essay.

Earlier in the twentieth century Henry St. John Thackeray had suggested the following divisions of the book based partly on contents (the end of 1 Kingdoms is the death of Saul; and 3 Kingdoms 2:11 marks the death of David) and partly on stylistic grounds: α = 1 Kingdoms; ββ = 2 Kingdoms 1:1–11:1; βγ = 2 Kingdoms 11:2–3 Kingdoms 2:11; γγ = 3 Kingdoms 2:12–21:43; and γδ = 3 Kingdoms 22:1–4 Kingdoms 24:15.[3] Because βγ and γδ display many similarities to each other and differences from the rest of Kingdoms, Thackeray speculated that two different translators were involved.[4] But the relationship of the different sections of LXX Kingdoms is connected to the larger problem of the so-called *Kaige*-Theodotion recension. Dominique Barthélemy analyzed a Greek scroll of the Minor Prophets (Book of the Twelve) found in the Judean Desert at Naḥal Ḥever and observed that this scroll, dating from the first century CE, stood apart from some LXX manuscripts by consistently showing the Hebrew גם/וגם for the Greek καίγε (*kaige*). This, along with other traits,[5] led Barthélemy to argue that the Naḥal Ḥever scroll was representative of a large-scale recension of

---

1. The text of 4Q51 appears in Cross, Parry, and Ulrich, *Qumran Cave 4: XII*.

2. Trebolle and Torijano ("Behavior," 101–17) put it this way: "When referring to the books of Kings, textual criticism of the LXX and textual criticism of the Hebrew text cannot be done independently. Both are so closely linked that it may be asked whether a critical edition of LXX should incorporate Hebrew variants—attested in Qumran and medieval manuscripts or reflected by the Aramaic, Syriac, and Vulgate versions—that agree with *Kaige* or with OG readings" (117).

3. Barthélemy, whose work on "Kaige-Theodotion" revolutionized the study of the Greek text of Kingdoms, accepted Thackeray's divisions; however, other scholars usually place the division between ββ and βγ at 2 Kingdoms 9:13 instead of 11:1.

4. Thackeray, "Greek Translators of the Four Books of Kings," 262–78; Thackeray, "Appendix I," 114–15.

5. These traits include rendering distributive איש with ἀνήρ rather than with ἕκαστος; rendering אין with οὐκ ἔστιν instead of οὐκ ἦν; and rendering אנכי by ἐγώ εἰμι to distinguish it from אני, which is simply rendered ἐγώ.

the Greek Jewish Scriptures carried out as early as the first century BCE.[6] The recension became known as *Kaige-Theodotion* or simply the *kaige* recension (KG). Barthélemy then observed that the majority manuscripts of βγ and γδ display the characteristics of the *kaige* recension, but the so-called Lucianic manuscripts[7] of βγ and γδ differed far less than the other manuscripts from the characteristics found in α, ββ and γγ. He therefore advanced the theory that the Lucianic manuscripts (designated as L in the rest of this article) represented an earlier stage in the textual history of βγ and γδ, and that the majority manuscripts represented the later *kaige* recension.

Prof. Muraoka agrees that Barthélemy's "thesis on the recensional character of the Greek text as represented by the majority textual tradition as against the minority group of L in the sections βγ and γδ must be said to stand on a rather firm foundation."[8] But Muraoka has also pointed out numerous similarities between the Lucianic and the majority manuscripts in βγ and γδ that did not appear in α, ββ or γγ.[9] Muraoka therefore agrees with Thackeray that two translators (at least) were involved in Kingdoms, but agrees also with Barthélemy that the material in βγ and γδ underwent a recension. The differences between the positions of Thackeray, Barthélemy and Muraoka are represented in the following chart.

---

6. Barthélemy, *Devanciers d'Aquila*.

7. The miniscule manuscripts of the LXX numbered 19, 108, 82, 93 and 127 (corresponding to b', b, o, c2, and e2 in the Larger Cambridge Septuagint) display similar readings and are hypothesized to reflect a Lucianic recension.

8. Muraoka, "Greek Texts of Samuel-Kings," 29–30.

9. Ibid, 40–45.

Thackeray

α – ββ – γγ	βγ – γδ
A → s	A → u
B → t	B → v

Barthélemy

A → s	A → u	B rell
	B → v	
B → t	A → s	boc₂e₂
	B → t	

Muraoka

A → s	A → u	B rell
B → t	B → v	
	C → y	
	D → z	
C → w	A → s	boc₂e₂
D → x	B → t	
	C → y	
	D → z	

Figure 9.1

The concept here is that certain Hebrew phrases (C, D) get translated one way (w, x) in sections α, ββ and γγ, and another way (y, z) in βγ and γδ, thus providing the evidence for there having been two translators. The presence of certain other phrases (A, B) that are translated the same way (s, t) throughout Kingdoms in the Lucianic manuscripts but which are translated differently (u, v) in βγ and γδ in those manuscripts that are otherwise similar to other texts in the *kaige* recension provides evidence of their having been a *kaige* recension in those sections of Kingdoms.[10]

---

10. An additional point needs making. This type of scholarship seeks to establish the earliest text we can plausibly reconstruct, not necessarily the one that is authoritative for worshiping communities. The Eastern Orthodox churches, for example, would argue that certain church figures had the authority to correct and clarify earlier texts and that the texts represented in the 1935 first edition of the Stuttgart *Septuaginta* have

Prof. Muraoka's article in this Festschrift is the third in a series of articles discussing the relationships between the Kaige (KG), the Lucianic (L) readings, the Masoretic Text (MT) and 4QSam^a (4Q51) in 2 Samuel 11–1 Kings 1, and assumes the basic relationship between KG and L described above.[11] In these articles, Muraoka makes heavy use of philology, the study of language in historical written sources. The relative paucity of classical Hebrew texts other than the Hebrew Bible complicates the task of analyzing the meaning of rare words in the Hebrew Bible. Hence text-critical scholars of the Old Testament often compare the evidence from cognate languages such as Aramaic, Ugaritic, Akkadian and Arabic—a process known as comparative philology—in order to ascertain the meaning of a Hebrew word.[12] And judicious use of the Versions[13] requires a knowledge of translation technique, which again involves philological analysis. For example, William Wevers has shown, by examining translation technique, that each book of the Pentateuch in the LXX derives from a different translator.[14]

Several of the contributors to this Festschrift, as well as the honoree himself, have made considerable contributions to Hebrew philology. Muraoka's *Semantics in Ancient Hebrew Database* discusses each lexeme with regard to seven factors: root and comparative material, formal characteristics, syntagmatics, the Versions, lexical/semantic fields, exegesis and conclusion.[15] John Hartley examines these factors in *The Semantics of Ancient Hebrew Colour Lexemes*, a nearly 300-page monograph that treats evidence from more than a dozen ancient languages.[16] Another Festschrift

---

greater authority than the Lucianic manuscripts.

11. Muraoka, "Philological Notes I"; Muraoka, "Philological Notes II."

12. Barr, *Comparative Philology*, for a critique of some abuses of comparative philology. With appropriate constraint, it remains a legitimate discipline, however.

13. The Versions refer to early translations of the Hebrew Scriptures, such as LXX (Greek), Peshitta (Syriac), Targums (Aramaic) and Vulgate (Latin).

14. Wevers, *Text History of Greek Genesis*; ibid., *Text History of Greek Deuteronomy*; ibid, *Text History of Greek Numbers*; ibid, *Text History of Greek Leviticus*; ibid, *Text History of the Greek Exodus*. In *Text History of the Greek Exodus*, 117–46, Wevers argues for a possible sixth translator for Exodus 35–40.

15. Muraoka, *Semantics of Ancient Hebrew*, ix-xii.

16. Hartley, *Semantics of Hebrew Colour Lexemes*. Hartley's discussion of formal characteristics range over noun patterns, verbal stems and various affixes; his discussion of syntagmatics concentrates on the range of nouns that the color lexeme modifies but also considers what nouns are the subject of verbal cognates of the color lexeme; the versions and comparative philological evidence considered by Hartley include sources in Greek, Syriac, Aramaic, Latin, Akkadian, Amharic, Demotic, Ethiopian, Ge'ez, Hittite, Mandaic, Persian, Sabaean, Tigrinya and Ugaritic; and his discussion of semantics incorporates the anthropomorphic research done on the basic color terms used by native speakers in languages from several different language families. Exegesis of the

contributor, David Clines, is the chief editor of the *Dictionary of Classical Hebrew*, which at eight volumes is the largest lexicon of ancient Hebrew to date, including entries for words absent from the Hebrew Bible but found in the Dead Sea Scrolls or various Ancient Near Eastern Inscriptions.[17] The Festschrift articles not only by Muraoka, but also by Profs. Beuken and Williamson, remind us how much contemporary commentary writers—like their forebears from late antiquity—owe to the painstaking work of philologists and text critics.

BIBLIOGRAPHY

Barr, James. *Comparative Philology and the Text of the Old Testament: with Additions and Corrections*. Winona Lake, IN: Eisenbrauns, 1987 [orig. 1968].

Barthélemy, Dominique. *Les Devanciers d'Aquila*. VTSup 10. Leiden: Brill, 1963.

Clines, David J. A. *The Dictionary of Classical Hebrew*. Sheffield: Sheffield Academic, 1994–2011.

Cross, Frank M., et al., eds. *Qumran Cave 4: XII*. DJD XVII. Oxford: Clarendon, 2002.

Hartley, John E. *The Semantics of Ancient Hebrew Colour Lexemes*. ANES 33. Leuven: Peeters, 2010.

Muraoka, Takamitsu. "The Greek Texts of Samuel-Kings: Incomplete Translations or Recensional Activity?" *AbrN* 21 (1982–83) 29–30.

———. *Semantics of Ancient Hebrew*. AbrNSup 6. Leuven: Peeters, 1998.

———. "Philological Notes on the David—Bathsheba Story I." In *In the Shadow of Bezalel: Aramaic, Biblical and Ancient Near Eastern Studies in Honor of Bezalel Porten*, edited by Alejandro F. Botta, 289–304. Leiden: Brill, 2013.

———. "Philological Notes on the David—Bathsheba Story II." In *Sophia Paideia, Sapienze e Educazione (Sir I, 27): Miscellanea di studi offerte in honore del prof. Don Mario Cimosa*, edited by Gillian Bonney and Raphael Vincent, 89–113. Rome: LAS, 2012.

Septuaginta. Alfred Rahlfs, ed. Stuttgart: Württembergische Bibelanstatt, 1935.

Thackeray, Henry St. John. "The Greek Translators of the Four Books of Kings." *JTS* 8 (1906–7) 262–78.

———. "Appendix I: The Books of Reigns: Table Showing the Characteristics of the Later Translator." In *The Septuagint and Jewish Worship: A Study in Origins*, 114–15. The Schweich Lectures, 1920. London: Oxford University Press, 1921.

Trebolle Barrera, Julio, and Pablo Torijano. "The Behavior of the Hebrew Medieval Manuscripts and the Vulgate, Aramaic and Syriac Versions of 1–2 Kings vis-à-vis the Masoretic Text and the Greek Version." In *The Text of the Hebrew Bible: From the Rabbis to the Masoretes*, edited by Elvira Martin-Contreras and Lorena Miralles-Maciá, 101–17. JAJSup 13. Göttingen: Vandenhoeck & Ruprecht, 2014.

---

specific passages in which a color lexeme occurs is followed by a conclusion concerning the lexeme's basic meaning, together with common extended meanings by figures of speech.

17. Clines, *Dictionary of Classical Hebrew*.

Wevers, James W. *Text History of the Greek Genesis*. AAWGPHK³ 81. Göttingen: Vandenhoeck & Ruprect, 1974.
———. *Text History of the Greek Deuteronomy*. AAWGPHK³ 106. Göttingen: Vandenhoeck & Ruprecht, 1978.
———. *Text History of the Greek Numbers*. AAWGPHK³ 125. Göttingen: Vandenhoeck & Ruprecht, 1982.
———. *Text History of the Greek Leviticus*. AAWGPHK³ 153. Göttingen: Vandenhoeck & Ruprecht, 1986.
———. *Text History of the Greek Exodus*. AAWGPHK³ 192. Göttingen: Vandenhoeck & Ruprecht, 1992.

10

Nathan's Ominous and Tragic Prophecy Becoming a Reality

2 Samuel 13:23-39[1]

—Takamitsu Muraoka

We wish to continue our philological study of the pericope 2 Samuel 11–13, beginning with 13:23.[2]

23) *L*: Καὶ ἐγένετο εἰς μετὰ δύο ἔτη ἡμερῶν καὶ ἦσαν κείροντες τῷ Αβεσσαλωμ ἐν Βασελλασωρ τῇ παρὰ Γοφραιμ. καὶ ἐκάλεσεν Αβεσσαλωμ πάντας τοὺς υἱοὺς τοῦ βασιλέως.

KG[3]: Καὶ ἐγένετο εἰς διετηρίδα ἡμερῶν . . . ἐν Βελασωρ τῇ ἐχόμενα Εφραιμ

---

1. It is a great honour and pleasure to present this modest study to John, an old friend and colleague with fond memories of our joint work on the database of Ancient Hebrew semantics.

2. The earlier installments are "David—Bathsheba story I"; "David—Bathsheba story II"; "Like father, like son."

3. In presenting the KG text only those parts of a given verse which differ substantially from *L* are given. *L* stands for the proto-Lucianic or Antiochene version and quoted from the text edited by Marcos Fernándes and Busto Saiz (with the exception of dispensing with breathing marks and accents for indeclinable proper nouns), KG for the Kaige recension quoted from A. Rahlfs's *Handausgabe of the Septuagint*, and MT for the Masoretic text quoted from *Biblia Hebraica Stuttgartensia*.

Nathan's Ominous and Tragic Prophecy Becoming a Reality

MT: וַיְהִי לִשְׁנָתַיִם יָמִים וַיִּהְיוּ גֹזְזִים לְאַבְשָׁלוֹם בְּבַעַל חָצוֹר אֲשֶׁר עִם־אֶפְרָיִם וַיִּקְרָא אַבְשָׁלוֹם לְכָל־בְּנֵי הַמֶּלֶךְ

KG's διετηρίς is a hapax in the LXX and unattested prior to it, probably motivated by a desire to express a single word in Hebrew with a single Greek word. The preposition εἰς[4] combined with a numeral usually underlines a fairly large number or quantity: "to the tune of, as many as"—εἰσ ἑξακοσίας χιλιάδας πεζῶν "as many as 600,000 foot-soldiers" Exod 12:37; "thousands" ib. 20:6; "3,000" ib. 32:28; "20,100" Jdt 2:5; "6,000" 2 Macc 8:1; ὡς ἡ ἄμμος ἡ ἐπὶ τῆσ θαλάσσης εἰς πλῆθος "like the sand on the sea-beach for abundance" 2 Kgs 17:11. The prolonged tension between the two brothers, possibly the hesitation on the part of Absalom as well, is thus emphasised. Two long years Absalom brooded over the matter, and after his return to Jerusalem his father would not meet him as long.

Syntactic analysis of גֹזְזִים and κείροντες is uncertain. Both could be viewed as a substantivally used participle, "shearers"[5] or a component of the periphrastic construction. In terms of meaning there is hardly any difference. Absalom's utterance as given in the next verse—הִנֵּה־נָא גֹזְזִים לְעַבְדֶּךָ and Ἰδοὺ δὴ κείρουσιν τῷ δούλῳ σου—favours the latter analysis, which is particularly true of the Greek rendering.[6] Thus the plural ויהיו and ἦσαν are impersonal.

The spelling Γοφραιμ in L suggests a place-name rather than the tribal name, and at 1 Sam 13:17 we find a place known as עָפְרָה Γοφερα and as situated in the proximity of Bethel.[7]

In 4Q51[8] we miss כל of לְכָל־בְּנֵי הַמֶּלֶךְ וַיִּקְרָא אַבְשָׁלוֹם in MT. The editors of the Qumran fragment dismiss the particle as secondary,[9] but it provides a vital piece of information for the story about to be told.

---

4. The selection of this preposition by the translator, however, may have been conditioned by the Lamed in his Hebrew *Vorlage*.

5. So Paul Teng in his assignment, "Comparison between MT, LXX[B], and LXX[L]," a written work submitted for my course on the Septuagint given at Torch Trinity Graduate University in Seoul early in 2014.

6. Compare Vulg. *ut tonderentur oves Absalom* with Pesh. *hwaw ga:zo:ze: lavša:lo:m*, similarly Targum Jonathan.

7. On Hebrew ע as preserving a Proto-Semitic ġ, cf. Joüon—Muraoka, *Grammar*, § 5 *l*. The place-name עָפְרָה is probably related to עֹפֶר "young hart," which in turn is related to *ǵufur* "young of mountain-goat." On a discussion from the perspective of historical geography, cf. McCarter, *II Samuel*, 333.

8. This Qumran fragment is quoted from Cross et al., *Qumran Cave 4 XII*.

9. Ibid., 149.

24) L: καὶ ἦλθεν Αβεσσαλωμ πρὸς τὸν βασιλέα καὶ εἶπεν Ἰδοὺ δὴ κείρουσιν τῷ δούλῳ σου, πορευθήτω δὴ ὁ βασιλεὺς καὶ οἱ παῖδες αὐτοῦ πρὸς τὸν δοῦλον αὐτοῦ.

KG: . . μετὰ τοῦ δούλου σου.

MT: וַיָּבֹא אַבְשָׁלוֹם אֶל־הַמֶּלֶךְ וַיֹּאמֶר הִנֵּה־נָא גֹזְזִים לְעַבְדֶּךָ יֵלֶךְ־נָא הַמֶּלֶךְ וַעֲבָדָיו עִם־עַבְדֶּךָ

The difference in wording of the concluding prepositional phrase represents a difference in perspective: L, which agrees with אל in 4Q51,[10] pictures Absalom as being there serving as the master of ceremonies. The 4Q fragment, however, agrees with MT in reading עבדך, and not עבדו.[11] In the matter of indirect address Biblical Hebrew is not strictly consistent; see Gen 42:11 cited below.

The indirect address in πορευθήτω δὴ ὁ βασιλεὺς in lieu of πορεύθητί δή, reproducing the Hebrew usage, is part of the typically biblical, honorific discourse system.[12] So are τῷ δούλῳ σου . . . πρὸς τὸν δοῦλον αὐτοῦ in lieu of μοι . . . πρὸς ἐμέ. In Septuagint Greek we also find παῖς used in a similar fashion as in οὐκ εἰσὶν οἱ παῖδές σου κατάσκοποι (Gen 42:11), preceded by πάντες ἐσμὲν υἱοὶ ἑνὸς ἀνθρώπου εἰρηνικοί ἐσμεν. However, this certainly does not apply to ὁ βασιλεὺς καὶ οἱ παῖδες αὐτοῦ as said by Absalom. L makes here a deliberate distinction, which is retained in KG, though MT uses עֶבֶד in both cases.

The particle נא probably helped the translator of L to analyse ילך as volitive, hence πορευθήτω, an imperative.[13]

25) L: καὶ εἶπεν ὁ βασιλεὺς πρὸς Αβεσσαλωμ Μή, τέκνον, οὐ μὴ ἔλθωμεν πάντες ἡμεῖς, ὅπως μὴ βαρυνθῶμεν ἐπὶ σέ. καὶ κατεβιάζετο αὐτόν Αβεσσαλωμ, καὶ οὐκ ἐβούλετο ὁ βασιλεὺς τοῦ πορευθῆναι καὶ εὐλόγησεν αὐτόν.

KG: . . . Μὴ δή, υἱέ μου, μὴ πορευθῶμεν πάντες ἡμεῖς, καὶ οὐ μὴ καταβαρυνθῶμεν ἐπὶ σέ. καὶ ἐβιάσατο αὐτόν, καὶ οὐκ ἠθέλησεν τοῦ πορευθῆναι . . .

MT: וַיֹּאמֶר הַמֶּלֶךְ אֶל־אַבְשָׁלוֹם אַל־בְּנִי אַל־נָא נֵלֵךְ כֻּלָּנוּ וְלֹא נִכְבַּד עָלֶיךָ וַיִּפְרָץ־בּוֹ וְלֹא־אָבָה לָלֶכֶת וַיְבָרְכֵהוּ

10. A reading shared also by OL and Vulg., as noted by McCarter, *II Samuel*, 330.

11. See Cross et al., *Qumran Cave 4 XII*, 149.

12. In Japanese a student would say to his teacher: *Sensei wa gozonji desu ka?* (= Does the teacher know?), meaning "Do you know, sir?" An honorific form can be applied by a master to himself, e.g., εἴσελθε εἰς τὴν χαρὰν τοῦ κυρίου σου "Share the joy of your master" (Matt 25:21), which can be translated literally into Japanese.

13. Vulg. is more explicit with its *veniat, oro*.

Nathan's Ominous and Tragic Prophecy Becoming a Reality 169

Τέκνον, definable as *direct offspring*,[14] by itself does not imply tender age; see its application to a daughter about to marry at Tob 7:17G[I] (|| θύγατερ). One does not know the age of Isaac addressed by his father with Τί ἐστιν, τέκνον; Gen 22:7 (בני). By selecting this word, not KG's υἱός, L might be wanting to indicate parental affection on the part of David, who was likely suspicious of Absalom's design.[15]

The editors of 4Q51 restore the beginning of the line concerned as אל אבשלום אל נא [נלך, probably because they do not see extra space for accommodating MT's אל בני, which may have been inadvertently lost as a homoioarcton. In any case, אל נא is indispensable.

4Q51 reads נכביד for MT נִכְבַּד. In Biblical Hebrew Hiph. הִכְבִּיד occurs at Neh 5:15 in the sense of "to make oneself burdensome, to impose oneself." But there are other stative verbs whose Hiph. has an ingressive value, e.g., יָמֶיךָ יַאֲרִיכֻן "your days will become long" Exod 20:12.[16] In Mishnaic Hebrew we do find an intransitive הכביד in שְׂעָרוֹ הִכְבִּיד "his hair became too heavy" (*m. Naz.* 1:2).[17]

L's imperfect κατεβιάζετο "he kept urging him" is more expressive than KG's plain aorist, ἐβιάσατο, though the MT's *wayyiqtol* form is normally constative, just stating that something happened in the past. For MT's וַיִּפְרָץ, 4Q51 reads ויפצר. For the sense of *to urge* the latter lexeme is well established. Since, however, the root פרץ occurs three more times (vs. 27, 1 Sam 28:23, 2 Kgs 5:23) the MT reading in our passage can hardly be dismissed as a scribal error,[18] and at 1 Sam 28:23 LXX uses παραβιάζομαι to render it.

For the variation between L οὐκ ἐβούλετο and KG οὐκ ἠθέλησεν, see our remark elsewhere.[19] The genitive article τοῦ had become a mere marker of the infinitive in the manner of English *to*, and scarcely partitive in value, cf. οὐ βούλεται ἡ γυνὴ πορευθῆναι (Gen 24:5) and ἐὰν δὲ μὴ θέλῃ (!) ἡ γυνὴ πορευθῆναι vs. 8.

Εὐλόγησεν αὐτόν "he wished him well," or in colloquial English, "he said, 'Have a nice party!'"[20]

---

14. Muraoka, *Lexicon*, s.v. 1.

15. Cf. Fokkelman, *King David*, 116.

16. For more examples, see Joüon–Muraoka, *Grammar*, § 54 d.

17. Mentioned by M. Jastrow, *Dictionary*, I 607. The editors of 4Q51, Cross et al., *Qumran Cave 4 XII*, 149, regard the MT form as representing archaic orthography, but this is a question of Hebrew verb morphology. Cf. ὡς μὴ βαρὺς αὐτῷ γένοιτο (Josephus *Ant.* 7.175).

18. If that is what the editors of 4Q51 mean with their "metathesis" (p. 151).

19. "Like father, like son," on 2 Sam 13:9.

20. According to Bar Efrat, שמואל ב, 141, a parting salutation, but Absalom would not leave it at that.

26) L: καὶ εἶπεν Αβεσσαλωμ Ἀλλὰ πορευθήτω δὴ μετ' ἐμοῦ Αμνων ὁ ἀδελφός μου. καὶ εἶπεν ὁ βασιλεύς Ἵνα τί πορεύεται μετὰ σοῦ;

KG: . . . Καὶ εἰ μή, πορευθήτω δὴ μεθ' ἡμῶν Αμνων . . . καὶ εἶπεν αὐτῷ ὁ βασιλεύς Ἵνα τί πορευθῇ . . .;

MT: וַיֹּאמֶר אַבְשָׁלוֹם וָלֹא יֵלֶךְ־נָא אִתָּנוּ אַמְנוֹן אָחִי וַיֹּאמֶר לוֹ הַמֶּלֶךְ לָמָּה יֵלֵךְ עִמָּךְ

A clause-initial וָלֹא signalling dissent or protest occurs also at 2 Kgs 5:17 with an analogous construction, וָלֹא יֻתַּן־נָא,[21] where LXX is similar to KG in our passage—Καὶ εἰ μή, δοθήτω δή. . . . On the other hand, an analogous use of clause-initial ἀλλά occurs at Gen 34:31 οἱ δὲ εἶπαν Ἀλλ' ὡσεὶ πόρνῃ (הַכְזוֹנָה) χρήσονται τῇ ἀδελφῇ ἡμῶν; "but should they treat our sister like a whore?" Renehan[22] shows that this usage of ἀλλά is as old as Homer: ὣς ἐφάμην, ὁ δέ μ' αὐτίκ' ἀμειβόμενος προσέειπεν· 'ἀλλὰ μάλ' ὤφελλες Διί τ' ἄλλοισίν τε θεοῖσι ῥέξας ἱερὰ κάλ' ἀναβαινέμεν. "So I said. Then he answered me promptly: 'You should have first offered fair sacrifices to Zeus and other gods before your embarking'" (*Od.* 4.471).

At the start of the story we are told that Absalom had sent an invitation to *all* the princes. Conceivably the king knew that Amnon had turned it down.

Since there is no good reason for supposing that אתנו "with us" (MT) or אתי "with me" (L) followed אחי, where 4Q51 breaks off, one must conclude that 4Q51 had no form of את or עם with a suffix here, most probably a scribal error,[23] seeing עִמָּךְ at the end of the king's reply demands a corresponding prepositional adjunct.

Whether L's *Vorlage* actually read אתי or עמי, the selection of the singular form reveals the true, dark nature of Absalom's design and would have more easily aroused the father's suspicion, hence עמך, and not עמכם.

KG's subjunctive πορευθῇ is deliberative of value: "what should he go for, I wonder?" and is superior to L's πορεύεται.

27) L: καὶ κατεβιάσατο αὐτὸν Αβεσσαλωμ, καὶ ἐξαπέστειλε μετ' αὐτοῦ τὸν Αμνων καὶ πάντας τοὺς υἱοὺς τοῦ βασιλέως. καὶ ἐποίησεν Αβεσσαλωμ πότον κατὰ τὸν πότον τοῦ βασιλέως.

KG: καὶ ἐβιάσατο . . ., καὶ ἀπέστειλεν . . .

MT: וַיִּפְרָץ־בּוֹ אַבְשָׁלוֹם וַיִּשְׁלַח אִתּוֹ אֶת־אַמְנוֹן וְאֵת כָּל־בְּנֵי הַמֶּלֶךְ

21. Noted by Wellhausen, *Text*, 188, and approved by Driver, *Notes*, 302—"We . . . excellently." In two other cases mentioned by Wellhausen, namely Judg 6:13 and 2 Kgs 10:15, we do not find וָלֹא.

22. *Lexicographical Notes* I, 22.

23. The editors of 4Q51 prefer the shorter reading, offering no argument for their preference.

4Q51 is again shorter, leaving אתו out, a result of inadvertent haplography.[24]

The concluding sentence in both *L* and KG is reconstructable as ויעש אבשלום משתה כמשתה המלך, which is generally assumed to have dropped out through homoioteleuton (המלך ... המלך). Since the king did not give a credible excuse for his absence, κατὰ τὸν πότον τοῦ βασιλέως must refer to the quality of foods and wines served. The precise value of the article in τοῦ βασιλέως is uncertain. Is it generic, 'a royal gala' or anaphoric, a kind of party David would have thrown? Cp. וְהִנֵּה־לוֹ מִשְׁתֶּה בְּבֵיתוֹ כְּמִשְׁתֵּה הַמֶּלֶךְ 1) Sam 25:36), which is significantly rendered καὶ ἰδοὺ αὐτῷ πότος ἐν οἴκῳ αὐτοῦ ὡς πότος βασιλέως, indicating the first analysis as preferable.

28) *L*: καὶ ἐνετείλατο Αβεσσαλωμ τοῖς παισὶν αὐτοῦ λέγων Ἴδετε, ὅταν εὖ ἔχῃ ἡ καρδία Αμνων ἐν τῷ οἴνῳ καὶ ἐρῶ πρὸς ὑμᾶς Πατάξατε τὸν Αμνων καὶ θανατώσατε αὐτόν· μὴ φοβεῖσθε, ὅτι ἐγὼ ἐντέλλομαι ὑμῖν. κραταιοῦσθε καὶ γίνεσθε εἰς ἄνδρας δυνατούς.

KG: ... τοῖς παιδαρίοις αὐτοῦ λέγων Ἴδετε ὡς ἂν ἀγαθυνθῇ ... καὶ εἴπω πρὸς ὑμᾶς ... μὴ φοβηθῆτε, ὅτι οὐχὶ ἐγώ εἰμι ἐντέλλομαι ὑμῖν; ἀνδρίζεσθε καὶ γίνεσθε εἰς υἱοὺς δυνάμεως.

MT: וַיְצַו אַבְשָׁלוֹם אֶת־נְעָרָיו לֵאמֹר רְאוּ נָא כְּטוֹב לֵב־אַמְנוֹן בַּיַּיִן וְאָמַרְתִּי אֲלֵיכֶם הַכּוּ אֶת־אַמְנוֹן וַהֲמִתֶּם אֹתוֹ אַל־תִּירָאוּ הֲלוֹא כִּי אָנֹכִי צִוִּיתִי אֶתְכֶם חִזְקוּ וִהְיוּ לִבְנֵי־חָיִל

Although in Septuagint Greek we do find a couple of times an indicative form in a ὅταν-clause such as ὅταν εἰσήρχετο (Gen 38:9) and ὅταν ἐκαθίσαμεν (Exod 16:3), the subjunctive is the norm. Hence ἐρῶ (future) is not co-ordinate with ἔχῃ (subj.), but the preceding καί is a calque of the apodotic *waw* in Hebrew, introducing an apodosis.

Both *L* and KG, in translating Absalom's order with two aorist imperatives joined with καί, appear to have analysed the *waw* as merely co-ordinating, which cannot be reconciled with the second verb in the perfect,[25] whether we read הֲמִתֶּם with MT or a synonymous Polel form, מתתם, so 4Q51. In other words, המתם or מתתם is co-ordinate with אמרתם, and not with הכו; by executing the order expressed with one imperative, the target of the operation, Amnon's death, would have been achieved. The future θανατώσετε with καί preceding or not would represent more accurate analysis of Hebrew. The subtlety and nicety of this Biblical Hebrew verb

---

24. So the editors of the fragment, Cross et al., *Qumran Cave 4 XII*, 150.

25. The rendition of KG "dann sollt ihr ihn töten" in *Septuaginta Deutsch* corresponds rather with MT.

syntax²⁶ sometimes escaped our Greek translators.²⁷ See, e.g., Gen 27:45: עַד־שׁוּב אַף־אָחִיךָ מִמְּךָ וְשָׁכַח אֵת אֲשֶׁר־עָשִׂיתָ לּוֹ וְשָׁלַחְתִּי וּלְקַחְתִּיךָ מִשָּׁם > ἕως τοῦ ἀποστρέψαι τὸν θυμὸν καὶ τὴν ὀργὴν τοῦ ἀδελφοῦ σου ἀπὸ σοῦ καὶ ἐπιλάθηται ἃ πεποίηκας αὐτῷ, καὶ ἀποστείλασα μεταπέμψομαί σε ἐκεῖθεν. Here is involved also a lexical-semantic aspect. The Hif. verb הִכָּה "to smite, hit, attack" is often used in the sense of "to smite fatally," hence "to smite *and* kill,"²⁸ hence sometimes translated with verbs such as ἀποκτείνω, e.g., τοὺς παῖδας ἀπέκτειναν ἐν μαχαίραις· σωθεὶς δὲ ἐγὼ μόνος ἦλθον τοῦ ἀπαγγεῖλαί σοι (Job 1:15), ἐξωλεθρεύω, e.g., αὐτοὺς πάντας ἐξωλέθρευσαν ἐν στόματι ξίφους (Josh 11:14).²⁹ But the *w-qataltí* syntagm in our passage suggests the preceding imperative הַכּוּ is meant as "attack, strike." Thus the construction is distinct from a case such as

עָלַי וְהֶחֱזַקְתִּי בִּזְקָנוֹ וְהִכִּתִי וַהֲמִיתִיו וַיָּקָם > ... ἐπάταξα καὶ ἐθανάτωσα αὐτόν (1 Sam 17:35).

L μὴ φοβηθῆτε, ὅτι ἐγὼ ἐντέλλομαι presupposes the absence of הלוא as the reconstructed 4Q51, whereas KG μὴ φοβηθῆτε, ὅτι οὐχὶ ἐγώ εἰμι ἐντέλλομαι suggests כי הלוא, which does not seem to occur in the Hebrew Bible.

The present tense, ἐντέλλομαι, implies that the suffix conjugation צִוִּיתִי was justly assigned performative value.³⁰

The two co-ordinated imperatives at the end of the verse in MT are rendered in both Greek versions with two present imperatives. Absalom is telling them how to act during the operation just about to start. According to L with its preceding present imperative, μὴ φοβεῖσθε, he saw that his men were visibly terrified. However, KG's μὴ φοβηθῆτε is a generic, negative command: "Don't you ever get scared."

In בני חיל L, with ἄνδρας δυνατούς, rightly identified a construct phrase expressing a quality. Then the use of υἱός would have sounded odd, which apparently did not bother the KG reviser, who selected the standard equivalent. By his time this Hebraic use of υἱός must have become acceptable;³¹ cf. υἱοὶ ἀνομίας (Ps 88:23); υἱοὶ ἄνομοι (Isa 1:4 ‖ σπέρμα πονηρόν).

It might be too cynical to suggest that Absalom was implying that a generous reward for his lads was in store. Even so, had his father told him of

---

26. See Driver, *Treatise*, §116.

27. So also Vulg. *Percutite eum et interficite* and Syr. *mḥa:ʼu(h)y ... w-quṭlu(h)y*, but Tg. *qṭulu w-tiqṭlun*.

28. This comes to an awkward expression in Tg. cited in the preceding footnote.

29. For other synonymous Greek verbs used in LXX, see Muraoka, *Index*, 277c–278a s.v. נכה hi.

30. On the notion of *performative*, see Joüon–Muraoka, *Grammar*, §112 *f*.

31. Cf. Muraoka, *GELS*, s.v. *3.

God's reproach conveyed to him through Nathan: "You have slain Uriah … with the sword … with the sword of the Ammonites" (2 Sam 12:9)?

29) L: καὶ ἐποίησαν οἱ παῖδες Αβεσσαλωμ τῷ Αμνων καθὼσ ἐνετείλατο αὐτοῖς. καὶ ἀνέστησαν πάντες οἱ υἱοὶ τοῦ βασιλέως καὶ ἐπέβησαν ἕκαστος ἐπὶ τὴν ἡμίονον αὐτοῦ καὶ ἔφυγον.

KG: … τὰ παιδάρια … καθὰ ἐνετείλατο αὐτοῖς Αβεσσαλωμ. καὶ ἀνέστησαν … καὶ ἐπεκάθισαν ἀνήρ … καὶ ἔφυγαν.

MT: וַיַּעֲשׂוּ נַעֲרֵי אַבְשָׁלוֹם כַּאֲשֶׁר צִוָּה אַבְשָׁלוֹם וַיָּקֻמוּ כָּל־בְּנֵי הַמֶּלֶךְ וַיִּרְכְּבוּ אִישׁ עַל־פִּרְדּוֹ וַיָּנֻסוּ

L's ἐνετείλατο αὐτοῖς agrees with 4Q51, which, as reconstructed by Cross et al., reads כאשר צוה להם without being followed by אבשלום.[32]

The use of ἕκαστος in L with distributive value is more idiomatic than KG's Hebraising ἀνήρ.

30) L: καὶ ἐγένετο, ὡσ αὐτοὶ ἦσαν ἐν τῇ ὁδῷ καὶ ἡ ἀγγελία ἦλθε πρὸς Δαυιδ λεγόντων Πέπαικεν Αβεσσαλωμ πάντας τοὺς υἱοὺς τοῦ βασιλέως, καὶ οὐχ ὑπολέλειπται ἐν αὐτοῖς ἕως ἑνός.

KG: καὶ ἐγένετο αὐτῶν ὄντων ἐν τῇ ὁδῷ καὶ ἡ ἀκοὴ ἦλθεν πρὸς Δαυιδ λέγων Ἐπάταξεν … , καὶ οὐ κατελείφθη ἐξ αὐτῶν οὐδὲ εἷς.

MT: וַיְהִי הֵמָּה בַדֶּרֶךְ וְהַשְּׁמֻעָה בָאָה אֶל־דָּוִד לֵאמֹר הִכָּה אַבְשָׁלוֹם אֶת־כָּל־בְּנֵי הַמֶּלֶךְ וְלֹא־נוֹתַר מֵהֶם אֶחָד

The syntagm <we-X-qatal> indicates that the clause הַשְּׁמֻעָה … אֶחָד בָאָה is co-ordinate with the preceding הֵמָּה בַדֶּרֶךְ and that וַיְהִי at the start of the verse is resumed with וַיָּקֻמוּ in the next verse: when the king arose, they were on the way and the rumour had reached him. This subtlety of the Hebrew syntax is not evident in either Greek version; καὶ ἡ ἀγγελία/ἀκοὴ ἦλθε could conceivably reflect וַתָּבֹא השמעה with free reversal of word-order.

The use of the genitive absolute, αὐτῶν ὄντων, is noteworthy. In Septuagint Greek this syntactic feature that has no exact correspondent in Hebrew or Aramaic is a mark of idiomatic Greek and stylistic elegance.[33]

The use of perfects in L, πέπαικεν … ὑπολέλειπται forcefully and dramatically conveys the news as still hot and zooms in on the catastrophic situation that had arisen. By contrast, the aorists in KG—Ἐπάταξεν … , καὶ οὐ κατελείφθη—are prosaic.

---

32. The editors of 4Q51 (151) prefer the shorter form as superior, though it is not easy to decide in a case such as this which is text-critically superior.

33. In translated books it occurs a little over 200 times. See Soisalon-Soininen, *Studien zur Septuaginta-Syntax*, 181–88.

Cross et al.³⁴ restore the end of the verse as וְלוֹא נוֹתַר מֵהֶם עַד אֶחָד. The text thus restored agrees almost verbatim with *L*. Cf. Judg 4:16*L* οὐχ ὑπελείφθη ἕως ἑνός for לֹא נִשְׁאַר עַד אֶחָד. As a matter of fact they could have gone a step farther and restore בָּהֶם instead of מֵהֶם; cf. 2 Sam 17:12*L* οὐχ ὑπολειψόμεθα ἐν αὐτῷ καὶ ἐν πᾶσι ἀνδράσι τοῖς μετ' αὐτοῦ οὐδένα for MT לֹא־נוֹתַר בּוֹ וּבְכָל־הָאֲנָשִׁים אֲשֶׁר־אִתּוֹ גַּם־אֶחָד.

31) *L*: καὶ ἀνέστη ὁ βασιλεὺς καὶ διέρρηξε τὰ ἱμάτια αὐτοῦ καὶ ἐκάθισεν ἐπὶ τῆς γῆς, καὶ πάντες οἱ παῖδες αὐτοῦ παρειστήκεισαν αὐτῷ διερρωγότες τὰ ἱμάτια αὐτῶν.

KG: . . . καὶ ἐκοιμήθη ἐπὶ τὴν γῆν, καὶ πάντες οἱ παῖδες αὐτοῦ οἱ περιεστῶτες αὐτῷ διέρρηξαν . . .

MT: וַיָּקָם הַמֶּלֶךְ וַיִּקְרַע אֶת־בְּגָדָיו וַיִּשְׁכַּב אָרְצָה וְכָל־עֲבָדָיו נִצָּבִים קְרֻעֵי בְגָדִים.

Some ancient readers of the Greek Bible may not have been perceptive enough not to wonder aloud why the king was so busy, standing up and next moment sitting down. Of course it may have been easier to rend his clothes standing. Even so, neither יקם nor ἀνέστη necessarily implies that until then the king was seated. By saying ἀναστὰς κάθισον καὶ φάγε "Sit up and eat" for MT קוּם־נָא שְׁבָה וְאָכְלָה (Gen 27:19) Jacob was not imposing physical exercise on his aged, bed-ridden father. The verb קום in Qal is idiomatically used in conjunction with another verb in urging one to act or in signalling an action taken with clear, firm intent, and this usage was imposed on ἀνίστημι.³⁵

If *L*'s *Vorlage* read וישכב as in MT, its rendering with καθίζω "to sit, seat oneself" is rather striking. This is the sole instance of this Hebrew-Greek correspondence in the entire Greek Old Testament. The translator might be mentally emending the text to וַיֵּשֶׁב, finding the use of שכב here odd. *L* wants to say that David, devastated at the news, could not hold himself upright and collapsed on to the ground or floor. Earlier the translator, also in a description of the king's grief over the loss of another prince of his, translates ³⁶שכב with καθεύδω: ἐκάθευδεν ἐν σάκκῳ ἐπὶ τὴν γῆν "he was lying asleep in sackcloth on the floor" for 4Q51 וישכב בשק ארצה וישכב. KG opted for a standard translation equivalent of שכב.

MT's כָל־עֲבָדָיו נִצָּבִים קְרֻעֵי בְגָדִים is clearly intended as a circumstantial clause, hence the use of an active participle, נִצָּבִים; when David tore his clothes, his servants were standing there, already having torn their clothes. This analysis of the situation is reflected in *L*'s use of the pluperfect

---

34. 148, 151.

35. See Joüon–Muraoka, *Grammar*, §105 *e*; and Muraoka, *Lexicon*, s.v. II 1 c.

36. We have identified this as a key-root for this part of the royal history, 2 Samuel 11–13; Muraoka, "David–Bathsheba story I," 290.

παρεστείκησαν³⁷ and the circumstantial active perfect participle, διερρωγότες. By contrast, KG's indicative aorist διέρρηξαν can give the impression as if the servants had copied their master's action.

4Q51 has preserved only the last word of the clause as בגדיו, on the basis of which McCarter³⁸ reconstructs the clause as כול עבדיו קרעו איש בגדיו.

As against בגדיו in 4Q51 no possessive suffix is attached in the corresponding form in MT, whereas both Greek versions have the plural suffix, which may be retroverted to בגדיהם. On the other hand the bare form is attested in a description of this well-known gesture, e.g., 2 Kgs 18:37 וַיָּבֹא אֶלְיָקִים ... אֶל־חִזְקִיָּהוּ קְרוּעֵי בְגָדִים Καὶ εἰσῆλθεν Ελιακιμ ... πρὸς Εζεκιαν διερρηχότες τὰ ἱμάτια, similarly Isa 36:22 (ἐσχισμένοι) and Jer 41:5 (LXX 48:5 διερρηγμένοι). The possessive suffix in בגדיו is required by the restored, distributive איש.³⁹ The use of the active form, διερρωγότες, is to be noted. See also its variant spelling διερρηχότες quoted above; also quoted above, διερρηγμένοι and ἐσχισμένοι are rather middle than passive. In any case all these participles agree in gender, number, and case with their respective personal subject, and not with τὰ ἱμάτια and the like. In view of the grammatical concord, the Hebrew syntagm of these examples is distinct from what we find in a case such as וְהִנֵּה אִישׁ בָּא מִן־הַמַּחֲנֶה מֵעִם שָׁאוּל קְרֻעִים (2 Sam 1:2 ... καὶ τὰ ἱμάτια αὐτοῦ διερρωγότα [nom.pl.]), where the active participle agrees with בְּגָדָיו. In terms of Hebrew syntax, in our case (2 Sam 13.31) and the above-quoted analogous cases, the participles are passive in form only, so unlike at 2 Sam 1:2, and they signify a result arising from a past action,⁴⁰ and this has been captured at וְהִנֵּה לִקְרָאתוֹ חוּשַׁי הָאַרְכִּי קָרוּעַ כֻּתָּנְתּוֹ διερρηχώς (pf. act. masc. sg.) τὸν χιτῶνα αὐτοῦ 2 Sam 15:32, where the translator must have noticed that the participle is not feminine, קרועה, in agreement with כתנתו. Furthermore, this Hebrew syntagm is to be kept apart from a formally similar one as in הָרֹפֵא לִשְׁבוּרֵי לֵב "the One who heals the broken-hearted" (Ps 147:3) or נְשֻׂא פָנִים "in high favour" (2 Kgs 5:1), in which we have an elliptical construction; the first instance can be rewritten as הָרֹפֵא לַאֲשֶׁר לְבָם שָׁבוּר, the construct phrase constituting an adjectival

---

37. This does not, *pace* McCarter, *II Samuel*, 331, presuppose נצבו. Nor does OL *et astabant ei* ויצבו עליו; in Biblical Hebrew √יצב is not used in Qal, and √נצב is confined to Nifal perfect or participle. One could, however, restore ויתיצבו, which does not suit the context in terms of meaning: "and they took their position."

38. *II Samuel*, 331, followed by Cross et al., *Qumran Cave 4 XII*, 151, where they suspect a conflation of two forms: נצבים עליו and קרעו איש בגדיו.

39. Ulrich, *Qumran Text*, 129, suspects a false attraction to the same form earlier in the verse. Nor is L, *pace* Ulrich, ibid., "polished Greek."

40. See Joüon—Muraoka, *Grammar*, §121 o.

adjunct just as with a genuine adjective as in אִשָּׁה יְפַת־מַרְאֶה=אִשָּׁה אֲשֶׁר יָפָה מַרְאָה (Gen 12:11).[41]

32): καὶ ἀπεκρίθη Ιωναθαν υἱὸς Σαμαα ἀδελφοῦ Δαυιδ λέγων Μὴ εἰπάτω ὁ κύριός μου ὁ βασιλεύς, ὅτι πάντα τὰ παιδάρια οἱ υἱοὶ τοῦ βασιλέως τεθνήκασιν, διότι ἀλλ᾽ ἢ Αμνων μόνος τέθνηκεν· ὅτι ἐν ὀργῇ ἦν αὐτῷ Αβεσσαλωμ ἀφ᾽ ἧς ἡμέρας ἐταπείνωσεν Αμνων τὴν ἀδελφὴν αὐτοῦ Θαμαρ.

KG: καὶ ἀπεκρίθη Ιωναδαβ . . . Δαυιδ καὶ εἶπεν Μὴ . . . τοὺς υἱοὺς τοῦ βασιλέως ἐθανάτωσεν, ὅτι Αμνων μονώτατος ἀπέθανεν· ὅτι ἐπὶ στόματος Αβεσσαλωμ ἦν κείμενος ἀπὸ τῆς ἡμέρας, ἧς ἐταπείνωσεν Θημαρ τὴν ἀδελφὴν αὐτοῦ·

MT: וַיַּעַן יוֹנָדָב בֶּן־שִׁמְעָה אֲחִי־דָוִד וַיֹּאמֶר אַל־יֹאמַר אֲדֹנִי אֵת כָּל־הַנְּעָרִים בְּנֵי־הַמֶּלֶךְ הֵמִיתוּ כִּי־אַמְנוֹן לְבַדּוֹ מֵת כִּי־עַל־פִּי אַבְשָׁלוֹם הָיְתָה שׂוּמָה מִיּוֹם עַנֹּתוֹ אֵת תָּמָר אֲחֹתוֹ

As against KG's τοὺς υἱοὺς L with its οἱ υἱοὶ obviously did not see את in MT's את כל הנערים. One would not know whether L is trying to harmonise the text with the following clause with the intransitive מֵת.[42]

Τὰ παιδάρια in either Greek version is in the same case as the following appositional phrase: nominative in L and accusative in KG. True, נערים in this story are Absalom's lads (vss. 28 and 29),[43] but in the report that had reached the king one would expect to find נערי אבשלום rather than הנערים. Moreover, though the S-O-V word-order is attested even in prose, one looks in vain for an argument for placing the subject up front here. In any event, KG with the singular ἐθανάτωσεν precludes such an analysis. Let us also note that both Greek versions are consistent in vs. 28 and 29 in their respective choice of παῖς (L) and παιδάριον (KG), whilst here L uses παιδάριον, nominative, obviously referring to the princes, and KG with πάντα τὰ παιδάρια has no conceivable argument for underlining that *all* of Absalom's lads had a hand in the slaughter *en masse*.

---

41. On this question, see Muraoka, "Status constructus" and Joüon—Muraoka, *Grammar*, § 129 *i-ia*.

42. In 4Q51 הנערים opens a new line (30) and the preceding line ends with a long lacuna which ends with כי, and the editors (p. 150) do not think that there is enough space to accommodate את כול. It depends, however, on how to restore the end of line 29. They restore אדוני המלך כי and account for the absence in MT of כי המלך as haplography (p. 151), by which they must mean the MT inadvertently dropped the two words. Seeing that 4Q51 and L do not always accord with each other, one could restore כי את כול without המלך.

43. As pointed out by McCarter, *II Samuel*, 331.

L διότι ἀλλ' ἢ Αμνων suggests כי אם אמנון; a haplography leading to the loss of אם due to the immediately following אמנון? See vs. 33.

Much ink has been spilled in the past over the concluding causal clause of the verse, עַל־פִּי אַבְשָׁלוֹם שׂוּמָה in particular. How did L arrive at 'Absalom was in anger at him [= Amnon]'? The feminine היתה cannot be reconciled with ἦν, and שׂוּמָה, also feminine, has not been translated. Significantly 4Q51 reads היה, the first word of a line (31).[44] The lacuna at the end of its preceding line is reconstructed, in part, by the editors of 4Q51 as כי על אף אבשלום.[45] Similarly McCarter[46] writes that part of the Hebrew text originally read על אף אבשלום היתה, referring to 2 Kgs 24:20 (= Jer 52:3) as a similar idiomatic expression, where we read כִּי עַל־אַף יְהוָה הָיְתָה בִירוּשָׁלַם וּבִיהוּדָה. In the text so reconstructed, however, one misses an indication as to who the target of Absalom's anger was.[47] Nor is it clear what or who the subject of היתה is. Neither his text nor the one as restored by Cross et al. can mean "Absalom was in anger." The clause cited from 2 Kgs 24, certainly identical in form, is just as vague[48]; the preposition ־בּ is best interpreted as indicating enmity. Its Septuagint rendition, ἐπὶ τὸν θυμὸν κυρίου ἦν ἐπὶ Ιερουσαλημ καὶ ἐν τῷ Ιουδα, is not very helpful, either. What is the subject of ἦν?[49] In the last analysis it appears to me that L is a product of despair, a contextually informed free rendering; על אף אבשלום היה/היתה cannot be made to mean "Absalom was in anger." The original Hebrew text may have read על פי אבשלום היה/היתה, which may have meant "he [= Amnon] / she [= Tamar] had always been (laid) on Absalom's lips," most probably in his private chamber, behind the closed doors. We would then have to reconstruct the Hebrew text שום היה and שומה היתה respectively. Important to note here is the masculine nominative participle κείμενος. KG then would represent על פי אבשלום היה שום.[50]

---

44. This 4Q51 reading is not mentioned by Fokkelman, *King David*, 119, and his translation "the killing of Amnon had become necessary in Absalom's eyes" does not convince.

45. I find the editors' comment incomprehensible: "אף is the subject of the verb [= היה] in 4QSama," for which they would have to delete על.

46. *II Samuel*, 331.

47. McCarter, ib., also mentions Jer 32:31 כִּי עַל־אַפִּי וְעַל־חֲמָתִי הָיְתָה לִּי הָעִיר הַזֹּאת לְמִן־הַיּוֹם אֲשֶׁר בָּנוּ אוֹתָהּ וְעַד הַיּוֹם הַזֶּה לַהֲסִירָהּ מֵעַל פָּנָי, which, however, is distinct with the grammatical subject of הָיְתָה explicitly mentioned. A third reference mentioned, Jer 24:3, must be a typo.

48. An attempt by König, *Syntax*, § 323 g, to resolve the issue does not convince.

49. The translation in *Septuaginta Deutsch* is hardly justifiable: "(weil) der Herr zornig war über Jerusalem und Juda." At Jer 52:3 only the Hexaplaric version is preserved and it is not significantly different from what we find at 2 Kgs 24:20.

50. Ulrich, *Qumran Text*, 103, plausibly argues for Amnon being the subject of היה.

33) L: καὶ νῦν μὴ θέσθω ὁ κύριός μου ὁ βασιλεὺς ἐπὶ τὴν καρδίαν αὐτοῦ ῥῆμα λέγων Πάντες οἱ υἱοὶ τοῦ βασιλέως τεθνήκασιν, ὅτι ἀλλ᾽ ἢ Αμνων μόνος τέθνηκεν.

KG: καὶ νῦν ὁ κύριός μου ὁ βασιλεὺς μὴ θέσθω . . . ἀπέθαναν, ὅτι ἀλλ᾽ ἢ Αμνων μονώτατος ἀπέθανεν.

MT: וְעַתָּה אַל־יָשֵׂם אֲדֹנִי הַמֶּלֶךְ אֶל־לִבּוֹ דָּבָר לֵאמֹר כָּל־בְּנֵי הַמֶּלֶךְ מֵתוּ כִּי־אִם־אַמְנוֹן לְבַדּוֹ מֵת

One cannot think of any reason why KG should deliberately depart from the word-order as we find in MT and put the subject up front. His *Vorlage* may have read so.[51]

As in the preceding verse, the wording בני המלך instead of בניך is due to the use of אדני המלך as a substitute for the second person singular.

34) L: καὶ ἀπέδρα Αβεσσαλωμ. καὶ ἀνέβη τὸ παιδάριον ὁ σκοπὸς καὶ ἦρε τοὺς ὀφθαλμοὺς αὐτοῦ καὶ εἶδε· ἰδοὺ λαὸς πολὺς πορευόμενος τὴν ὁδὸν τὴν Σωραιμ ὄπισθεν αὐτοῦ ἐκ μέρους τοῦ ὄρους ἐν τῇ καταβάσει· καὶ παρεγένετο ὁ σκοπὸς καὶ ἀπήγγειλε τῷ βασιλεῖ καὶ εἶπεν Ὁρῶν ἑώρακα ἄνδρας ἐκ τῆς ὁδοῦ τῆς Σωραιμ ἐκ μέρους τοῦ ὄρους.

KG: . . . καὶ ἦρεν τὸ παιδάριον ὁ σκοπὸς τοὺς ὀφθαλμοὺς αὐτοῦ καὶ εἶδεν καὶ ἰδοὺ . . . ἐν τῇ ὁδῷ ὄπισθεν αὐτοῦ ἐκ πλευρᾶς τοῦ ὄρους . . . εἶπεν Ἄνδρας ἑώρακα ἐκ τῆς ὁδοῦ τῆς Ωρωνην ἐκ μέρους τοῦ ὄρους.

MT: וַיִּבְרַח אַבְשָׁלוֹם וַיִּשָּׂא הַנַּעַר הַצֹּפֶה אֶת־עֵינָו [עֵינָיו] וַיַּרְא וְהִנֵּה עַם־רַב הֹלְכִים מִדֶּרֶךְ אַחֲרָיו מִצַּד הָהָר

It is often said the first clause is out of place here, dislocated from vs. 37. However, at this point in the story, Absalom is still the principal player, and it is not unreasonable to record here his flight following the success of the operation engineered by him. Besides, at vs. 37 the wording is ואבשלום בָּרַח and positioned at the start of the verse so that it is presented as a circumstantial clause and background information over what had taken place earlier. Exactly the same information is repeated in vs. 38 in the same word-order and again up front. In these two verses ויברח אבשלום would be out of place.

L's ἀνέβη is unique. The remaining letters of 4Q51 leave no space for it, say ויעל. Only Jacob of Edessa's (7th cent.) Syriac translation from a Greek version attests to it.[52]

The concluding part of MT starting with מִדֶּרֶךְ is generally agreed to be hopefully amiss. Even though 4Q51 has not preserved the text after

---

51. Vulg., Syr., and Tg. all accord with MT.
52. *wa-sleq ṭalya*: etc.; see Salvesen, *Jacob of Edessa*, 127.

נֵעַר ה[א וַיִּשׁ], its editors allow for ample space which would accommodate what lies behind both Greek versions after τὴν ὁδὸν (L) or τῇ ὁδῷ (KG). A widely accepted emendation largely based on the Greek versions reads: הֹלְכִים בְּדֶרֶךְ חֹרֹנַיִם בַּמּוֹרָד וַיָּבֹא הַצֹּפֶה וַיַּגֵּד לַמֶּלֶךְ וַיֹּאמֶר אֲנָשִׁים רָאִיתִי מִדֶּרֶךְ חֹרֹנִים מִצַּד הָהָר.[53]

It is difficult to choose between a *Vorlage* that can be reconstructed for L and KG respectively: רָאֹה רָאִיתִי אֲנָשִׁים and אנשים ראיתי. With the former the watchman is trying to impress on the king that he actually saw the crowd, and is not reporting a mere hearsay.

35) L: καὶ εἶπεν Ιωναθαν πρὸς τὸν βασιλέα Ἰδοὺ οἱ υἱοὶ τοῦ βασιλέως παραγεγόνασιν· κατὰ τὸ ῥῆμα τοῦ δούλου σου, οὕτως γέγονεν.

KG: καὶ εἶπεν Ιωναδαβ . . . πάρεισιν· κατὰ τὸν λόγον τοῦ δούλου σου, οὕτως ἐγένετο.

MT: וַיֹּאמֶר יוֹנָדָב אֶל־הַמֶּלֶךְ הִנֵּה בְנֵי־הַמֶּלֶךְ בָּאוּ כִּדְבַר עַבְדְּךָ כֵּן הָיָה

36) L: καὶ ἐγένετο ἐν τῷ συντελέσαι αὐτὸν λαλοῦντα, καὶ ἰδοὺ οἱ υἱοὶ τοῦ βασιλέως παραγεγόνασιν καὶ ἦραν τὴν φωνὴν αὐτῶν καὶ ἔκλαυσαν, καὶ ὁ βασιλεὺς καὶ πάντες οἱ παῖδες αὐτοῦ ἔκλαυσαν κλαυθμὸν μέγαν σφόδρα.

KG: καὶ ἐγένετο ἡνίκα συνετέλεσεν λαλῶν, καὶ ἰδοὺ οἱ υἱοὶ τοῦ βασιλέως ἦλθαν καὶ ἐπῆραν . . ., καί γε ὁ βασιλεὺς . . .

MT: וַיְהִי כְּכַלֹּתוֹ לְדַבֵּר וְהִנֵּה בְנֵי־הַמֶּלֶךְ בָּאוּ וַיִּשְׂאוּ קוֹלָם וַיִּבְכּוּ וְגַם־הַמֶּלֶךְ וְכָל־עֲבָדָיו בָּכוּ בְּכִי גָּדוֹל מְאֹד

In the description of the arrival of the survived princes L retains here παραγεγόνασιν for בָּאוּ, whereas KG alters πάρεισιν to ἦλθαν, a sensible alteration, since in vs. 35 the present tense was more fitting in a direct speech with the princes in sight, whereas here we have a narrative from the author's perspective.

37) L: καὶ Αβεσσαλωμ ἀπέδρα, καὶ ἐπορεύθη πρὸς Θολμι υἱὸν Αμιουδ βασιλέα Γεδσουρ εἰς γῆν Χαλααμα. καὶ ἐπένθησεν ὁ βασιλεὺς ἐπὶ τοὺς υἱοὺς αὐτοῦ πάσας τὰς ἡμέρας.

KG: . . . ἔφυγεν καὶ ἐπορεύθη πρὸς Θολμαι υἱὸν Εμιουδ βασιλέα Γεσσειρ εἰς γῆν Χαλααμα. καὶ ἐπένθησεν ὁ βασιλεὺς Δαυιδ ἐπὶ τὸν υἱὸν αὐτοῦ πάσας τὰς ἡμέρας.

MT: וְאַבְשָׁלוֹם בָּרַח וַיֵּלֶךְ אֶל־תַּלְמַי בֶּן־עַמִּיחוּר [עַמִּיחוּד] מֶלֶךְ גְּשׁוּר וַיִּתְאַבֵּל עַל־בְּנוֹ כָּל־הַיָּמִים

---

53. Cf. Wellhausen, *Text*, 189f.; Driver, *Notes*, 304; McCarter, *II Samuel* 332.

The editors of 4Q51[54] convincingly reconstruct בא]רץ חי[לם, which accords with L. Moreover, their reconstructed text allows space for either המלך or דוד, but not for both as in KG. On the other hand, one expects a subject to be mentioned for ויתאבל.

According to McCarter[55] the first clause is out of place. However, Absalom's flight is a vital piece of information in the unfolding story. The syntagm <we—x—qatal> indicates the clause as circumstantial, co-ordinate with the following וַיֵּלֶךְ; the information on his destination forms the background for the following וַיִּתְאַבֵּל, which latter takes up the narrative broken with וַיִּבְכּוּ . . . מְאֹד (vs. 36).

L's ἐπὶ τοὺς υἱοὺς αὐτοῦ "over his sons" as against KG's ἐπὶ τὸν υἱὸν αὐτοῦ (= MT) is rather difficult to comprehend. Even if the translator supposedly misread בנו as בְּנָו, the plural form is harsh here.

In Classical Greek the verb πενθέω "to mourn, bemoan" takes an accusative. So in Septuagint Greek except here, Hos 10:5 ἐπ' αὐτόν (MT עליו), 2 Chr 35:24 ἐπὶ Ἰωσιάν) (על יאשיהו), and ἐπ' αὐτούς 1 Macc 2:39. It looks like a Hebraism.[56]

38) L: Καὶ Αβεσσαλωμ ἔφυγε καὶ ἀπῆλθεν εἰς Γεσσειρ· καὶ ἦν ἐκεῖ ἔτη τρία.

KG: Καὶ Αβεσσαλωμ ἀπέδρα καὶ ἐπορεύθη εἰς Γεδσουρ . . .

MT: וַאַבְשָׁלוֹם בָּרַח וַיֵּלֶךְ גְּשׁוּר וַיְהִי־שָׁם שָׁלֹשׁ שָׁנִים

In the light of the first half of vs. 37 the repetition of ואבשלום ברח here appears to be superfluous. Driver[57] surmises an inadvertent transposition, restoring the original sequence as 37b, 37a, 38b, 39. There is no difficulty with what we have identified above as a circumstantial clause in 37a following the mainline clause (37b).

For the first time L uses φεύγω in a description of Absalom's flight, whereas earlier in vss. 34 and 37 we read ἀπέδρα < ἀποτρέχω; MT is consistent with ברח. In vss. 34 and 37 his destination is given, but here with "and he was there three years" one learns that he had found a temporary, safe haven there, φυγαδεῖον.[58]

39) L: καὶ ἐκόπασε τὸ πνεῦμα τοῦ βασιλέως Δαυιδ τοῦ ἐξελθεῖν ἐπὶ Αβεσσαλωμ, ὅτι παρεκλήθη ὑπὲρ Αμνων τοῦ υἱοῦ αὐτοῦ τοῦ τεθνηκότος.

---

54. Cross et al., *Qumran Cave 4 XII*, 148, 150.
55. *II Samuel*, 332: "This intelligence is out of place."
56. Cf. Rev 18:11 πενθοῦσιν ἐπ' αὐτήν.
57. *Notes*, 305.
58. In his *Jewish Antiquities* 7.180, Josephus, apparently referring to this verse, writes: φεύγει . . . τρισὶν ὅλοις ἔτεσι αὐτῷ καταμένει "he escaped . . . stayed with him three whole years." One does not know why KG varied ἔφυγεν to ἀπέδρα.

KG: καὶ ἐκόπασεν τὸ πνεῦμα τοῦ βασιλέως τοῦ ἐξελθεῖν ὀπίσω Αβεσσαλωμ, ὅτι παρεκλήθη ἐπὶ Αμνων ὅτι ἀπέθανεν.

MT: וַתְּכַל דָּוִד הַמֶּלֶךְ לָצֵאת אֶל־אַבְשָׁלוֹם כִּי־נִחַם עַל־אַמְנוֹן כִּי־מֵת.

Since the days of Wellhausen[59] the grammatical difficulty of the feminine verb followed by דוד has been resolved by emending the latter to read רוח in line with the Greek versions, and now this reading has been confirmed by 4Q51, which reads רו[ח המלך.

There is, however, no agreement as to what the first clause means. On one hand, Driver[60] offers "And *the spirit of the king longed* to go forth unto Absalom." On the other hand, McCarter[61] renders: "King [David's] enthusiasm for marching out against [him] was spent," for David was no longer angry at his son and was in a reconciling mood.[62] Bar-Efrat[63] objects to such a view by drawing attention to the hard efforts Joab would have to invest in the sequel with a view to reconciliation between David and Absalom as well as the king's persistent refusal to grant an audience to his son as long as two years. Bar-Efrat adheres to the Masoretic pointing of the verb as Piel, suggesting the meaning "to finish," in fact, however, in an intransitive sense of "to come to an end."[64] This is lexicographically unlikely. The sense preferred by Bar-Efrat is that of the verb in Qal. Furthermore, by saying that David's anger ceased to burn within him, Bar-Efrat is contradicting himself.

How about ἐκόπασε(ν) here? In my *Lexicon* I have defined one of its two senses as "to lose strength and cease to be troublesome or noxious."[65] A paradigmatic study shows that its grammatical subjects are flood water (Gen 8:1, 8, 11), the sea with its mounting waves (Jonah 1:11, 12), fire (Num 11:2), and destructive plague (Num 16:48, 50, Ps 105:30). The infuriated vigour of the king can be easily added to this list. Hence "the king had no mental strength left to go after Absalom" is suggested as a possible translation.[66]

---

59. *Text*, 223; Ulrich, *Qumran Text*, 190–91, 223.

60. *Notes*, 305, f.n. 4, where his literal rendering reads: *"failed* with longing to ..."

61. *II Samuel*, 335. For his "against" McCarter finds support in L's ἐπί. Whether or not KG's ὀπίσω suggests that his *Vorlage* read אַחֲרֵי, the Greek preposition, like English *to go after*, can signify a hostile intent, cf. Gen 44:4 ἐπιδιώξον ὀπίσω (אַחֲרֵי) τῶν ἀνθρώπων.

62. Id., 344.

63. שמואל ב, 148. He also justly points out that the Hebrew verb here denotes intense desire in Qal, but not in Piel as in MT.

64. Ibid.: מלשון כילה = גמר, פסק.

65. *Lexicon*, s.v. 1.

66. *Septuaginta Deutsch* is problematic with its "... hörte allmählich auf, Abessalom zu zürnen," although a second sense of the verb is "to cease, stop what one is doing,"

παρεκλήθη ὑπὲρ Αμνων cannot possibly mean that someone called on the king to offer him condolences, but rather David, who had already mourned over the decease of his beloved, eldest son (vs. 37), slowly came to terms with the reality, Amnon's death. His fatherly sixth sense must have alarmed him over what Absalom had up his sleeve, and yet he sent Amnon away. The father ought to have got down to the bottom of this tragic fratricide. The culprit's rape and violation of a half-sister was also a virtual fratricide. The root cause can be traced to David's murder of Uriah, which Nathan prophesied was bound to unleash a series of tragic deaths and murders in the royal family.[67] The first casualty was the innocent, infantile prince.

BIBLIOGRAPHY

Bar-Efrat, Shimon. שמואל ב:מקרא לישראל. Jerusalem: Magnes, 1996.
Cross, Frank Moore. et al. *Qumran Cave 4 XII. DJD XVII.* Oxford: Clarendon, 2005.
Driver, Samuel R. *A Treatise on the Use of the Tenses in Hebrew and some other Syntactical Questions.* 3rd edition. Oxford: Clarendon, 1892.
———. *Notes on the Hebrew Text and the Topography of the Books of Samuel.* Second edition. Oxford: Clarendon, 1913.
Fernández Marcos, Natalio and José R. Busto Saiz. *El texto antioqueño de la biblia griega, I 1–2 Samuel.* Madrid: Instituto de Filología, 1989.
Fokkelman, Jan. *King David: Narrative Art and Poetry in the Books of Samuel.* Vol. 1. Assen: Van Gorcum, 1981.
Jastrow, Marcus. *A Dictionary of the Targumim, the Talmud Babli and Yerushalmi, and the Midrashic Literature.* New York: Pardes, 1950.
Joüon, Paul, and T. Muraoka. *A Grammar of Biblical Hebrew.* Subsidia biblica 27. Rome: Pontifical Biblical Institute Press, 22006.
König, Friedrich E. *Historisch-comparative Syntax der hebräischen Sprache.* Leipzig: Hinrichs, 1897.
McCarter, P. Kyle, Jr. *II Samuel.* AB 9. Garden City, NY: Doubleday 1984.
Muraoka, Takamitsu. "The Status Constructus of Adjectives in Biblical Hebrew." *VT* 27 (1977) 375–80.
———. *A Greek-English Lexicon of the Septuagint.* Leuven: Peeters, 2009.
———. *A Greek-Hebrew / Aramaic Two-way Index to the Septuagint.* Leuven: Peeters, 2010.
———. "Philological Notes on the David–Bathsheba Story I." In *In the Shadow of Bezalel: Aramaic, Biblical, and Ancient Near Eastern Studies in Honor of Bezalel*

---

but that is not what כלה Piel means; its meaning is rather "to complete what one started doing" as in 1Chr 27:24 הֵחֵל לִמְנוֹת וְלֹא כִלָּה, fittingly rendered ἤρξατο ἀριθμεῖν ἐν τῷ λαῷ καὶ οὐ συνετέλεσεν. David had not even started a pursuit. Thus Vulg. "*cessavitque . . . persequi*" is questionable. And whence "zürnen"? MT's וַתְּכַל is also questionable.

67. Cf. Bar Efrat, שמואל ב, 140: "The murder is a punishment for Amnon ... and likewise a punishment for David for his murder of Uriah ... , just as the rape of Tamar was a punishment for David for his deed against Bathsheba."

Porten, edited by Alejandro F. Botta, 289–304. Culture and History of the Ancient Near East 60. Leiden: Brill, 2013.

———. "Philological notes on the David-Bathsheba story II." In *Sophia—Paideia. Sapienza e Educazione (Sir 1,27). Miscellanea di studi offerti in onore del prof. Don Mario Cimosa*, edited by Gillian Bonney and Raphael Vincent, 89–113. Nuova biblioteca di scienze religiose 34. Rome: LAS, 2012.

———. "Καθὼς ὁ πατήρ, καὶ ὁ υἱός 'Like father, like son." Forthcoming.

Renehan, Robert. *Greek Lexicographical Notes: A Critical Supplement to the Greek-English Lexicon of Liddell-Scott-Jones*. Untersuchungen zur Antike und zu ihrem Nachleben 45. Göttingen: Vandenhoek & Ruprecht, 1975.

Salvesen, Alison. *The Books of Samuel in the Syriac Version of Jacob of Edessa*. Monographs of the Peshitta Institute of Leiden 10. Leiden: Brill, 1999.

Soisalon-Soininen, Ilmari. *Studien zur Septuaginta-Syntax: Zu seinem 70. Geburtstag am 4. Juni 1987*. Edited by Annneli Aejmelaeus und Raija Sollamo. Annales Academiæ Scientiarum Fennicæ B/237. Helsinki: Suomalainen Tiedeakatemia, 1987.

Ulrich, Eugene. *The Qumran Text of Samuel and Josephus*. Harvard Semitic Monographs 19. Missoula, MT: Scholars, 1978.

Wellhausen, Julius. *Der Text der Bücher Samuelis untersucht*. Göttingen: Vandenhoek & Ruprecht, 1871.

11

Commenting on the Unknown
Reflections on Isaiah 9:7–20

—H. G. M. Williamson

As a distinguished commentator, John Hartley knows well the problem that inevitably occurs from time to time in a text from over two thousand years ago, namely that despite our best endeavours we have reluctantly to conclude that in the current state of affairs we simply do not know what it means. The reasons vary. The Hebrew text may be corrupt, or, if not, using words or idioms whose meaning is no longer known. Perhaps there are historical allusions to events of which we have no independent knowledge, so that we cannot contextualize the incident or understand how the allusion relates to the broader course of events. Or there may be images or figures of speech which are no longer transparent. The question then presents itself to the commentator: what should I say?

In my observation of many commentaries from many periods and written for many levels of readership, the least likely answer is simply to confess ignorance. Popular commentaries for pastors or lay people perhaps have a mistaken belief that the perspicacity of Scripture seems incompatible with confessing ignorance, or (speaking cynically) that it is unlikely to boost sales in the market if preachers cannot find the short-cuts to sermon preparation that they are looking for. More scholarly commentaries may list a number of possibilities that have been entertained by previous commentators and then choose what seems to them the most attractive. I have no wish to be critical: I have done this myself from time to time! But is it responsible?

ISAIAH 9:7-20 AS A WHOLE

Isaiah 9:7-20 [NRSV 8-21] provides a good test case.[1] As the text stands, it is a poem in three clear stanzas. The refrain in vv. 11, 16, and 20 [NRSV 12, 17 and 21] makes that clear, and the stanzas are of roughly (though not exactly) equal length. The same refrain appears also in 5:25 and 10:4, on which basis many commentators draw other material into what they consider to have been the 'original' poem as well. In my view, as I have tried to explain in detail elsewhere, this is a mistake so far as 10:4 (and hence 10:1-4 as a possible stanza) is concerned.[2] In 5:25, however, the refrain is followed by what seems to be a convincing candidate for the concluding stanza of our poem. The stanzas in ch. 9 move from one degree of partial judgment to another, and now in Isa 5:26-29 we have a stanza where the predominant tenses move into the imperfect (hence future) with the description of a final judgment from which recovery is not possible.[3]

However, no repeat of the refrain is needed after that as the refrain indicated that more is yet to come, whereas by the time 5:29 has been reached such an expression would no longer be meaningful. This being so, the refrain in 5:25 must have originally followed another stanza, most of which is now lost to us. The immediately preceding line perhaps speaks of an earthquake.[4] If the fourth stanza did end that way, it would suit very well as a form of judgment approaching a final climax, but it must be admitted

---

1. Throughout this article I shall refer to the verse number in the Hebrew text. Where different, the verse numbers in the NRSV are given in square brackets following.

2. See "'An Initial Problem.'"

3. There has been much debate, especially in older commentaries, as to whether 9:7-20 should be construed as descriptive of past judgments, preceding the final one that is yet to come (5:26-29), or whether they too are all prophetic. Either view has some explaining to do in terms of the verbal "tenses" used, but in my opinion, which seems now to be shared by the large majority of other commentaries, the former is far more probable. The brief comments by H. Donner, *Israel unter den Völkern*, 70, have been decisive: the number of *waw*-consecutive forms should be the overriding consideration; see previously K. Fullerton, "Isaiah's Earliest Prophecy." For fuller documentation of recent scholars in agreement with this, see A. Lange, *Vom prophetischen Wort*, 76-77 n. 61.

4. So correctly Kissane, "The Qumrân Text of Isaiah," though I cannot accept his wider suggestion that the earthquake is referred to in every stanza.

that this is speculative and that not all commentators by any means follow this brief summary.[5]

These additional speculations are not strictly germane here, as I shall discuss only 9:7–20 [NRSV 9:8–21], where there is little controversy in terms of composition. In my opinion, half a line (or a line and a half) has probably been lost by accident from the middle of v. 8 [NRSV 9]. It is difficult to account satisfactorily for the state of the Hebrew text in any other way.[6] Also, v. 14 [NRSV 15] is a later explanatory addition and therefore not part of the earliest form of the text.[7]

The three stanzas that we have in Isa 9 seem to plot a plausible story of increasing sin and increasing judgment. In the first stanza the accusation is the one so familiar in Isaiah of human hubris ("pride and arrogance of mind"; see especially, for instance, 2:10–19) expressed by a dogged determination to overcome damage already caused in some unstated way. The punishment has been the incursion of foreign enemies: "Aram from the east and Philistines from the west."[8] The second stanza, vv. 12–16 [NRSV 13–17], observes that military defeat leads to the disappearance of normal civic leadership and hence the breakdown of civil society, a scenario which finds a close parallel in the opening verses of ch. 3. Consequently, the Lord will no longer show the clemency and compassion otherwise expected. The third stanza, vv. 17–20 [NRSV 18–21], takes us even farther into the mire as,

---

5. For a fuller discussion of these matters with some attention also to alternative views, see my *Commentary on Isaiah 1–27*, 1: *Isaiah 1–5*, 400–403.

6. For full justification for this conclusion (which is shared by a number of others), see the forthcoming second volume of my ICC commentary. For the moment we may note that *wyd'w* has no object clause or phrase and so has to be taken as an absolute— "and they will know/experience (it)"—rather than the expected "and they will know x/that . . . ." Then the second line simply says "in pride and in greatness (insolence) of heart, saying." As it stands, this should qualify "and they will know," but this is not convincing, because it combines a good quality (acknowledgment of God's word) with a sinful response (pride) in a manner hard to understand. Also, in a poem of generally regular length lines, this second line is suspiciously short. RV renders "And all the people shall know, even Ephraim and the inhabitant of Samaria, that say in pride and in stoutness of heart, ..." This tacitly moves *l'mr* to the start of the second line (see Rashi and Kimḥi), which of course is indefensible. There is a good possibility that 1QIsa^a's reading of *wyr'w* "and they did evil," represents an earlier reading, but even then it does not eliminate all the difficulties. Other proposed emendations are less plausible.

7. This conclusion is very widely agreed by commentators, but see especially Goshen-Gottstein, "Hebrew Syntax."

8. I take the name "Rezin" in verse 10 [NRSV 11] to be a later historicizing gloss; MT's "adversaries of Rezin" is clearly unsuitable in the context; with others I emend to *ṣryw*. The close parallelism with *'ybyw* in the second half of the line strongly supports this, and the emendation has the further advantage of restoring the expected line-length.

with the image in particular of destructive fire, we find the country becoming embroiled in internecine strife. The description of cannibalism, whether intended as literal or metaphorical, employs extremely severe language. It is thus reasonable to conclude that these three stanzas (regardless of what others may once have followed them) form a coherent sequence. Furthermore, the underlying thought on several points closely coincides with what we know elsewhere of Isaiah's outlook. So far, with allowance made for some difficult textual issues and details of exegetical uncertainty, the picture is therefore reasonably clear.

Problems arise, however, at the point where we begin to try to pin down more precisely the apparent historical allusions included within the passage. Without being exhaustive, I shall simply indicate the range of opinions which these allusions have evoked in previous scholarship.

The First Stanza

In the first stanza, particular attention has fallen on v. 11 [NRSV 12]. Following a more general indication in the previous verse that God has raised up adversaries against them, it continues, "Aram from the east and Philistines from the west, and they have devoured Israel in a single gulp."

Commentators have suggested a variety of possible historical settings to account for this reference. Kaiser thinks that the Philistines devouring the northern kingdom might refer to Saul's wars (1 Sam. 13–14; 31), though the collaboration with Aram reminds him of the period of the Judean king Joash (I presume he is referring to 2 Kgs 12:18, not 12:8, as printed).[9] Wildberger suggests that the reference is to events in the relatively distant past (he mentions the ninth century in particular),[10] and Donner similarly finds here a general reference to incursions in the ninth and the first half of the eighth centuries,[11] whereas most commentators think of the more recent past. Blenkinsopp, for instance, thinks of the reign of Jeroboam II or just after, mainly by association with the implications of Amos 1:3-5 and 6:13-14 (see too 2 Kgs 14:22-29).[12] Procksch makes a strong case for the last years of Menaḥem's reign; unlike his successor Pekah, who adopted an anti-Assyrian stance and so allied with Aram to invade Judah, Menaḥem appears to have

---

9. Kaiser, *Das Buch*, 212–13.

10. Wildberger, *Jesaja 1–12*, 212; see too Fey, *Amos und Jesaja*, 98; Vollmer, *Rückblicke und Motive*, 139.

11. Donner, *Israel unter den Völkern*, 71–72; see too Skinner, *Isaiah, Chapters i-xxxix*, 79; Fohrer, *Jesaja 1–23*, 148; Høgenhaven, *Gott und Volk*, 46.

12. Blenkinsopp, *Isaiah 1–39*, 218.

been a loyal vassal who could well have roused the ire of Aram and the Philistines at the time when they were putting together an anti-Assyrian coalition.[13] No independent evidence exists that they invaded Israel at this time, however, as Gray observes[14] (and he is right to note that the reference to a Philistine attack during Ahaz's reign in 2 Chr 28:18,[15] to which he might have added defeat at the hands of Aram in v. 5, relates to Judah, not Israel, as the present passage demands). This is not a fatal objection, as the books of Kings omit other significant campaigns involving the northern kingdom, the battle of Qarqar during Ahab's reign being the classic example. Those who retain the MT "enemies of Rezin" are, of course, obliged to date these events later, following the Assyrian conquest of Aram and Israel; Beuken, for instance, refers specifically to the first Assyrian conquest in 732 bce.[16] Sweeney, it should be noted, makes this the starting point for his bold hypothesis that the series of events referred to throughout 9:7–20 should be taken in reverse chronological order, albeit all in connection with the Syro-Ephraimite war.[17] Thus he links Isa 9:11 [NRSV Isa 9:12] to the period following the Assyrian invasion, vv. 12–16 [NRSV 13–17] to the removal of Israelite leadership following Hoshea's coup, and vv. 17–20 [NRSV 18–21] to the pre-war period. As ingenious as Sweeney's links to references and allusions in the Assyrian annals are, the analysis is implausible. Not only does its starting point depend on what I regard as an unlikely text but the whole flow flies in the face of everything that the reader would expect, especially if familiar with the closest formal parallel, namely Amos 4:6–12, which seems to move resolutely from the past to the present.

Given the wide diversity of opinions, it is difficult to reach any firm conclusion (even more so if the poem was originally directed at the whole of Israel and not just the northern kingdom). The most satisfying result rhetorically would be to find here a reference to the closing years of Menaḥem's reign, as something within the memory of the audience seems probable (I cannot see how the parallel with Amos 4:6–12 can be invoked to imply a

13. Procksch, *Jesaia I*, 103–4; see similarly Dillmann, *Jesaia*, 96–97; Fullerton, "Isaiah's Earliest Prophecy" (a very full presentation of the case of which Procksch appears to have been unaware); Fischer, *Das Buch Isaias*, 89; Scott, "Chapters 1–39," 235; Eichrodt, *Der Heilige*, 115; Gottwald, *All the Kingdoms of the Earth,*, 153. For a recent analysis of the Biblical account of Menaḥem's reign, albeit without reference to the present passage, see Dubovský, "Menaḥem's Reign."

14. Gray, *Isaiah I-XXVII*, 184.

15. The historical value of this note has in any case been sharply questioned by Na'aman, "In Search of Reality," and he thinks that the Chronicler may precisely have been influenced by our verse (51).

16. Beuken, *Jesaja 1–12*, 264.

17. Sweeney, *Isaiah 1–39*, 192–95.

longer time span); it furnishes the only possible scenario where Aram and the Philistines might have acted jointly against Israel. No such action is actually known to us from those years, however, so we are left with the quandary of whether to eliminate the possibility from consideration or simply to acknowledge that it might not have been recorded in our extant sources.

The Second Stanza

The second stanza is tricky to deal with because some commentators find a great deal more secondary material in it than I have allowed above. Because most reconstructed versions include the breakdown in civil society, we may fasten on that element as relatively uncontroversial. As with the preceding stanza, a number of suggestions have been offered, including the revolution of Jehu (2 Kgs 9–10), which was still vividly remembered shortly before Isaiah's day (Hos 1:4),[18] the period following the fall of Jehu's dynasty,[19] the aftermath of Tiglath-Pileser III's invasion in 732 after the Syro-Ephraimite war (this with what I regard as a mistaken geographical understanding of v. 13 [NRSV 14]),[20] and the general descent into anarchy in the final years of the northern kingdom's existence, as attested especially in Hosea.[21]

The Third Stanza

The third stanza initially confronts us with how to interpret the language of cannibalism in vv. 19–20 [NRSV 20–21]. Cannibalism is mentioned several times in the Hebrew Bible (whether literally or not) to express an extreme state of distress, such as the conditions of people undergoing siege

---

18. Fohrer, *Jesaja 1–23*, 148; Wildberger, *Jesaja 1–12*, 220.
19. Eichrodt, *Der Heilige*, 115–16.
20. Donner, *Israel unter den Völkern*, 72–73, thought on the one hand that Isaiah had in mind in v. 13 [NRSV 14] the Assyrian annexation of part of the territory of Israel in 733; on the other hand he proposed that "head and tail" could well be based on Egyptian usage, where head is often used geographically for the forward frontier of a country and where tail can refer to the hinterland of a region. Similarly he saw the palm branch and the papyrus as parts of the Egyptian insignia for the country. This broad approach was followed later by Ockinga, who qualified it in only minor respects: "*rōš*," 31–34. This approach has been criticized by Niccacci, "Isaiah xviii–xx," 230, though his own solution is rather too general: he sees both phrases as merely an expression of totality, "something complete." Equally, Wildberger, *Jesaja 1–12*, 219, followed by Bjørndalen, *Untersuchungen zur allegorischen Rede*, 224, questioned whether a Judean audience would have been in a position to understand these subtleties.
21. E.g., Clements, *Isaiah 1–39*, 68.

(Lev 26:29; Deut 28:53, 55; 2 Kgs 6:28–29; Jer 19:9) or severe post-conflict famine (Lam 4:10). Micah 3:3 uses it figuratively to express the lack of social justice within a class-based system; and in Isa 49:26 it comes closer to our present verse in reference to Israel's oppressors devouring one another (surely not eating their own flesh). References in Ps 27:2 and Job 19:22 concern attacks on an individual by his enemies. More pictorial allusions occur at Zech 11:9–16 and Eccl 4:5. All these seem less extreme than Isaiah 9:19–20 [NRSV 20–21], however, where the whole point is to emphasize the complete depravity of the situation. The first two lines lean towards exaggeration for rhetorical effect. The use in parallel of "on the right" and "on the left" indicates comprehensiveness while "remained hungry" and "was not satisfied" underline the rapacious appetite that drove the barbarity.

It is not easy to interpret this unusually strong form of condemnation. In Micah the issue is one of social justice, but Isa 9:20 [NRSV Isa 9:21] suggests something more in the realm of inter-tribal rivalry. Obviously land seizure would be one possibility, but is a rather weak cause unless accompanied by some significant level of violence. Perhaps, in view of the foregoing paragraphs, we should link the accusation rather with the turbulent closing years of the kingdom of Israel, when there were several *coups d'état* which involved bloodshed and violence and thus effectively civil war (cf. 2 Kgs 15). Wildberger's commentary surveys several more specific suggestions on verse 20 [NRSV 21] within that general framework, but all suffer from the disadvantage that no surviving historical sources directly refer to specifically tribal conflicts, which is what the verse seems to imply.

The further consideration in this verse that "together they are set against Judah" is taken by a few scholars to be a later addition. For instance, Clements writes that it comprises "a redactor's addition who has sought to bring out more forcefully that the final defeat of the Northern Kingdom arose because the people there refused to reunite with Judah and accept the Davidic monarchy."[22] In his view, the original prophecy concerned only the Northern Kingdom in its final decade. Considering that this kind of Judean gloss is familiar in Hosea, it is perhaps surprising that this suggestion has not been more widely adopted. Sparks, for instance, is strongly tempted, but ultimately decides against, even though explicitly without conviction.[23] Presumably it is not so certain as Clements maintains that the poem originally referred exclusively to the Northern Kingdom.[24] Moreover, a Judean author

---

22. Clements, *Isaiah 1–39*, 69. See too, though for different reasons, Becker, *Jesaja*, 149.

23. Sparks, *Ethnicity and Identity*, 198.

24. In my opinion, based on Isaiah's use of names elsewhere in his eighth-century writings, the heading to the poem in v. 7 [NRSV 8] includes Judah as well as the

such as Isaiah would himself no doubt be interested in his observations' effects on his own nation. It seems to me, furthermore, that the first line of the verse on its own would have been a curiously weak poetic ending to the stanza.

Assuming that the line is an integral part of the poem, many commentators not surprisingly see here a reference to the Syro-Ephraimite invasion: it was only in times of common enmity that this fraternal strife was set aside. Wildberger finds this difficult, however, on the ground that the poem looks back to past events ("das ist chronologisch aber doch schwierig, zumal bereits auf diese Ereignisse *zurück*geblickt wird," not a strong objection, as this can apply to the invasion in any case); he therefore proposes instead the battle between Amaziah of Judah and Jehoahaz of Israel (2 Kgs 14:8–14).[25] This seems even less likely, however, since in that case it was Judah, not the Northern Kingdom, which was the aggressor.

A more serious objection to the Syro-Ephraimite theory at this point is that it fits less well with the specifically tribal identity of Ephraim and Manasseh and that there is no reference to the Syrian partner in the coalition. As others have pointed out, there were likely border skirmishes several times through the history of the divided monarchy,[26] so that here Oswalt is more likely correct: he does not think it the case that any specific event is here in view, any more than in the case of the inter-tribal fratricide of the first line. "It is more likely that he was referring to the long history of hatred between the northern and southern parts of the nation."[27]

EVALUATION OF OPTIONS

Where does this survey of widely divergent views leave us? Two possible honest but challenging options seem open. First, we could admit ignorance concerning the apparently historical references and attribute them to some form of social memory rather than annalistic history. All societies accumulate an abundance of such familiar narratives whose relation to what we today would consider "history" is usually quite uncertain. They often contribute in powerful ways to moral example or to national or regional identity, and the examples in the present passage might fall into the same category.

---

northern kingdom; so too, for instance, Procksch, *Jesaia I*, 102; Kratz, "Israel in the Book of Isaiah," 119–22.

25. Wildberger, *Jesaja 1–12*, 222.

26. Fullerton, "Isaiah's Earliest Prophecy," 34–35; Oded, "Historical Background"; Tomes, "Reason."

27. Oswalt, *Isaiah Chapters 1–39*, 258.

While disconcerting for the commentator, at least no obviously false historical identifications would be made with the comparatively sparse amount of historically reliable data available. The challenge for this approach, however, is the oddity of so many examples of this nature occurring together within a short passage and, moreover, the unlikelihood that these particular examples all fall naturally into the category of material which would lend itself to being among the building blocks of Israel's social memory.

An alternative approach therefore deserves mention, namely that instead of specific historical references here, the examples cited are all of a paradigmatic but imaginary nature. How might this suggestion be supported?

In the case of v. 11 [NRSV 12], the two foreign nations mentioned may simply have been chosen as examples of traditional enemies in general.[28] That the same two nations also feature twice elsewhere (in Amos 9:7 and Ezek 16:57) as stereotypical and classic neighbouring enemies, strongly favors this approach.

A similar result can be reached in the later stanzas as well.[29] In the second, the description of the breakdown of society in a time of disaster is clearly based on elements that are also familiar elsewhere. The combination of "head and tail"[30] is repeated with an exact repetition also of the following pair at 19:15 where they seem to refer to agents unable to do anything for Egypt. Separately, in Deut 28:13, in a passage descriptive of potential blessings, God promises Israel that she can be the head and not the tail, amplified by the explanation that she will be on top and not at the bottom; conversely, in v. 44, in a passage descriptive of potential curses, a stranger may become the head and Israel the tail. All this suggests common idiom. From literary considerations, the second stanza of our poem is likely based in particular on Isa 3:1–9, where again Isaiah envisaged the collapse of society in all its dimensions as the inevitable consequence of destructive judgment. Interestingly, he begins there too by referring to the removal of "staff and

---

28. See, for instance, Kruger, "Another Look," and, apparently independently, Childs, *Isaiah*, 84, 86.

29. The only exception would be one that falls outside our immediate passage in Isaiah 9, namely what I regard as the original final stanza of the poem in 5:25b–29; there, the move to a prediction of an Assyrian invasion seems to become clear. This might be expected, however: paradigmatic examples of past disasters give way to the probability of a real and actual threat in the present—a powerful hermeneutical move.

30. Kruger, "Another Look," 138, notes the occurrence of both words in 7:4, 8, 9, and so suggests that there is a possible reference here to the *coups d'état* in the last years of the existence of the Northern Kingdom. They do not occur there as a pair, however, and in any case the composition of Isaiah 7 was later than that of the present passage, so that if anything this would have been the later author's interpretation of the present reference, not the reverse; see my *King, Messiah and Servant*, 73–112.

stay," which could be compared rhetorically with the 'head and tail' of v. 13 [NRSV 14] here. With general memories of past disasters he is concerned mainly to show how the failure to heed warnings has only one inevitable result—the total collapse of civilized society.

In the third stanza, a minor consideration behind the choice of Manasseh and Ephraim may have been that these patriarchal characters were brothers with each other but not with the remaining patriarchs[31] and also that the tribes were the largest and most powerful. Even more pertinently, Kruger points out that there are indications of tension between these two tribes from the earliest times, according to our present sources (see Jud. 6:35; 8:1), so that a paradigmatic or exemplary form of reference could easily have been intended.[32]

In that case, virtually all the suggested historical occasions will be involved generally, but none specifically. This last position, which should in any case be maintained along with any other, has the virtue that the focus of attention in the poem as a whole is less on the acts of judgment than on the spread of sins which evokes them as developed systematically from one stanza to the next.

Furthermore, the forms of expression in each case seem deliberately chosen to convey a sense of comprehensiveness. The point about Aram and the Philistines states that they come "from the east" and "from the west." The leaders of society are described as 'head and tail,' again a spatial metaphor that serves as a vivid merismus for totality, indicative in particular of high and low rank. The same may be true of the more enigmatic "palm branch and reed," the one being considered tall and majestic, the other lowly and insignificant; in vv. 15-16 [NRSV 16-17] we find an admirable amplification, first in terms who should lead and who should be led, which is close to the sense of head and tail in Deuteronomy 28, and then to young men and orphans and widows, which match well with what little we glean elsewhere about the symbolism of palm branch and reed. I conclude, therefore, that these two phrases refer metaphorically to the totality of the population, first in political terms and then in terms of social status. Finally, the tribes mentioned in v. 20 [NRSV 21] were the most powerful in the northern kingdom and those by whom the nation as a whole could be named. Equally, the repetition in reverse order is suggestive of totality.

Attention to possible historical allusions has often distracted attention in the commentaries from these kinds of literary device to the detriment of our understanding of the poem as a whole. Only when we stop chasing

---

31. See further Sparks, *Ethnicity and Identity*, 196-98.
32. Kruger, "Another Look," 139.

twenty-first century obsessions for tangible reference and admit that "we do not know" shall we find ourselves liberated both to explore the more poetic dimensions of the text and, in hermeneutical mode, to adopt a paradigmatic interpretation which in fact allows for a more legitimate application of underlying theological principles.

BIBLIOGRAPHY

Becker, Uwe. *Jesaja—von der Botschaft zum Buch*. FRLANT 178. Göttingen: Vandenhoeck & Ruprecht, 1997.
Beuken, Willem A. M. *Jesaja 1–12*. HThKAT. Freiburg: Herder, 2003.
Bjørndalen, Anders J. *Untersuchungen zur allegorischen Rede der Propheten Amos und Jesaja*. BZAW 165. Berlin: de Gruyter, 1986.
Blenkinsopp, Joseph. *Isaiah 1–39*. AYBC 19. Garden City, NY: Doubleday, 2000.
Childs, Brevard S. *Isaiah*. OTL. Louisville: Westminster John Knox, 2001.
Clements, Ronald E. *Isaiah 1–39*. NCBC. London: Marshall, Morgan & Scott, 1980.
Dillmann, August. *Der Prophet Jesaja*. KHAT. 5th ed. Leipzig: Hirzel, 1890.
Donner, Herbert. *Israel unter den Völkern*. VTSup 11. Leiden: Brill, 1964.
Dubovský, Peter. "Menaḥem's Reign before the Assyrian Invasion (2 Kings 15:14–16)." In *Literature as Politics, Politics as Literature: Essays on the Ancient Near East in Honor of Peter Machinist*, edited by D. S. Vanderhooft and A. Winitzer, 29–45. Winona Lake, IN: Eisenbrauns, 2013.
Eichrodt, Walter. *Der Heilige in Israel: Jesaja 1–12*. BAT 17 (First Series). Stuttgart: Calwer, 1960.
Fey, Reinhard. *Amos und Jesaja: Abhängigkeit und Eigenständigkeit des Jesaja*. WMANT 12. Neukirchen-Vluyn: Neukirchener, 1963.
Fischer, Johann. *Das Buch Isaias übersetzt und erklärt: Kapitel 1–39*. Vol. 7 of HSAT 7. Bonn: Hanstein, 1937.
Fohrer, Georg. *Jesaja 1–23*. 3rd ed. ZBK. Zürich: TVZ, 1991.
Fullerton, Kemper. "Isaiah's Earliest Prophecy against Ephraim." *AJSL* 33 (1916–17) 9–39.
Goshen-Gottstein, Moshe H. "Hebrew Syntax and the History of the Bible Text: A Pesher in the MT of Isaiah." *Textus* 8 (1973)100–106.
Gottwald, Norman K. *All the Kingdoms of the Earth: Israelite Prophecy and International Relations in the Ancient Near East*. New York: Harper & Row, 1964.
Gray, G. B. *A Critical and Exegetical Commentary on the Book of Isaiah I–XXVII*. ICC. Edinburgh: T & T Clark, 1912.
Høgenhaven, Jesper. *Gott und Volk bei Jesaja: eine Untersuchung zur biblischen Theologie*. AThDan 24. Leiden: Brill, 1988.
Kaiser, Otto. *Das Buch des Propheten Jesaja, Kapitel 1–12*. ATD 17. Göttingen: Vandenhoeck & Ruprecht, 1981.
Kissane, Edward J. "The Qumrân Text of Isaiah, ix, 7–9 (1QIsa)." In *Sacra Pagina: Miscellanea Biblica Congressus Internationalis Catholici de Re Biblica I*. BETL 12–13, 1:413–18. Gembloux: Duculot, 1959.
Kratz, Reinhard G. "Israel in the Book of Isaiah." *JSOT* 31 (2006) 103–28.
Kruger, Paul A. "Another Look at Isa 9:7–20." *JNSL* 15 (1989) 127–41.

Lange, Armin. *Vom prophetischen Wort zur prophetischen Tradition: Studien zur Traditions- und Redaktionsgeschichte innerprophetischer Konflikte in der Hebräischen Bibel*. FAT 34. Tübingen: Mohr Siebeck, 2002.

Na'aman, Nadav. "In Search of Reality behind the Account of the Philistine Assault on Ahaz in the Book of Chronicles." *Transeuphratène* 26 (2003) 47–63.

Niccacci, Alvieri. "Isaiah xviii–xx from an Egyptological Perspective." *VT* 48 (1998) 214–38.

Ockinga, Boyo G. "*rōš wĕzānāb kippāh wĕ'agmôn* in Jes 9,13 und 19,15." *BN* 10 (1979) 31–34.

Oded, Bustenay. "The Historical Background of the Syro-Ephraimite War Reconsidered." *CBQ* 34 (1972) 153–65.

Oswalt, John N. *The Book of Isaiah Chapters 1–39*. NICOT. Grand Rapids: Eerdmans, 1986.

Procksch, Otto. *Jesaja I*. KAT 9 (First Series). Leipzig: Deichert, 1930.

Scott, R. B. Y. "The Book of Isaiah, Chapters 1–39." In *The Interpreter's Bible*, edited by G. A. Buttrick, 5:156–381. New York: Abingdon, 1956.

Skinner, John. *The Book of the Prophet Isaiah, Chapters i–xxxix*. Cambridge: Cambridge University Press, 1897.

Sparks, Kenton L. *Ethnicity and Identity in Ancient Israel: Prolegomena to the Study of Ethnic Sentiments and Their Expression in the Hebrew Bible*. Winona Lake, IN: Eisenbrauns, 1998.

Sweeney, Marvin A. *Isaiah 1–39 with an Introduction to Prophetic Literature*. FOTL 16. Grand Rapids: Eerdmans, 1996.

Tomes, Roger. "The Reason for the Syro-Ephraimite War." *JSOT* 59 (1993) 55–71.

Vollmer, Jochen. *Geschichtliche Rückblicke und Motive in der Prophetie des Amos, Hosea und Jesaja*. BZAW 119. Walter de Gruyter, 1971.

Wildberger, Hans. *Jesaja 1–12*. 2nd ed. BKAT 10. Neukirchen-Vluyn: Neukirchener, 1980.

Williamson, H. G. M. *Variations on a Theme: King, Messiah and Servant in the Book of Isaiah*. Carlisle, UK: Paternoster, 1998.

———. *A Critical and Exegetical Commentary on Isaiah 1–27, 1: Isaiah 1–5*. ICC. London: T & T Clark, 2006.

———. "'An Initial Problem': The Setting and Purpose of Isaiah 10:1–4." In *The Book of Isaiah: Enduring Questions Answered Anew. Essays Honoring Joseph Blenkinsopp and His Contribution to the Study of Isaiah*, edited by R. J. Bautch and J. T. Hibbard, 11–20. Grand Rapids: Eerdmans, 2014.

PART 3

Relevance of Biblical Commentary

12

Exegetical Evidence for Non-Solar and Non-Sequential Interpretations of the Genesis 1 and 2 Creation Days[1]

—Miles V. Van Pelt

QUESTIONS CONCERNING THE ORIGIN and age of the universe are older than the biblical text itself. Additionally, the relevance of these questions and the implications for their answers continue to shape modern worldviews. Almost every field of learning has attempted to make their own contribution to the issue. Approaches have included phenomenological, philosophical, historical, literary, theological, and even artistic investigations, to name just a few. In each case, the biblical text of Genesis 1 and 2 has played a role, even if only as ideological foil. For this reason, a proper understanding of the text is essential, both in terms of what it teaches, and what it does not teach.

The purpose of this paper is to identify and interact with some of the exegetical evidence from Genesis 1 and 2 supporting those interpretations

---

1. This author owes an immeasurable debt of gratitude to Professor John E. Hartley. I arrived on the campus of Azusa Pacific University in the fall of 1989, a veritable academic catastrophe. Professor Hartley ignited in me a passion for the rigorous study of the biblical text, taught me how to write, and most profoundly, taught me the classical Hebrew language. His life and work, both inside and outside the classroom, continue to bear fruit in my life even after over twenty-five years.

of the creation days that are non-solar and non-sequential. This evidence will also demonstrate the exegetical validity for other literary interpretations of the creation days, in opposition to the solar-sequential hypothesis.[2]

POINT ONE

Genesis 1:2 provides the explicit, organizing framework for the presentation of creation days in Genesis 1. Properly understood, this verse accounts for the logic behind the presentation of days and establishes a priority for non-chronological interpretations of those days.

The text of Gen 1:2 consists of three disjunctive (noun) clauses, each of which describes the state of the earth *prior* to day one. The first disjunctive clause describes the state of the earth as תֹּהוּ וָבֹהוּ or "formless and empty" (NIV).[3] This two-fold designation divides the presentation of creation days into two triads: days one through three and days four though six. In the first triad, days one through three, God makes that which is formless (תֹּהוּ) into that which is formed. He makes the uninhabitable into that which is habitable. In the second triad, God makes that which is empty (בֹהוּ) into that which is filled. The description of the earth as תֹּהוּ וָבֹהוּ is, therefore, more than anecdotal background information. It is, rather, a macro-structuring device for the presentation of the six days in Genesis 1, and this begins to provide the basis for a logical, thematic interpretation of creation days.

The second and third disjunctive clauses in 1:2 describe aspects of the formless and empty earth in terms of an already existing water mass, understanding תְּהוֹם and הַמָּיִם as synonyms in this context.[4] In the second disjunctive clause, darkness resides over the surface of the deep and in the third disjunctive clause, the Spirit of God is described as hovering over the waters. This single reference to darkness (וְחֹשֶׁךְ), and the two-fold reference to watery elements—the deep (תְהוֹם) and the waters (הַמָּיִם)—identify ad-

---

2. The designation "solar-sequential hypothesis" is intentional. The "solar-sequential" nomenclature aptly characterizes the interpretation of the creation days as an ordered series of twenty-four hour periods. It also avoids use of the term "literal" as a label; suggesting that other interpretations are "non literal" in the sense that the biblical text is not taken seriously. I confess, however, that the "hypothesis" affix is winsomely polemical. There is no good, exegetical rationale for designations such as the "literal day interpretation" in opposition to the "framework hypothesis." Perhaps this slight adjustment will provide an opportunity for some to walk a mile in the shoes of another.

3. Other translations include "without form and void" (KJV, RSV, ESV), "formless and void" (NASB), and "without shape and empty" (NET). The Septuagint translation is ἀόρατος καὶ ἀκατασκεύαστος. An English translation like "uninhabitable and uninhabited" captures the alliteration and euphony of the original תֹּהוּ וָבֹהוּ.

4. Cf. Exod 15:8; Isa 51:10; Ps 33:7; 106:9; 135:6; Job 28:14; 38:16.

ditional structuring features for the days within the first triad. One creation day in the first triad will address the issue of darkness and two creation days will address the issue of waters.

On day one, light was created in opposition to darkness and then the two were divided, the one from the other. On day two, the רָקִיעַ was created in order to provide a vertical division of the waters, those below and those above the רָקִיעַ. On day three, the waters were divided a second time, but this time horizontally, as the means by which dry ground appeared. This analysis recognizes that the three disjunctive clauses of 1:2 provide the logic behind the presentation of the Genesis creation days, forming the formless (days one through three) and filling the empty (days four through six) in the categories of darkness and light (day one), waters and sky (day 2), and waters and dry land (day 3). Recognition of the architectural significance of Gen 1:2 for the construction of the creation days is an important factor in properly interpreting the nature of these days.

This identification of the structural design behind the presentation of creation days in Gen 1:2 is reinforced by the explicit and obvious connection between the days in each of the two triads. This connection is one of "ruling." That is to say, the elements of the second triad of days (four through six) are characterized as "ruling over" the realms of the corresponding days of the first triad (one through three).[5] The greater light and the lesser light (day four) "rule" over the day and the night (day one). The fish and the birds (day five) "fill" and so rule over the waters and the sky (day 2). Finally, the land animals and humankind (day six) "fill," "rule over," and "subdue" the dry land and those other aspects of creation subordinated to their dominion (day six). Thus, the elements created, made, formed, or brought forth on days four through six are described as ruling over those realms created by division on days one through three.

Note also that days three and six each contain two acts of creation. This type of organization demonstrates, for any interpretational scheme, the close literary and thematic correspondence between the days. It is certainly evidence for intentional literary design. In days one through three, the formless becomes formed and in days four through six, that which was formed becomes filled. The first triad of days emerges *by division* according to the scheme identified in 1:2. The second triad of days emerges *by filling* each of the respective realms with the "rulers" of that realm. The significance

---

5. The language of dominion in the second triad of creation days is pervasive and diverse. It includes the two-fold use of the noun מֶמְשָׁלָה in 1:16, the verbs משׁל in 1:18, רדה in 1:26 and 1:28, and כּבשׁ in 1:28. To this list, we may add the identical creation mandates from days four and five, 1:22) פְּרוּ וּרְבוּ וּמִלְאוּ and 1:28), as an appropriate expression of dominion within each of the narrated episodes.

of understanding this aspect of the construction of the creation days is the notable absence of chronology or sequencing. This reality does not prevent understanding the presentation of the creation days according to the solar-sequential hypothesis. This has yet to be demonstrated. It does, however, identify the possibility for recognizing other organizational schemes.

A SECOND POINT

In addition to identifying the architectural design behind the presentation of creation days, Gen 1:2 also provides evidence that the six days of Genesis 1 do not comprehend the totality of God's creative work. Before the first fiat of day one, there existed the earth (הָאָרֶץ), darkness (חֹשֶׁךְ),[6] and the waters (תְהוֹם and הַמָּיִם). It is also clear from Gen 1:1 that God created these things (cf. Exod 20:11; Acts 14:15; Col 1:16), but when? The only indication in the text is that the earth, darkness, and the waters were created by God and existed for some unspecified period of time prior to day one. This often-overlooked reality may suggest a purpose for the presentation of the creation days other than discrete, solar sequencing. The elimination of totality as part of the rationale behind the presentation of days complicates the issue of sequencing, though it does not entirely preclude the possibility.

Because the six days of creation described in Gen 1:3–31 do not comprehend the totality of God's creative work, it becomes significant to observe that the temporal modifier בְּרֵאשִׁית in Gen 1:1 is grammatically indefinite, "in *a* beginning." A first-year Hebrew student would have no trouble identifying this prepositional phrase as indefinite. In fact, the translation "in *the* beginning" is grammatically indefensible. Attempts to interpret this phrase as semantically determined in spite of its syntax remain wanting.[7]

---

6. Some object to the notion that darkness is a created thing, preferring to understand darkness simply as the absence of light. Such a preference, however, is unsupported by the biblical data. In Isa 45:7a, it is recorded (in the first person!) that Yahweh created (ברא) darkness (חֹשֶׁךְ), using the same verb and noun combination found in Genesis 1.

7. The syntax of Gen 1:1 is rather straightforward. The indefinite modifier בְּרֵאשִׁית is fronted and then followed by the clausal predicate (בָּרָא), subject (אֱלֹהִים), and two definite direct objects (אֵת הַשָּׁמַיִם וְאֵת הָאָרֶץ). Another, more sophisticated interpretation of the clausal syntax of Gen 1:1 appears in the work of Robert D. Holmstedt, "Restrictive Syntax." Holmstedt argues that the fronted modifier בְּרֵאשִׁית is followed by an asyndetic relative clause. In constructions of this type, the relative clause is understood as restrictive, providing information about the modified construction that works to identify, describe, or clarify the referent. Thus, the רֵאשִׁית of Gen 1:1 is a רֵאשִׁית *in which God created the heavens and earth*, nothing else. The clause syntax simply does not allow for conjecture regarding the nature of this particular beginning from the

An indefinite interpretation of this construction recognizes the eschatological orientation of Gen 1:1 by pointing readers forward to subsequent beginnings (cf. Mark 1:1; 2 Cor 5:17; Gal 6:15; Col 1:8, 15; 1 John 3:8, 11; Rev 3:14; 21:6; 22:13). "Put another way, the grammar of Gen [1:1] points forward only; it does not comment about whether this basic creative event was unique or whether there were others like it ... Grammatically, the introduction to Genesis simply indicates that this is the particular [רֵאשִׁית] from which the rest of the story as we know it unfolds."[8] This type of interpretation argues for a plain, grammatical-historical interpretation of the text in its context. God alone created everything in the categories of heaven (invisible) and earth (visible). He ordered it (days 1–3), filled it (days 4–6), and reigns over it (day 7). But this interpretation also spares readers from the temptation to force the Genesis creation account into unrealistic, unscientific theories regarding the absolute beginning of the universe.

A THIRD POINT

The relationship between days one and four precludes a strict solar and sequential interpretation of the creation days.[9] On day one, God created the light by divine decree, separated that light from the darkness, and then named the light "day" and the darkness "night." Then, on day four, God decreed the existence of the light sources (מְאֹרֹת)[10] and set them in the expanse of the heavens. The question becomes, "from where did the light of day one come if not from the light sources identified on day four?" Perhaps there is a scientific explanation for the existence of light prior to the existence of the sources of light, but the biblical text is unaware of any such explanation.

---

perspective of God, who never had a beginning.

8. Holmstedt, 66.

9. The problem of the relationship between days one and four is well known. For example, Augustine, in *City of God* (Book XI, chapter 7), states, "We see, indeed, that our ordinary days have no evening but by the setting, and no morning but by the rising, of the sun; but the first three days of all were passed without sun, since it is reported to have been made on the fourth day. And first of all, indeed, light was made by the word of God, and God, we read, separated it from the darkness, and called the light Day, and the darkness Night; but what kind of light that was, and by what periodic movement it made evening and morning, is beyond the reach of our senses; neither can we understand how it was, and yet must unhesitatingly believe it."

10. The Hebrew noun מָאוֹר occurs only 19 times in the Hebrew Bible (Gen 1:14, 15, 16 (3x); Exod 25:6; 27:20; 35:8, 14 (2x), 28; 39:37; Lev 24:2; Num 4:9, 16; Ezek 32:8; Ps 74:16; 90:8; Prov 15:30). Its range of meaning includes "source of light" (*HALOT*), light-bearer (BDB), or luminary (*HALOT*, BDB).

In fact, in the narration of day four, the three-fold purpose of the light is explicitly described, two times each:

(1) to divide between the day (light) and the night (darkness);

| 1:14ab: | לְהַבְדִּיל בֵּין הַיּוֹם וּבֵין הַלָּיְלָה |
| 1:18ab | וּלֲהַבְדִּיל בֵּין הָאוֹר וּבֵין הַחֹשֶׁךְ |

(2) to rule over (mark) the day and the night;

1:16b	אֶת־הַמָּאוֹר הַגָּדֹל לְמֶמְשֶׁלֶת הַיּוֹם
1:16b	וְאֶת־הַמָּאוֹר הַקָּטֹן לְמֶמְשֶׁלֶת הַלַּיְלָה
1:18aa	וְלִמְשֹׁל בַּיּוֹם וּבַלַּיְלָה

(3) to shine light upon the earth.

| 1:15b | לְהָאִיר עַל־הָאָרֶץ |
| 1:17b | לְהָאִיר עַל־הָאָרֶץ |

The narration of day four characterizes the sun, moon, and stars as the *sources* for the earth's light, the *instruments* for dividing light from darkness, and the *markers* for seasons, days, and years. A logical conclusion from such a description is that days one and four describe the same events. This identity is reinforced by the correspondence in the description of each days' events. On both days one and four, God divides (בדל) the light from the darkness, producing day and night. The correspondence is striking and warrants illustration:

Day One	(1:4b)	וַיַּבְדֵּל אֱלֹהִים	בֵּין הָאוֹר	וּבֵין הַחֹשֶׁךְ
Day Four	(1:14ab)	לְהַבְדִּיל	בֵּין הַיּוֹם	וּבֵין הַלָּיְלָה
Day Four	(1:18ab)	וּלֲהַבְדִּיל	בֵּין הָאוֹר	וּבֵין הַחֹשֶׁךְ

The selected comparison of days one and four above demonstrates the identity of creative activity on each day. Additionally, the purpose behind describing a single event on two non-contiguous days has been identified. In Gen 1:2, the presentation of days is identified as logical, not chronological. The presentation of light on day one corresponds to the description of the earth as תֹהוּ or formless (first triad). The formless darkness is "formed" by its separation from light. The presentation of light on day four corresponds to the description of the earth as בֹהוּ or empty (second triad). The empty realm is filled with the sun, moon, and stars. Another possible way to think about the appropriate relationship between days one and four is that of agent and instrument. On day one, God identifies himself as the "agent" of light's creation. On day four, God identifies the instruments of light's production. The polemical impact of this description on the worldview of the original audience would have been clear.

Appreciation of the non-sequential arrangement of the six creation days also helps to explain the concluding refrain for each day, "it was evening and morning, a [the] 'numbered' day." According to a solar-sequential interpretation of the biblical text, the appearance of an evening, morning, or solar day would have been impossible before the fourth day; the establishment of which being the explicit consequence of that day. To think otherwise appears to impugn the veracity of the biblical account.

A FOURTH POINT

The use of the singular noun יוֹם in Gen 2:4, as a reference for the time within which God had created, provides a challenge for the careful reader.[11] Did God create heaven and earth in a single day, as 2:4 seems to indicate, or did God create in six days according to the narrative in Genesis 1? Is the word "day" in 2:4 to be taken any less "literally" than its use in Genesis 1? It is also helpful to recall that the previous two verses, 2:2–3, mention the seventh day three times and, in Gen 1:3–2:3, the noun יוֹם appears fourteen times. Contextually speaking, therefore, the use of the word יוֹם in 2:4 should not be considered unmotivated or ambiguous. What then would motivate the use of the singular noun in this context given the clear plurality of days in the previous account?

Some have suggested that the use of the singular noun יוֹם in this particular syntactical environment constitutes a generic temporal reference best translated as "when."[12] The NIV is one example of this type of translation for the Hebrew construction בְּיוֹם עֲשׂוֹת יְהוָה אֱלֹהִים אֶרֶץ וְשָׁמָיִם, "*when* the Lord God made the earth and the heavens." The NASB represents an alternative translation, "*in the day* that the LORD God made earth and heaven."[13] Which translation is to be preferred in this context? The NIV is harmonistic, eliminating a potential contradiction for those who would advocate the solar-sequential hypothesis. The NASB translation, however, creates a problem for the "literal" reader. The evidence below will suggest that the singular noun יוֹם in 2:4 should be translated and interpreted as a single day, equal in status to the "days" of Gen 1:3–2:3.

---

11. See the work by Hodge, *Revisiting,* 70–98.

12. See, for another example, Harris, "Length," 109. Harris states, "I would rather argue that *bᵉyom* of Gen 2:4 is a prepositional phrase simply meaning an indefinite 'when.'"

13. The NET Bible corresponds to the NIV. The ESV is similar to the KJV, RSV, NRSV, and NASB in its rendering of the text at this point.

First, the construction בְּיוֹם plus the Infinitive Construct occurs sixty-four times in the Hebrew Bible,[14] six times in Genesis and twenty-one times in the remainder of the Pentateuch. When the noun יוֹם is rendered definite according to the rules that govern the Hebrew construct chain and the event referenced is past, not future, the word יוֹם appears to refer to a specific, single day.[15] For example, in Gen 21:8, "Abraham made a great feast, *on the day* Isaac was weaned."[16] The construction בְּיוֹם הִגָּמֵל אֶת־יִצְחָק describes the specific day on which Abraham celebrated the feast. As such, the translation of בְּיוֹם as "when" may not necessarily be supported by the subsequent occurrences of this construction throughout the Hebrew Bible.

Second, the construction בִּימֵי (the preposition בְּ prefixed to the masculine plural construct form of יוֹם) plus the Infinitive Construct occurs two times in the Hebrew Bible (Ruth 1:1; 2 Chron 26:5) as an alternative to the construction under consideration. In each case, the temporal reference is an unspecified period of time greater than a single day. The two instances of this construction in the book of Ruth, one singular and one plural, serve as helpful illustrations. The beginning of Ruth 1:1, וַיְהִי בִּימֵי שְׁפֹט הַשֹּׁפְטִים, contains the construction with the plural form of יוֹם (בִּימֵי) which clearly indicates a period of time greater than a single day. Second, in Ruth 4:5, בְּיוֹם־קְנוֹתְךָ הַשָּׂדֶה מִיַּד נָעֳמִי, the construction with the singular form of יוֹם (בְּיוֹם) clearly designates a single, solar day. Unfortunately, the overall rate of distribution in the Hebrew Bible for the plural construction does not provide a substantial measure of certainty. It does indicate, however, the possibility of the plural idiom for references to periods of time greater than a single day. One wonders, therefore, what would motivate the author of 2:4

---

14. Gen 2:4, 17; 3:5; 5:1, 2; 21:8; Exod 10:28; 32:34; Lev 6:13; 7:16, 36, 38; 13:14; 23:12; Num 3:13; 6:13; 7:1, 10, 84; 8:17; 9:15; 30:6, 8, 9, 13, 15; Deut 21:16; Josh 9:12; 10:12; 14:11; 1 Sam 21:7; 2 Sam 21:12; 1 Kings 2:8, 37, 42; Isa 11:16; 14:3; 30:26; Jer 7:22; 11:4, 7; 31:32; 34:13; Ezek 16:4, 5; 20:5; 24:25; 28:13; 31:15; 33:12 (2x); 34:12; 36:33; 38:18; 43:18; 44:27; Amos 3:14; Obad 11 (2x), 12; Nah 2:4; Ps 20:10; Ruth 4:5; Neh 13:15. Verse references listed above correspond to the Hebrew Bible divisions.

15. An example of an indefinite, non-past construction appears in Lev 13:14, וּבְיוֹם הֵרָאוֹת בּוֹ בָּשָׂר חַי יִטְמָא, "but on a day when [or whenever] raw flesh appears on him, he will be unclean." An example of a definite, non-past construction appears in Gen 2:17, בְּיוֹם אֲכָלְךָ מִמֶּנּוּ מוֹת תָּמוּת, "on the day that you eat from it, you will certainly die." Note that the action portrayed by מוֹת תָּמוּת may be interpreted as inceptive, since Hebrew usually does not morphologically mark the inchoative aspect.

16. וַיַּעַשׂ אַבְרָהָם מִשְׁתֶּה גָדוֹל בְּיוֹם הִגָּמֵל אֶת־יִצְחָק (Gen 21:8). Two additional examples that may contribute to our understanding of Genesis 1 appear in Gen 5:1–2. In Gen 5:1b, it is recorded, בְּיוֹם בְּרֹא אֱלֹהִים אָדָם בִּדְמוּת אֱלֹהִים עָשָׂה אֹתוֹ, "In the day God created man, he made him in the likeness of God. In Gen 5:2b, it is stated, וַיִּקְרָא אֶת־שְׁמָם אָדָם בְּיוֹם הִבָּרְאָם, "he called their name 'man' on the day they were created."

to select the singular form of the noun given the proliferation of "days" in the immediate context?

Third, the construction בְּ plus the Infinitive Construct with an intervening noun occurs 78 times in the Hebrew Bible (excluding the combination בַּעֲבוּר, 8 times). In 66 cases, the intervening noun is יוֹם (64 singular and 2 plural). The remaining nouns include: כֹּל (3 times), עֵת (1 time), שָׁנָה (3 times), and תְּחִלָּה (3 times). Note that, including יוֹם, four out of the five different nouns refer to time or periods of time. This indicates that, if the author of 2:4 had desired to indicate an unspecified period of time, a number of other nouns were available to indicate such a reality. The selection of יוֹם over שָׁנָה, עֵת, or תְּחִלָּה should be considered intentional and meaningful because there were other options available to the author.

Fourth, the combination of the preposition בְּ and the Infinitive Construct, without any intervening noun, is an unmarked, generic temporal construction. This unmarked construction occurs 729 times in the Hebrew Bible, 43 times in Genesis and 149 times in the remainder of the Pentateuch. In unmarked constructions of this type, the preposition בְּ is frequently translated as "when," indicating an unspecified period of time. Therefore, the use of the noun יוֹם in this context is marked, indicating a specific temporal reality in an otherwise unspecified temporal construction. Its inclusion must be interpreted as purposeful.

We might wonder if the author was confused or simply unsophisticated in his narrative technique at this point. Or, given the non-obligatory nature of the noun יוֹם in this construction, perhaps the author was expressing a level of sophistication by identifying an organizing element of the Genesis 1 creation account, suggesting that the so-called "days" of Genesis 1 constitute the names for the six creation actions/episodes without any necessary solar or sequential implication. One thing is clear, however. Translations that maintain the potential contradiction, "in the day," are to be preferred.

A FIFTH POINT

The numerical labelling of the days of creation does not require a strict solar-sequential interpretation. Unfortunately, some of the more popular English translations (e.g., KJV, NIV, ESV) complicate the issue by providing inaccurate renderings of the sequencing system presented in Genesis 1 (e.g., the first day, the second day, etc.).

In the Hebrew text, days one through five are enumerated with indefinite constructions. In fact, the Hebrew expressions for days two through five are unique to Genesis 1—a second day, a third day, a fourth day, a fifth day. For day one, the indefinite construction is best translated as "a single day," "day one," or even "a certain day," but certainly not as "the first day." The summary chart displays the Hebrew data from Genesis 1:1–2:3 with an English translation and the appropriate grammatical labels: anarthrous (indefinite) or articular (definite).

Summary of Day Designations in Gen 1:1—2:3

Hebrew	Verse	Translation	Grammar
יוֹם אֶחָד	1:5	*a* single day, day one	anarthrous
יוֹם שֵׁנִי	1:8	*a* second day	anarthrous
יוֹם שְׁלִישִׁי	1:13	*a* third day	anarthrous
יוֹם רְבִיעִי	1:19	*a* fourth day	anarthrous
יוֹם חֲמִישִׁי	1:23	*a* fifth day	anarthrous
יוֹם הַשִּׁשִּׁי	1:31	*the* sixth day	articular
בַּיּוֹם הַשְּׁבִיעִי	2:2	on *the* seventh day	articular
בַּיּוֹם הַשְּׁבִיעִי	2:2	on *the* seventh day	articular
אֶת־יוֹם הַשְּׁבִיעִי	2:3	*the* seventh day	articular

Day One. The noun יוֹם appears with the cardinal (not ordinal!) אֶחָד thirty one times in the Hebrew Bible.[17] In the singular, this designation occurs twenty eight times and normally describes a single, unidentified day.[18] For example, in Gen 33:13, "If they are driven hard for *one day*, all the flocks will die." Or, in Zech 3:9, "I will remove the iniquity of this land in *a single day*" (ESV). In three instances (Gen 27:44; 29:20; Dan 11:20), the construction is plural (יָמִים אֲחָדִים), and in every instance an indefinite period of time is indicated ("a few days" [NASB, KJV, RSV, ESV, NIV, NET], "a while" [RSV, ESV, NIV, NET]). If the author of Genesis 1 had wanted to characterize day one as "*the first* day," an appropriate construction was certainly available (e.g., בַּיּוֹם הָרִאשׁוֹן; cf. Ex 12:15–16; Lev 23:7, 35, 39–40; Num 7:12; 28:18; Deut 16:4; Judg 20:22). The designation יוֹם אֶחָד does not necessarily designate an absolute first day, but rather a certain, single day. In Gen 1:5, a translation like "the first day" is simply unwarranted and indefensible. Regardless of whether or not it was "the first day," the author did not choose to identify it as such in the biblical text.

---

17. Gen 1:5; 27:44–45; 29:20; 33:13; Lev 22:28; Num 11:19; 1 Sam 2:34; 9:15; 27:1; 1 Kings 5:2; 20:29; Is 9:13; 10:17; 47:9; 66:8; Jonah 3:4; Hag 1:1; Zech 3:9; 14:7; Esth 3:13; 8:12; Dan 11:20; Ezra 3:6; 10:13, 16–17; Neh 5:18; 8:2; 2 Chr 28:6. In Gen 12:18, the construction יוֹם אֶחָד וְעֶשְׂרִים לַחֹדֶשׁ refers to *the* twenty-first day of the month.

18. In late biblical Hebrew, the construction is used for dating and appears to function as an ordinal, thus "the first day of the month" (cf. Hag 1:1; Ezra 3:6; Neh 8:2).

Days Two through Five. The numerical labels for days two through five are also indefinite, "a [x^th] day." As stated above, these particular constructions in Genesis 1 are unique in the Hebrew Bible.[19] For example, the English expression "[on] the third day" is normally expressed in Hebrew as בַּיּוֹם הַשְּׁלִישִׁי, a determined noun followed by the determined ordinal adjective. In Genesis 1, however, the construction יוֹם שְׁלִישִׁי is indefinite, an anarthrous noun followed by an anarthrous ordinal adjective. Given the unique nature of the constructions in Genesis 1, it is difficult to achieve absolute certainty with regard to significance. What is clear is that these numerical designations situate days two through five into an indefinite series relative to day one, itself an indefinite single day. Given these grammatically indefinite designations for days one through five, it is not unwarranted to understand the reason for this juxtaposition as the result of a literary strategy for the days identified in Gen 1:2 (described in Point One above), not necessarily a chronological, solar sequential scheme.

Days Six and Seven. The exact expression, "the sixth day" (יוֹם הַשִּׁשִּׁי), a determined construct chain, is unique to the biblical literature, and it is unique to the corresponding numerical constructions of Genesis 1, representing the final, climactic day of God's creative work.[20] This determined construction represents one of the several literary devices employed by the biblical author to highlight the significance of day six in the creation account.[21] Day seven is also designated with a determined expression, "the seventh day."[22] In fact, as the summary table above demonstrates, day seven

---

19. The noun יוֹם with the ordinal "second" occurs 15 times (Gen 1:8; Ex 2:13; Lev 13:5, 33, 54; Num 7:18; 29:17; Josh 6:14; 10:32; Judg 20:24–25; Jer 41:4; Ezek 43:22; Esth 7:2; Neh 8:13). The noun יוֹם with the ordinal "third" occurs 32 times (Gen 1:13; 22:4; 31:22; 34:25; 40:20; 42:18; Ex 19:11, 16; Lev 7:17–18; 19:6–7; Num 7:24; 19:12, 19; 29:20; 31:19; Josh 9:17; Judg 20:30; 1 Sam 30:1; 2 Sam 1:2; 1 Kings 3:18; 12:12; 2 Kings 20:5, 8; Hos 6:2; Esth 5:1; 2 Chr 10:12). The noun יוֹם with the ordinal "fourth" occurs 7 times (Gen 1:19; Num 7:30; 29:23; Judg 19:5; Ezra 8:33; Neh 9:3; 2 Chr 20:26). The noun יוֹם with the ordinal "fifth" occurs 4 times (Gen 1:23; Num 7:36; 29:26; Judg 19:8).

20. The noun יוֹם with the ordinal "sixth" occurs 6 times in the Hebrew Bible (Gen 1:31; Ex 16:5, 22, 29; Num 7:42; 29:29). The construction in Gen 1:31 is unique, a construct chain with the determined ordinal number in the absolute position. The five subsequent occurrences consist of the definite noun followed by the definite ordinal adjective, בַּיּוֹם הַשִּׁשִּׁי (the object of the preposition בְּ in each instance).

21. In addition to the unique designation יוֹם הַשִּׁשִּׁי, the prominence of day six in Genesis 1 is signified by: (1) word count allotment; (2) double creation day (similar to day four); (3) creation of humanity in the image of God; (4) extended commentary (recapitulation) of day six in Genesis 2.

22. The exact expression, "*the* seventh day" is not unique to Genesis 2, but represents a standard formula. This construction (with and without the preposition בְּ) appears some 48 times in the Hebrew Bible (Gen 2:2–3; Ex 12:15–16; 13:6; 16:26–27, 29–30; 20:10–11; 23:12; 24:16; 31:15, 17; 34:21; 35:2; Lev 13:5–6, 27, 32, 34, 51; 14:9,

is labelled as "the seventh day" three times, once again a literary convention highlighting the significance of the seventh day in the Genesis creation account. It is significant to observe, therefore, that among the days of creation, days six and seven are the least likely days to constitute a singular, solar period consisting of twenty-four earthly hours. With regard to day six, the events recorded for this day in Genesis 2 appear to extend beyond a single earthly day (see The Seventh Point below). With regard to day seven, it lacks the termination formula of the previous six days (see The Sixth Point below). Evidence of this type points, once again, to the literary significance of the numbering scheme and allows for the possibility of interpreting the data in a way other than strict, solar sequencing, at least from an earthly (visible realm) perspective.

THE SIXTH POINT

The presentation of the seventh day in Gen 2:1–3 appears to preclude a solar interpretation of that day. Even the casual reader will recognize the one glaring omission from the seventh day narration, the concluding refrain that appears in each of the previous six days, "and it was evening and morning, a/the 'numbered' day." Because of this, a literal reading of the account would require that this seventh day has not literally ended. Accordingly, if the seventh day of creation is non-solar, then it is possible that the previous six days are also non-solar days. Later biblical texts, including Psalm 95 and Hebrews 4, recognize the enduring nature of the seventh day of God's rest. In Ps 95:11, it is recorded that the wilderness generation from the book of Exodus failed to enter into God's rest (אִם־יְבֹאוּן אֶל־מְנוּחָתִי). Then, Hebrews 4:1–11, after quoting Gen 2:2 and Psalm 95, indicates that the possibility of entering into God's Sabbath rest is still open for the people of God (see especially 4:1, 3, 6, 9, 11). In other words, the seventh day of God's Sabbath rest continues, even now, as a present reality. As such, this final numbered day in the creation account has extended well beyond a single, solar day.[23]

39; 23:3, 8; Num 6:9; 7:48; 19:12, 19; 28:25; 29:32; 31:19, 24; Deut 5:14; 16:8; Josh 6:4, 15; Judg 14:15, 17–18; 2 Sam 12:18; 1 Kings 20:29; Esth 1:10).

23. "There is the strongest presumption in favor of the interpretation that this seventh day is not one that terminates at a certain point in history, but that the whole period of time subsequent to the end of the sixth day is the Sabbath of rest alluded to in Gen. 2:2." Murray, *Principles of Conduct*, 30 (quoted by Harris, "Length," 110). The eventual closing of this day, according to the New Testament, is an eschatological reality occurring in two stages. The first stage in the termination of the seventh day is connected to Christ's crucifixion, with his words τετέλεσται, "it is finished" (John 19:30). The second and final stage in the closing of the seventh day is similar, occurring

Exegetical Evidence for Non-Solar and Non-Sequential Interpretations 211

The subsequent connection between the seventh day of God's Sabbath rest and the ordinance for man's Sabbath observance becomes important for the interpretation of the first six creation days.[24] In Exod 20:11, the command for the people of God to remember the Sabbath day is grounded in God's pattern of work and rest during the creation week. The people of God are to work for six solar days (Exod 20:9) and then rest on the seventh solar day (Exod 20:10). If, therefore, it can be maintained that God's seventh day rest in Gen 2 extends beyond the scope of a single solar day, then the correspondence between the "day" of God's rest and our "day" of observance would be analogical, not identical. In other words, if day seven is an unending day, still in progress, then our weekly recognition of that day is not temporally identical. As such, there is no reason to maintain that the same could not be true for the previous six days, especially if the internal, exegetical evidence from Genesis 1 and 2 supports this reality. In fact, once the questionable solar-sequential constraint is removed from the interpretation of the creation days, the internal textual contradictions are eliminated without recourse to extra-biblical, anti-scientific, theoretical polemicizing.

THE SEVENTH POINT

The account in Gen 2:4–25 appears to represent an expanded treatment of God's creative work on day six in Gen 1:24–31. A comparison of the events portrayed in each account reveals a number of solar and/or sequential discrepancies not easily accounted for by the solar-sequential hypothesis.

First, Gen 2:5 indicates that irrigation and cultivation were the necessary prerequisites for the appearance of vegetation. It is recorded that neither wild (שִׂיחַ הַשָּׂדֶה) nor cultivated (עֵשֶׂב הַשָּׂדֶה) vegetation existed at that time because God had not caused it to rain and man did not exist to work the ground.[25] In the Genesis 1 account, however, vegetation (דֶּשֶׁא and עֵשֶׂב מַזְרִיעַ זֶרַע and עֵץ פְּרִי) preceded man's creation by some three "days" (cf. Gen 1:11). The problem of sequencing presented by the comparison of Gen 2:5 with Gen 1:11 spans multiple creation days (days three and six).

---

in connection with the termination of this present world and the advent of the world that is to come, γέγοναν, "it is done" (Revelation 21:6).

24. For this point, I am indebted to the work of Ross, "Framework Hypothesis," 128–30.

25. For the translation of שִׂיחַ הַשָּׂדֶה as "wild vegetation" and עֵשֶׂב הַשָּׂדֶה as "cultivated" vegetation, see Futato, "Because It Had Not Rained," 2–4. Additionally, for a discussion of how Gen 2:5 identifies God's use of ordinary providence during the six creation days, see Kline, "Because It Had Not Rained."

Second, the creation of man in Gen 2:7 is distinguished from the creation of woman in 2:21–22. These accounts are separated from each other by the construction of the garden in Gen 2:8–17 and God's making of the animals in Gen 2:19–20. Note, of course, the use of the *wayyiqtol* verbal conjugation in 2:7, 8, 9, 15, 16, 18, 19, 20, 21 (2x), 22 (2x). In the Genesis 1 account, however, the creation of man *and* woman (together!) in 1:27 follows the creation of the animals in 1:25. Once again, note the use of the *wayyiqtol* verbal conjugation at the beginning of each verse to indicate the so-called sequence of events. The problem of sequencing presented by the comparison of Gen 2:7, 21–22 with Gen 2:19–20 occurs within a single day (day six). The creation of the woman is separated from that of the man by the creation and naming of the animals after an unspecified period of time.

Third, in 2:19, the text indicates that God created the birds (כָּל־עוֹף הַשָּׁמַיִם) with the other animals (כָּל־חַיַּת הַשָּׂדֶה) at the same time on what appears to be the same day. Note once again the use of the *wayyiqtol* verbal conjugation (וַיִּצֶר). In the Genesis 1 account, however, the creation of the birds (and fish) occurs on day five (1:20–21) and the creation of the remaining animals occurs on day six (1:25). The problem of sequencing presented by the comparison of Gen 2:19 with Gen 1:20–21 and 1:25 spans multiple creation days. In fact, according to Genesis 1, the order of creation was birds, then animals, and then man. In Genesis 2, however, the order of presentation is man, then animals and birds. Note that the orders of presentation are reversed and this "rearrangement" is not simply internal to day six, but crosses the boundary between days five and six.

Fourth, in Gen 2:20, it is recorded that the man named every beast, bird, and living creature of the field as they were presented to him by God in an attempt to identify the one who would be his helper. Given that this naming event occurred prior to the creation of the woman, the text implies that the man named every living creature that was created by God in less than a single, solar day according to the solar-sequential hypothesis. Estimates of the number of species currently in existence range from two to one hundred million. How the man would have named even a fraction of these animals in a single day is well beyond comprehension. If we gave the man all twenty-four hours in the day and conservatively estimated five million species, then the man would have had to name 3,473 animals per minute or 58 animals per second. Calculations of this type certainly border on the absurd, but it does make a point. The events of day six presented in Genesis 2:4–25 could not have transpired on a single, solar day.

The above comparison of selected events from Genesis 1 and 2 have identified a number of difficulties occasioned by a strict solar and sequential interpretation of the creation days. Additionally, the number of proposed

Exegetical Evidence for Non-Solar and Non-Sequential Interpretations 213

solutions is not far from the number of species identified above. A few of the basic solution categories are, however, worth mentioning. Some propose that the events of Genesis 1 are presented sequentially while the events of Genesis 2 are presented logically or thematically.[26] One could also propose, however, that the events of Genesis 2 are sequential while the events of chapter 1 are presented logically or thematically. The problem for each of these solutions, however, is the lack of any explicit markers that identify a shift from chronological to logical or logical to chronological, especially given the pervasive use of the *wayyiqtol* verbal form.[27] Each account must maintain its own integrity while, at the same time, not contradicting the other. As such, another common solution is harmonization, usually with the events of Genesis 1 serving as the grid into which the events of Genesis 2 are harmonized.[28] However, most attempts at harmonization include the use of one's apocryphal imagination and, therefore, must be rejected *prima facie*.

One final option for consideration is that neither Genesis 1 nor Genesis 2 are arranged in a strictly chronological manner but that each is arranged logically.[29] A solution of this type would recognize the significance of Gen 1:2 as providing the logical framework for the presentation of creation days in Genesis 1. Similarly, it would also recognize the significance of Gen 2:5 as providing the logical framework for the presentation of events in the remainder of that chapter.[30]

Like Gen 1:2, Gen 2:5 provides readers with a set architectural blueprints for the subsequent material. The two-fold problem is identified in 2:5a, "all wild vegetation was not yet on the earth and all cultivated vegetation was not yet growing." Next, the text identifies the two reasons for these

26. One fine example of this approach is presented by Young, *Studies in Genesis 1*. He states, "Genesis two may well serve as an example of a passage of Scripture in which chronological considerations are not paramount . . . It is obvious that a chronological order is not intended here . . . In chapter two events are narrated from the standpoint of emphasis . . . Hence, we should not make the mistake of trying to force its 'order of events' into harmony with the order of events given in chapter one" (74).

27. The *wayyiqtol* verb conjugation occurs 76 times in Genesis 1 and 2, 50 times in Genesis 1 and 26 times in Genesis 2.

28. An excellent example of this approach is presented by C. John Collins, "*Wayyiqtol*."

29. Futato, "Because It Had Not Rained." I am indebted to Futato's work for identifying the significance of Gen 2:5–7 as the organizing rubric for the presentation of material in Gen 2:5–25.

30 Gen 2:4, like Gen 1:1, constitutes the introduction to a new section. Note the correspondence between these two "beginnings."
Gen 1:1 בְּרֵאשִׁית בָּרָא אֱלֹהִים אֵת הַשָּׁמַיִם וְאֵת הָאָרֶץ
Gen 2:4a אֵלֶּה תוֹלְדוֹת הַשָּׁמַיִם וְהָאָרֶץ בְּהִבָּרְאָם

problems: "because the Lord God had not caused it to rain on the earth and there was no man to cultivate the ground." The lack of wild vegetation is explained by the lack of rain, and the lack of cultivated vegetation is explained by the non-existence of man. Accordingly, 2:6–7 addresses these problems in this logical sequence. In 2:6, the problem of irrigation is solved by the rain cloud rising from the earth and watering the entire surface of the ground. Then, in 2:7, the problem of cultivation is solved by God's creation of man as the cultivator. Futato states that "Gen 2:5–7 is quite logical, highly structured, and perfectly coherent:

Problem	Reason	Solution
1) No wild vegetation	1) No rain	1) God sent rain
2) No cultivated grain	2) No cultivator	2) God formed a cultivator"[31]

The implications of this architectural structure for the entire chapter is summarized by the following outline:

OUTLINE: GENESIS 2:4–25

2:4 Heading
  2:5 Twofold Problem (no vegetation): (1) no rain, (2) no man
  2:6 The sending of rain
  2:7 The creation of man
    2:8–14 More vegetation and irrigation (garden and rivers)
    2:15–25 More vegetation and cultivation (garden and woman)

SUMMARY AND CONCLUSION

The seven points presented above identify some of the more interesting and substantial evidence supporting non-solar and non-sequential interpretations of the Genesis 1 creation days. We have highlighted the creation of the sun, moon, and stars on day four, the numbering of each day, the enduring nature of the seventh day, the translation of בְּיוֹם in Gen 2:4, and the naming of the animals in Genesis 2 as mitigating against a solar interpretation of the creation days. Similarly, we have compared the accounts of days one and four, considered the presentation of events in Genesis 1 and 2, and identified a number of potential discrepancies for strict sequential interpretations. It would appear, therefore, that the days of Genesis 1 are not to be interpreted as solar, sequential days. Rather, they provide readers with a literary, thematic framework for understanding the work of God that

---

31. Futato, "Because It Had Not Rained," 10.

has become the sabbatical pattern for the life of God's people.[32] Perhaps the articulation of days in Genesis 1 and 2 can be understood in a way similar to God's revelation of the plans for the Tabernacle, as something patterned after an invisible, heavenly reality (cf. Exod 25:9, 40). In fact, Gen 1:1–2 and 2:1–3 sets the narration of the six creation days into a framework exhibiting a heavenly orientation. In other words, the creation account is told from the perspective of the invisible realm, not the visible realm. Given this heavenly (invisible realm) orientation, it might be best to understand the days of Genesis 1 as the so-called "days of heaven" (Deut 11:21; Ps 89:30 [English 89:29]; cf. also Ps 90:4; 2 Pet 3:8), representing the *reality* behind the *copy* of our own earthly days.

"What kind of days these were it is extremely difficult,
or perhaps impossible to determine."

—AUGUSTINE, *CITY OF GOD*, 11.7.

BIBLIOGRAPHY

Augustine, *The City of God*. A Select Library of the Nicene and Post-Nicene Fathers of the Christian Church, First Series, vol. 2. Edited by Philip Schaff. Translated by Marcus Dods. Buffalo, NY: Christian Literature Company, 1887.

Collins, C. John. "The *Wayyiqtol* as 'Pluperfect': When and Why." *Tyndale Bulletin* 46 (1995) 117–40.

Futato, Mark D. "Because It Had Not Rained: A Study of Gen 2:4–25 and Gen 1:1–2:3." *WTJ* 60 (1998) 1–21.

Harris, R. Laird. "The Length of the Creation Days in Genesis 1." In *Did God Create in Six Days?*, edited by Joseph A. Pipa, Jr. and David W. Hall, 101–11. Taylors, SC: Southern Presbyterian Press, 1999.

Hodge, B. C. *Revisiting the Days of Genesis: A Study of the Use of Time in Light of Its Ancient Near Eastern and Literary Context*. Eugene, OR: Wipf & Stock, 2011.

Holmstedt, Robert D. "The Restrictive Syntax of Genesis i 1." *VT* 58 (2008) 56–57.

Kline, Meredith G. "Because It Had Not Rained." *WTJ* 20 (1958) 146–57.

Murray, John. *Principles of Conduct*. Grand Rapids: Eerdmans, 1957.

---

32. It is interesting to note at this point that the origin of the seven-day week is uniquely biblical. Naturalistic timetables would include diurnal (or daily), lunar (or monthly), seasonal (or agricultural), or annual (or yearly). The pattern of the seven-day week does not derive from general revelation but, rather, is the product of God's sabbatical imprint on time made known to us in the biblical text.

Ross, Mark. "The Framework Hypothesis: An Interpretation of Genesis 1:1–2:3." In *Did God Create in Six Days?* edited by Joseph A. Pipa, Jr. and David W. Hall, 122–28. Taylors, SC: Southern Presbyterian Press, 1999.

Young, Edward J. *Studies in Genesis 1*. Phillipsburg, NJ: P&R Publishing, 1999 [1964].

13

Ḥerem versus Hospitality in the Story of Rahab

—Victor H. Matthews

Two major concepts stand in counterpoint within the Story of Rahab and the capture of the city of Jericho (chapters 2 and 6). The first is *ḥerem* and the other is hospitality. In this story and the follow-up episode involving Achan (Joshua 7), *ḥerem* appears to function as an absolute principle demanding total obedience and total destruction of the targeted city, its inhabitants, and their possessions. Interspersed within the narrative is the story of Rahab, who should, according to God's commanded *ḥerem*, die with the other inhabitants of Jericho. However, the social principle of hospitality overrides this apparent absolute and therefore saves Joshua's spies from detection and death. It also leads to a compact between Rahab and the spies that spares her and her family's lives. Of course, there is also Rahab's statement of faith in her transactional dialogue with the spies—a further wedge between the *ḥerem* command and the need to demonstrate that the faithful (whether Canaanite or Israelite) can be protected from God's judgment. In order to understand the interaction of these two concepts in these narratives, we shall explore both the hospitality protocol and the imposition of the *ḥerem* command.

NARRATIVE USE OF THE HOSPITALITY PROTOCOL

When social patterns are created and become so familiar that any deviation from the established pattern results in a form of social dissonance, that deviation can also serve in a story as a catalyst for crisis and resolution. That is apparently the case with the depiction of the hospitality protocol in the biblical narratives. Hospitality is a social transaction, an exchange of gifts in the form of food, lodging and conversation, and, best of all, a period of nonaggression and rest.

As a gift exchange, it involves strategies for both parties. Hosts stood to benefit from the honor attached to making the invitation and to providing a comfortable stay for the guest. And guests obtained respite from the journey and a chance to exchange news about the area through which they were travelling. However, at times, as in 1 Kgs 13:7–10, the gift of hospitality was overridden by a higher concern or the need to travel on your way.

The hospitality ritual certainly obligated hosts to treat strangers properly so that they would receive similar treatment when they travelled. But it was more than simply an amenity extended by individual households; in more populated areas it served as a village's most important form of foreign policy.[1] Villages could use hospitality to determine whether strangers (individuals or groups) were friends or enemies. The offer of hospitality factored into improving the distribution of resources, labor, and goods, preventing war, and keeping the peace.[2] And in those instances when tensions and uncertainty were generated by the presence of a potentially hostile stranger, hospitality helped neutralize any potential threat. The code of courtesy within the social ritual also contains an element of unease since either party might be suppressing animosity or even masking treachery or evil intent.[3] With that background, we can now formulate the biblically based elements of a social protocol for hospitality, using events in Gen 18:1–18.

In this narrative, the head of household or village must react to the appearance of strangers within the sphere of responsibility (basically line of sight) for that household or village (Gen 18:1–5). Although a traveler does not have to accept hospitality, it is likely that most would welcome the opportunity to rest, wash their feet, have a meal, and share news (Gen 18:5b-8). To protect both sides of this social transaction, certain rules were formulated and presumably enforced that prevented either the host or the guest from taking unfair advantage of each other. For example, the host

---

1. Matthews and Benjamin, *Social World*, 82.
2. Herzfeld, "'As in Your Own House,'" 77.
3. Herzfeld, "Afterword," S212–S213.

cannot ask the guest anything personal and the guest must not request anything tangible of the host. In this way the host obtains honor for his household by providing the invitation, and the guest is prompted to accept by the benefits of a temporary safe haven to rest, have a meal, and enjoy an exchange of conversation, within strict limits. The guest, however, once the invitation has been accepted, is obligated to set aside any potential or latent hostility and grant the host the honor due him and his household/village for the short time that they are together.

Protocol of Hospitality[4]

(1) A sphere of responsibility comprised a zone of obligation for both the individual encampment and the citizen of a village or town within which they must offer hospitality to strangers. The size of the zone is of course smaller for the individual encampment than for the urban center.

(2) The object was to transform the stranger from a potential threat to a temporary ally and thus forestall any hostilities.

(3) The invitation of hospitality could only be offered by the male head of household or a male citizen of a town or village.

(4) This invitation's time span could be extended, if agreeable to both parties, on the renewed invitation of the host. However, it was not an indefinite invitation.

(5) The stranger had the right of refusal, but had to do so diplomatically to prevent a loss of honor for the host or hostilities ensuing.

(6) Once the invitation is accepted, the roles of the host and the guest are set by the rules of custom.

    (a) The guest must not ask for or appear to desire anything.

    (b) The host provides the best available care and provisions despite what he may have modestly offered in the initial invitation.

    (c) The guest is expected to reciprocate with news, predictions of good fortune, or gracious responses or a blessing based on what he has been given.

    (d) The host must not ask personal questions.

(7) The guest remains under the protection of the host until he/she has left the zone of obligation of the host and the host accompanies the guest to that area.

Curiously, all other biblical examples deviate from the social practices described in Abraham's encounter with the three "strangers."[5] In every other

---

4. This protocol is a modified version of the chart appearing in Matthews, "Hospitality and Hostility," 11. Some of the changes are based on remarks in Jenei, "Abraham's Hospitality," 19–21.

5. See the use of some of the provisions of the hospitality protocol in Job's oath of clearance in Job 31:31–32. The appearance of a wisdom example suggests the protocol was well established and operative in ancient Israel.

instance, elements of what may have been normative social rituals are incomplete or violated in some way, presumably as a signal to the audience that a story is not in fact "normal." Why do all of these hospitality stories except Gen 18:1–18 violate the protocol in some way? The answer may be found in the sacred and rigid character of this social ritual, which makes any violation so shocking it compels the audience to consider the story more carefully. In the process, it shakes them out of their mental image of a formal set of social rituals and forces them to take each element and variation as central to the plot's theme.

Narrative	Characters	Violation of Hospitality Protocol
Gen 19:1—16	Lot and angels/Sodom	Resident-alien offers hospitality
Joshua 2	Rahab and 2 spies	Woman offers hospitality
Judg 4:17—22	Yael and Sisera	Woman offers hospitality
Judg 19:1—10	Levite and father-in-law	Repeated extensions, no blessing by guest
Judg 19:14—21	Levite and Ephraimite	Resident-alien offers hospitality
1 Sam 25:2—12	David and Nabal	Nabal refuses to host David's men on a feast day
2 Sam 12:4	Rich man and traveler	Rich man takes client's lamb to feed guest
1 Kgs 13:11—19	Two prophets	Old prophet pursues other prophet outside his sphere
1 Kgs 17:9—16	Elijah and widow	Elijah demands water and bread of the widow
2 Kgs 4:8	Elisha and Shunemite	Only invitation and meal mentioned

Table 13.1

For instance, in Gen 19:1–16 and in Judg 19:14–21, a resident-alien offers hospitality. He has no legal right to do so; it is reserved for citizens of the town or village. Similarly, in Judg 4:17–22 and Joshua 2, the protocol is violated when women (Jael and Rahab) participate in the hospitality ritual.[6] In 2 Sam 12:4, Nathan describes a host who takes a lamb from his poor client rather than his own flock to feed his guest, an action that infuriates David. The story of David and Nabal (1 Sam 25:2–12) also contains a protocol variation, although the associated political implications appear to

6. See Davidson, "Gazing (at) Native Women," 79–92.

take precedence here over the norms of hospitality. David's men arrive on a feast day, when largesse would generally be shared with all comers, and they suggest that Nabal owes David a favor for protecting his shepherds. Nabal rejects their claim, insults David by suggesting he is an outlaw with no entitlement to either an association with an honorable household or his stores of food, and sends them away empty-handed.

For women, such as Abigail or Rahab, in the ancient Near East or the Middle East today to be involved in this form of social transaction is unusual and eye-raising.[7] In this instance, Rahab is forced to intercede on behalf of her household since there is no mention of her husband or another male within her household.[8] In addition, as a prostitute she does not initially function as a host in the sense of the hospitality protocol until changing from the role of running her business to become a spokesperson whose intent is to protect her family by (1) hiding Joshua's spies, and (2) transacting a pact with them that will let the spies and ultimately her family live. Rahab's transactional dialogue with the spies is similar to that bargained for by Abigail (1 Sam 25:23–35) when her husband, Nabal, turns David's men away without hosting them. In each instance, the unusual factor of a woman talking for the family and bargaining for its safety must be considered a literary device to get the audience's attention and to contrast with the king of Jericho's failure to make peace with Joshua, and Nabal with David.

Embedding the Rahab story into basically a *ḥerem* narrative magnifies the shock to the audience. The blending of two very different stories that in some ways complement each other allows the narrative as a whole to: (1) demonstrate once again the power of the divine warrior (Josh 2:10—11 and 6:1—21), (2) use *ḥerem* as form of cultural cleansing, and (3) appear as an alternative voice/opinion calling out, as it does in Jonah 4:10—11, for preserving or at least considering the value of all people and all of God's creation.

ḤEREM PROTOCOL

Ḥerem is the social opposite of hospitality, a principle which enables the stranger to survive hostility and destruction. *Ḥerem* is one dimensional, requiring a single-minded determination to destroy completely those persons

---

7. Van Nieuwenhuijze, *Sociology of the Middle East*, 287; Matthews, "Female Voices," 9–11.

8. Bird, "The Harlot as Heroine," 125, refers to Rahab as "a kind of legal outlaw," who stands outside the normal social protocols and has more freedom to speak and represent her household.

and their property who are outside the group. If God had chosen to apply the principle in the story of the flood, no effort would have been made to save Noah and his family, and when Abraham made his plea for Sodom (Gen 18:20–33) there could be no basis for God's negotiating the possibility of the city's survival.

The Deuteronomistic Historian (DtrH), surveying the Hebrews' failure to offer *ḥerem* sacrifices throughout the land, considered this an act of disobedience to Yahweh and a primary cause why Israel never became a single people worshipping its one divine patron at one sanctuary. According to the *ḥerem* principle, Yahweh had commanded the Hebrews to clear away the seven nations of Canaan (Deut 7:1–6). No mercy was to be given them after their defeat and no covenant negotiated. The Hebrews were to "utterly destroy them" (Deut 7:2).[9]

The language of the DtrH is unequivocal, in contrast to that found in the book of Exodus which allows the Hebrews to deal with the indigenous peoples of Syria-Palestine in different ways. For example, a stipulation in the Covenant between Yahweh and Israel (Exod 19:1—24:18) commands them to drive the indigenous peoples out of their lands gradually (Exod 23:20–33), rather than utterly destroy them. This prevented them from becoming a "snare" to Israel without need for a command to commit genocide.

Jericho was not the only site in Syria-Palestine where the Hebrews offered *ḥerem* sacrifices. Throughout the book of Joshua, Yahweh commands them to *utterly destroy* the inhabitants of each place they conquer (Josh 8:26; 10:1, 28, 35–40; 11:11–21). In order to understand what is at stake in the embedded Rahab narrative, let us consider how the principle of *ḥerem* is described and detailed elsewhere in the biblical text:

---

9. There are five uses of the phrase "utterly destroyed" in the book of Deuteronomy (Deut 2:34, 3:6, 4:26; 7:2). There are ten in the book of Joshua (Josh 2:10; 8:26; 10:1, 28, 35, 37, 39, 40; 11:20–21) all reflecting a common phrase employed by the DtrH.

Text	Interpretation
Lev 27:28–29 No property that "has been devoted to destruction for the LORD, be it human or animal, or inherited landholdings may be sold or redeemed . . . No human being who has been devoted to destruction can be ransomed; they shall be put to death."	This post-exilic legal statement reflects the exclusivist thinking of the returned exiles and the restored priestly community. If we consider the invocation of *ḥerem* in Joshua 6 to also be Josianic (sixth century BCE), then the justification for Jericho's total destruction demonstrates the interest of the (Josianic) DtrH editor in cleansing the land of cultural contaminants. The Holiness Code simply reinforces that view point for anyone questioning the value or the necessity of "devoting" an entire city to destruction. Of course, it also removes the possibility that Rahab and her family could be "redeemed" by righteous action (i.e. hospitality). That further strengthens the contention of a separate, post-exilic DtrH edition that refuses to allow *ḥerem* to be transcended in importance by hospitality.
Num 18:14–19 In assigning the Levitical portion of the sacrifice, the people are told that "every devoted thing in Israel shall be yours . . . But the firstborn of human beings you shall redeem, and the firstborn of unclean animals you shall redeem."[A]	When considering the implications of human sacrifice, the decision is made to claim the first-born for God as a devoted entity along with everything else, but a loop hole is provided to redeem these children. Perhaps this represents a softening of *ḥerem* in Numbers and should therefore be excluded from our consideration of "devoted" things.

Text	Interpretation
Deut 7:26 An Israelite can be tainted by contact with or possession of an "abhorrent thing" (in this case images of other gods made of gold and silver), and for this crime can be "set apart for destruction like it." **Deut 13:12–18** This chapter deals with idolatry and those who advocate the worship of other gods. Israelites in a town allotted to them in the Promised Land have become "scoundrels" (*bĕnî belîʿal*) and commit the above. So, the charges been proven, they and their town are to be "utterly destroyed" along with everything in it including the livestock. The spoil is placed in the "public square" and offered as "whole burnt offering" and the place is never to be rebuilt (compare the curse against Jericho's gate in Josh 6:26). In fact they are told not to "let anything devoted to destruction stick to your hand" or face God's wrath.	These two passages relate to what happened to Achan, who stole from the loot "set apart" at Jericho (Josh 7:1, 11–26). Thus, through physical contact an Israelite is transformed into the abhorrent thing and must be destroyed or the entire nation be subject to destruction (Deut 20:16–18).[B] The argument can therefore be made that the abhorrent "other" (images and those who worship them) must be destroyed so as not to become a stumbling block of coveting or revering. The question, however, is can the Samaritans and other "people of the land" in the post-exilic period be excluded because their worship practices and places do not correspond to those of the second temple Israelites (see Ezra 4:1–3; Neh 2:20). There is also the matter of Josiah's treatment of Bethel as a place like the one described in Deut 13:12–18 that must be destroyed because of its idolatry (i.e. Jeroboam's golden calf).
Josh 22:10–34 A dispute arises over the building of an altar by the Trans-Jordanian tribes on the east bank of the Jordan River. The argument is invoked that their action is similar to Achan's breach of faith "in the matter of the devoted things" (v. 20).[C]	This addresses whether a sacrificial altar can be built for Yahweh outside the region of Canaan.[D] The Trans-Jordanian tribes curiously argue that their altar was constructed in "fear that in time to come your children might say to our children, 'What have you to do with the Lord, the God of Israel?'" (v. 24). The resolution of the dispute then comes with the altar identified not for sacrifice, but as a "witness" (much like the pillar built by Laban and Jacob in Gen 31:44–49 and the stone set up by Joshua at Shechem in Josh 24:27) that the tribes in Canaan and those in Transjordan have a common worship of, and devotion to, Yahweh.

Ḥerem versus Hospitality in the Story of Rahab

Text	Interpretation
1 Sam 15:2–33 The term *ḥerem* only appears in v. 21, but the command is given in vv. 2–3 to "go and attack Amalek, and utterly destroy all that they have; do not spare them, but kill both man and woman, child and infant, ox and sheep, camel and donkey."	Saul fails to carry out *ḥerem*, taking "sheep and cattle, the best of the things devoted to destruction, to sacrifice to the LORD your God in Gilgal." The war against the Amalekites results from their opposition to Israel in the wilderness (Exod 17:8–14). Such an after-the-fact campaign seems like "overkill," and more likely reflects either current problems with them in Saul's time or the need to once again use them as the generic for all Canaanites (see Num 14:25, 43–45; 24:20) or is once again part of DtrH's perpetual problem with Amalek (see Deut 25:17–19), a biblical thread that even stretches into the time of Esther with Haman the Agagite. Typically, failure to obey God's command to the letter is a cardinal sin in DtrH, as the prophetic complaint "it is better to obey than sacrifice" (1 Sam 15:22) echoes. As with Achan, Saul's problem is laying hands on "devoted" items that should have been destroyed.
Isa 34:5 In Isaiah's "judgment on the nations" oracle the divine sword is to "descend upon Edom, upon the people I have doomed to judgment."	Edom is once again singled out as the enemy neighbor (cf. Ps 108:9; Jer 49:17; Ezek 25:13). Similarly to that against the Amalekites, the desire for revenge is accomplished by "devoting" them to utter destruction.

  A. Compare Ezek 44:29 where the consignment of "devoted" things is assigned to the Levites of the restored temple.
  B. Clements, "Achan's Sin," 116.
  C. Stern, "The Biblical Ḥerem," 154–55.
  D. What immediately comes to mind is the case of the Elephantine temple that dates to the time of Nehemiah and the eventual resolution that they would not rebuild without the consent of the Jerusalem authorities. See Elephantine Papyrus TAD A4.7, and Porten, *Elephantine Papyri*, 140–41.

Table 13.2

226 Part 3: Relevance of Biblical Commentary

LITERARY ANALYSIS

In the narrative containing the Story of Rahab it is possible to separate out the portions that relate to *ḥerem* and those associated with hospitality:[10]

Ḥerem: Josh 6:1–17a, 18–21, 26–27

Hospitality: Josh 2; 6:17b, 22–25

These distinct sections function as a counterpoint somewhat awkwardly reconciled after the description of apparent total destruction in 6:21, when Joshua instructs the two spies to remove Rahab and her family from their house (6:22–23) followed by a recapitulation of destructive activity (6:24–25). I tend to agree with Jacques Briend,[11] who contends that the Rahab narrative was integrated into the document when the account about Jericho (Joshua 6) was already elaborated,[12] and therefore had no actual influence on its composition. In looking at Josh 6:22–23, 25, he concludes that v. 25 is in fact an older conclusion on the fate of Rahab than that found in vv. 22–23. These verses call to mind the terms of the oath found in Josh 2:12, 17, 20, and thus explains why Rahab and her house escaped the destruction of Jericho. So it is likely that the account in Joshua 2 only made its way into the overall narrative at a later date, but prior to the sixth-century Deuteronomic redaction.

Assuming then that the *ḥerem* section can stand freely on its own as an independent narrative, it depicts Yahweh as "the commander of the army of the Lord" (Josh 6:17), who orders Joshua to "devote" the city and all its inhabitants to "the Lord for destruction." What is apparent here is that victory only comes through complete obedience. The concept of complete victory as defined by complete destruction stands as a corollary to the command "devour all the peoples that the LORD your God is giving to you, showing them no pity" (Deut 7:16–26).

When Yahweh commissions Joshua to take the land, the only appropriate response is for him to have complete faith in the divine warrior's ability to assist him and then go and take the land as ordered. Instead Joshua

---

10. Countering this argument, Sherwood's aim in "A Leader's Misleading," 61, is to demonstrate that Joshua 2 is not an interpolation or later addition to the narrative of Josh 1–11, but rather an argument by the narrator that allows chapter 1 and chapter 2 to dovetail together with the emphasis being an "invitation" to the Israelites to "join in transforming Canaan into the Land" with God's help. Rahab in that sense serves as a vehicle "providentially" supplied by Yahweh to preserve the lives of the spies.

11. Briend, "Sources of the Deuteronomistic History," 374.

12. Stern, "The Biblical *Ḥerem*," 145, suggests this is evidence of the pre-deuteronomic composition of most of Joshua 6 due in part to the omission of the list of the ethnic groups typical of the later *ḥerem* passages.

chooses to send out a reconnaissance mission first.[13] While modern military strategists require reconnaissance as a natural preparation for battle, ḥerem war in the world of the Bible forbids it. Reconnaissance missions determine the strength of the enemy, which in ḥerem war is totally irrelevant. Warriors were expected to go into ḥerem war at a disadvantage in order to highlight the victory as divine rather than human. For example, Jerubbaʻal (Gideon) twice reduces the size of the tribe mustered to defend Israel against the Midianites (Judg 7: 1—8:28). Likewise, Deuteronomy (Deut 13: 13–19) assumes that the size of a city convicted of treason is of no consequence to the punitive expedition ordered against it.[14]

Israelite leaders may use prophets (1 Kgs 22:5), divination (2 Kgs 13: 15), necromancy (1 Sam 28:6), and the ephod with its *Urim* and *Thummim* (1 Sam 30:7–8; 1 Sam 28:6) to prepare for ḥerem war, but not spies. Reconnaissance characterizes warriors as petty (Num 13:1—14:15), cowardly (Deut 1:19–46), greedy (Judg 1:22–26), and heretical (Judg 18:1–31).[15] Going into battle against a superior opponent is intended to be an act of faith and an opportunity to highlight the victory as Yahweh's, not Israel's.

Magnus Ottosson interprets the sending of the spies as part of the "Mosaic praxis" that establishes Joshua "as equal to Moses" and as "a continuation of Moses' actions when Joshua and the people approached 'Canaanite' territory."[16] He makes an interesting point that the two spies were sent because of the juridical nature of the oath sequence, which requires two individuals to actually contract a treaty with Rahab (see Deut 17:6; 21:17; 1 Kgs 21:10, where "two men" appear as witnesses). However, in this instance there is no divine command to send out spies and therefore Joshua is guilty of a breach of faith when he orders them to go.

This disparity in what Ottosson calls the "Mosaic praxis" is what provides the opening for the intrusion of the hospitality narrative. In fact the hospitality theme here plays on elements of the story of God's inspection tour of Sodom and Gomorrah in Gen 18:16–22 and its continuation in Gen 19:1–15. In both narratives two "spies" are sent to check out the

13. Note that God instructs Moses to employ tribal representatives to spy out the land in Num 13:1–2. Joshua, in contrast, makes the decision to uses spies on his own. Sherwood, "A Leader's Misleading," 51, n. 31, draws an intertextual parallel between Num 13:1; Deut 1:22–28; and Joshua 2. He tries to harmonize the first two passages, but I think it is better to acknowledge that DtrH is protecting Moses' reputation in Deut 1 by portraying the people as villains while the Numbers 13 passage has God instructing Moses to send spies and in that way retains divine control over tactics and further highlights the theme that the people will fail when they demand or suggest tactics.

14. Benjamin, *Deuteronomy and City Life*, 113–37.

15. Polzin, *Moses and the Deuteronomist*, 85–91.

16. Ottosson, "Rahab and the Spies," 420.

city and determine whether it will be subject to divine destruction. In addition, there is a didactic element in both narratives. In Gen 18:17–19, God tells Abraham about the intention to examine and possibly destroy Sodom and Gomorrah so that he will be better able to "charge his children and his household after him to keep the way of the Lord by doing righteousness and justice," something Abraham has already demonstrated earlier in the chapter by following the proper protocols of hospitality (Gen 18:1-8).

The Rahab story, like that of Lot in Sodom (Gen 19:1–38), demonstrates that hospitality transcends the *ḥerem* command. In the end, both Lot's and Rahab's deliverance from a doomed city is due to their assisting endangered strangers. And, just to be clear and to remove the stigma of "seduction" raised by some commentators,[17] Rahab does not approach the spies "decked out like a prostitute, wily of heart" (Prov 7:10) or offer her perfumed bed for their entertainment and pleasure. More to the point, Rahab's action in hiding them is reminiscent of Lot's insistence that the two visitors he encounters in Sodom's city gate should not remain in the *reḥōb* as they suggest, not being a safe place (Gen 19:3). This shows quick thinking on Rahab's part when the king's men demand that she serve as their agent and turn over the Israelites (Josh 2:3–7). Though a reason is lacking here, it is supplied in her faith-based monologue before the spies in vv. 8–11.

Rahab's motivation for hiding the men could arise from multiple causes including problems she had with the local authorities or perhaps military intelligence she heard from her customers.[18] For our purposes, however, the question is whether hiding the spies constitutes a form of hospitality. Do brothel or business owners automatically become hosts when a guest agrees to accept their services or products? Can Rahab expect the same honor that Lot or Abraham received in offering hospitality? If hospitality is at its base about preventing conflict, then the sense of mutual agreement and benefits obtained are at least as important as the obtaining of an honorable name. But, remember that in Josh 6:25 the reason for her survival is that "she hid the messengers."[19] In that sense, she does perform the role of host by protecting her guests, who can be considered guests both by patronizing her business and their willingness, if not voiced, to be hidden by her.

It is possible that the hospitality story ends with the misdirection of the guards in Josh 2:7 just as it seems to end with the blinding of the crowd

---

17. Hawk, "Strange Houseguests," 90, 96.

18. Gillmayr-Bucher, "'She Came to Test Him,'" 143, simply concludes that Rahab is "a typical *zōnah*" for she "shows no loyalty to her king or her people" and "she seeks her own advantage."

19. Hawk, "Strange Houseguests," 94, notes that *mal'akîm* in Josh 6:25 is the same term used in Gen 19:1 for the "men" that Lot encounters.

in Gen 19:11. In that case, the shift in dialogue in Gen 19:12–23 and Josh 2:8–14 marks another phase of the narrative that centers on transactional dialogue. In the Rahab story, this transaction remarkably involves a Canaanite woman vividly reciting the deliverance history of the Israelites. She reminds the spies of God's mighty acts and explains that, on hearing these stories, her household had been convinced that Yahweh "is indeed God in heaven above and on earth below" (Josh 2:8–11).[20] And, just as a result of their mission to Sodom, the angelic spies in Sodom will determine that Lot is the only righteous man in that city (Gen 19:12–14), so Joshua's spies find only Rahab and her household worthy of protection and therefore agree to her request for a pact that would save their lives when the city is destroyed (Josh 2:12–14).

While the outcome of the spies' mission determines the fate of the two cities, both narratives also include oath-taking as an important element.[21] Abraham successfully negotiates with God to destroy Sodom and Gomorrah only if fewer than ten righteous men are found there (Gen 18:20–33). While an oath is not directly mentioned, God gives the divine word and that serves as an equivalent. In comparison, in the Rahab narrative the spies swear an oath to her to protect her and her family (Josh 2:12–14). They also warn her to keep her bargain to preserve them until they can escape, telling no one, and then that she must keep her family all together during the attack and signal their presence with a red cord (a clear parallel to the blood-stained doorpost in the Passover event of Exod 12:22–23; Josh 2:17–21). The oath is also referenced twice in Josh 6:17b and vv. 22–25 as the basis for Rahab's survival.[22]

Particularly interesting about this oath-taking process is how it complements the hospitality protocol. Just as a stranger becomes a guest and someone the host is to protect, the oath between Rahab and Joshua's spies also transforms her from a foreigner into a member of the Israelite

---

20. McKinlay, "Rahab: A Hero/ine?" 51, assumes that Rahab's words have been put in her mouth by the editor, but notes that "her words . . . are heard as the very guarantee of Israelite success. This is the theological affirmation that needs to be heard—by the spies, by Joshua, and by each succeeding Israelite audience."

21. Note the similarity with the story of the Gibeonite deception in Joshua 9. Both narratives cite the power over Egypt and the defeat of the Amorite kings as the basis for their actions (Josh 2:9–10; 9:9–10). In neither case is God consulted (see Josh 9:14) about making this pact, but once it has been enacted it must be fulfilled (although note the spies do warn Rahab that she must stay within her house to survive the sack of Jericho, a further parallel with the Passover). Again, the oath or vow is the key to the stories and like hospitality is a compact with the force of divine sanction.

22. Compare Gen 19:10 where Lot's house functions as his sanctuary against the predatory citizens of Sodom.

community. Gillmayr-Bucher points to Rahab's request for ḥesed since she in turn had shown ḥesed to the spies (vv. 12–13; see Gen 21:23; Judg 8:35; 2 Sam 2:6; 10:2 = 1 Chron 19:2).[23] I would suggest that ḥesed in this context is what Britt refers to as an exilic and post-exilic strategy "to combine literary convention with innovation: familiar, liturgical language about the covenant with Yahweh" in order "to affirm the tradition [of divine concern] even despite the horrors of circumstance."[24] Ḥesed is treaty language and the basis for mutual agreement. And, in this case true reciprocity is possible based on a life for a life.

Thus, this free exchange of peace and mutual respect embodied in the concept of ḥesed allows the spies to consider Rahab acceptable as, if unexpected, a treaty partner. In other words, Rahab has created a new mental image that transforms her identity from an enemy "other" into a friendly ally.[25] Although biblical law strictly forbids such a treaty with a Canaanite (see Exod 23:32; 34:15; Deut 7:2), Rahab obtains a new status (compare Ruth's transformation ritual in 1:16—17) and in the process provides DtrH with a legal loophole based upon the offer of ḥesed as a form of hospitality.[26]

CONCLUSIONS

Polzin removes the individuality of Rahab by asserting that "it is not because of Rahab's merit that she and her household will continue to occupy the land, but because of the wickedness and lack of faith of Israel."[27] McKinlay, goes even further by describing Rahab as simply a narrative creation, saying if she sounds like an Israelite in her discourse on the mighty acts of God, it is because "she is an Israelite construct and constructed as a pawn of the text which makes her into the all-important Other, and so a significant part

---

23. Gillmayr-Bucher, "'She Came to Test Him,'" 145–46. Tikva Frymer-Kensky, "Reading Rahab," 61, labels her as a "resourceful outsider, Rahab the trickster, is a new Israel."

24. Britt, "Unexpected Attachments," 306.

25. Gillmayr-Bucher uses as background for this position the work of Denis-Constant Martin, "The Choices of Identity," 5–20. Martin notes that "one proposes one's identity in the form of a narrative in which one can re-arrange, re-interpret the events of one's life in order to take care both of permanence and change, in order to satisfy the wish to make events concordant in spite of the inevitable discordances likely to shake the basis of identity." This is of course what every group or national storyteller does and it serves Rahab's purposes as well as the spies, who wish to escape a dangerous situation.

26. Bird, "Harlot as Heroine," 129, 131–32, does not use of the term hospitality, but does refer to ḥesed as the basis for Rahab's actions and those of the spies.

27. Polzin, *Moses and the Deuteronomist*, 88.

of the justification for the dispossession of her people's land."[28] If McKinlay is correct about this lack of ethnic identity until the choice of Yahwism is made, then Rahab becomes the model for what is expected of the Israelites and becomes DtrH's "poster child" for determining who is an Israelite in much the same way that Ruth achieves that status through her faithful behavior.[29]

However, I would argue that giving Rahab credit for right behavior does not change her status as a real character. She is more than a construct of the DtrH. She functions as true host and thereby gains honor and life for her household. Her protection of the spies functions at both the theological and social level. With that said, it is possible to say that *ḥesed* transcends *ḥerem*, and that hospitality can be equated with *ḥesed*. Both these terms refer to a pact or covenant and a set of social obligations.

It is also possible that a larger or alternative theological principle is at work here predicated on the universality of Yahweh. At stake here is the concept evidenced in the very difficult questions that God asks Job (38—41) and Jonah (4:9–11) about divine sovereignty over creation, which in turn mitigates against exclusion of non-Israelites from God's concern and care if they demonstrate righteous behavior.[30] This is consistent with the assertion of Yahweh's total majesty in Isa 42:5–9 as creator of all things and the bold statement in Isa 45:5, "I am the Lord, and there is no other."

Therefore, it may be that the key to the hospitality/*ḥerem* issue is (1) recognition of Yahweh as the only god, and (2) right behavior and right speech that demonstrate membership in a larger faith community that can include non-Israelites even though they are not part of the covenant community of Israel. For those who resist recognizing Yahweh's sovereignty and continue to worship other gods, as the inhabitants of Sodom or Jericho do, they demonstrate their lack of righteousness and are destroyed. But those Canaanites who profess their recognition of Yahweh's power, as Rahab and the Gibeonites do (Josh 9:6–14), survive the conflagration that consumes their neighbors. Furthermore, the case made in the Story of Rahab is that those showing hospitality to strangers are blessed with an enduring title to

---

28. McKinlay, "Rahab: A Hero/ine?" 52–53.

29. Matthews, "Determination of Social Identity," 49–54. The story of Ruth allows a non-Israelite to make a statement of faith and opens up a social mechanism for her cultural absorption into the Israelite community in Bethlehem. However, her full identity is not achieved until she has proven her righteousness through care for her mother-in-law, hard work, and submission to Israelite law.

30. Jonah's short-sighted and exclusivistic attitude is condemned when God asks why the prophet is more concerned about the demise of a bush that had given him shade than about Nineveh and its one hundred twenty thousand inhabitants.

the land, whereas those who carry out *ḥerem* sacrifice against strangers, like the households of Joshua and Josiah, ultimately forfeit their land to strangers like Assyria and Babylon.[31] Therefore in the final redaction of the Book of Joshua, the DtrH endorses hospitality rather than *ḥerem*, to ensure an enduring title to the land once the exile ends.

BIBLIOGRAPHY

Benjamin, Don C. *Deuteronomy and City Life: Form Criticism of Texts with the Word CITY in Deut 4:41–26:19*. Lanham, MD: University Press of America, 1983.

Bird, Phyllis. "The Harlot as Heroine: Narrative Art and Social Presupposition in Three Old Testament Texts." *Semeia* 46 (1989) 119–39.

Briend, Jacques. "The Sources of the Deuteronomistic History: Research on Joshua 1—12." In *Israel Constructs Its History: Deuteronomistic Historiography in Recent Research*, edited by Albert de Pury et al., eds., 360–86. JSOTSup 306. Sheffield: Sheffield Academic, 2000.

Britt, Brian. "Unexpected Attachments: a Literary Approach to the Term ḤSD in the Hebrew Bible." *JSOT* 27 (2003) 289–307.

Clements, Ronald E. "Achan's Sin: Warfare and Holiness." In *Shall not the Judge of All the Earth Do What Is Right?: Studies on the Nature of God in Tribute to James L. Crenshaw*, edited by David Penchansky and Paul L. Redditt, 113–26. Winona Lake, IN: Eisenbrauns, 2000.

Davidson, Steed V. "Gazing (at) Native Women: Rahab and Jael in Imperializing and Postcolonial Discourses." In *Postcolonialism and the Hebrew Bible: The Next Step*, edited by Roland Boer, 79–92. Semeia Studies 70. Atlanta: Society of Biblical Literature, 2013.

Frymer-Kensky, Tikva. "Reading Rahab."In *Tehillah le-Moshe: Biblical and Judaic Studies in Honor of Moshe Greenberg*, edited by Mordechai Cogan, et al, 57–67. Winona Lake, IN: Eisenbrauns, 1997.

Gillmayr-Bucher, Susanne. "'She Came to Test Him with Hard Questions': Foreign Women and Their View on Israel." *BibInt* 15 (2007) 135–50.

Hawk, L. Daniel. "Strange Houseguests: Rahab, Lot, and the Dynamics of Deliverance." In *Reading between Texts: Intertextuality and the Hebrew Bible*, edited by Danna N. Fewell, 89–97. Louisville: Westminster John Knox, 1992.

Herzfeld, Michael. "'As in Your Own House': Hospitality, Ethnography, and the Stereotype of Mediterranean Society." In *Honor and Shame and the Unity of the Mediterranean*, edited by D. D. Gilmore, 75–89. Washington, DC: American Anthropological Association, 1987.

---

31. In its final redaction, the tone of the book of Joshua changes during the early exile (597—538 BCE). Instead of celebrating without reserve the victories of Joshua, indictments are injected against the leaders of the people, especially Josiah, for forfeiting Yahweh's covenantal gifts of land and children by negotiating treaties with surrounding states. These alliances did not protect and provide for the land and its people, but fueled relentless wars and brutal famines and epidemics that ultimately led to the destruction of Judah and Jerusalem, and the deportation of their people.

———. "Afterword: Reciprocating the Hospitality of These Pages." *Journal of the Royal Anthropological Institute* 18 (2012) S210—S217.
Jenei, Péter. "Abraham's Hospitality: Social Scientific Biblical Criticism, the Ancient Custom of Hospitality and an Interpretation of Gen 18:1–16." *Sapientia Logos* 6 (2014) 1–34.
Martin, Denis-Constant. "The Choices of Identity." *Social Identities* 1 (1995) 5–20.
Matthews, Victor H. "The Determination of Social Identity in the Story of Ruth." *BTB* 36 (2006) 49–54.
———. "Female Voices: Upholding the Honor of the Household." *BTB* 24 (1994) 8–15.
———. "Hospitality and Hostility in Genesis 19 and Judges 19." *BTB* 22 (1992) 3–11.
Matthews, Victor H., and Don C. Benjamin. *Social World of Ancient Israel, 1250–587 BCE*. Peabody, MA: Hendrickson, 1993.
McKinlay, Judith E. "Rahab: A Hero/ine?" *BibInt* 7 (1999) 44–57.
Nieuwenhuijze, C. A. O. van. *Sociology of the Middle East: A Stocktaking and Interpretation*. Leiden: Brill, 1971.
Ottosson, Magnus. "Rahab and the Spies." In *DUMU-E2-DUB-BA-A: Studies in Honor of Åke W. Sjöberg*, edited by Hermann Behrens, et al., 419–27. Philadelphia: University Museum, 1989.
Polzin, Robert. *Moses and the Deuteronomist: a Literary Study of the Deuteronomic History*. New York: Seabury, 1980.
Porten, Bezalel. *The Elephantine Papyri in English: Three Millennia of Cross-cultural Continuity and Change*. Documenta et monumenta Orientis antiqui 22. Leiden: Brill, 1996.
Sherwood, Aaron. "A Leader's Misleading and a Prostitute's Profession: A Re-Examination of Joshua 2." *JSOT* 31 (2006) 43–61.
Stern, Philip D. *The Biblical Ḥerem: A Window on Israel's Religious Experience*. Brown Judaic Studies 211. Atlanta: Scholars, 1991.

14

As a Commentator, One Might Ask, "What Would Jeremiah or John Say?"

—*John E. Goldingay*

In a commentary I am writing, I tentatively translate Jer 2:5–14 as follows:

> Yahweh has said this:
> What wrongdoing did your ancestors find in me,
>   that they went far away from me.
> They went after emptiness and became emptiness,
>   and didn't say "Where is Yahweh,
> The one who brought us up from the country of Egypt
>   and enabled us to go through the wilderness,
> Through a country of steppe and pit,
>   a country of drought and deep darkness,
> A country through which no one passed
>   and where no human being lived?"
> I enabled you to come into a country of farmland
>   to eat its fruit and its good things.
> But you came and defiled my country;
>   you made my possession an outrage.
> The priests didn't say, "Where is Yahweh?";
>   the people controlling the Teaching didn't acknowledge me.

> The shepherds rebelled against me,
>> the prophets prophesied by Ba'al
>> and followed beings that couldn't achieve anything.
> Therefore I shall contend with you more (Yahweh's declaration),
>> and contend with your grandchildren.
> Because cross over to the shores of Cyprus and see,
>> send off to Qedar and observe well,
>> see if something like this has happened.
> Has a nation changed its gods,
>> when those are not gods?
> But my people have changed my splendor
>> for what doesn't achieve anything.
> Be devastated at this, heavens,
>> shudder, be utterly desolate (Yahweh's declaration).
> Because my people have done two bad things:
>> they've abandoned me,
>> the fountain of running water,
> To dig themselves cisterns,
>> breakable cisterns,
>> that can't [hold] water.

But as well as translating Jeremiah's words, as a commentator I also ask, "What would Jeremiah himself say if standing in a seminary or Christian university courtyard, instead of simply being talked about there and being written about in my office?"

The time we live in is somewhat like Jeremiah's. Sometimes people say the church in the United States is in exile. While that seems an exaggeration, the church is weaker and less influential than it used to be. It is indeed on the way to exile, and we are therefore living at a moment not unlike Jeremiah's time. He performed most of his ministry in the decades before the exile, when there was a possibility of avoiding that fate. In that context, Jeremiah's analysis of Judah's situation is transferable to ours.

In the passage quoted, Jeremiah lays out the basics of his four-decade-long message, asking the question we ourselves might ask: "Why are we in a reduced state, why are we a shadow of our former self?" For Jerusalem, the first reason was that they have forgotten their gospel, the good news, the story of what God did for them, the story about the God who brought them out of Egypt and gave them the land, and they hadn't asked where God was when things went south. Secondly, they gave up on God's written word. The people controlling the Teaching, the Torah, didn't acknowledge me, Yahweh says. The written word of God was not shaping their relationship with God and their lives. Thirdly, they turned to other spiritual resources. They abandoned the fountain of running water, and dug for themselves cisterns that couldn't hold water. Jeremiah's metaphor works brilliantly because the best water supply is a spring or a well, from which people get fresh water, but sometimes they have to make do with a tank to collect water in the winter and use during the summer. A leak in the tank then has deathly implications. How stupid to give up a spring and choose to rely on a tank, specifically a tank that leaks? Yet Israel did so in turning from Yahweh.

That was because they thought the culture around them had the answer to their key needs, and so assimilated to the culture. They needed a deity who could make crops, flocks, herds, and families grow, a god relevant to everyday life. They questioned whether Yahweh was a better answer than Ba'al, who specialized in these agricultural concerns. Israel thus assimilated how it lived its religious life to the surrounding culture. Everyday pressures had made people forget about the story of who they were and made them abandon the written word of God designed to shape them. They gave up on the gospel and assimilated to the culture. Or perhaps more subtly, they continued to call God Yahweh, but they had so changed Yahweh's nature to that of Ba'al that in effect they were worshiping Ba'al.

Today, I imagine Jeremiah denouncing similar factors affecting the church. We, too, have assimilated to our culture. Our everyday needs are different, but the result is the same. Israel couldn't be sure about its everyday outer needs. In Western culture we are more preoccupied with our abstract, inner so-called needs, needs that *our* culture encourages us to think about. Where will I get my significance? What can I do to make myself count? Does anyone care about me and understand me? Where can I find intimacy? Such questions evidence our internal isolation and emptiness.

We then try to make the gospel focus on those needs. We do so in worship, which becomes the way we deal with our emptiness and our isolation. Worship is redesigned to make us feel good. Discussion about God is not done to change our hearts and actions but to make us feel good. Worship abandons the reading of scripture, because that's boring. I recently talked with a pastor from a "Bible Church," part of a movement intended to have the emphasis its name implies. This pastor ironically said that they don't usually read the Bible as such nowadays in his "Bible Church." Bible reading happens only in the context of the sermon. I visited a mega-church a while ago and it was the same there. And at a Pentecostal church. So it's not surprising that many students arrive at college or seminary never having read the Bible.

Likewise, worship ignores the gospel story, because those events happened a long time ago and don't seem relevant. So one can sit through a whole worship service without hearing any reference to the gospel events—to the way God created the world, delivered Israel, sent Jesus to live and die for us, and raised him from the dead. As Israel forgot the gospel and gave up on God's written word because it was so concerned with its personal needs, so it is happening to us.

There's a tragic paradox here. We need to be brought out of ourselves by seeing our lives set in the context of a bigger picture, a bigger story, the gospel story. But we are so overwhelmed by our emptiness, isolation, and insignificance that we don't pay attention to this bigger story. So we turn God into someone whose focus is on meeting those needs. In worship we use many of the same words our forebears used, the words God and Lord and Jesus, but the content we read into them comes from the contemporary context. A New Age person could come into worship and find ninety or even one hundred percent of what we say and do quite acceptable.

And that is unacceptable! We short-circuit the process whereby God gives content and meaning to our lives. We make God a quick fix for our needs. But quick fixes don't work. The only fix that works is the gospel story and the scriptures where we find that story—the very things our worship services have given up on.

We have devised a religion to enable us to give expression to our individual sad selves and we hope it will make us feel better, but it doesn't. We leave worship just as sad as when we arrived. Next, we think that more of the same is the solution. If only we make the worship livelier, it will work. This is trying to get a drink from a tank with no water. We have focused on our immediate felt needs and given up on the gospel story that made us what we are. We are focused on me, rather than on God, on scripture, on the church, on the gospel, and on our calling on God. We have assimilated to the culture, as Israel did, and forgotten the big picture. We think the gospel is just about me and God—especially about me.

Another way we compensate for our sense of lost-ness, insignificance, and loss of conviction about the gospel is a concern about social justice. Jeremiah would be enthusiastic about that passion, of course, though he would worry that we have taken our understanding of social justice from our culture, too, and we have not thought out how the Bible looks at the topic. We think it's obvious what social justice means, we share the conviction of the culture that it can be achieved, and yet we are on our way to the same fate as overcame the enthusiasts for social justice in the 1920s. It's another factor threating the demise of the church over the next decade or two.

The parents of many of the present generation knew the gospel and knew the Bible, and they sought to apply it by an involvement with social justice. But the current generation lacks that background in the gospel and the Bible, so it will inevitably simply assimilate to the culture and its social concerns, read those back into the Bible, and lose the real gospel about God. Fifty or sixty years ago, some surface similarity existed between Christian values and the values of the culture, which the church attempted to Christianize or look for signs of redemption within. But the culture has now moved further and further from a Christian perspective. We long ago reached a point when the church needed to become the embodiment of an alternative vision for being human, but it failed to make that revolutionary move. Consequently, Jeremiah would warn us that we will now die of assimilation to the culture.

I am writing just after Pentecost, and another way of speaking about going into exile is to speak of the withdrawal of the Holy Spirit. In a class a little while ago we were studying Psalm 51 with its prayer, "Don't take your Holy Spirit from me." A student commented, "How great to know that now God wouldn't ever take his Holy Spirit from us." In Anglican prayer we pray that prayer every day. Are we misguided? God will never randomly abandon us. God can be trusted. But can we forfeit the Holy Spirit's presence?

The question came home afresh when my wife and I went around many cities in Turkey exceptionally important in Christian history: the cities to which John sent letters (Revelation 2–3), the cities Paul visited in his missionary journeys, the cities where the church agreed on its creeds, and finally Patmos, the island in sight of Turkey where John sat in confinement. Nowadays in that part of the world, you wake up each day to the call of the minaret. Virtually nowhere is there a Christian community. The Eastern Mediterranean was the cradle of the development of Christian faith, but the church is gone. The situation looks rather similar in Europe. Did God not take his Holy Spirit away from these churches?

Having asked what Jeremiah would say, I now want to ask what the John of the book of Revelation would say if here in a seminary or a Christian college instead of just being commented on. From Patmos, John looked across at the country whose churches in those gigantic Roman cities were on his heart. So what did John do?

Revelation implies that he worshiped and prayed. Certainly he wrote, because Revelation is the fruit of his time there. What useless things to do, worship and pray and write! Like Jeremiah, John had been able to preach earlier in his life, but eventually he had to stop. Both Jeremiah and John were taken into confinement, into exile. The communities they cared about got destroyed. Yet the writings of both of them have had an influence and importance way beyond their day. Whether Jeremiah or John thought they might have that influence, I do not know.

As regards the commentaries and other books that I write, or anything I say as a professor, I am quite gloomy. They make a difference to the occasional individual but likely have little long-term effect on most. The examples of Jeremiah and John at least give me hope that something I write might benefit the church the other side of its coming exile. When we talk about scholarship and research, and even master's level study, as professors we sometimes speak of introducing people to the scholarly conversation. But for the most part the scholarly conversation is empty. One thing you can be sure of is that today's new insights will seem hopelessly outdated to tomorrow's scholarship. In the world of scholarship there is much talk of intertextuality, which can mean a conversation between texts in which they are their own world, with no points of contact with a real world outside the texts. The scholarly conversation is uncomfortably parallel. It doesn't link with a real world outside the articles in scholarly journals. Jeremiah and John would want their commentators not to contribute to a scholarly conversation but to write something that's true and something that will help the church the other side of its coming exile.

If the church is to evade that fate or be restored after that exile, God has to be the one who makes this happen. That fact might heighten the importance of the worship and prayer that John stresses, and also the importance of not having the Holy Spirit being taken from us. In the United States, when there is a new movement of the Spirit the tradition is to start a new church rather than let it empower the existent churches. Unfortunately, this lets the existent churches off the hook and lets the new churches do what they like.

I recently asked a friend who is a pastor in a big Pentecostal church, though not himself from a Pentecostal background, how the traditional marks of Pentecostalism surface in his church. They don't feature, he said, because the church wants to be seeker-friendly, to reach outsiders, people on the church's fringe. Once, in a dinner conversation with students about some of these questions about the Holy Spirit, one of them sounded so bemused that she reminded me of the believers in Ephesus who hadn't even heard that there was a Holy Spirit. Christian faith becomes something we do, which suits us Americans, because we like to be in charge, to be in control. Or it becomes something we think about, which suits us theologians and commentators.

On the basis of all these considerations, I suggest an agenda for commentators and other theologians. Rather than quashing or downplaying the Holy Spirit, pray for the pouring out of the Holy Spirit on the church. Get people to read the Bible. Get them to think about the culture in a way that doesn't surrender the importance of the unique Christian story, the story of God's creating the world, God's involvement with Israel and God's activity in Jesus. Get them to rethink and rework social justice in a way that doesn't mimic the culture but reflects the radically different way a prophet such as Jeremiah conceives it. Teach people to lead worship in a way that reflects the gospel and gives prominence to Scripture. Write about things that matter, that will last, and that are true. Let all be preparation for the church's coming exile, or even for a renewed outpouring of the Holy Spirit that could avert exile.

15

Biblical Commentary as an Exercise in Counterpoint

The Book of Job, Prosperity, and Liberation

—*Alissa Jones Nelson*

IN SITTING DOWN TO write this article, I unearthed an old paper I wrote for John Hartley's "Hebrew Poetry and Wisdom Literature" class.[1] I have moved at least 11 times since my undergraduate days, yet these eight sheets of paper have travelled with me, from California to Europe to Japan and back to Europe again. This is a testament to the fact that both this course and Dr. Hartley (I still cannot quite bring myself to call him John) made a lifelong impression on me. I can safely date the beginning of my love for the book of Job, the topic of my Ph.D. thesis and still a topic of my research, back to that class.

The paper, written by a lowly first-year Hebrew student, was (not so creatively) titled "*Mišpat*: Job's God of Justice."[2] Rereading the paper to-

---

1. There is a date on the paper, which I refuse to disclose; however, one could make an educated guess when one discerns that I have the paper in hard copy only, and that I had to add the Hebrew vowel pointing to the typed copy by hand.

2. I received an A for the paper, although that did not prevent Dr. Hartley from covering the entire text with blue ink and indicating where I might have done better. On the back of one page, the last of his extensive comments, is the following paragraph: "This material and insightful presentation accords well with your goal of illuminating

day, and disregarding paragraphs and sections that I cringe at now, I am pleasantly surprised to find entire paragraphs in this paper, written when I was 20 years old, that guide my opinions and research today. I cannot take much credit for this; it is in large part due to Dr. Hartley's careful guidance, encouragement, and criticism. These did not end with that paper, or indeed with the course itself. Several years later when I returned to California for the SBL Annual Meeting, presenting my very first academic paper as a first-year Ph.D. student, Dr. Hartley was in the audience. When I asked him afterwards what he thought of the paper, which was of course on Job, he replied with characteristic frankness that he didn't understand much of it, but that he found it very interesting, and I certainly seemed to know what I was talking about.

John Hartley taught me many things, among them the importance of kindness as a scholarly skill. At the same SBL panel mentioned above, I encountered an early-career academic, a fellow presenter, who took the opportunity during the discussion portion of the session to tear my paper, and consequently my fragile first-year graduate student self, to shreds. It was a difficult 30 minutes, and Dr. Hartley's invitation to lunch after the session was something that kept me going that day. He taught me by example something that I have only recently learned to articulate: In academia, everyone is smart. There is no point distinguishing yourself by trying to be the smartest, but you can distinguish yourself by being kind. Dr. Hartley is certainly both.

My research and opinions, both professional and personal, have undergone many changes since my undergraduate and early graduate days. In keeping with the spirit with which he offered his critical (in both senses) encouragement after that SBL presentation, I offer here a variation on a theme, a counterpoint to my years as a student at Azusa Pacific University and to what I learned from Dr. Hartley, with points of harmony and points of dissonance. I consider this the most suitable homage to a mentor who so elegantly communicated what he thought and so effectively encouraged me to think for myself.

INTRODUCTION

Whatever one's opinion of Prosperity theology and its proponents, one cannot deny that it has provoked both national and international debate. In

---

for people the biblical text. May you have a blessed journey on this path." My journey has taken many unexpected turns since then, but I remain blessed and encouraged by the comments nevertheless.

September 2006, *Time* magazine's cover posed what has become a critical question for many: "Does God Want You to be Rich?"[3] In "academic" circles, and particularly in biblical commentary, one can easily malign, dismiss or ignore some of the more questionable theological products of the North American megachurch. Contextual engagement, however, requires that one address those issues that participate in the shaping of the wider contexts of which "academic" biblical studies is a part and with which it interacts. Several recent calls for conversation and serious engagement between Prosperity theology and its opponents[4] provide the impetus for this reflection, which will engage the issues Prosperity theology raises by instigating a dialogue between Prosperity and Liberation theologies in the context of commentary on the book of Job.

THE ORIGIN AND SPREAD OF PROSPERITY THEOLOGIES

The provenance of Prosperity theology is still a subject of some debate. Most commentators trace its philosophical basis to Norman Vincent Peale's *The Power of Positive Thinking*, first published in 1952, which was and remains an influential text in the North American psyche. Theologically, Prosperity theology rose to prominence in the work of Kenneth Hagin, whose debt to E. W. Kenyon is estimated in greater or lesser degrees,[5] and was further popularized in its various forms by Kenneth and Gloria Copeland, Oral Roberts, and Robert Schuller, among others.

Significantly, Mark Hellstern argues that the origins of Prosperity theology can be found much earlier than the mid-twentieth century, and that the theology is in fact "as old as Jamestown and Massachusetts Bay."[6] At the beginning of the seventeenth century, the Puritans and the first settlers at Jamestown viewed material prosperity as an end goal of their "new Jerusalem," although material prosperity was seen as a goal for the good of the community rather than the individual. The concept of double (positive and

---

3. Van Biema and Chu, "Does God Want You To Be Rich?"

4. See Folarin, "Prosperity Gospel in Nigeria"; Piedra, "Theology of Grace"; Smith, "Communication"; Starner, "Prosperity Theology."

5. On this point, see Anderson, "The Prosperity Message"; see also Phiri and Maxwell, "Gospel Riches"; Piedra, "Theology of Grace"; Kim, "A Bed of Roses"; Starner, "Prosperity Theology."

6. Hellstern, "The 'Me' Gospel," 79. On this point, see also Anderson, "The Prosperity Message," 73.

negative) retribution was key to this theology.⁷ This theological focus found its counterpart in the self-improvement theories that became the focus of eighteenth-century American philosophy in the so-called Age of Reason. "It would require only a matter of time for self-improvement to evolve into self-promotion and self-aggrandizement," as evidenced in later arguments for "Manifest Destiny."⁸ North America's individualistic philosophy of life, the concept of pulling oneself up by one's own bootstraps, spilled over into its religion as well. Early nineteenth-century religious revivals stressed pietism, individualism, reductionism, and anti-intellectualism in North American religion, values which are still reflected in current Prosperity movements.⁹ The American Industrial Revolution created an even greater need for the moral justification of wealth, which had already begun in the mid-nineteenth century. In this era, concepts of self-help became closely aligned with the idea of upward social mobility and economic success as evidence of moral merit. Thus the rich adopted a Christian version of 'survival of the fittest,' which argued that the poor deserved to be poor and that charity therefore constituted interfering with God's just punishment of moral failure. Historically, "[i]t seems that during times of economic growth and prosperity [North] Americans make the most obvious attempts to justify their materialistic bent by claiming divine sanction."¹⁰ Peale's work in the 1950s is another manifestation of over 300 years of Prosperity Theology. Contemporary prosperity preachers such as Creflo Dollar, T. D. Jakes, and Joel Osteen are thus "variations on a very old, very well-developed [North] American theme."¹¹

Many of the diatribes against Prosperity theology take account solely of the more extreme manifestations of this particular perspective. Like Liberation theology, which is more properly referred to as Liberation theolog*ies*, Prosperity theology is a complex phenomenon with many incarnations. The basic tenets Prosperity theologies hold in common are: 1) God desires prosperity for all of God's children; 2) the promise of prosperity in the Abrahamic covenant is extended to include Christians after the death and resurrection of Christ; 3) the practice of "positive confession" or "name it and claim it" is the means of obtaining the material blessings associated with health and wealth; and 4) related to this, the concept of "seed faith" is giving in faith more than one can reasonably afford in order to reap better

7. Hellstern, "The 'Me' Gospel," 82–83.
8. Ibid., 84.
9. Ibid., 84–85.
10. Ibid., 87.
11. Ibid., 87–88.

returns. These various aspects are emphasized in greater or lesser degrees in different Prosperity teachings. The concept of "seed faith" is perhaps most obviously open to abuse by greedy church hierarchies as well as by believers who, it is argued, give only or primarily in order to receive. Nevertheless, even among some of the more easily lampooned Prosperity theologians, "prosperity is not seen as financial blessing alone, but as spiritual, mental, and physical prosperity also."[12] Furthermore, in the more moderate perspectives, financial prosperity is not given to believers to allow them to live in luxury, but rather to enable them "do something about the poverty in the world."[13] The good news for the poor, according to Kenneth Copeland, is that God does not want the poor to be poor anymore.[14]

This message in particular has popularized Prosperity theologies as a significant theological export, evidenced by the exponential growth of prosperity churches recorded in Latin America,[15] Africa,[16] and Asia[17] in the past thirty years. Both Claudio de Oliveira Ribeiro[18] and Paul Gifford[19] note the irony of the fact that a theology apparently devised to justify the wealth of the rich and the poverty of the poor has been so enthusiastically embraced in contexts of poverty around the world. In Latin America, particularly in urban contexts, many of the poor have "voted with their feet" and are abandoning the traditionally dominant Catholic churches in favor of Neo-Pentecostal churches, many (though not all) of which preach prosperity.[20] Many scholars of religion in Latin America offer some version of

12. Anderson, "The Prosperity Message," 77.

13. Copeland, "Prosperity Puzzle," 4. See also Anderson, "The Prosperity Message," 77.

14. Copeland, "The Whole Gospel," 2.

15. Particularly in Brazil and Guatemala, with recognized growth also in Costa Rica, Chile, Argentina, and Peru.

16. Particularly, although not exclusively, in Nigeria and South Africa.

17. Particularly, although not exclusively, in South Korea.

18. Ribeiro, "Has Liberation Theology Died?"

19. Gifford, "Theology and Right Wing Christianity."

20. The extent of and reasons for this migration are hotly debated among theologians, scholars of religion, and sociologists alike, but the fact of the migration itself is widely acknowledged. See Bastian, "Religious Transnationalisation"; Buckley, "Promises of Riches"; de Oliveira Ribeiro, "Has Liberation Theology Died?"; Berge Furre, "Crossing Boundaries"; Garrard-Burnett, "Transnational Protestantism,"; Garrard-Burnett, "The Third Church"; Kenny, *Substitute for Catholicism*, 1–24; Levine, "The Future of Christianity"; Martin, "Capitalist Society"; Llana, "Wealth Gospel Propels Poor Guatemalans"; Oro and Seman, "Brazilian Pentecostalism"; Piedra, "Theology of Grace"; Quiroz, "Suffering"; Smith, "Politics and Religious Fundamentalism." Furthermore, many who abandon their Catholic parish churches in favor of Neo-Pentecostal alternatives may eventually abandon the institutional church, although not necessarily

the adage, "Liberation theology opted for the poor, and the poor opted for Pentecostalism."[21] I shall explore some surprising convergences between Liberation and Prosperity theologies in the interests of flagging the relevance and importance of considering a variety of "vernacular" perspectives in the production of biblical commentary.[22] The book of Job, a biblical text often deployed against Prosperity theologies, has some potentially surprising resonances with prosperity ideals as well.

THE BOOK OF JOB: MUTUAL CHALLENGES

The most well-known work on the book of Job from the perspective of Liberation theologies is Gustavo Gutiérrez's *On Job: God-Talk and the Suffering of the Innocent*.[23] For Gutiérrez, the question at issue in the book of Job is the question of "how we are to talk about God from within a specific situation—namely, the suffering of the innocent."[24] This question relates to the book's discussion of the retribution doctrine and how a person might serve God gratuitously.

In Gutiérrez' view, the book of Job presents gratuitous service of God as a possibility not just for one person, but for all who believe. This possibility "implies the loving and completely free meeting of two freedoms,

---

the Christian faith, altogether. "To join an evangelical church breaks the traditional commitment to Catholicism, and then people become free to be 'without religion.' Those who leave the church do not necessarily become atheists; in many cases they become free 'consumers' of religious 'commodities.' They do not trust churches any more. They believe in God (or whatever) and invent their own religious diet, based on their own personal feeling and understanding." See de Aquino and de Oliveira, "'Overpragmatism,'" 19–21.

21. See Llana, "The Fiesta Spirit." Important differences exist between Pentecostal and Neo-Pentecostal or "second wave" churches; not all Neo-Pentecostal churches preach Prosperity theologies, and not all Prosperity theologies are associated with Neo-Pentecostal churches. Unfortunately, there is no consistent system of reference to these various movements among commentators, and it is sometimes difficult to discern to which of these various movements the term "Pentecostal" is meant to refer.

22. This paper will not concern itself with the extent of this trend. I recognize that the movement from Catholic to Pentecostal churches, particularly those that preach prosperity, is well-documented, but I also acknowledge that its provenance, pervasiveness, and significance are all hotly debated issues that vary according to context. Nevertheless, I consider that these issues have been adequately treated elsewhere. See note 18 above.

23. Gutiérrez, *On Job*. Other significant contributions include those of Elsa Tamez and Enrique Dussel, which space restrictions prevent me from including in the current discussion. See Tamez, "Father of the Needy"; Tamez, "A Letter to Job," 50–52; Dussel, "The People of El Salvador."

24. Gutiérrez, *On Job*, xviii.

Biblical Commentary as an Exercise in Counterpoint 247

the divine and the human."²⁵ Through this application of the principle of gratuitous love, "Job begins to free himself from an ethic centered on personal rewards and to pass to another focused on the needs of one's neighbor. The change represents a considerable shift."²⁶ Job's answer to the doctrine of retribution is that it simply does not reflect real life.²⁷

The doctrine of retribution is problematic for any advocate of the poor who must face the argument that the poor are poor according to their own just punishment for "sin," their own laziness, or their own greed. The character of Job exposes the false premises on which this argument is based, and Gutiérrez seizes upon this as confirmation that the poor suffer innocently and that a doctrine of retribution is not only insufficient but also unjust in the face of such suffering. Gutiérrez claims that Job 24:2–14 demonstrates the fact that Job "sees that the question being debated does not concern him alone" and furthermore "that this poverty and abandonment are not something fated but are caused by the wicked, who nonetheless live serene and satisfied lives."²⁸ In this passage, Gutiérrez claims, Job realizes his own solidarity with the poor, and this realization adds a new dimension to his complaint.²⁹

For Gutiérrez, the closing chapters of the book of Job particularly emphasize the importance of the relationship between God's revelation and God's gratuitous love.³⁰ These chapters reject the doctrine of retribution, and Guttiérrez argues that Job concerns not only the possibility of a person exercising gratuitous love of God but God's gratuitous love of humanity, which is not based on any merit or demerit. God's restoration of Job's wealth in the epilogue is interpreted as evidence of this gratuitous love. Tangentially, God's choice to reveal Godself specifically to the poor, not based on any merit or intrinsic worth of the poor but simply according to God's "free and unmerited love," is viewed as a demonstration of the relationship between God's revelation and God's gratuitous love.³¹

Gutiérrez' commentary postulates that, through careful exegesis of Job's speeches in the final chapters of the book, the reader comes to understand that "two languages—the prophetic and the contemplative—are required" if one is to speak of God accurately in contexts of suffering, and that

25. Ibid., 4.
26. Ibid., 31.
27. Ibid., 32.
28. Ibid., 32.
29. Ibid., 34.
30. Ibid., xi.
31. Ibid., xii–xiii.

these two languages must be "integrated into a single language."³² In Job's second response to God (Job 42:2-6), contemplative language "expresses the gratuitousness of God's love," e.g., the plans of God and the fact (as opposed to the content) of God's response to Job, while "prophetic language expresses the demands this love makes," e.g., Job's repudiation (as Gutiérrez interprets it) of dust and ashes.³³ Thus contemplative language helps one understand God's preferential love for the poor, which arises out of God's gratuitous love for people who are "living in an inhuman situation that is contrary to God's will," that is, the plan of God which is the subject of God's first speech to Job.³⁴ In concert with contemplative language, prophetic language emphasizes the importance of action on behalf of the poor as a recognition of the requirements of God's gratuitous love.³⁵ These insights find ample opportunity for application in the contexts of Liberation theologies.³⁶

32. Ibid., 94.

33. Ibid., 87–92, 95. Gutiérrez argues that Job abandons his retributive outlook in favor of the expanded horizon presented to him by the divine speeches. Job's final response to God does not express "contrition but *a renunciation of his lamentation and dejected outlook.*" Thus "Job begins to see the way by which he is to go to meet God and others." See Gutiérrez, *On Job*, 86, italics in original.

34. Ibid., 94.

35. Ibid., 94.

36. On the translation of the difficult passage in 42:2–6, see Morrow, "Consolation," 218–23. This chapter will not dwell on the Hebrew variants and the philological arguments surrounding the translation of this verse; a brief discussion will suffice. The ambiguity arises from nearly every Hebrew word in this particular verse. The Hebrew word *ma'as* can be variously translated as "reject," "refuse," "despise," "abhor," or "melt away." The second verb, *nikham*, can mean "to be sorry," "to console oneself," "to console another," "to be moved to pity," "to repent," or "to regret." The absence of a clear object, i.e., something which Job clearly rejects or repents *of*, has led many commentators to interpret this verse not as a reference to repentance but rather to the more positive connotation of changing one's mind based on experience, in this case Job's personal experience of encounter with God in the whirlwind. Nevertheless, the key question of whether or not Job is here expressing remorse cannot be unambiguously decided. In addition to the translation of these verbs, the translation of the Hebrew preposition *'al*, which can variously mean "on account of," "concerning" or "upon" in a spatial sense, presents a potential problem for translators. In this case the translation of this preposition is largely dependent upon the meaning the translator ascribes to the phrase "dust and ashes." Is "dust and ashes" a literal reference to the earth broadly or more narrowly to the ash heap on which Job has been sitting, or is it a metaphorical reference to human mortality or to mourning rites? Each of these translations has precedents in the Hebrew Bible as well as in the book of Job itself. How the translator interprets this phrase largely determines the way in which the preposition is translated. Thus this ambiguous verse provides us with an example of the truism that every translation is an interpretation. It also provides us with a basis on which to argue that those interpreters who assert that translations which conflict with their own preferred translation are "nonsense" or that they "distort the point of the book of Job" are based on subjective understandings

In attempting to find alternative interpretations of Job from the perspective of Prosperity theologies, I was surprised at the dearth of such material.[37] Part of the explanation is that Prosperity traditions use the biblical text differently, often involving superficial prooftexting and making the Bible a symbol of authority rather than a text to be closely studied and interpreted. While Prosperity theologies emphasize the Bible's importance, they do not place a corresponding importance on a close reading of the text itself, or indeed on the production or consumption of academic biblical commentary. The book of Job is generally taken by opponents of Prosperity theologies to be a direct contravention of Prosperity principles.[38] Nevertheless, a few voices recognize that the book of Job might not be such an easy opponent of Prosperity theologies after all. Among these, there is potential for an unlikely alliance between Prosperity theologies and the commentary work of David J. A. Clines.[39]

In his early work on Job, Clines argues that the retributional principle, while it is challenged throughout the dialogues, seems to be reinstated in the epilogue. In his more recent work on the subject, Clines has softened his position to indicate the lack of direct reference in the text itself to Job's

---

of what "the point" of the book of Job is rather than on objective semantic arguments, because the semantics are themselves ambiguous. For me, this very ambiguity is one of the chief attractions of the book of Job, and one of the reasons for arguing that its ambiguity should be preserved in commentary. See Wilson, *Job*, 467–68; Hartley, *The Book of Job*, 534–36; Fokkelman, *Major Poems*, 325–31; Gordis, *The Book of Job*, 491–92; Driver and Gray, *Book of Job*, 348, 373.

37. Even a search of sermons given in relevant contexts yields very little material on the book of Job, or on biblical texts in general, apart from a series of ubiquitous prooftexts. This lack of material surprised me. I assumed that Prosperity theologians would attempt to answer the charges leveled against them by their opponents, particularly as relates to the book of Job, which is usually cited in its entirety and very unambiguously as a proof against the validity of Prosperity theologies. Instead, I discovered that the large majority of sermons and literature in these churches is centered around predetermined theological issues rather than around the biblical text itself. The text is primarily a reference to supplement extant theology, a tool with which to make positive confessions, and a weapon to be used against the incursions of the devil rather than a basis upon which to counter the arguments of one's opponents.

38. See Benfold, *Why Lord?*, 49–60; Byassee, "Be Happy," 20–23; Collective authorship, "Statement on Prosperity Theology"; Gifford, "Right Wing Christianity," 36; Randerson, "God's Purpose"; Waters, "Reflections."

39. This is not to suggest that Clines himself supports the ideals or principles of Prosperity theology; in fact, his own position is oppositional to these principles and is quite complex. See Clines, "Quarter Days Gone"; see also Clines, "Job's Fifth Friend." Nevertheless, Clines' work does provide some ground on which proponents of Prosperity theologies may take their stand. His work merely provides the basis here for my own attempt to play devil's advocate and problematize simplistic oppositions in the production of biblical commentary.

renewed wealth as a reward; nevertheless, Clines leaves his options open on this point.[40] He prefers to conceptualize the epilogue's relationship with the poetic dialogues as one of deconstruction. The poetry serves "to prove over and over again that the doctrine of retribution is wrong," but the last eleven verses of the book (42:7–17) "deconstruct the second philosophy in the direction of the first."[41] Thus "the epilogue deconstructs the book as a whole."[42] Clines rightly points out that to understand the source or nature of a discrepancy, i.e., understanding the epilogue as secondary material, is not to eliminate the discrepancy. It must still be addressed. Furthermore, contrary to some arguments, Clines finds the epilogue very relevant to the theology of the book as a whole. It could be argued that the book of Job "ends up by giving assent to the very dogma it set out to annihilate."[43] Significantly, "[t]he very fact that the ending of the book of Job is not normally regarded as logically incoherent with what precedes it is an evidence that the contradiction is an *undermining*," that is, a deconstruction.[44] Finally, the interpreter has "no firm ground to stand on ... each of the philosophies [the book] actually does assert is undermined by the other."[45] This in no way suggests that Clines's interpretation explicitly supports Prosperity theologies. It does, however, underscore an ambiguity in the text itself which such interpreters could capitalize on. Although biblical scholars may rally around the idea that Prosperity theologians give only superficial and therefore problematic attention to the biblical texts, it would appear that biblical scholars and their commentaries have in fact done the work of Prosperity theologians for them, at least in this instance.

Some outspoken opponents of Prosperity theologies also find the epilogue potentially problematic as an instance of retributional ideas creeping back into the book of Job.[46] What these opponents fail to grasp is the subtlety of some of the more moderate Prosperity theologies. According to these proponents, prosperity is God's desire for *all* Christians; in these less extreme perspectives, it is not a matter of poverty being a punishment for personal sin, but of poverty as the result of a lack of active faith. The acquisition of an active faith, manifested in positive confession, raises the

---

40. Clines, "Does the Book of Job Suggest." See also Clines, "Job's Fifth Friend," 245–47.

41. Clines, "Deconstructing the Book of Job," 69–70.

42. Ibid., 70.

43. Ibid., 70–71.

44. Ibid., 71.

45. Ibid., 73.

46. See Randerson, "God's Purpose," 1.

believer out of poverty into the prosperity that God wants for all of God's children. It is not a matter of repenting personal sin, as Job's friends urged. Rather, it is a matter of faith, of positive confession in spite of circumstantial realities, which brings prosperity. Seen in this light, the parallels with Job's situation become increasingly obvious: Initially, Job is an example of a prosperous and godly individual.[47] This upright and believing individual is struck down for no discernible reason (as far as he himself is aware) and experiences both suffering and material privation. That individual continues, however, to espouse faith in God and to confess that faith in positive terms (as in Job 19:23–27) despite the negative emotions that suffering elicits. This faith eventually merits a response from God as well as restored health and, significantly, a *doubling* of that individual's material assets.[48] All of this is perfectly consistent with a more moderate form of Prosperity theology. In this view, the theme of the book of Job "is that God will ultimately bless the righteous [person] with prosperity when he [or she] trusts the Lord to the end and when he [or she] understands that the blessing is not his [or her] own but God's."[49] It is the final clause of the previous sentence that separates the proponents of more moderate Prosperity theologies from their more polemical, and hence more visible, brothers and sisters in the faith.

Hence, although Job has often been taken as a definitive rebuttal of retributional theology, this does not preclude its use as textual support for Prosperity theologies. Furthermore, the assumption that the book decisively refutes the principle of retribution has been called into question. Gutiérrez' attractive reading of the book of Job assumes that the doubling of Job's wealth in the epilogue is a manifestation of the gratuitousness of God's love. He does not acknowledge the ambiguity and potential subversion identified by Clines, but assumes the death of retributional theology. Similarly, a Prosperity perspective would have trouble reconciling its interpretation with Gutiérrez's interpretation of Job's struggle as a move toward solidarity with the poor. It is necessary for a Prosperity perspective to emphasize Job's individual faith relationship with God and to de-emphasize Job's commitment to a community of people who supposedly lack the faith to achieve what Job achieves in the end. Yet each of these aspects is arguably present in the text itself.

The prevailing interpretation, widespread in popular magazine articles and evangelical sermons, on websites, discussion forums, and personal blogs, seems to be that the book of Job in its entirety refutes Prosperity

---

47. Grogan, "Liberation and Prosperity Theologies," 121.
48. This would arguably correspond to the concept of seed faith, as discussed above.
49. Lee, "The Case for Prosperity Theology," 27.

theologies. Job's friends are identified as early proponents of Prosperity theologies, while Job stands against their theological positions. There are also a minority of voices who believe that the book of Job supports the notion that if one maintains one's faith and continues to claim one's share of God's blessings even in seemingly hopeless situations, then one is materially rewarded in the end. However, these ostensibly dissonant interpretations may be more harmonious than they initially appear.

READING TOGETHER: DISCOVERIES OF CORRESPONDENCE

Both Liberation and Prosperity theologies are predicated on the notion that God values and desires certain things for a certain group of people. For Liberation theologies, this group is "the poor," which includes all marginalized persons and groups, with emphasis on particular groups in particular contexts to a greater or lesser degree. In most Liberation theologies, God desires liberation not just for the Christian poor but for all poor persons. Prosperity theologies argue that God wants to "bless" all of God's children (exclusively construed in this perspective to be Christian believers) with material prosperity and full mental, physical, and spiritual health. In both cases, God's desire has a quasi-universal application; in the former theologies, it is applied to all of the world's poor, while in the latter, it is applied to all of the world's Christians. In both cases, there are behavioral expectations associated with the benefits offered. Liberation theologies argue that the poor must be conscientized and empowered to understand and resist their oppression in solidarity with other conscientized and empowered individuals who "opt for the poor." Prosperity theologies argue that all Christian believers must be conscientized and empowered to understand and claim the blessing of prosperity that faith in God necessarily offers. Both perspectives believe strongly in the importance of conscientization and empowerment. Both also insist on the universality of their particular ethical perspectives. Both recognize poverty as an evil. Where they differ is in their separate articulations of ultimate goals and the means by which to reach them. Nevertheless, it is significant that, perhaps despite appearances, these two perspectives are based on similar universalist foundations and similarly universal ethical assertions.

Both perspectives assume that God has the welfare of God's followers uppermost in God's mind; the question is not whether God rewards God's servants, but in what manner God does so. They disagree about the nature and timing of the reward, but agree that reward is forthcoming. Liberation commentaries on Job argue that God supports those who struggle against oppression, those who sit on the ash heap. In this context, the book of Job provides hope that God ultimately supports the liberation struggle and is therefore a God of justice. Prosperity theology argues that God's blessing of Job in the final verses of the book indicates that faith and positive confession are ultimately rewarded materially, even if periods of suffering punctuate the believer's life. Both theologies can agree that God does not want the poor to be poor, and that God wishes to rectify their suffering in this life, not the next.

I would also argue that both Liberation and Prosperity theologies make selective use of the biblical text generally, and of the book of Job in particular. Therefore the argument that either of these perspectives ignores textual counterevidence can and should be applied equally to the other perspective. As any collection of biblical commentaries demonstrates, both liberation and prosperity are key themes in the Old Testament or Hebrew Bible generally,[50] and in the book of Job in particular. Interpretation of the biblical text does not definitively support either perspective. Furthermore, both Liberation and Prosperity theologies postulate that the biblical text is directly applicable to contemporary life and contemporary struggles. While Liberation theologies generally are more apt to take into account historical speculations about the original context(s) of the biblical text(s) in question, both perspectives assume a certain level of direct correspondence and relevance between biblical and contemporary issues, whether these are liberation struggles or questions of health and wealth.

Furthermore, both Liberation and Prosperity theologies argue for a holistic view of salvation.[51] In the purview of Liberation theologies, salvation is a matter of spiritual, physical, social, and psychological well-being, and the Kingdom of God must begin to be realized in this life, although many Liberation theologies would agree that it must await its complete fulfillment in the next. Prosperity theologies see salvation as a matter of both the spiritual and the physical, with particular emphasis on the material. The spiritual aspects of salvation are not denied, but the physical aspects (health and wealth) are emphasized in reaction to a perceived de-emphasis of these aspects in the Christian tradition. The holistic concepts of salvation variously propounded by both Liberation and Prosperity theologies are consistent with the connotations of the Hebrew concept of salvation, although Liberation theologies are closer to the biblical idea of *shalom*, which includes the

---

50. See Grogan, "Liberation and Prosperity Theologies," 121, 127–28.

51. On the holistic nature of Prosperity theologies, see Anderson, "The Prosperity Message," 72–83. See also Phiri and Maxwell, "Gospel Riches," 23–29.

wholeness not only of the human person but of the community and the natural world as part of the concept of prosperity.[52]

Both Prosperity and Liberation theologies are interested in resistance to domination. The former tradition views domination primarily as a spiritual issue, one which can be addressed through faith and positive affirmations; the latter tradition views it as a systemic social issue, which can be solved through active religious and political resistance. Harold Wells argues that Neo-Pentecostal and Liberation perspectives "are far from antithetical; indeed they are potentially very congenial in that both place great emphasis on 'experience' in the life of faith, and both have relevance to circumstances of poverty and oppression."[53] The same argument could also be applied more specifically to Prosperity theologies, which are taught in many Neo-Pentecostal communities. The polarization between reason and emotion, manifested in a perceived polarization between Liberation and Prosperity theologies, respectively, needs to be overcome.[54] Both Liberation and Prosperity perspectives evince and could be united around what Wells refers to as a "spirit of resistance." Both offer resources that can be utilized politically. The challenge, particularly in communities that preach prosperity, is activating those resources.

Both Liberation theologies and Prosperity theologies offer hope to the poor.[55] If the concept of liberation propounded by Prosperity theologies is contrary to that propounded by Liberation theologies, then both concepts of liberation should be called into question. Financial security is a form of liberation. If prosperity for some simply means "a roof over their heads, clothes to wear, enough food to eat, do we then think differently about

---

52. See Warners and Borst, "Flourishing Creation."

53. Wells, "Resistance," 170.

54. Ibid., 171.

55. Perhaps the most common pragmatic argument against Prosperity theologies is that they do not work for everyone. This is certainly true; there are many people who leave these churches as a direct result of being disappointed in their financial expectations. Nevertheless, success stories do circulate, and with the concrete aid of the church, many adherents do prosper. Many others reap the more modest financial benefits associated with the lifestyle promoted by these (primarily) Neo-Pentecostal communities: an emphasis on hard work, an avoidance of alcohol and gambling, the need for a solid family life, and an end to sexual promiscuity and prostitution. Over time, this lifestyle promotes increased financial stability by combining a decrease in spending with an increase in both income and emotional/psychological support. Thus, while the received benefits may not align with the grandiose promises associated with seed faith and positive confession, they are nevertheless tangible and appreciable, and this is sufficient for many. See Llana, "Wealth Gospel Propels Poor Guatemalans." See also Williams, "Heresy," 33–34; Oro and Seman, "Brazilian Pentecostalism"; Sang-Bok, "Bed of Roses."

it?"[56] Have Liberation theologies failed to offer immediate solutions to the concrete problems of material privation faced by the poor? If the poor are voting with their feet and joining Prosperity churches as a result of pressing material needs, what other solutions to those immediate needs can be offered by alternative hermeneutical perspectives?

In spite of a wealth of recent work that would appear to answer the question in the negative, scholars are still asking whether Liberation theology has died.[57] My question is not, "What do Liberation theologies do now?" but rather, "What (else) do Liberation theologies have to offer?" Have we simply entered a "post-liberation theology era"[58] in which "a new kind of liberationist agenda" represented by Prosperity theologies addresses new needs in new contexts?[59] If we recognize the problematic nature of Prosperity theologies that "may be seen as lending religious justification to victimizing economic processes, at the same time as [they render] spiritual and practical support to the victims of these processes," how do we address this discrepancy?[60] Can Liberation theologies offer a means by which to meet the felt needs discussed above based on an ethic of community and solidarity, without calling for further sacrifice and delay on the part of those who have already sacrificed too much and delayed too long? If so, on what basis? If not, how can these theologies hope to survive?

JOB AS A CALL TO ACTION: READING JOB FROM AN ACTIVIST'S PERSPECTIVE

The extent to which Prosperity theology stifles political activism is debatable. Scholars largely agree that Prosperity theology frequently encourages individualistic pursuit of health and wealth at the expense of community solidarity and concern with political issues, including the political structures that contribute to the creation and maintenance of poverty in the neo-liberal ideals of late capitalism and globalization. Political passivity evidently rises among adherents to Prosperity theologies in Africa,[61] in

---

56. Phiri and Maxwell, "Gospel Riches," 29.
57. Ribeiro, "Has Liberation Theology Died?" 304–14.
58. Garrard-Burnett, "The Third Church in Latin America," 268.
59. Lee, "Almighty Dollar," 232.
60. Stålsett, "On-Time Deliverance," 209.
61. See Gifford, "Right Wing Christianity"; see also Gifford, "Expecting Miracles."

African American communities,[62] and in Latin America.[63] Nevertheless, counter-arguments also exist.[64] While some scholars argue that Prosperity theologies are highly individualistic, others note that they are nevertheless an aspect of a larger community in which the success stories of some adherents influence and encourage others, in which the principle of seed faith encourages a continual flow of resources between and among members of the congregations, and in which charity is actually encouraged, since material manifestations of prosperity are meant to be shared, not hoarded.[65] While Takatso Mofokeng argues that charity has the potential to cover up the structural injustices which create the need for charity in the first place, Michael Kenny argues that personal empowerment, as fostered by Prosperity theologies, is a necessary precursor to community empowerment, solidarity, and action for change.[66]

In the Latin American contexts we have been considering here, arguments surrounding the political effects of Prosperity theologies vary from increased political quietism, to increased (if authoritarian) activism, to arguments that no change in political activity is discernible.[67] With such a wide range of arguable effects, each based on electoral and sociological evidence, we could postulate that it is not Prosperity theologies themselves that significantly alter patterns of political participation among their adherents but rather that Prosperity theologies have various effects in various contexts, determined not only by the theologies themselves but also by the social standing of the adherent as well as a wide variety of both personal and external factors.[68] If this is the case, then the argument that Prosper-

62. See Franklin, "The Gospel of Bling"; see also Harris-Lacewell, "Righteous Politics."

63. See Furre, "Crossing Boundaries," 39–51; see also Esperandio, "Globalization and Subjectivity."

64. See Bastian, "Religious Transnationalisation"; see also Coleman, "Conservative Protestantism"; Coleman, *The Globalisation of Charistmatic Christianity*; Cox, "Spirits of Globalization"; Doak, "Liberation Theology"; Lee, "Prosperity Theology"; Quiroz, "Suffering in Latin America; Young "The Case for Prosperity Theology."

65. See Anderson, "The Prosperity Message," 72–83.

66. See Mofokeng, "The Prosperity Message and Black Theology"; see also Kenny, *Substitute for Catholicism*, 28–37. On the importance of individual empowerment as a virtue of Prosperity theologies, see Coleman, "America Loves Sweden"; Gifford, "Expecting Miracles," 20–24; Llana, "Fiesta Spirit"; Esperandio, "Globalization and Subjectivity"; Stålsett, "On-Time Deliverance."

67. See Buckley, "'Purse Strings"; see also Ribeiro, "Has Liberation Theology Died?"; Furre, "Crossing Boundaries"; Levine, "The Future of Christianity"; Martin, "Capitalist Society"; Esperandio, "Globalization and Subjectivity"; Smith, "Communication."

68. See Garrard-Burnett, "Transnational Protestantism," 117–125; see also Garrard-Burnett, "The Third Church in Latin America."

ity theologies necessarily and universally increase political quietism among their adherents is no longer tenable.

The basic tenets of both Liberation and Prosperity theologies have positive values in the political arena. Liberation theologies encourage a long-term view in which structural change, political alternatives to capitalist structures and neo-liberal values, and the solidarity of individual activists are all seen as essential tools in the alleviation or even elimination of poverty. These are worthy and necessary goals, but it must be admitted that the long-term focus leaves something to be desired in terms of immediate relief for those who need it. Prosperity theologies appear to fill this gap, at least in the estimation of many of their adherents. Prosperity churches encourage immediate individual empowerment as well as meeting the immediate existential needs of adherents by providing everything from free meals after services, to help finding jobs, to entrepreneurial classes and small business loans, to gifts of land.[69] Furthermore, Prosperity theologians argue that these changes filter through to the wider community, lifting individuals out of poverty, allowing them to pass on newfound wealth to their family and church communities, thus raising living standards for entire communities.[70] While little evidence of such a widespread impact in countries such as Guatemala or Brazil exists,[71] it must be remembered that these movements are still, broadly speaking, in their early days.

While opponents of Prosperity theologies argue that these theologies primarily attract those who are already upwardly mobile, particularly middle-class adherents, demographic evidence increasingly suggests that "the poor" are also attending Prosperity churches in increasing numbers.[72] Furthermore, certain elements of Prosperity churches are particularly attractive to the poor and the marginalized, including a de-emphasis on reading the biblical texts and a corresponding emphasis on memorization and prooftexting, which appeals to those who are illiterate, and potential continuity with certain so-called "indigenous" religious concepts of the spirit world, demonic oppression, and exorcism. Liberation theologies face a liability here, as they have only recently come to take seriously indigenous religiosity as a potentially positive factor in their theologies and are also heavily text-

---

69. See Furre, "Crossing Boundaries"; see also Llana, "Wealth Gospel Propels Poor Guatemalans"; Esperandio, "Globalization and Subjectivity."

70. See Phiri and Maxwell, "Gospel Riches," 23–29; see also Llana, "Wealth Gospel Propels Poor Guatemalans."

71. See Llana, "Wealth Gospel Propels Poor Guatemalans;" see also Arlene Sanchez Walsh, "Prosperidad."

72. See Martin, "Capitalist Society"; see also Kenny, *Substitute for Catholicism*, 25–26.

centered, with an emphasis on the reading and interpretation of the Bible. I do not wish to argue that biblical interpretation *should* be a liability; as a student of biblical hermeneutics writing this chapter for a volume devoted to biblical commentary, I would argue the opposite. However, textuality *has* become a liability for what I still consider to be an important theological and hermeneutical movement, and as such, the appeal of a more superficial use of the biblical texts must be seriously addressed.

Furthermore, the tangible shortcomings of Liberation theologies must also be honestly addressed.[73]

> In the 1970s and 1980s, especially in Brazil, many groups and theologians were expecting to see power coming from poor people's movements. Enthusiasm was great, and there were many cooperative efforts by popular movements hoping for real and lasting change. It has not happened. The situation of the poor in the 1990s has not improved but worsened. The power of neo-liberalism has brought a feeling of powerlessness, weakness and despair among the poor as the possibilities of social changes have not been realized. Now more than ever, the option for the poor must be grasped. This option means being committed in costly ways, living a life of instability and risk, without a chance to be in power or to get power. It is a spiritual and prophetic calling to follow the way of Christ.[74]

Is it any wonder that this call for costly commitment, for "living a life of instability and risk, without a chance to be in power or to get power," is not often appealing to the poor, who already live lives of instability and risk, who are searching for stability and empowerment, both of which they often seem to find more readily in Prosperity theologies than in this brand of Liberation theology? This may be a sad realization for those who support the laudable long-term goals of structural change and the challenge to neo-liberal globalization, but it is nonetheless a growing contemporary reality. While I agree with Liberation perspectives that the long-term solutions related to the alleviation of poverty require a renunciation of neo-liberal late capitalism, the immediate solution for the hungry is to become part of the system, to become consumers in the market, and Prosperity theologies offer a community in which to accomplish this. In the urban contexts where Prosperity theologies primarily flourish, it is much easier to embrace

---

73. On the debate over the failure of CEBs (*Comunidades Eclesiales de Base*) to achieve lasting political change, and their consequent abandonment by both the poor and the Catholic hierarchy, see Levine, "The Future of Christianity in Latin America"; Garrard-Burnett, "Transnational Protestantism."

74. Ribeiro, "Has Liberation Theology Died?" 310–11.

the values of individualism and competition than to maintain a communal solidarity which seems passé, related to the rural communities which many have left, or been forced to leave, behind.[75] For many people in these contexts, Neo-Pentecostal churches offer a vibrant new community, and Prosperity theologies offer a convenient and effective new theology.

CONCLUSION

In light of these pressing contemporary realities, I read Job as a call to action. The very deconstructability of the book itself, the fact that it can legitimately be read as both a retributional and an anti-retributional text, underscores the difficulty of choosing one or the other of these interpretations. If I incline to the latter perspective personally, I must remind myself that I have never been hungry nor faced the loss of my home or even my income. In short, I have never been driven to the extremes that seem to motivate both Job and his friends, both Liberation and Prosperity adherents. Political activists perhaps argue too easily for the importance of the long-term view. This ethical problem leads me to reject a simplistic opposition between these two interpretive perspectives in particular, as well as to advocate for more complexity in the genre of biblical commentary generally. The drive towards hermeneutical harmonization is not automatically a positive good in the production of commentaries; counterpoint as a hermeneutical method, as practiced in this article, offers a fertile complexity in the genre of biblical commentary and challenges both "academic" and "vernacular" readers of the Bible to take each other's perspectives on the text more seriously.[76]

I see political activism as a necessary element in the potential solution of the contemporary dilemmas facing both Liberation and Prosperity perspectives; related to this, I see a need for incorporating both the long-term views of Liberation theologies and the immediate gratification demanded by Prosperity theologies. I choose both. And lest this seem like the easy way out, I refer my readers back to Job. It cannot be easy to be the individual who simultaneously maintains that God is both his greatest tormenter and his only hope, to accept that the Lord gives and takes away, and to hold blessing and cursing in tension, while ultimately managing to please the God who receives both from one's lips. This is a complex and difficult text, read in a complex and difficult contemporary context, and it could provide a basis on

---

75. Ibid., 305–7.

76. For a more detailed theoretical discussion of this hermeneutical method, which I elsewhere refer to as contrapuntal hermeneutics, see Nelson, *Power and Responsibility*.

which to propose complex and difficult action in the production of biblical commentary as well as in a wider response to global poverty.

BIBLIOGRAPHY

Anderson, Allan. "The Prosperity Message in the Eschatology of Some New Charismatic Churches." *Missionalia* 15.2 (1987) 72–83.

Benfold, Gary. *Why Lord? The Book of Job for Today*. Epsom, UK: Day One, 1998.

Buckley, Stephen. "'Prosperity Theology.'" In "Pulls on Purse Strings: Promises of Riches Entice Brazil's Poor." *Washington Post* (13 February 2001), http://www.rickross.com /reference/universal/universal19/html.

Byassee, Jason. "Be Happy: The Health and Wealth Gospel." *Christian Century* (July 12 2005) 20–23.

Clines, David J. A. "Job's Fifth Friend: An Ethical Critique of the Book of Job." *BibInt* 12 (2004) 232–50.

———. "Deconstructing the Book of Job." In *The Bible as Rhetoric: Studies in Biblical Persuasion and Credibility*, edited by M. Warner, 65–80. London: Routledge, 1990.

———. "Does the Book of Job Suggest that Suffering Is not a Problem?" Paper presented at the Symposium for the 100th Birthday of Gerhard von Rad, *Das Alte Testament und die Kultur der Moderne*, Heidelberg, 18–21 October 2001. Online: http://www.shef.ac.uk/bibs/DJACcurres/ProblemSuffering.pdf.

———. "Quarter Days Gone: Job 24 and the Absence of God." In *On the Way to the Postmodern: Old Testament Essays, 1967–1998*, 2:801–19. JSOTSup 293. Sheffield: Sheffield Academic, 1998.

Coleman, Simon. "America Loves Sweden: Prosperity Theology and the Cultures of Capitalism." In *Religion and the Transformations of Capitalism*, edited by Richard H. Roberts, 161–79. London: Routledge, 1995.

———. "Conservative Protestantism and the World Order: The Faith Movement in the United States and Sweden." *SR* 54 (Winter 1993) 353–73.

———. *The Globalisation of Charismatic Christianity: Spreading the Gospel of Prosperity*. Cambridge Studies in Ideology and Religion 12. Cambridge: Cambridge University Press, 2000.

Collective Authorship, "Statement on Prosperity Theology and Theology of Suffering." *ERT* 20 (1996) 5–13.

Copeland, Kenneth. "How You Can Solve the Prosperity Puzzle." *Believers Voice of Victory* (July 1986) 4.

———. "The Whole Gospel." *Believer's Voice of Victory* 13 (April 1985) 2.

Cox, Harvey. "Spirits of Globalization: Pentecostalism and Experiential Spiritualities in a Global Era." In *Spirits of Globalization: The Growth of Pentecostalism and Experiential Spiritualties in a Global Age*, edited by S. Stålsett, 11–22. London: SCM, 2006.

de Aquino, Jorge L. F., and Gustavo G. S. de Oliveira. "'Overpragmatism,' Denominationalism,Fundamentalism, Liberalism—and the Evangelical Way." *Transformation* 21 (2004) 19–21.

Doak, Brian R. "Liberation Theology." In *Encyclopedia of Pentecostal and Charismatic Christianity*, edited by Stanley M. Burgess, 293–96. Routledge Encyclopedias of Religion and Society. New York: Routledge, 2006.

Dussel, Enrique. "The People of El Salvador: The Communal Sufferings of Job." *Concilium* "Job and the Silence of God" 169 (1983) 61–68.

Esperandio, Mary Rute Gomez. "Globalization and Subjectivity: A Reflection on the 'Universal Church of the Kingdom of God' in a Perspective Drawn from Psychology of Religion." In *Spirits of Globalization: The Growth of Pentecostalism and Experiential Spirtualties in a Global Age,* edited by S. Stålsett, 52–64. London: SCM, 2006.

Fokkelman, J. P. *Major Poems of the Hebrew Bible: At the Interface of Prosody and Structural Analysis.* Vol. IV, *Job 15–42.* Assen: Van Gorcum, 2004.

Folarin, George O. "Contemporary State of the Prosperity Gospel in Nigeria." *AJT* 21 (2007) 69–95.

Franklin, Robert M. "The Gospel of Bling." *Sojourners* (January 2007) 19–23, 46.

Furre, Berge. "Crossing Boundaries: The 'Universal Church' and the Spirit of Globalization." In *Spirits of Globalization: The Growth of Pentecostalism and Experiential Spirtualties in a Global Age,* edited by S. Stålsett, 39–51. London: SCM Press, 2006.

Garrard-Burnett, Virginia. "The Third Church in Latin America: Religion and Globalization in Contemporary Latin America." *LARR* 39 (2004) 256–69.

———. "Transnational Protestantism." *Journal of Interamerican Studies and World Affairs* 40 (1998) 117–25.

Gifford, Paul. "Expecting Miracles: The Prosperity Gospel in Africa." *Christian Century* (July 10, 2007) 20–24.

———. "Theology and Right Wing Christianity." *JTSA* 69 (1989) 28–39.

Gordis, Robert. *The Book of Job: Commentary, New Translation and Special Studies.* New York: The Jewish Theological Seminary of America, 1978.

Grogan, Geoffrey. "Liberation and Prosperity Theologies." *SBET* 9 (1991) 118–32.

Gutiérrez, Gustavo. *On Job: God-Talk and the Suffering of the Innocent.* Translated by Matthew J. O'Connell. Maryknoll, NY: Orbis, 1987.

Harris-Lacewell, Melissa V. "Righteous Politics: The Role of the Black Church in Contemporary Politics." *Crosscurrents* (Summer 2007) 180–96.

Hartley, John E. *The Book of Job.* NICOT. Grand Rapids: Eerdmans, 1988.

Hellstern, Mark. "The 'Me' Gospel: An Examination of the Historical Roots of the Prosperity Emphasis within Current Charismatic Theology." *FH* 21.3 (1989) 78–90.

Kenny, Michael Stephen Francis. "Is Pentecostalism a Substitute for Catholicism in Brazil?" M. thesis, University of St. Andrews, 2008.

Kim, Sang-Bok David. "A Bed of Roses or a Bed of Thorns." *ERT* 20 (1996) 14–25.

Lee, Shayne. "Prosperity Theology: T. D. Jakes and the Gospel of the Almighty Dollar." *Crosscurrents* (Summer 2007) 227–36.

Lee, Young Hoon. "The Case for Prosperity Theology." *ERT* 20 (1996) 26–39.

Levine, Daniel H. "The Future of Christianity in Latin America." (Paper presented at a workshop on "Trajectories in Modern Christianity" held at the School of Oriental and African Studies. University of London, February 2007.

Llana, Miller. "How Pentecostals Brought 'The Fiesta Spirit' to Church in Latin America: A Look at the Religion's Theological Roots and How the Faith Took Hold in the Region." *CSM* (17 December 2007). Online: http://www .csmonitor.com /2007/1217/p25s04-woam.html.

———. "Wealth Gospel Propels Poor Guatemalans: 'Prosperity Theology' is Empowering People to Help Themselves Out of Poverty." *CSM* (17 December 2007), http://www.csmonitor.com /2007/1217/p01s02-woam.html.

Martin, David. "Evangelical Religion and Capitalist Society in Chile: Historical Context, Social Trajectory and Current Political and Economic Ethos." In *Religion and the Transformations of Capitalism: Comparative Approaches*, edited by R. Roberts, 215–27. London: Routledge, 1995.

Mofokeng, Takatso. "The Prosperity Message and Black Theology: A Response to Allan Anderson." *Missionalia* 15 (1987) 84–86.

Morrow, William S. "Consolation, Rejection, and Repentance in Job 42:6." *JBL* 105 (1986) 211–25.

Nelson, Alissa Jones. *Power and Responsibility in Biblical Interpretation: Reading the Book of Job with Edward Said*. London: Equinox, 2012.

Oro, Ari Pedro, and Pablo Seman. "Brazilian Pentecostalism Crosses National Borders." In *Between Babel and Pentecost: Transnational Pentecostalism in Africa and Latin America*, edited by A. Corten and R. Marshall-Fratani, 181–95. Indianapolis: Indiana University Press, 2001.

Phiri, Isaac, and Joe Maxwell. "Gospel Riches." *Christianity Today* (July 2007) 23–29.

Piedra, Arturo. "Theology of Grace and Theology of Prosperity." *Reformed World* 55 (2005) 326–354.

Quiroz, Pedro Arana. "Suffering in Latin America." *ERT* 20 (1996) 77–87.

Randerson, Richard. "Prosperity Theology Thwarts God's Purpose." Sermon delivered at Holy Trinity Cathedral, Auckland, New Zealand, 29 October 2006. Online: http://www.holytrinity.org.nz/377.php.

Ribeiro, Claudio de Oliveira. "Has Liberation Theology Died? Reflections on the Relationship between Community Life and the Globalization of the Economic System." *The Ecumenical Review* 51 (1999) 304–14.

Samuel, Driver R. and George B. Gray. *A Critical and Exegetical Commentary on the Book of Job*. ICC. Edinburgh: T & T Clark, 1977.

Sanchez-Walsh, Arlene. "First Church of Prosperidad," *Christianity Today* (6 July 2007). Online: http://www.ctlibrary.com/ct/2007/july/13.26.html.

Smith, Dennis A. "Communication, Politics and Religious Fundamentalism in Latin America."Paper presented as a contribution to the panel "Religious Responses to Neoliberalism in Latin America" at the Conference for the Latin American Studies Association, Montreal,Quebec, September 2007. Online:http://www.pcusa.org/missionconnections/letter/smithd/smithd_0709_fundamentalisms.pdf.

Stålsett, Sturla J. "Offering On-Time Deliverance: The Pathos of Neo-Pentecostalism and the Spirits of Globalization." In *Spirits of Globalization: The Growth of Pentecostalism and Experiential Spiritualties in a Global Age*, edited by S. Stålsett, 198–212. London: SCM Press, 2006.

Starner, Rob. "Prosperity Theology." In *Encyclopedia of Pentecostal and Charismatic Christianity*, edited by S. Burgess, 392–97. New York/London: Routledge, 2006.

Tamez, Elsa. "A Letter to Job." In *New Eyes for Reading: Biblical and Theological Reflections by Women from the Third World*, edited by J. S. Pobee and B. Von Wartenburg-Potter, 50–52. Geneva: World Council of Churches, 1986.

———. "From Father of the Needy to Brother of Jackals and Companion of Ostriches: A Meditation on Job." *Concilium* "Job's God" (2004) 103–111.

van Biema, David, and Jeff Chu. "Does God Want You To Be Rich?" *Time Magazine* (10 September 2006). Online: http://www.time.com/time/magazine/article/0,9171,1533448,00.html

Warners, Dave, and Larry Borst. "The Good of a Flourishing Creation: Seeking God in a Culture of Affluence." *PSCF* 57.1 (2005) 24–33.

Waters, Larry J. "Reflections on Suffering from the Book of Job." *BibSac* 154 (1997) 436–51.

Wells, Harold. "Resistance to Domination as a Charism of the Holy Spirit." In *Spirits of Globalization: The Growth of Pentecostalism and Experiential Spiritualties in a GlobalAge*, edited by S. Stålsett, 170–82. London: SCM, 2006.

Wilson, Gerald H. *Job*. NIBC. Peabody, MA: Hendrickson, 2007.

www.ingramcontent.com/pod-product-compliance
Lightning Source LLC
Chambersburg PA
CBHW070242230426
43664CB00014B/2382